MASTER
MECHANICS
&
WICKED
WIZARDS

MASTER MECHANICS & WICKED WIZARDS

Images of the American Scientist as Hero and Villain from Colonial Times to the Present

Glen Scott Allen

University of Massachusetts Press

AMHERST

LC 2009007124
ISBN 978-1-55849-703-0 (paper); 702-3 (library cloth)

Designed by Dennis Anderson
Set in Warnock Pro by Binghamton Valley Composition
Printed and bound by Sheridan Books, Inc.

Library of Congress Cataloging-in-Publication Data

Allen, Glen Scott, 1950–
Master mechanics & wicked wizards : images of the American scientist as
hero and villain from colonial times to the present / Glen Scott Allen.
p. cm.
Includes bibliographical references and index.
ISBN 978-1-55849-702-3 (lib. cloth : alk. paper) —
ISBN 978-1-55849-703-0 (pbk. : alk. paper)
1. Science in popular culture—United States—History.
2. Science in mass media—United States—History.
3. Scientists—United States—History.
I. Title.   II. Title: Master mechanics and wicked wizards.
Q127.U6A6815 2009
509.73—dc22
2009007124

British Library Cataloguing in Publication data are available.

For my parents,
Shirley and Glen

CONTENTS

Illustrations follow pages 84 and 148

ACKNOWLEDGMENTS

FIRST OF all I want to thank my wife, Inna, for her unfailing support and encouragement over the years it took to complete this work. I also wish to thank the tireless members of my reading group, Mark Osteen, Ron Tanner, and Ned Balbo, whose suggestions and insights contributed in ways too numerous to count; Bruce Wilcox, director of the University of Massachusetts Press, whose infinite patience and invaluable suggestions were vital in seeing this book through to completion; Paul Jenkins and the other editors at *The Massachusetts Review*, who published the original essay that eventually grew into this book; and Charles Berger, whose encouragement of a graduate student's naïve curiosity provided the initial inspiration for many long years of research. And finally, thanks to all my colleagues who offered constructive criticism to the various drafts and presentations of this material over the course of its evolution.

MASTER
MECHANICS
&
WICKED
WIZARDS

INTRODUCTION

ONE SCENE from an old black and white film best summarizes what this book is about: a tall, thin man wearing a white lab coat bends over the prone body of a bulky giant. He is surrounded by huge Tesla coils filling the air with branching electrical sparks, and tall glass tubes of bubbling liquids. Scurrying about him is a hunchback assistant who whispers, "Yes, master" to his every command, throwing one enormous switch after another. The thin man in the lab coat bends over the prone body; his face is emaciated, intensely pale, shining with mad intensity. He listens for a moment, eyes darting wildly. Then he raises his head and, his voice rising hysterically, screams, "It's alive! It's *alive*!!"

This is of course the creation scene from James Whale's 1931 *Frankenstein*, a scene as famous in its iconography and mythological power as perhaps any in cinematic history. And, though the same scene had been played out in dozens of variations for over a century before Colin Clive made it famous (as Henry Frankenstein, with Boris Karloff as the Monster), it is that particular actor and his mad, gaunt visage which has become the exemplar of the Frankenstein myth and all it entails, and that particular scene with its atmosphere of transgression and power which has become the exemplar of the Mad Scientist and all that character entails.[1] Yet, though many books have been written about Whale's artistic agenda in *Frankenstein*, others about the less artistic agenda of the many imitations to follow, and still others about the sociological, psychological, aesthetic, ethical, and moral agendas in the Gothic novel which inspired them all—Mary Shelley's *Frankenstein*—still rarely are questions asked about why that *particular* image became so indelibly etched into the American public consciousness.

Why, for instance, must Dr. Frankenstein always be *thin*? Why not a stout Frankenstein? Why must he appear, in manner and looks, so aristocratic, so *foreign*? Why is his only companion a subservient hunchback? Why is he always working in a decrepit castle? For that matter, why is he never, ever *blonde*?[2]

This book began with a relatively simple question, much like those I've just listed. However, it was a question inspired by a book rather than a film. The book was Paul Boyer's *By the Bomb's Early Light*, which examines in great detail the effect of the A-bomb on 1950s American culture. Several sections in

Boyer's book are devoted to chronicling the political and social failure of the Los Alamos scientists in their attempts to limit and control the "monster" they had unleashed; but in the wealth of the statistics, quotes, analyses, and opinions, one question seemed to me to go unanswered: Why had the immense admiration that America expressed for the A-bomb scientists at the end of World War II evaporated *so quickly* and *so thoroughly*? So quickly that by 1949, the "father of the atomic bomb," Robert Oppenheimer, was an outsider to most of the committees and organizations charged with determining the future of atomic weapons; and so thoroughly that by 1954, he'd lost his government security clearance and was portrayed in the popular media as a traitor.

The routine answer is that the politically active Manhattan Project scientists, like Robert Oppenheimer, became in the public media associated with the international Communist "conspiracy." It was the Communists who were the real threat, this traditional analysis claims; higher-profile scientists like Oppenheimer were just handy scapegoats.

Yet this traditional answer struck me as unsatisfying. For one thing, while only a minority of the A-bomb scientists actually participated in "Atoms for Peace" and other political movements, the acrimony expressed in the popular and even intellectual media of the time seemed directed at nearly all of them. And, while "guilt by association" seems a possible explanation for how suspicion of a small group of atomic scientists could contaminate the public's perception of scientists generally, it did not explain why public fear of Russian Communists would so "naturally" transform into fear of *American* scientists. Furthermore, though certainly the Pentagon and much of the American political spectrum expended great energy convincing Americans that the "Reds" were a threat to the Western democracies, the historical record indicates that the fear and loathing expressed in the media toward the Manhattan Project scientists in fact arose *before* the Red Scares of the '50s were in full swing.

But even more perplexing to me was why the American public—let alone the Pentagon—would consider the Communists not just an ideological menace, but a military one. Given our overwhelming victories in Europe and the Pacific, as well as our technological and military advantages, why were *we* afraid? I simply could not accept the conventional wisdom that the rampant, deep-seated anxiety evident across the media, and the almost savage vilification of scientists who had only the day before been national heroes, were in response to an enemy separated from us by half a world, an enemy that could not possibly be planning to invade America. How on earth, I wondered, could the very superpatriots who pointed to our triumph in the war as evidence of our superior culture feel at the same time that our culture was so *vulnerable* as to be seriously threatened by the Soviet Union, a nation completely absorbed in the rebuilding of its own devastated society—a nation that couldn't possibly consider attacking us, lest they suffer atomic retaliation that they at that time could not match? What exactly could *they* do to *us*? In fact, the Communists' sole offensive weapon seemed to be the quite ethereal ability to "influence" our minds, "undermine" our values, and "infiltrate" our institutions. So the question kept nagging at me: what did we have to fear?

And it was in this very rhetoric of the "silent menace" that eventually I found the answer to my question: for of course the most insidious threat is the one that you cannot see, the one that is invisible and unsuspected. It isn't the barbarians at the gates who present the greatest danger; it is the barbarians already *inside* the gates, the ones posing as ordinary citizens.

It was from this realization not a great leap to the suspicion that there was concealed in this decade-long spectacle of social paranoia a Nietzschean reversal of hierarchy: perhaps the supposed "fellow travelers" among the A-bomb scientists were in fact the *chief* evil, albeit an unconscious one, and the Russian and Chinese Communists the convenient scapegoats. That is to say, perhaps during the period 1945–1959, when anti-scientist sentiment in America reached a peak, the American popular culture attacked a certain segment of the American scientific community not as a feint or out of frustration, but because it felt instinctively that *they* were the real enemy. And perhaps this intracommunal threat of American scientists was linked to the extracommunal enemy of Russian Communists as a kind of national, subconscious justification for demonizing and ostracizing people who were, after all, Americans.

However, like so many other simple questions and their first-order answers, this one, too, seemed incomplete: for where would such American "instincts" come from in the first place? Sensing a threat, why would the popular culture turn so swiftly on American *scientists*? Why not war profiteers, scaremongering militarists, selfish monopolists, or corrupt politicians? Why immediately focus all our anxiety and ferocious media satire on a segment of our society that, according to our cultural mythology, we admire, even idolize as with those icons of the American scientist, Benjamin Franklin and Thomas Edison?

At first there seemed no logical connection between questions such as these that implied sweeping sociological generalizations and the far simpler ones as to why Frankenstein was always imagined with a thin face and an accent. But soon I began to wonder if there might not be a link, if somehow both didn't represent an attitude buried deep within our cultural consciousness. Why *did* the Frankenstein myth evidence such longevity, represented in American text and drama and film hundreds of times—why should it seem so *familiar* to us? Why should it not only be instantly recognizable as a fusing of centuries-old legends and phobias, but also seem to capture a cultural fear which apparently transcends any one American era?

Frankenstein—the name immediately summons up not merely popular images of a shambling Boris Karloff in elevator boots, but also a complex of attitudes about everything from technological arrogance to parental responsibility, from hope in scientific achievement to fear of the consequences that achievement will bring, from fascination with exceptional genius to fear of transgressive hubris. . . . Confronted with the almost inexhaustible depth of momentous themes raised by the novel, as well as the cottage industry it spawned, one thinks of Voltaire's comment about God: without Mary Shelley's *Frankenstein*, perhaps it would have been necessary for us to invent one.

Given the strength of this myth in our culture, perhaps it was not surprising that, when the public media turned on the atomic scientists after World War II, the first trope they should wield as a club was that of Frankenstein. And by then, the name referred not just to the Herr Doctor, and not even just to his creation, but to the entire morality play of intellectual arrogance and the obsessive self-destruction it inevitably engenders—an argument (or perhaps "assumption" is a better word) which runs throughout Western master narratives from Oedipus to Faust.

I'd begun by wondering how well-respected geniuses could so quickly become vilified outsiders and why a Gothic ghost story which makes more reference to Milton than Newton could become a universally recognized warning about the dangers and limits of science, and wound up by investigating the vein of American anti-science rhetoric which begins with the Puritans and runs wide and strong through two-and-a-half centuries of American popular media. While my initial investigations were focused on the immediate post–World War II period, I soon found I had to expand my research: back to the Colonial portrayals of "natural philosophers" and their practices, and forward to the contemporary representation of scientists and scientific ethics in print, film, and television. All of this because I'd stopped to wonder what exactly made a mad scientist "mad."

Much has been written of late about the "mad scientist" figure. Such treatments tend to focus on the historical development of the character, from shamans to scientists.[3] While some create fairly elaborate categories and subgroups (Roslynn Haynes, for instance, offers no less than seven "types" of mad scientists), none have focused specifically on the historical development, composition, and influence of the trope over the roughly 300 years of American culture. Those texts which have examined the relationships between American science and "mad" scientists have typically based their arguments on three general axioms: 1) the American public views scientists as a fairly homogeneous group; 2) Americans admire science and fear its innovators less than other national cultures; and, 3) whatever suspicion or even dislike there is in American culture toward scientists is merely the general response of all people when faced with the unknown.

However, this book will question these axioms. Some of the more specific questions I began to ask myself were: Are all American scientists equally suspect, or does the public see divisions within the scientific community? Why are certain scientific innovations acceptable, even laudable, while others generate an almost instantaneous backlash of paranoia and condemnation? Is there a particularly *American* cultural response at work here? And if so, how is this cultural response linked to American cultural influences, such as Puritanism, pragmatism, even capitalism? I also began to wonder to what extent that formula might be reversed, specifically, to what extent has American culture shaped American scientific practice?

One might even question if there can be a particularly "American" science, or if science is in fact subject to the sorts of cultural influences that all other forms of social practice are. Even though the analysis of the history, practice, and philosophy of science has become a central theme of contemporary Cultural Studies, one of the earliest twentieth-century contributions to this field was Michael Polanyi's *Science, Faith, and Society* (1946). Polanyi, a chemist, argued: "Any account of science which does not explicitly describe it as something we believe in is essentially incomplete and a false pretense. It amounts to a claim that science is essentially different from and superior to all human beliefs that are not scientific statements—and this is untrue."[4] Though this assertion has become so oft-quoted as to be a commonplace in books, articles, and websites about the philosophy of science, when Polanyi wrote it in 1946 it was considered deeply controversial, if not heretical.

And in fact, it is still typically assumed by modern scientists that science is an "ideology-free zone," an endeavor that is universal in its methods and goals: transnational, transhistorical, transcultural. The advent of Cultural Studies as a recognized and respected academic field may have brought this assumption into greater contestation in recent years, but the debate between cultural relativists and traditional scientists still rages. My perspective, as expressed in this work, is as follows: science is an activity conducted by human beings, and therefore it is an activity affected by all things human: beliefs, prejudices, biases, traditions—ideology. None of this is to argue that an apple dropped in America falls any differently than an apple dropped in Russia; rather, it is to argue that what that dropped apple *means* to an American might well be different from what it means to a Russian; that the ways in which this "fact" is integrated into both languages and cultures might also be quite different; and that, although the apple hits the ground with the same force in both countries, the *cultural* impact it has is not necessarily the same.[5]

For this reason I have chosen to analyze texts that are, first, almost exclusively American, and second, that circulate in the "popular" culture—fiction, films, art, newspapers, magazines, television, advertising—rather than essays and books by scientists themselves. Far better, I think, to use expressions of cultural attitudes that are indirect and "unconscious" rather than explicit and didactic, as then the underlying premises are taken to be axiomatic; and, as most popular texts are constructed not so much to convince as persuade, as entertainment rather than argument, then the unconscious assumptions implicit in those texts might be taken as the deepest roots of that culture's ideology.

In selecting these "indirect" cultural texts, I primarily focus on those books, films, and other "texts" that were popular in their time, and especially those that have proved popular beyond their time. In other words, though a book or film may offer a representation of scientists that is powerful or engaging in one way or another, unless that text circulates, its cultural impact is minimal. By somewhat reverse reasoning, then, I'm assuming that those texts with the widest circulation have had the greatest impact on, and made the greatest contribution to our imaginings about what kind of people good and bad scientists are.

And in all cases I am particularly interested in the *image* of scientists, how they are *imagined* to look, to dress, to behave. After all, that tableau of Frankenstein bent over the misshapen form of his creation has had more to do with sculpting the American conception of "mad" science than have all the treatises written by and about scientists over the last three centuries. That iconographic image and others like it form the basis of popular American conceptions of science, good, bad, and mad, regardless of how little such images have to do with how science is actually practiced. Therefore, much of this book is devoted to close readings of such images, from political cartoons of the 1700s, to the covers of science fiction "pulps" of the 1930s, to posters for science fiction films of the 1990s. My methodology, then, is to examine not only the details of these images, but also the implicit assumptions resident in those details for what they tell us about our culture's hopes and fears about science, what it can do for us, what it can do to us.

AT THIS point, it is important to make clear what this book is not. It is not a collection of biographies of famous American scientists; it is not a history of scientific and technological evolution in America; nor is it my intention to settle long-standing controversies about the lives or actions of individual scientists. My analyses throughout will focus on the *public perceptions* of American scientists, not on their private realities. For instance, whether or not Benjamin Franklin actually practiced what he preached isn't really germane to my argument here; rather, what is important is our *received image* of Franklin, the extent to which the public believes in this iconic Franklin, and the ways in which this icon influenced Colonial attitudes toward science and those who practiced it.

Of course, some scientists and science historians might object to my use of figures like Benjamin Franklin and Thomas Edison as icons of the American scientist. While agreeing that they are epitomes of innovators and inventors, they might still insist that they both lacked the formal education and rigorous methodology of "genuine" scientists. However, ask any average American to name a famous American scientist, and you are liable to elicit Franklin or Edison at the top of the list. In other words, regardless of how scientists themselves define what it means to be a "genuine" scientist, the public at large has certain key and very firm images of what that term describes; and it is those public images I will analyze in this book, rather than the standards applied within the profession itself.

Such scholars might also object that the topic of the difference between theoretical and practical science has been thoroughly examined previously. However, I would respond that this split within the scientific community has typically been portrayed as a split between science and technology, or pure and applied science; and I would agree that those differences *within the scientific community itself* have been examined quite exhaustively. However, that is not the distinction I analyze in this book. Rather, I am interested in exhuming and scrutinizing artifacts from the broader community of the American popular culture—artifacts as far back as Benjamin Franklin's *Almanac,* and as recent as Steven Spielberg's *Artificial Intelligence: A.I.*—for what they tell us about how the theory/practice dichotomy is perceived by the average American. Furthermore, as I will argue, I believe the "pure" vs. "applied" dichotomy employed, however contentiously, throughout the sciences is in fact a distinction without a difference; especially in the minds of the American public, for whom technology *is* science.

This book is a chronological analysis of the popular and lasting *images* of scientists in the American culture, and what those images tell us about broad and deep cultural beliefs and prejudices regarding who American scientists should and shouldn't be, and what they should and shouldn't do. Thus, this book is composed as a sustained argument on this issue, with each chapter representing an analysis of a particular historical period or text, and each presenting a step toward a final conclusion.

My essential argument is that there is a fundamental anti-intellectualism in American attitudes toward and practice of what would seem to be our most intellectual pursuit, science. I contend that the portrayal of the scientist in American popular culture typically takes one of two forms: either that of a heroic figure with mastery over technology who utilizes that skill in the service of his community to achieve relatively limited goals of reform; or that of a villain whose arrogance is rooted in the intellect and who seeks, to the detriment of his community, some sort of totalizing revolution. The first type is an inventor who produces practical or at least material outcomes which serve the traditional goals of American progress; and the second is a theoretician whose work is abstract and with a value either unclear or threatening to the average citizen, as it implies a critique or even an overturning of that traditional idea of progress.

I have labeled these two types the Master Mechanic and the Wicked Wizard. The first is obvious enough, as its character embodies our fascination with and desire for mastery over technology. The second is more subtle, but the term captures, I hope, the sinister aura of this character in American culture, as well as conveying my assertion that this sinister aura is created by that character's display of intellectual prowess, a prowess that is usually communicated in rhetoric that strikes us as more closely aligned with magic than science. The wizard, through incantations, summons powers dark and esoteric, powers that seem to operate outside the boundaries of "natural" material laws. The wizard is also perceived as someone who stands outside the social laws of everyday communities: he is isolated, independent, alien.

It is important to emphasize that I am not suggesting that there is a fundamental truth to either of these stereotypes, only that there is a *perceived* truth to them. Is this a "cop out"? To such a question I can only respond that the truth or falsehood of these stereotypes isn't really relevant to my thesis; demonstrating their existence over more than two hundred years of American history is. In other words, whether or not the category Master Mechanic accurately captures Edison's true character isn't my focus; what is important is whether the general public *imagines* Edison in those terms. It would be another book entirely that would attempt to establish the extent of discontinuity between these public perceptions and the private realities (an attempt that I believe would prove ultimately futile). What I will be arguing is that the *perceived* truth of these stereotypes has had and continues to have profound effects on American culture, even on the kinds of science which are and are not practiced in our country.

The organizational scheme for arranging these cultural artifacts and their analyses is, with one exception—the Colonial period—chronological. One might wonder why I saved the earliest period for the penultimate chapter. I want to reproduce for the reader my own "journey" from specific and narrowly contextualized questions to general and largely historical conclusions; I also want to present the evidence essentially as I encountered it, so that the theory derived from that evidence seems as grounded and convincing to the reader as it does to me. Rhetorically, I believe the ultimate destination at which I arrive is clearest and most convincing when it is presented as the end point of my investigations, rather than as their point of departure. The roots of the American cultural tendencies investigated here seem to me most evident *as* roots after we have a full description of the various branches they have produced.

Writing this book was like building a bridge: I knew where I wanted to get to and where I must begin from, and it was a matter of connecting those two points. But as with any bridge—especially one almost three hundred years long—it is impractical to build supports every inch of the way. Instead, I have tried to pick key moments in that span and support my argument solidly at those moments. If I have sacrificed depth for breadth in my analysis, I can only hope that the overall consistency of my evidence and argument convinces the reader that I am on to something, even if I haven't explicated every detail of what that something is. And in some instances I am merely "connecting the dots": some of the points I make about particular historical tendencies have been made by very able scholars who came before me, but typically in the narrower contexts of those periods or themes. I owe a tremendous debt to these other writers, without whose research and insight I never could have completed this work. I only hope I have extended that research and those insights in ways they would find consistent and convincing. And I hope other scholars still to come will find inspiration here to continue and expand in this area.

SIMON PURE AMATEURS

1

American Scientists of the
Early Nineteenth Century

IT WAS a typically dreary Boston November day of 1849 when Dr. George Parkman stepped out of his fashionable home in East Cambridge and headed for Harvard College. The foul weather didn't improve his mood. He was angry, and he was in a hurry. He stopped at a market on Merchant's Block—a long, narrow street of butcher shops, bakeries, and produce stands—then decided he didn't have time to collect his groceries and said he'd pick them up later. At a refreshment stand in East Cambridge he inquired when the next omnibus would leave for Boston, and seemed quite put out when he was told it would not be for another hour.

His anger and haste were those of a man fed up with excuses; he was planning to have it out with someone who owed him the considerable sum of $470, but seemed unwilling or unable to repay him. He'd brought the necessary papers to either settle the debt or ruin the debtor's career, and he meant to do one or the other before the day was over. It was around 4:00 in the afternoon when Parkman finally reached the Harvard Medical College. Shaking off the chilling rain, he entered the building . . . and was never seen alive again.

Dr. Parkman's disappearance didn't go unnoticed. He was, after all, a member of one of Boston's most prominent Brahmin families. Suspicion quickly fell on one John Webster, a professor of chemistry at Harvard who, it was known, had borrowed money from Parkman, among others, and who had complained recently of how closely Parkman was pressing him. A janitor at the Medical College took it upon himself to do a little investigating and, digging beneath Webster's laboratory, quickly made a horrifying discovery: pieces of a dismembered human body.

Webster's trial was significant as it was one of the first in the country where forensic evidence—primarily Parkman's teeth—was used to obtain a conviction. A year after Parkman's murder, Webster was convicted and hanged. In addition to the grisly details of the murder—Webster was even at one point suspected of cannibalism—the trial also received considerable publicity due to the victim's social standing in the Boston community, as well as the fact that both victim and murderer were on the faculty of the country's most prestigious college, Harvard.[1] And it is that latter aspect of the case that is most relevant to the thesis of this book. It is difficult to decide which is the more surprising aspect of the case: that, even teaching at the best American college of the time, Webster could barely make ends meet; or that someone of his limited talents was teaching at Harvard in the first place.

John Webster was slightly portly and sported the muttonchop sideburns in fashion at the time, as well as a pair of scholarly round spectacles. He'd been born into a fairly wealthy family, only to find the fortune had evaporated by his adulthood. He obtained his medical training at Harvard, and even practiced medicine for a time in the Azores, where he met his wife. But back in Boston, his private medical practice failed, and he was forced to take a position as lecturer in chemistry at Harvard, a position Parkman had been instrumental in obtaining for him. In his eventual confession, Webster admitted he'd been driven to the desperate act of braining Parkman by his unsupportable debts. His salary as a Harvard professor was around $1,200 per year; among the highest for professors anywhere in the country, yet utterly insufficient, he complained, to maintain the lifestyle of a member of the Cambridge elite, a lifestyle to which all Harvard faculty members were expected to aspire. But whereas Webster was known socially as possessing "a mild, kind and unassuming disposition, with eminently social feelings and manners of uncommon affability," a local paper, the *Boston Daily Bee*, suggested that, as a professor, he was "tolerated rather than respected, and has only retained his position on account of its comparative insignificance." As a teacher he was described as, at best, "lackluster," and his general knowledge of his subject was politely referred to as "limited."[2] Yet Webster, homicidal tendencies aside, may stand as a perfect representative of the average American scientist of his time.

In the first few decades of the nineteenth century, two key conditions in American culture dominated the formation of a distinctly American image of science and scientists: 1) the "amateur" status of most American scientists, which was quite different from that of the professional European scientist; and 2) an American reverence for technology, which led to a preference for practical over theoretical science and scientists. These two factors were the result of a number of cultural practices and exigencies of the time: nascent institutions of higher learning; a completely consumer-driven publishing industry; limited scientific professional organizations and employment opportunities; cultural mythologies and antipathies about class and labor; anti-elitist political ideologies; even geographic resources and requirements. But before I discuss these factors, it may be useful to briefly examine how terms like "scientist" and "technology" first entered the American public discourse.

It may come as something of a surprise to discover that the word "scientist" did not come into public usage until approximately 1840, when it was coined by William Whelwell of Cambridge (England) to describe "someone who seeks knowledge and organizes it to some useful purpose"[3] (Note the near-cautionary phrase "useful purpose"). Before this, the person we would today call a scientist was variously designated an artist, craftsman, chemical experimenter, "natural philosopher," or even just "philosopher." And the word "technology" wasn't widely circulated until the publication of Jacob Bigelow's *Elements of Technology* in 1829, wherein it was defined as "the application of science to the useful arts"[4] (again, note the modifier "useful").

At the time of Webster's trial, the difference between the European and American scientific communities was the difference between well-trained, hierarchically specialized, full-time university faculties, and self-taught, loosely organized groups of local hobbyists. In 1846, Germany alone funded a score of modern scientific and technical universities; American had none.[5] France had the Ecole Polytechnique and the Académie des Sciences, and England the Royal Society, Cambridge, and Oxford, while the closest America came was Harvard College, which still offered no graduate training in the sciences and provided only such undergraduate preparation as people like Webster could supply.[6]

Not only had American scientists nowhere to study, they had nowhere to publish. Up until 1846, when the Smithsonian Institute and the Yale Scientific School were founded and began their own publications, the only regularly published journal available to American researchers was the *American Journal of Science*, which itself depended heavily on summarizing European articles.[7] Even with the gradual growth of American science as a national community, American scientists tended to be more of the gathering-classifying-Louis Agassiz strain than the philosophers and theorists more prevalent in Europe. As of 1846, at least 15 percent of the leading American scientists were still "simon pure amateurs."[8] Until the founding of the informal group in Boston known as the Lazzaroni—which would become the core of the American Association for the Advancement of Science—there was no national organization of "natural philosophers" in America to correspond to England's Royal Society. The closest American corollary was the American Philosophical Society, founded by Benjamin Franklin in 1745 in Philadelphia. Franklin wrote that the purpose of the APS was "the promoting of Useful Knowledge, especially as it respects the Agriculture, Manufactures, and Natural History of North America."[9] In other words, the APS wasn't particularly interested in theorizing, or in paying much attention to the scientific advances made beyond America's borders. As for either disciplining or distributing scientific articles, there was no central body to sit in judgment of research or publishing standards or classroom curricula, or to serve as "spokespeople" for a national scientific community.

The first major event in American history that began a development of such a community came with the end of the Mexican War in 1848, when over a million acres of new territory was added to the country. The desire of nearly every practicing American scientist was to get out there and explore it—particularly as most American scientists of the time were botanists, biologists, and geologists. (Mathematicians, chemists, and physicists totaled only a little over 25 percent of the practicing American scientists of 1850, and even by 1876 there were fewer than 20 nationally publishing American physicists.[10]) Setting a trend that would become an American trademark, many university professors of the time moonlighted as "consultants," offering their services as soil analysts, patent advisers, decipherers of complicated scientific tables, and the like. Most university professors were, like Webster, so severely underpaid that they often had to rely on collecting fees directly from their students. Only by making some sort of alliance with the business community could science professors make enough money to continue doing "real science," on the side.[11]

European scientists considered their American cousins impatient, diffuse, and so eager for new discoveries that they didn't bother to thoroughly investigate those already made. Said one British astronomer: "Few, indeed, are the American investigators who have followed up their subject during their whole lives . . . as Europeans have done." In fact, many American scientists sensed this as a "national tendency"; even Benjamin Gould of the AAAS warned in 1869 of "our national fault—want of thoroughness." One European naturalist charged that "Neither [Henry D.] Rogers nor any other American have a mind for purely scientific researches; they look for practical result." Rogers did not disagree; he, too, complained that "the great demand in the United States is for applied science, not theoretical science."[12]

Many manufacturers bragged of how scientific research had little or nothing to do with their practical advancements. Charles Goodyear, for instance, made a point of telling all and sundry that his success had absolutely nothing to do with "chemical knowledge," but depended entirely on "trial and error"; and years later Edison would express a similar sentiment regarding his light bulb. In fact, his famous statement that his genius was "1 percent inspiration and 99 percent perspiration" can be read as a testimonial to the primacy of practice over theory.

These years also witnessed the introduction of countless "pseudosciences" into the popular American culture. For instance, both phrenology and mesmerism were accepted in the United States as scientific practices with, according to literary historian Taylor Stoehr, an enthusiasm even greater than they had received in Europe: "The public . . . seemed willing to pay the price for any scientific demonstrations or treatments so long as there was something tangible to show for it, something 'practical'—a cranial character reading, marked on a card like a dentist's chart, or a circumstantial account of the condition of one's liver, diagnosed by a clairvoyant who in the trance state became a sort of human fluoroscope."[13] Most of these pseudosciences were characterized by Americans as "reformist" movements whose goal wasn't profit or the expansion of scientific knowledge so much as the betterment of the practitioner and his community. Of course, quacks with fancy titles and fancier rhetoric had been part of the American cultural landscape from its inception, often with impressive results. Samuel Thomson of South Carolina was an autodidact who considered traditionally educated doctors to be charlatans, preached heartily against bloodletting, and made a fortune selling "distillates" of vegetables. He also recommended severe regimes of purging and sweating; yet by 1838, it is estimated that 1 in 6 Americans were "Thomsonians."[14] Even mesmerism was aligned less with spiritualism and other supernatural practices of ill repute than with "social sciences" which offered supposedly empirical evidence of human "interconnectedness," as imagined in R. W. Emerson's essay "The Over-Soul." Stoehr summarizes the fervor that greeted mesmerism particularly as follows:

> But a certain success attended it. . . . It was human, it was genial, it affirmed unity and connection between remote points, and as such was excellent criticism on the narrow and dead classification of what passed for science; and the joy with which it was greeted was an instinct of the people which no philosopher would fail to profit by. . . . There was a breath of new air, much vague expectation, a consciousness of power not yet finding its determinate aim.[15]

Emerson and many other American philosophers and writers of the time looked upon mesmerism and its fellows as, if not substantiated, at least novel and progressive enough in concept to warrant respect and investigation. In Hawthorne's *House of the Seven Gables*, Clifford Pyncheon effuses over mesmerism, claiming that "the harbingers of a better era are unmistakable. Mesmerism, now! Will that effect nothing, think you, towards purging away the grossness out of human life? . . . These rapping spirits . . . What are these but the messengers of the spiritual world, knocking at the door of substance?"[16] Part of the popularity of these pseudosciences arose from their (supposedly) eminent self-help practicality. As Stoehr puts it, "There was a moral cast to such activities, even when they amounted to nothing more than

a new system of shorthand or of memorizing dates."[17] During the same period, the writings of social reformists like Horace Mann, Samuel Howe, Henry
Ward Beecher, Horace Greeley, and William Cullen Bryant were printed in
Sunday news supplements and inexpensive magazines. These speakers and
dozens less well known but with the same "pitch" made the town hall lyceum
tour to large and enthusiastic audiences, and the most popular topic was social reform—though, interestingly enough, apparently little reference was
made by these speakers to more professional and more traditionally scientific
social theories, such as Auguste Comte's new "positivist" science of society,
which he called Sociology.

Another important difference between the public perceptions of science in
Europe and America was the need in this country to make science "popular," a
requirement seen by European scientists as quite irrelevant to their work. "In
England," the Royal Astronomer said to the American Maria Mitchell in 1857,
"we do not need to make science popular." And many American scientists resented this difference. "I dislike writing for the public," grumbled James Hall in
1846. James Dana, too, complained that, in order to meet the "vulgar appetites
of the people," he had to "dilute" his scientific writings with "unsophisticated"
vocabulary. However, these somewhat snide professional objections to dumbing-
down science received little sympathy from those government officials responsible for overseeing scientific reports. Stoehr writes: "In 1851 Commander Charles
Wilkes objected to the uncompromisingly professional way in which Torrey and
Gray proposed to write up his expedition's botany. 'The Library Committee [of
Congress] intend the work for the people . . . and not for any class of scientific
men.'"[18] American poets, too, had very little use for the technical details and specialized rhetoric of professional scientists: even as Whitman listened to the
"learn'd astronomer," instead of feeling curiosity for factual knowledge he grew
"tired and sick," and preferred to look at the stars "in perfect silence" (or, one
might offer, in perfect ignorance).[19]

In other words, from the beginnings of science in this country as even a semi-
organized profession, the public reception and perception of the scientist tended
to favor the independent amateur over the university professor, the practical inventor over the abstract theoretician, the average tinkerer over the highly trained
specialist. In fact, any exclusionary association of scientific professionals was
seen in many quarters as dangerously aristocratic. In a congressional speech
against the bill to establish the national Smithsonian Institution—a bill we would
expect even in those times to encounter no resistance—one senator warned that
it would be "one of the most withering and deadly corporations, carrying with it
all the features of an aristocracy."[20] Several points in that statement are worthy of
notice: that a professional organization of scientists is seen not as bringing rigor

and discipline to American science, but rather as a "withering and deadly" force; that such a group is most easily comparable to a "corporation," a business model apparently being the most ready analogy to come to the senator's mind; and finally, that professionalism is a synonym for "aristocracy," suggesting that standards, discipline, and institutionalized expertise are somehow inseparable from class bias, arbitrary exercises of power, and inherited privilege.

THE SCIENTIFIC community itself must be held partly responsible for maintaining this taint of the "aristocrat" attached to any suggestion of professionalizing the practice of American science. By and large, American colleges considered the sort of "applied" science practiced outside their ivy-covered walls to be antithetical or even somehow corrosive to the kind of science they supported. Robert Bruce reports, "When the bright young chemistry professor Ira Remsen in 1872 asked Williams College for a small room to do research in, the president admonished him, 'You will please keep in mind that this is a college not a technical school. . . . The object aimed at is culture, not practical knowledge.' "[21]

Not unaware of the increasing popularity and influence of the pseudosciences in this country, in 1838 a group of scientists in Boston formed the Lazzaroni, an exclusive society whose membership was be limited to the "best scientific minds of the country" and whose purpose was to keep the "progress of science" from being threatened by "charlatanism and quackery."[22] The founding members of the Lazzaroni—Alexander Bache, Benjamin Pierce, and the Harvard botanist and insatiable collector Louis Agassiz—were not only interested in distinguishing "true" from "practicing" scientists, they also had an explicit political agenda. In 1848, after changing their name to the American Association for the Advancement of Science, they stated their primary goal as "increasing government funding for the purer *rather than* industrial" sciences (italics added). And yet, even though the core of the Lazzaroni were to be the "best scientific minds," the AAAS membership included clergy, journalists, farmers, librarians, doctors—even lawyers.

Though the AAAS never achieved the level of influence the members hoped for—they had to settle for exerting control over who was hired at certain key institutions and universities, such as Harvard—perhaps their most lasting accomplishment was the robust resentment they managed to engender in the American scientific community, especially among those not originally anointed to their by-invitation-only club. Joseph Leidy, one of the first 50 members of the National Academy of Sciences, said of the Lazzaroni: "It appears to me nothing more than the formation of an illiberal clique, based on Plymouth Rock."[23] And yet, even though the Lazzaroni were known in certain circles as "The Cambridge

Clique," their charter remained essentially unchanged as the constitution of the AAAS until 1920.

Thus did the nineteenth-century American scientific community itself provide evidence for a certain social differentiation *within* the sciences, with the Lazzaroni providing the very sort of "aristocracy" of scientists that the senator, as well as the American public at large, seemed to fear. This split between the "pure" Lazzaroni scientists and the "applied" technicians and engineers would gradually become, in the American popular as well as scientific psyche, the difference between the engineer as "democratic" if not outright working class, and the theoretician as elitist, aristocratic, and therefore vaguely foreign. And thus certain political agendas—and even certain kinds of science—became identified with the exclusionary airs of the Lazzaroni. The early American scientific elitism of the Lazzaroni, however well intentioned it may have been at the time, gradually served to enhance the average American's image of at least one type of scientist—the theorist—as someone isolated from the mainstream of middle-class American life, and eventually transformed the relatively moderate distinction between the practical and the theoretical scientist into the radical distinction between the Reformer and the Revolutionary.

Sir Peter Medawar, writing about "Anglo-Saxon" attitudes toward science, reminds us that "in England it was Francis Bacon who first made the distinction between basic and applied science, the former increasing our understanding of nature, the latter our power over it."[24] Medawar goes on to say that the "notion of *purity* has somehow been superimposed upon the concept of a distinction between the two kinds of science, creating a distinction between 'polite and rude learning.'" Decades later, the physicist I. I. Rabi would characterize these two scientific cultures as follows:

> There is first the creative intellectual activity which constantly pushes back the boundaries of our understanding of natural phenomena; second, there is an industrial activity which applies the results of scientific knowledge and understanding to satisfy human needs and whimsies. Only the first is what I call the "science of physics" proper; the second is only the side of physics which has been called "the inheritance of technology."[25]

Here, from one of the chief A-bomb wizards himself, is the distinction between Technology and Science, between Technician and Scientist—between Doer and Thinker. In fact, a common sentiment expressed by those drafted into the A-bomb ranks was that "the Manhattan Project was essentially engineering rather than science."[26] J. J. Thompson put the distinction between the two groups this way: "research in applied science leads to reforms; research in pure science to revolutions."[27] In other words, applied scientists are capable only of building new gadgets; pure scientists, on the other hand, are capable of conceiving entirely new societies.

In the nineteenth century, this split had already become institutionalized in the European university-based scientific community. The differing functions of "applied" and "pure" science were taken for granted, and assigned different responsibilities—and different departments—in the university. However, as American science was to come to this type of structure relatively late in the nineteenth century, the split between the two kinds of scientists tended to form along lines more loosely defined as "social," as is evidenced by the relatively narrow membership of the Lazzaroni, which resulted in their presenting themselves as a sort of New England–scientific FFV, rather than as a congregation of professionals dedicated to maintaining high standards.

A FAIR question to ask at this point might be, didn't this portrayal of scientists represent a distrust of *all* things new, a general anxiety about the Industrial Revolution? And was there anything particularly *American* about it?

In fact, the American public's distrust of the kind of theoretical, elitist scientist represented by the Lazzaroni was not exhibited toward all scientific offspring of the new industrial age. To a large extent, American anti-technologists like Hawthorne and Melville, and even eventually Emerson, were quite out of step with the American public. The American faith in, even reverence for technology was distinctly the opposite of our distrust of and distaste for theoretical scientists, and was demonstrably different from the European attitude toward the increasing mechanization of society.

There are several reasons for this differential in the popular response to industrial mechanization in America vs. Europe. In many ways, the labor situation in America was the exact opposite of that in England. America of the mid-1800s was experiencing a labor scarcity rather than a surplus, and seemed to possess nearly unlimited raw materials and "undeveloped" territory. Technology in this country was seen as the key to supplementing labor power and "conquering" the wilderness, rather than, as in England, replacing human labor and defiling the landscape. As Bruce notes, "Technological unemployment held no terrors for Americans. American workers welcomed the labor-saving technology that Europeans resisted."[28]

Additionally, the American public was fascinated with all this new technology, as is evidenced by the fact that technological fairs were all the rage of the mid-century. The first national technology "fair" was held in 1846 in Washington and was essentially a display of the latest advancements in steam power. It was such a success that another was held in New York only a few years later, in 1853—partly as a national answer to the World Exhibition of 1851 in London, but also because, in the few intervening years, many innovations had been made in steam and other technologies. What was chiefly celebrated at these American fairs was inventiveness: manufacturing processes and the machines that automated them, from steel and lumber to rubber and cloth. These technology fairs were designed to appeal to a consumer mentality and in fact made little effort to represent the state of American science.[29] (I will return to this subject in chapter 3.) And as the public enthusiastically embraced any and all displays of the new technology—technology advertised as the essence of American ingenuity and progress—there grew up in the public mind an identification with science and technology so strong that, unlike in Europe, one became a synonym for the other: "The line between science and technology seems to have been less sharp and invidious in America than in Europe, where rigidly defined hierarchies were traditional," writes Bruce. "Practical work carried no public stigma in the New World, and science (as some scientists complained) had no aristocratic standing."[30] At best, it might be said that there was in America no cultural "predilection" toward granting the scientist "aristocratic" standing; but at worst, it might be argued that there was a tremendous cultural bias *against* any such attitude. To most Americans, the true scientific heroes were the inventors: men with little or no formal training who nonetheless, through sheer individual initiative and "Yankee ingenuity," created mechanisms which performed tasks trivial to major, and which could be seen as visibly contributing to the increased productivity of the entire community rather than merely the personal reputation of some individual (though that was, of course, an "unavoidable" byproduct—see chapter 3).[31]

The general term to describe such scientists seemed to be "engineers." Such a designation was only partly accurate. Though these scientists applied engineering principles to bridges, buildings, railway lines, canals, roads, the telegraph—that is, all the expanding networks of a growing nineteenth-century technostate—the vast majority of these practicing civil and manufacturing engineers, until well after the Civil War, had little or no university training whatsoever; most had learned their trade through apprenticeships with older, equally layman engineers, or in the Army. However, American colleges, while slow to see this need for trained engineers as an opportunity—and still slower to add graduate curricula in the theoretical sciences—eventually began to establish the technical schools that would provide the basis for America's astounding technological advances of the late nineteenth and early twentieth centuries. These years saw the founding of the Franklin Institute in Philadelphia, the Rensselaer Polytechnic in Troy, New York, and the Cooper Institute in New York City, all schools devoted exclusively to training engineers. By the late 1870s, there were *eighty-five* engineering schools in the country—and still less than a dozen well-credentialed graduate programs in the theoretical sciences.[32]

Even as there were few places to either train or work as a theoretical scientist, there were even fewer places to publish theoretical scientific work. With the exception of half a dozen scholarly journals, most scientific magazines of the time were aimed at an audience of amateur mechanics and inventors. *Scientific American* was one of them, and was not viewed by scientists as a properly scientific journal but rather as an "everyman's" magazine touting the latest technological wonders. In an article about *The Manufacturer and the Builder*, a long-running and very widely read nineteenth-century version of *Popular Mechanics*, Daniel Weber discovers a consistent editorial ideology that went beyond merely honoring the skilled laborers in American society. In fact, "their only 'political' stance seems to have consisted of a passionate demand that the nation recognize that the symbol of all national progress is the mechanic." Moreover, the editors clearly felt that progress was a result of a particular *kind* of scientific knowledge: "There is one vital reservation . . . to this impulse to regard science as Truth, for the editors considered only practical scientific knowledge to be of any lasting value. . . . The advantage of practical over theoretical knowledge was apparently one of the major factors in the mechanic's superiority." Weber goes so far as to suggest that "the publishers and editors of *The Manufacturer and the Builder* were unconsciously attempting to create an archetypical national hero in the 'mechanic.' "[33]

And in this attempt they certainly did not represent a minority, or even merely a rural perspective. From an editorial about the "new sciences" in the *New York Times* of 1859: "The Professor is no longer the near-sighted, thin-faced and clean-shaven man, in rusty black, that he was. Now he wears a beard [and] is discovering gold-diggings, indicating new mines, and pointing out to capitalists the wealth of unannounced coal measures."[34] Even from the sophisticated perspective of America's premier metropolis, New York City, the "new" scientist was imagined as someone who had escaped the university laboratory, had given up reading books (which had made him nearsighted), and traded the lifestyle of the aesthete for that of a healthy, rugged outdoorsman. Most important, this *American* scientist had found his proper place in the American community, as a sort of resource scout for the capitalist. And he had grown a beard for good measure.

Such an image is indeed a far cry from the gaunt, pale, crazed Dr. Frankenstein of filmic infamy, screaming into the raging lightning storm, "It's alive!" If this "new" American scientist is to be considered the standard for what an American scientist ought to be and do, and even how he ought to look (of course noting that the figure is always a "he"), we might wonder to what extent this image was circulated and admired in other media of the nineteenth century: how his wider life—that life he'd left behind before he'd forsaken his laboratory and glasses, grown a beard, and "lit out for the territories"—was imagined, and to what extent his personal life was considered formational to his professional life. These are the questions I will examine in the next chapter.

SEX AND THE SINGLE MAD SCIENTIST

2

Domesticating Scientific Passion in Nineteenth-Century American Fiction

IF ONE was asked for the image of the iconographic mad scientist of the nineteenth century, one might reasonably respond that such an image could be found in the character of Mary Shelley's Victor Frankenstein as described in the Introduction—an image that would become the model for countless mad scientists of books and films in the next 150 years. However, many of the character traits, rhetoric, and even "props" that mark Victor as a mad scientist in these later books and films aren't to be found in the original novel bearing his name. In fact, we can find most of these trappings in the work of Nathaniel Hawthorne, as in these opening lines of his short story "The Birthmark":

> In the latter part of the last century there lived a man of science, an eminent proficient in every branch of natural philosophy.... In those days when the comparatively recent discovery of electricity and other kindred mysteries of Nature seemed to open paths into the region of miracle, it was not unusual for the love of science to rival the love of woman in its depth and absorbing energy... The higher intellect, the imagination, the spirit, and even the heart might find all their congenial aliment in pursuits which ... would ascend from one step of powerful intelligence to another, until the philosopher should lay his hand on the secret of creative force ... [Aylmer] had devoted himself, however, too unreservedly to scientific studies ever to be weaned from them by any second passion. His love for his young wife might prove the stronger of the two; but it could only be by intertwining itself with his love of science, and uniting the strength of the latter to his own.[1]

Nathaniel Hawthorne's work is generally considered archetypically American Romantic fiction, with its focus on metaphysical dilemmas, its structural foundations in Puritan allegory, and its indictment of modern technology. And

23

his stories are always distinguishably American in their settings—more American, I would argue, than the strikingly European milieux of Edgar Allan Poe's stories, with their decrepit ancestral halls, medieval dungeons, subterranean crypts, and general tone of age and decay.

Yet certainly there are many parallels between Hawthorne's stories and much of the European Gothic fiction of the period. One thinks, for instance, of the obsession in the Gothic with the megalomaniacal, narcissistic persona of a protagonist wrestling with stupendous problems of hubris, God, and Nature—a recurrent theme in Hawthorne. Time and again, the protagonist of a Hawthorne tale is a "chemical experimenter" or a "natural philosopher" or a "psychical researcher" who has pursued a line of scientific investigation to an extreme—an extreme that threatens not only his own life, but also the lives of his family.

Hawthorne's "Birthmark" sets the standard for this dynamic. The plot of "The Birthmark" pits Aylmer's scientific knowledge—which is in fact, with mentions of "charms" and "enchantment," much more closely aligned to the mysticism of the medieval alchemist than the empiricism of the enlightenment scientist— against all the powers of Nature, as symbolized by the crimson handprint on the cheek of his wife, Georgiana. And the central term for this conflict, as presented in those opening lines, seems to be "passion": the first passion of the "higher intellect, the imagination, the spirit, and even the heart" for scientific investigation; and a second passion—if such is the right word, given the relative neutrality of the prose about it—for his young wife. In this confrontation between laboratory and hearth, while the latter might somehow "intertwine" itself with the former, the narrator suggests no possibility of the domestic passion ever eclipsing the scientific one. Though Aylmer's wizardry (his library consists of the works of alchemists like Albertus Magnus, Cornelius Agrippa, and Paracelsus, but not scientists like Newton or Davy) is ostensibly directed to making Georgiana's beauty "perfect," in fact his chief motivation seems to be a desire to demonstrate that he is more powerful than the forces of Nature that have stamped their mark on his wife's cheek.

It is also remarkable that so many of the tropes we associate with the entire Frankenstein genre appear nowhere in Mary Shelley's novel, but in fact originate in "The Birthmark." For instance, while Victor works alone, it is Aylmer who has a deformed and slavish assistant, Aminadab: "a man of low stature, but bulky frame, with shaggy hair hanging about his visage, which was grimed with the vapors of the furnace." Aylmer even makes a brief allusion to achieving Frankenstein's goal when he says, of Georgiana's "case," "I have already given the matter the deepest thought—thought which might almost have enlightened me to create a being less perfect than yourself."[2] Aylmer has a secret laboratory which he jealously guards and which he insists his wife must not enter. And of course, when his mystical machinations finally succeed and the birthmark fades, so does his wife's life; thus he is even more directly responsible for murdering his domestic tranquility than is Victor Frankenstein.

We find many of these same themes in another Hawthorne story, "Ethan Brand," particularly the opposition between the passion for learning and that for love. Brand begins as a happily married and domestically contented lime-burner, a perfectly respectable practitioner of a fundamentally practical trade. However, as the result of a pact made with the devil wherein Brand is to increase his intellectual abilities manyfold, he becomes a "cold observer, looking on mankind as the subject of his experiment." In Brand we have a Faustian figure, someone who makes the transition from "good" manual and, most important, familial productivity to "wicked" cerebral and isolated intellectual searching: "Thus Ethan Brand became a fiend. He began to be so from the moment that his moral nature had ceased to keep the pace of improvement with his intellect."[3] Note the assertion that Brand's intellectual "improvement" in and of itself is not at fault; rather, it is the *pace* of that improvement which is somehow to blame for Brand's fall, the implication being that moral improvement will quite naturally lag behind intellectual progress. Thus Brand's "dehumanization" is really a process of unnaturally accelerated intellectualization. Additionally, the particularly American sensibility of the story seems especially repelled by a lack of any obvious, practical product from Brand's self-damning intellectual investigations, rather than by his transgression of any moral or communal laws (a distinctly American reaction I will explore further in my discussion of Ahab's character in *Moby Dick*). Still, I would argue that the primary sin Brand commits, as far as the story is concerned, is his self-willed alienation from his family and community, which is presented as an essentially inevitable by-product of his hyper-intellectualization.

Yet another example of this formula in Hawthorne is the oft-anthologized story "Rappaccini's Daughter." Despite the European setting that distinguishes it from most of Hawthorne's other "mad scientist" stories, the basic elements so evident in "The Birthmark" and "Ethan Brand" can be found again here, but with an important twist: rather than scientific passion serving to seduce the scientist away from his family, Rappaccini—a widower, one should note—actually turns his scientific knowledge *against* his family, in the person of his daughter. By raising his daughter among poisonous flowers of his own creation, Rappaccini has created someone immune to those poisons. However, his daughter is as a consequence fatally poisonous to all other humans. It could be argued that Rappaccini as Creator/Father in fact poisons what is figured explicitly as the Garden of Eden of his hearth and home (and literal garden) with his scientific passion. This use and one might say abuse of the myth is taken so far that, in one scene, a drop of poison from one of the flowers actually kills a reptile, marking Rappaccini as even more venomous than the Garden's original serpent.

In fact, all males in this story are unified by the blindness of their passion, regardless the object of that passion. The young man who is the nominal hero of the story has his passion for the daughter figured in the same hypnotic terms that characterizes the scientist's passion for investigation in other Hawthorne stories: "It mattered not whether she were angel or demon; he was irrevocably within her sphere, and must obey the law that whirled him onward."[4] Furthermore, the creation of the flowers themselves is seen as perverse, something outside the sanctified familial boundaries of normal reproduction: "Their gorgeousness seemed fierce, passionate, and even unnatural. . . . Several [blooms] also would have shocked a delicate instinct by an appearance of artificialness indicating that there had been such commixture, and, as it were, adultery, of various vegetable species."

Rappaccini himself is described as a "tall, emaciated, sallow, and sickly-looking man, dressed in a scholar's garb of black," with "a face singularly marked with intellect and cultivation, but which could never . . . have expressed much warmth of heart." And the story clearly codes this cold intellect as a true scientist: "Her father . . . was not restrained by natural affection from offering up his daughter in this horrible manner as the victim of his insane zeal for science; for, let us do him justice, he is as true a man of science as ever distilled his own heart in an alembic." If the narrator is doing Rappaccini "justice" in praising him as a "true man of science," the first half of the statement makes it a very curious kind of praise, indeed. Significantly, Rappaccini's opposite number, Signor Pierro Baglioni, is also a professor, but Baglioni has no program for revolutionizing life and is rather presented as a modest practitioner of medicine. And, while he is also described as elderly, he is of a "genial nature, and habits that might almost be called jovial," as well as being "portly" rather than emaciated.[5]

But by far the worst sin Rappaccini commits is removing his daughter from the human community, for throughout the tale the emphasis is on the solitude of his daughter's unnatural existence. And her young lover's horror at the end isn't revulsion so much at his transformation into a poisonous creature, but rather at his transformation into a fellow *isolato*. "Accursed one! . . . finding thy solitude wearisome, thou hast severed me like wise from all the warmth of life and enticed me into thy region of unspeakable horror!" Thus it is separation from community that is the worst result of Rappaccini's experiment. "They stood, as it were, in an utter solitude, which would be made none the less solitary by the densest throng of human life." And to gild the lily, as it were, the story has the mad scientist gloat over his demented triumph of enforced alienation: "My science and the sympathy between thee and him have so wrought within his system that he now stands apart from common men, as thou dost . . . from ordinary women." Even Rappaccini's love for his daughter is presented as perverted by his cold, calculating obsession with science: "Oh, how stubbornly does love—or even that cunning semblance of love which flourishes in the imagination, but strikes no depth of root in the heart. . . ."[6] When the daughter dies, she is seen as a victim of intellectual investigation which has transgressed some sort of normal boundaries: "thus the poor victim of man's ingenuity and of thwarted nature, and of the fatality that attends all such efforts of perverted wisdom. . . ."[7] Note that such a transgression is linked to a "thwarting" of nature, that wisdom gained from such transgressions is automatically assumed to be "perverted," and that the imagination is marked as the site of this transgression and consequent perversion—all topics to which I will return later.

Thus in Hawthorne the scientist's passion for exploring—and consequently and apparently necessarily deforming—Nature always results in the abandonment of the communal regulation of production and the familial modes of reproduction. As critic Taylor Stoehr has noted:

> Hawthorne's stock figure . . . is an isolated man whose mentality and special pursuits tear him away from the warmth of (usually female) society until he hardens into a frozen or petrified monster. . . . Hawthorne repeatedly plays upon a contrast between the human warmth of domesticity and the self-defeating coldness and abstraction of egotistical endeavor. . . . In Hawthorne's work clinical detachment . . . is always a symptom of moral disease.[8]

With such characters as Aylmer, Brand, and Rappaccini, as well as Goodman Brown, Chillingworth, Maule, Westervelt, Gromshawe, and Dolliver, Hawthorne explored and extended the "mad scientist" repertoire of cultural archetypes, firmly rooting these figures in the American cultural consciousness.

But it is not just Hawthorne who viewed American scientists—or as they would have been called then, natural philosophers—in such a condemnatory light. This treatment of not just scientists but of scholars of almost any stripe is practically omnipresent in American Romantic fiction. Think for instance of the demented chemical experimenters in Poe, or of Washington Irving's hapless teacher, Ichabod Crane, or of the dandified and over-educated easterners in James Fenimore Cooper's stories of the frontier, who seem more misplaced Europeans than "true" Americans.

Certainly one of the most wicked aspects of most American mad scientist characters of this period is their distinctly European and aristocratic bearing. From explicit references to titles and nobility, as in "Rappaccini's Daughter," to more veiled applications of this trope, such as the fake nobleman in Melville's

Confidence Man, these early versions of American "mad scientists" are often tainted by an aristocratic and autocratic attitude which smacked of the artificial nature represented in the estates of Europe rather than the "wide open frontier" nature of America. However, subtle alterations were necessary to adapt certain European motifs to American audiences. For instance, while the European protagonists of Shelley and E. T. A. Hoffmann are usually Counts or Barons, in American fiction they become Doctors and Professors—thus emphasizing an elitism attained (or perhaps indoctrinated?) by education. And Hawthorne's megalomaniacs actually possess ancestral titles, own estates, are often entrusted with young female wards, and display a most *haut monde* knowledge not just of botany and medicine, but also of brandy and cigars.

But perhaps the most significant representative of all American mad scientists is a character not Hawthorne's at all; and I'm speaking here of the maddest mad scientist of them all, Melville's Captain Ahab. This particularly American thematic of the irreconcilable dichotomy between the natural, communal, productive, and tranquil commitment to domestic stability and the unnatural, selfish, counter-productive, and overzealous obsession of scientific passion is perhaps best set forth in *Moby Dick*.[9]

The emphasis in *Moby Dick* on the domestic realm as the only possible counterbalance to Ahab's autocratic and, importantly, over-intellectualized madness is certainly in keeping with the theme of anti-domestic isolation running through this period's "mad scientist" fiction. Ahab's obsession with "striking through" what he believes is the façade of Nature, and the hubris represented in his quest for vengeance on the symbol of that Nature, the White Whale, are perfect examples of the transgressive beliefs and outsized egos of these figures—figures which are typically, as with Ahab, coded through their ideology, speech, dress, and mannerisms as European. However, Ahab's counterpoint in the novel can be found in a character of fundamentally American pragmatism—his first mate, Starbuck.

Starbuck is the one member of the *Pequod* crew alert to the dangers posed to their community by Ahab's monomania, and the only member capable of dissuading Ahab from his plan of vengeance. It is in "The Symphony" that Starbuck comes closest to diverting Ahab, when he offers Ahab an ideal image of the domesticity awaiting him back on shore:

> "why should any one give chase to that hated fish! Away with me! let us fly these deadly waters! let us home! Wife and child, too, are Starbuck's—wife and child of his brotherly, sisterly, play-fellow youth; even as thine, Sir, are the wife and child of thy loving, longing, paternal old age! Away! let us away!"[10]

Ahab responds with the only substantive mention of his family in the entire book:

"I have seen them—some summer days in the morning. About this time—yes, it is his noon nap now—the boy vivaciously wakes; sits up in bed; and his mother tells him of me, of cannibal old me; how I am abroad upon the deep, but will yet come back to dance him again."[11]

And Ahab himself suggests it is his years at sea and his single-minded and solitary dedication to whaling that have hardened his heart and left him more interested in pursuing metaphysical vengeance than domestic serenity:

"for forty years has Ahab forsaken the peaceful land, for forty years to make war on the horrors of the deep! Aye and yes, Starbuck, out of those forty years I have not spent three ashore. When I think of this life I have led; the desolation of solitude it has been; the masoned, walled-town of a Captain's exclusiveness, which admits but small entrance to any sympathy from the green country without—oh, weariness! heaviness!"[12]

It is interesting, too, that what defeats Starbuck in his attempts to alter Ahab's self-destructive course are Ahab's flights into metaphysical theorizing about free will vs. determinism; at such moments Starbuck feels himself "over-matched" and quietly slinks away, apparently more afraid of theory than suicide. And, rather than Ahab's sinister demeanor, mad rhetoric, and self-destructive ravings, Starbuck seems most horrified by Ahab's attributing conscious malevolence to the "dumb brute" that is, in Starbuck's eyes, a necessary and respected component of the commonsensical and *mechanistic* industry that is whaling:

"I am game for his crooked jaw, and for the jaws of Death too, Captain Ahab, if it fairly comes in the way of the business we follow; but I came here to hunt whales, not my commander's vengeance. How many barrels will thy vengeance yield thee even if thou gettest it, Captain Ahab?"

[Ahab]: "my vengeance will fetch a great premium here!" [striking his chest]

"Vengeance on a dumb brute!" cried Starbuck, "that simply smote thee from blindest instinct! Madness! To be enraged with a dumb thing, Captain Ahab, seems blasphemous."[13]

What most offends Starbuck is the *inefficiency* of Ahab's madness. In other words, Ahab's first sin (according to Starbuck) appears to be the abstraction of the white whale into a mythical being, rather than treating it as a mere commodity to be harvested, manufactured, and distributed; and, conjointly, seducing the crew to join this perverted abstraction and away from their manual and practical function as workers in the whaling industry.[14] Thus finally it is the lack of any *practical* outcome to Ahab's obsession that horrifies Starbuck, at least as much as if not more than his commandeering of the *Pequod* community to serve his personal vendetta. Though Ahab's roots can certainly be traced through Hawthorne to Hoffmann and Shelley, and so to European

myths and anxieties about mad alchemists and rhetorically seductive megalomaniacs, there is something fundamentally *American* about the character
Starbuck, and about Starbuck's particular discomfort with the anti-utilitarian
and hyper-intellectual aspects of Ahab's scheme.

That Ahab views the world as a gigantic mechanism and all the living organisms as components of that machine is made clear by his rhetoric throughout the book, as exemplified in this scene from "Sunset":

> "but my one cogged circle fits into all their various wheels, and they revolve. . . .
> The path to my fixed purpose is laid with iron rails, whereon my soul is grooved
> to run. Over unsounded gorges, through the rifled hearts of mountains, under
> torrents' beds, unerringly I rush!"[15]

However, that Ahab is as much if not more wizard than rationalist is also made
clear throughout by his frequent use of magical rituals, such as the scene where
he commands the harpooners to cross their lances and chant "Death to Moby
Dick!"; or when he extinguishes the demonic St. Elmo's fire with his bare
hands; or when he nails the gold coin to the mast not as a symbol of the practical profit Starbuck seeks, but as a talisman focusing his hypnotic control of
the crew.

It may in fact be the chief irony of *Moby Dick*'s reception that, in a tale
Melville intended to be a dire warning about the seductive and potentially
apocalyptic power of the New Technology, the popular American imagination
found instead a warning of the danger of the New Intellect. In many ways,
Ahab is the progenitor of what would become the mad scientist archetype in
the countless "invader" films of the 1950s: aristocratic in dress, speech, and
mannerisms; arrogant and reserved with his fellow men; isolated from his family and community; and, finally, someone whose monomaniacal passion for
pushing through the "pasteboard mask" of nature leads to his own destruction
as well as that of his entire community—or almost his entire community for,
after all, Ishmael does "escape alive to tell thee."

IF AHAB is perhaps best conceived as first and foremost a particularly American Frankenstein, then it is worth examining in some detail the reception of
the European novel which generated perhaps the most durable image of the
mad scientist in both cultures, if not worldwide.[16] Mary Shelley's *Frankenstein;
or, The Modern Prometheus* was first printed in England in 1818, to an immediately enthusiastic audience, and a surprisingly diverse one for what was in
some ways merely a modern Gothic ghost story. It was as if every group in European society saw in the figure of Victor's revivified monster an incarnation of
their particular and worst nightmare.

Chris Baldick has traced the use of the monster as a trope across a broad spectrum of European political and social discourses, from Carlyle's warnings about the increasing "mechanization" of the human spirit, to political cartoons wherein the monster appears as the embodiment of various rampaging hordes—everything from French revolutionaries to Irish rebels. Baldick finds that one thing all these images have in common is that the "monster," whatever it represents, is always an ugly and awkward assemblage of various parts of other organisms or organizations, an aggregate that would not naturally occur as a "whole."[17] For most Europeans, the Frankenstein monster as trope created an alignment in public discourse between esoteric technology and monstrous "anatomies," organic and social, and served as a "ready-made" symbol for their anti-technology sentiments.

An indication of the novel's popularity is the fact that within three years of its publication there were fourteen productions of plays, English and French, which were either near-literal adaptations of the plot or based on the same elements (by 1990 that number had risen to nearly 90).[18] The most successful of the time was *Presumption: or, the Fate of Frankenstein* (1823), adapted from Shelley's novel by Richard Brinsley Peake. We might first note the transformation of title and subtitle: whereas Shelley's subtitle focused on the aspiration of the mythological figure of Prometheus (*Frankenstein, or The Modern Prometheus*), the play's obvious interest is in the scientist's punishment; and it introduces a new level of ambiguity into the question of protagonist, for exactly which Frankenstein—creator or creature—is more keenly the victim of fate? Also, according to Stephen Forry, the most "newsworthy" aspect of this as well as nearly every other production was what in modern terms we would call the "packaging" of the Monster. Through innovative makeup (green-tinted skin, enlarged head and features), costuming (elevated shoes, and, in one production, a tattered hangman's noose left somehow inexplicably around the creature's neck), and lighting techniques (a heavy dependence on footlights to achieve an effect familiar to any child who's ever held a flashlight below his chin to spook his friends), the monster was made the center of the story. In fact, Thomas Potter Cooke's portrayal of the monster in *Presumption* completely stole the show in London—so much so that there were letters in the newspapers and demonstrators outside the theater protesting that the "monstrousness" of the monster was too graphic and shocking for something open to general audiences.

The most famous French version was called *Le Monstre et le magicien* (1826), a title which nicely indicates the true star of the play by giving the monster top billing. Interestingly enough, as Forry notes, reviews of the play's debut in Paris "immediately equated the Creature with mob violence," and "on the English stage . . . Frankenstein immediately became associated with unbridled revolution, atheism, and blind progress in science and technology. . . . Percy Shelley's reputation as a revolutionary and atheist certainly preceded and tainted the reception of his wife's first novel."[19] This was an analogy that, as Baldick chronicles, became quite common in the use of the monster as, indeed, a warning, in this case of social revolution or disorder.

But this figuring of the creature as a one-man mob does *not* appear in American renditions of the story. Perhaps one explanation is that, until the draft riots of the Civil War, Shays's Rebellion was the closest the new nation had come to mob violence (and of course in most places this country was too sparsely settled to generate much of a mob anyway). In American plays and eventually films, the only role of a "mob" is the literal one of the peasants who chase the monster with torches, and thus represent not revolution but ignorance and prejudice in the face of new technology, aligned more with the Luddites of the English textile mills than the Sans-culottes of the French Revolution.

Forry also points out that the first plays tended to emphasize the "demoniacal aspects of the Creature, elaborated the alchemical overtones of Frankenstein's experiments, and expanded the sinister context of the laboratory." In fact, most of the later film images with which we are so familiar were originally created by the requirements of the stage: the need to entertain and impress an audience, confine the action to a few readily constructable locales, and concentrate on simple and physical conflicts between characters that might be choreographed for the stage, rather than the complex and abstract conflicts within and between the characters' psyches that form the majority of the novel. Forry believes most of the early plays reduced "the character of Frankenstein to that of a simple hubristic overreacher condemned for challenging God's order, [which] transformed the novel into a simplistic moral allegory."[20] For instance, from a playbill for *Presumption: or, the Fate of Frankenstein*: "The striking moral exhibited in this story, is the fatal consequence of that presumption which attempts to penetrate, beyond prescribed depths, into the mysteries of nature."[21]

Many of these plays added a character absent from the novel, a laboratory assistant (who would eventually become the infamous Igor of countless film productions), and for which we find the model not in *Frankenstein*, but instead in the figure of Aminadab from "The Birthmark." However, whereas in "The Birthmark" Aminadab's deformity is presented in a positive light, something that increases his identification with the earth and the forces of Nature which he believes placed the mark on Georgiana as a sign of their power—power with which Aminadab believes Aylmer is locked in a futile contest for supremacy— in the play and film versions of *Frankenstein* the assistant represents Victor's deformed soul and is a physical manifestation of the ugliness in Frankenstein's character which would motivate him to such blasphemous behavior. Also, in terms of the dynamics of plays, the assistant was required as a dramatic foil, sometimes even as comic relief, yet another way in which the actualities and specifics of the novel are lost to the requirements of dramatic formula.[22] However, in another American departure, the assistant is largely absent until James Whale's film version of 1931, as though Americans found the assistant either irrelevant or superfluous—or perhaps because, for Americans, Victor as Inventor doesn't necessarily possess a deformed soul.[23] (More about this national distinction in a moment.)

Another of those novelistic actualities that would be sacrificed to the requirements of dramaturgy is the monster's ability to speak. Whereas in the novel the monster not only teaches himself to read and write and eventually quotes Milton to Victor and in many ways outmatches him rhetorically, in nearly every play and film adaptation to follow the monster is capable of nothing more than grunting, or at the most monosyllabic utterances such as "friend" and "good." It would be safe to say that, in the popular imagination, the monster is always and must always be speechless, and that the thought of an articulate monster runs violently counter to the public's conception of everything that makes him monstrous. One might take from this that, in the popular cultural imagination, speech is evidence of a soul, which is of course what the monster is theorized to be missing as he is created "unnaturally" (see chapter 12 for an extended discussion of this issue). In other words, the putative moral message of the novel—and the explicit moral message of most of the plays and films made from it—is the "presumption which attempts to penetrate, beyond prescribed depths, into the mysteries of nature," and thus the monster, as the physical representation of that unnatural penetration must, *a priori*, be soulless. In fact, one of the earliest film portrayals of the story was titled *Life Without a Soul* (1915).

Forry also argues that the monster, like Caliban in *The Tempest*, "represents nature devoid of nurture." Certainly Victor's chief crime is to abandon the monster "at birth," as it were, and to leave its nurturing up to Nature; which in fact Nature does very handily, providing it with food, clothing, fire, and reading material—all aspects of the novel's treatment of the relationship between the monster and Nature which would suggest that, at least as far as the novel is concerned, the monster may be uniquely constructed and animated, but it is certainly not "unnatural." However, as Forry points out, whereas Prospero "redeems [his] Creature by claiming 'this thing of darkness I acknowledge mine,' Frankenstein can never claim the image of darkness that he has unleashed."[24] And this failure of compassion and empathy is ultimately what leads to Victor's destruction as well as that of his familial community.

Of course the "monstrousness" of the monster accounts to a large extent for the popularity of the Frankenstein myth and the industry which sprang up around it—though it is curious that the visualization of the monster became fixated with details of its construction which do not in fact have any basis in the novel. Shelley's monster is vaguely described as large—Victor having chosen supersize body parts in order to make the surgery easier (a choice made great sport of in Mel Brooks's *Young Frankenstein*)—and with "yellow skin" that "scarcely covered the work of muscles and arteries," "lustrous black" hair, teeth of a "pearly whiteness," "watery eyes," and "shriveled complexion and straight black lips"; but nowhere in the novel is there any mention of the iconic neck electrodes or the fliptop lid that were made famous by James Whale's 1931 *Frankenstein*—features which in the popular imagination now come to symbolize not just the monster, but the very name Frankenstein. In fact, if one enters any costume shop and asks for a Frankenstein mask, one is unlikely to be presented with the mask of a cultured, aristocratic, handsome Swiss medical student, i.e., Victor Frankenstein. Rather, the green skin, the iron electrodes protruding from the neck, the half-dead, heavily lidded eyes, the flat skull, the prominent hackwork surgical stitches . . . all are now trademarks of everything Frankensteinian.

In fact, it could be argued that the creature, at least as conceived in the novel, isn't a monster at all; at least, not in the modern sense of the word: a malevolent entity enacting death and destruction for its own sake, and without any deeper psychological motivation. Rather, while Shelley's (and Victor's) creation is certainly represented as a grotesque being, something drastically ill-formed and therefore "monstrous" to behold, it is a monster more importantly in the sense of the word's Latin root, *monstrum*, a portent or warning; and in its modern meaning, a demonstration—specifically of Victor's hasty and irresponsible methodology in first constructing the creature, and then in abandoning him.

But such fine linguistic distinctions are essentially absent from the Creature's popular image, where its physical monstrousness is its defining feature. The first photographic images of the monster appeared in New York in 1873, and strangely anticipate the depiction of the monster in Edison's brief one-reeler of 1910, wherein the creature looks like a cross between the Scarecrow and the Tin Man from *The Wizard of Oz*. Significantly, this first filmic version of the novel begins with Dr. Frankenstein leaving wife and kids to go build the monster, with much melodramatic crying and wringing of hands.[25] I would argue that this scene presents the key to Frankenstein's "original sin," at least in American eyes, as that of the abandonment of the communal and tangible domestic realm for the solitary and theoretical world of the laboratory—even though both that domicile and that laboratory are missing from the novel. Thus, from the very first installment of what would grow to become an almost limitless fascination in film with mad scientists and their progeny, the figure of the mad scientist is represented as someone whose soul is torn between his love for his wife and his passion for his intellect—with the intellect the clear and undisputed winner every time. Thus the eternal love triangle is given a modern, and more sinister meaning.[26]

Of course, by far the most recognized version, even today, is James Whale's *Frankenstein*, made for Universal Studios in 1931 and starring Boris Karloff as the Monster and Colin Clive as Henry (changed from the novel's Victor for reasons never explained) Frankenstein. Forry suggests that the general look of makeup and scene were greatly influenced by earlier films, such as *Der Golem* (1920), *The Cabinet of Dr. Caligari* (1920), and *The Phantom of the Opera* (1925), all of which set a standard of cadaverous faces for both Victor and the monster. Also contributing to the iconic image of Victor is the near-emaciated form of the protagonist in all these films, perhaps again for the dramatic effect it brought to the presentations, but also perhaps to make the creature seem even bigger. And Whale adds the assistant figure, Igor, rescued from the obscurity of Peake's *Presumption* of a century before.

In yet another departure from the novel, Whale (and all his imitators) focuses on the creation scene, the one described in my Introduction and which concludes with Colin Clive's famous "It's alive! It's *alive!*" Again, this reaction, as well as the entire scene, is something absent from the novel; thus we should examine the actual creation—or rather animation—scene from Shelley's novel in order to compare it to the popularized version which has become as integral a component of the myth as the transposition of Frankenstein's name onto the monster's visage:

> It was on a dreary night of November, that I beheld the accomplishment of my toils. With an anxiety that almost amounted to agony. I collected the instruments of life around me, that I might infuse a spark of being into the lifeless thing that lay at my feet. It was already one in the morning; the rain pattered dismally against the panes, and my candle was nearly burnt out, when, by the glimmer of the half extinguished light, I saw the dull yellow eye of the creature open; it breathed hard, and a convulsive motion agitated its limbs.[27]

And that's it. Nothing about electrical bolts zapping across the room, nothing about bubbling cauldrons or glowing test tubes, and certainly nothing about hunchback assistants scurrying to and fro to activate the complicated machinery apparently thought absolutely necessary in order to instill something as mysterious and fundamental as life. Given the relatively low-key rhetoric of this scene—especially when considered against the elevated, one might even say melodramatic and clearly Gothic tone of much of the rest of the novel— this particular moment is obviously not, for Shelley, the climax of the narrative, or even a defining moment. Rather, everything proceeds in the novel from

Victor's *reaction* to this moment: his abandonment of the monster, his refusal to take responsibility for its education or integration into society, and his continuing and seemingly irrational denial of any connection between the monster and himself. Clearly the focus of Shelley's interest is not on the animation of the monster—not even, I would argue, on the supposed moral transgression of the experiment—but rather on the consequences of Victor's abrupt and complete rejection of his accomplishment.[28]

However fervently Victor tries to deny any association with his creature, links between the two are emphasized throughout the novel. In fact, the identification of Victor's name with the monster's image, while it might seem to merely represent a fundamental ignorance about the actual text, could in fact be seen as a perfectly logical reading of that text. The theme of doubles, or *doppelgangers*, is much evident throughout European as well as American Gothic literature, and has been thoroughly documented by any number of critics.[29] Martin Tropp, for instance, points out that the monster is nearly always active only during Victor's various fits of nervous collapse and *ennui*, as though only one of them can physically manifest their joint psyche at any one time.[30]

Curiously, however, this eminently exploitable thematic isn't really explored until Whale's *Frankenstein*, where it is hinted at throughout the film and finally made clearly, if not didactically evident in the "through the windmill shot," when the camera shifts back and forth between Victor's face and the Monster's seen staring at one another through the rotating panes of a windmill. But this concept of their linked existence—a fundamental motif in the novel—would disappear from subsequent film treatments until it was made the center of the entire creation-animation scene in a made-for-television version, TNT's *Original Frankenstein*.[31] In this depiction, the Monster is not just Victor's metaphorical double, but is in fact literally created from him through a complicated (and tragically under-explained) process of "magnetic cloning."

There were, of course, cultural traditions that informed Shelley's "construction" of her monster novel. In Victor Frankenstein, passionate-if-naive chemical experimenter, Shelley was in fact drawing on a long European tradition of sinister, near-mythical folk villains: Albertus Magnus, Cornelius Agrippa, Dr. Faust—all essentially magician-shaman figures. And stories of "doomed experimenters and obsessive chemists" were in fact particular favorites of early nineteenth-century audiences. Balzac, the arch realist himself, wrote a popular story entitled "La Recherche de l'Absolu" (1834). Interestingly enough for my argument here, in this story about an obsessive search for the "absolute," what is sacrificed is primarily the scientist's domestic harmony. Baldick sees this theme, too, in the work of E. T. A. Hoffmann, which focuses on a "complex involving the fusion of productive labour and sexual obsession," but a sexual obsession which, as in Hawthorne, seduces the experimenter's sexual passion away from its "natural" target, his wife, and focuses it instead into the "unnatural" passion for penetrating "beyond prescribed depths."

Most important, the "striking moral exhibited" by most of the American versions is that obsessive *intellectual* labor not only leads to an alienation from one's family, but is in and of itself fundamentally suspicious. A quote from *Presumption* that was to have served as a key moment in Whale's screenplay—but which was later revised to a milder admonition that what he is doing is "mad"— had Waldman, the good scientist, advising Victor to turn back from his "unholy" investigations: "You make yourself equal to God—that was the sin of the fallen angel."[32] In other words, Victor is linked here with Satan—which is yet another corruption of the novel, as in Shelley's version it is the monster who compares himself to Satan, *Paradise Lost* having served as one of the key texts in his self-education.

Thus, in the early European dramatic conceptions of the novel, Victor's chief crime was to be the same as in *Presumption*, and that was the crime of hubris. Yet in American versions of the myth that charge never really stuck. Rather, in the popular refiguring presented in countless film versions for American audiences, it is Victor's placing himself apart from his familial community, rather than above his larger social community, that marks this scientist as incurably mad and irredeemably bad.

One might in fact ask if the novel itself even considers Victor "mad." Victor certainly is high-strung and given to extremes of both anger and repose, always either violently threatening the monster with destruction, or floating in a kind of serene ennui (usually when contemplating mountains and trees in true Romantic form). And it is true that the primary motivation for his project, to create a "new species [that] would bless me as its creator and source," suggests more than a touch of megalomania. But it could be argued that Victor isn't *exactly* crazy—at least not in the twentieth-century sense of the mad scientist who creates in order to wreak havoc or gain power. And after all, the polarity of his feelings and reactions is perfectly in keeping with the dynamics of most Romantic texts.

But ultimately it isn't necessary, at least to my purposes here, to measure Victor's madness by modern standards. Rather, what is important is that Victor is *perceived* in the popular culture as the *sine qua non* of the Mad Scientist, and that for much of the American population—most of whom have never read the novel—the image that comes to mind when they hear the phrase "mad scientist" is Colin Clive hunched over that hulking body, eyes wide, mouth agape, quivering with megalomaniacal glee over his grotesque accomplishment. And thus, in the popular zeitgeist, Frankenstein *is* the model for all mad scientists to come, regardless of whether or not the novel from which he sprang supports this diagnosis.

More important, there are in fact reasons to consider Victor a "mad" scientist, at least in terms of the American understanding of a Wicked Wizard—which is a scientist who, first and foremost, abandons his domestic pleasures and responsibilities in order to pursue his intellectual obsessions: a choice that is, axiomatically, insane. And the novel does support this reading. If the family is seen as the site for "natural" sex and reproduction, then the novel clearly condemns Victor's attempt to leave that territory. Victor is given the opportunity to end the monster's campaign of revenge by creating a female mate for him, and he even begins to work on a female creature. But when faced with the prospect of an actual mating of the two, he envisions their progeny as an entire race of monsters. (This is a curious conclusion for someone who has supposedly studied biology and physiology as closely as Victor, for he ought to know that, since his creations are merely surgically reconstructed versions of normal humans, there would in fact be no biological reason that their offspring would not be perfectly normal humans.) However, Victor's revulsion at the thought of their sexual mating and its consequences is perfectly consistent with the condemnation of "unnatural" sexual reproduction which runs throughout the novel, from the absence of biological mothers to the near-incestuous relationship between Victor and his semi-sister/fiancée, Elizabeth.

Just as thoroughly as the novel explores and condemns all "unnatural" versions of mating and reproduction, it also explores and ultimately condemns obsessive intellectual labor which removes—or more properly seduces—the experimenter away from his family as the site of acceptable concentration of effort and reproduction of self. And this formula was laid down not just by Hawthorne and Shelley, but by other early nineteenth-century literature as well.

For instance, in Hoffmann's "Sandman": "moreover, as is always supposed to be the case with such laboratory experimenters, your father, altogether absorbed in the deceptive desire for higher truth, would have become estranged from his family."[33] Notice first that the father's search is characterized as a "desire," and particularly a deceptive desire. Second, note the suggestion that to search for "higher" truth is to (nearly automatically) be deceived. And finally, that the search itself takes on the figure of a seductress, a homewrecker who "estranges" the father from his proper family duties. Clearly the danger here is the threat presented to proper and familial sexual relations by obsessive and (most important) solitary intellectual labor.[34]

In accounting for differences between the European and American reactions to and adaptations from *Frankenstein*, we also have to examine the differing formulation and practice of Romanticism in the two cultures. For

Europe, *Frankenstein* came at the moment of peak Romantic reaction against the latest scientific discoveries and technological inventions that would eventually culminate in the Industrial Revolution. The science of Frankenstein—or what the public saw as the science of the novel—seemed to embody, literally, all that the Romantics considered dangerous about scientific practices, practices that sought to demystify and deface rather than celebrate and enhance Nature. After all, the novel is centered on breaching the most mysterious and powerful natural boundary of all, death.

Frederick Amrine writes of how post-Enlightenment science was envisioned as a practice formulated to draw bright lines between that which properly fell under the rubric of empiricism and all other human activities practiced by men who were somehow beyond normal human society. Goethe, for instance, reacting to what he saw as this scientific reductionism, sought a "fundamentally new scientific method that does not simply exclude qualities from the domain of scientific inquiry, but instead strives to explore them in a rigorous and systematic fashion."[35] Amrine suggests that Romanticism developed at least in part as a reaction to this new science, and that the Romantics saw Newton as their chief enemy. He also suggests that this reaction of the Romantics was partly due to the fact that Newtonian science abstracted time, "making all moments equal, whereas the romantic wants to find certain elevated, transcendental moments which are unlike all others, that cannot be generalized or quantified."[36]

It could also be argued that, aside from or perhaps as a direct and logical consequence of the new science, the real enemy of the Romantics was materialism, the reduction of the esoteric and mystical Nature to literally *matériel*, mere matter that acted and was acted upon in ways completely comprehensible and predictable. And thus in this view the chief enemy of Romanticism would indeed have been Newton and his clockwork universe, and the chief inheritor of this viewpoint was no longer a natural philosopher—a title which would have at least retained the aura of a metaphysician engaged with deeper meanings of powerful natural forces—but rather the mechanical technician, someone entirely dedicated to the analysis and control of this clockwork universe. In other words, the Master Mechanic.

However, materialism as such was never a problem in mainstream America in the same ways it was in Europe, for reasons to do with the differing roles of technology and labor in the two cultures (see chapter 3). Thus American romanticism (small r) was not culturally disposed to attack the empiricism of the new science, or the technological wonders it offered to a nation with an apparently infinite appetite for technology. Unable to criticize the methods or tools of this new empirical and pragmatic science, American anti-technologists could only criticize its goals; but as any practical goal that benefited the community and increased the nation's productivity in ways easily understood by the popular imagination was to be admired, no matter the method or tools, then ultimately only *impractical* goals could be appropriate targets of opportunity for such criticism.

How did American romanticism define *impractical* goals? I think we see the answer to this question in the work of Hawthorne and the other American Romantics and Trancendentalists: impractical goals were those which sought the outflanking or subversion of the natural, material, manual, and communal labor required to transform the wilderness into utopia—goals achieved through an unnatural indulgence in abstract, intellectual endeavors, endeavors that motivated the scientific "theorist" to live outside the confines of natural communities, such as his or her family and social network.

This reaction went even to the bedrock of the language that was used to construct the new science, as well as the language used to critique it. Stuart Peterfreund writes of the movement among the Romantics aiming to achieve a "perfect" language, a language that had been lost in the Fall and had been replaced by poetic language too dependent on metaphors, which at least the American Romantics considered a lesser language as it was perforce further removed from contact with actual Nature. In this view of the dynamics of metaphor, the word no longer perfectly matches the thing, and thus is suspect.[37] One might even see in such a reaction a precursor to the markedly American development of Pragmatism, which sees metaphor as a linguistic "tool"; and the development of new linguistic tools to keep pace with innovations is a perfectly pragmatic necessity. This conceptualization is in contrast to the European critique, which involved theories questioning the very logic of the tools themselves.[38]

Of course 1859—a year we might mark as the ending of American romanticism with the growing threat of the Civil War—saw the publication of Darwin's *Origin of Species*, a work which implicitly argued that the biological existence of humankind was separable from its spiritual existence, and thus which separated God from not only the daily reality of that biological existence, but also from any serious study of that existence, as well.[39] In Darwin's schema, all evidence of evolution reduces, or at least reconstructs God as something more akin to Newton's "cosmic clockmaker" than the Romantics' (and later the Trancendentalists') notions of an omnipresent and vital force reflected in all of Nature and ascertained through an anti-rational or Gnostic appreciation of that Nature. As Linda Bergman writes, "Darwin's theory . . . explicitly demands that we see God not as a creator of specific beings or even as a designer of types, but at most as the remote originator of the natural law that set creation going, and it represents nature as a force more powerful than God and more immediately involved in creation."[40] In a sense it could be argued that *Species* creates a new Nature, a force independent of both God and humankind; a sentient Nature which not only manipulates humankind through forces ancient and powerful and to ends which only it fully comprehends, but which also actively resists human efforts to understand and control those forces. And the Romantics resented and resisted what they saw as this new science's dogmatic program to demystify this Nature, to reduce it to formula, to autopsy it and of course in service of that autopsying, kill it; as the famous lines from Wordsworth have it: "Our meddling intellect / Mis-shapes the beauteous form of things: / We murder to dissect."

Still, there were some similarities in the European and American reaction to *Frankenstein*. Much as it had been in Europe, the monster trope in America was used as a figure in nearly every discourse warning of any process, trend, product, political or social movement that threatened to "control men" rather than be controlled by them; and in this function it appeared in treatises everywhere, from Emerson and Thoreau's philosophy to Margaret Fuller's early American feminism. Fuller, for instance, warned against attempting to construct an "American" literature to respond to—or compete with—the calls for a European literature ringing out in England and France. The American experience had not yet, Fuller argued, coalesced sufficiently to allow such a creation: "Without such ideas, all attempts to construct a national literature must end in abortions like the monster of Frankenstein, things with forms, and the instincts of forms, but soulless, and therefore revolting."[41]

However, while Europe saw in *Frankenstein* a warning about the evils of the Industrial Revolution, or the evils of Irish rebellion, or even the evils of democracy, largely the reception of the novel and its tropes was quite different in America.[42] Whereas in England, Carlyle's pessimism fueled such popular revolts against technology as the Luddites, the American public's attitude toward technology was best expressed in essays such as Timothy Walker's "Defense of Mechanical Philosophy," published in 1831—an argument which encountered little resistance and much enthusiastic support. In fact, the very technology that presented such a threat to European philosophers was seen by Americans as a necessary precursor to the spiritual enlightenment Carlyle and the other European technology doomsayers so longed for. Walker spoke for the majority of Americans when he wrote, "We deny the evil tendencies of Mechanism, and we doubt the good influence of [Carlyle's] mysticism."[43] Furthermore, while in Europe the figure of Prometheus—clearly Victor's mythological "father"—was taken to be a trope of hubris appropriately punished, the classical figure represented nearly the opposite to most Americans, who considered Prometheus a bold, clever hero—someone more on the order of Ulysses than of Sisyphus. In Bruce's words, "To Americans the stealer of fire from the gods triumphed in the final reckoning."[44] Wrote one American magazine editor in an enthusiastic, if narrow review of the novel: "To the Prometheus of the nineteenth century, no rewards are esteemed excessive, no dignities too exalted."[45]

Yet these distinctly American attitudes toward Promethean boldness and ascendant technology create a problem in terms of our accounting for the developing American mad scientist trope in fiction; for, if Americans found nothing cautionary in the tale of Prometheus, and nothing threatening in the rise of the new technology, then what exactly about the story did they see as frightening, evil, let alone "mad"?

The first part of our answer can be found in the plot of *Frankenstein*, which presents Victor, his fiancée, and his creature as three points in an "eternal triangle" wherein Victor's passion for Elizabeth is brought into competition with his passion for creature building—and the former is found wanting. This theme in particular was picked up and expanded upon by the novel's American audience. In nearly every stage production, the role of the fiancée was expanded, and in later productions she was typically written simply as Victor's wife. In fact, as previously mentioned, Edison's famous "lost" silent adaptation of *Frankenstein* begins with a scene where the Dr. leaves his wife and children.

Why code scientific endeavor as something that *necessarily* competes with the passion for mate and family? One might answer that such a dynamic is simply "good drama," or that emphasis of this aspect of the plot is necessary to reduce the tale to, as Forry said, a "simplistic moral allegory." Perhaps it was even assumed that an American audience could better relate to the monster as home wrecker than metaphysical dilemma. But such simple answers don't seem to go nearly far enough. For one thing, the emphasis on the virtues of the hearth as a palliative to the dangers of the laboratory, à la Hawthorne and Melville, is a distinctly American addition to the myth. Furthermore, since Americans were *not* offended by Victor's philosophical boldness or technological mastery, one wonders why this particular tale would become so oft-quoted a trope in the genre of American *anti*-science fiction; or why, for that matter, there even developed such a genre in American fiction at all.

Which brings us back to the work of Hawthorne. The mad scientists in Hawthorne's work, as well as in that of so many other writers of the period, are egoists whose intellectual passions can be realized only in efforts that are solitary, heavily dependent on writing and books, and fundamentally derived from the energies of the imagination. Thus by all properly Puritan laws of family, mind, and spirit (cultural forces I will discuss at length in the penultimate chapter), they are outlaws, and thus figures whose desire for achievement must be aligned with results which are a threat to their communities. And of course at the figurative center of those communities sits the family. The obsessive experimenter working long hours all alone in a laboratory is an individual who is beyond surveillance by even his closest relatives (again a theme much evident in Puritan ideology to be examined later). Moreover, the product of that solitary labor is not materially apparent, is not a device or a gadget that might easily be seen to increase the efficiency of the community. Whatever intellectual talents these mad scientists are admitted to possess are therefore figured as *wasted* talents, waste which inevitably returns—like some monstrous repressed memory, or Victor's abandoned creature—to wreak havoc on the people closest to them, destroying not only their families and communities but their entire world, so that not even the mad scientists themselves will "live to tell thee."

Thus, I argue, Frankenstein as trope, inspiration, portent, and model evolved in the American marketplace to stand for—and against—ideas and prejudices quite different from those it had meant for its European audiences. Primarily, it came to represent everything that was *un*-American about certain kinds of scientific practices, i.e., overly intellectual scientific practices. By the last third of the nineteenth century, set against this monster of the imagination run amuck, was the trope for all *good* American scientific practice: all the marvelous technological gadgets produced by the explosion of invention and innovation enabled by first steam and then electric power. From the conclusion of the Civil War to the beginning of World War I, these Great Independent Master Mechanics would offer the American consumer a "cabinet of wonders" produced in their workshops and "invention factories," thus cementing themselves and their products in the minds of that American consumer as the epitome of scientific achievement—of, that is, *practical* scientific achievement.

A CABINET OF WONDERS

3

Selling American Science in
the Nineteenth Century

THE SCIENTIST stands before a thick red velvet curtain, pulling it slightly aside to offer a glimpse of what lies beyond. We see a seemingly endless row of shelves rising from floor to ceiling. We can't quite make out their contents, but from the rapt attention of several people gazing at them, we assume whatever is on display is captivating. At the man's feet are arrayed massive bones of some prehistoric beast, and on a small table is draped the body of a large bird: peacock? condor? We can't be certain. In fact, an overall aura of mystery hangs about the painting, making us eager to accept the man's invitation and explore beyond the frontier of that lifted veil.

The painting is *The Artist in His Museum* (1822) by Charles Willson Peale (1741–1827). Though Peale would become one of the foremost naturalists of his time, his true passion was for painting, as evidenced by the names he chose for four of his sixteen children: Raphaelle, Rembrandt, Rubens, and Titian. Through his fervent fund-raising work for the American rebels, he became portrait painter to Colonial celebrities such as Jefferson, Hamilton, Franklin, and Hancock; and of course the most famous portrait of George Washington is by Peale, one of over sixty he made of America's pre-eminent Founding Father. But he also used his wealth and influence to finance expeditions into the wild frontier of the new nation, and placed the results, alongside his paintings, in a gallery first called the Philadelphia Museum, but which eventually became known and renowned as the Peale Museum. Peale's vision of New World science is nicely encapsulated in *The Artist in His Museum* as an "art" meant to fascinate as it educates, entertain as it elucidates. And Peale's painting stands as perhaps the best icon of how American science and American scientists were perceived for most of the nineteenth century.

The triumph of the image of Master Mechanics as the "good American scientist"—as opposed to the Wicked Wizards of Hawthorne et al. as "bad" and therefore implicitly (and often explicitly) not "American scientists"—became solidified in the second half of the nineteenth century by the ways in which American science was sold—which was often concomitant with the ways America itself was sold. Several cultural trends and forces can be identified as establishing the ascendancy of this image of American science as technology to be consumed, and therefore the American scientist as inventive salesman: the popularity and structure of technology fairs; the presentation of technology as the key to the exploitation of the American frontier; the rise of Pragmatism as the preeminent American philosophy; representations of the Great Independent inventors in the public media; and the foregrounding of technological innovation in utopian literature and movements

Strikingly absent from this picture is any association of this new technology with public universities or other institutionalized expertise. Building on the already well established American distrust of "book learning," the public came to not only *not* associate the concept of formal education and theoretical sophistication with scientific—or more properly technological—exploration and advancement but, if anything, to view formal education as an impediment to technological invention and social progress. As evidenced by their ubiquitous designation as "independents," the much-publicized corps of Great Independent inventors was set in the public's mind in stark contrast with theoreticians, who were characterized in the literature and public media as "dependent" on universities, cliques, and formal training.

Chief among the forces communicating these two divergent images of scientists to the American public were technology fairs. As previously stated, the first American foray into the highly competitive world of science and technology exhibitions was the Technology Fair of 1846 in Washington, which was soon followed by the New York "Crystal Palace" exhibition of 1853, seen as the American national answer to London's World Exhibition of 1851. The New York fair was intended to showcase new technology as the chief and most representative accomplishment of a young, vital democratic New World. As Walt Whitman wrote in "Song of the Exposition":

> . . . a Palace,
> Loftier, fairer, ampler than any yet,
> Earth's modern wonder, History's Seven out stripping,
> High rising tier on tier, with glass and iron facades,
> Gladdening the sun and sky – enhued in the cheerfulest hues,
> Bronze, lilac, robin's-egg, marine and crimson
> Over whose golden roof shall flaunt, beneath thy banner, Freedom.

The other two major fairs with a similar purpose were the Centennial International Exhibition in Philadelphia in 1876 (where total attendance topped ten million), whose entire *raison d'être* was the celebration of the Democracy's first century of progress; and the World Columbian Exhibition in Chicago in 1893 (with an attendance of over twelve million), which was meant to rival the metropolises of Europe in its grandeur. All the American exhibitions were essentially advertising venues for the latest manufacturing machinery, and were constructed more along the lines of county fairs than scientific conferences. Entertainment was their chief aim, and what nod they paid to education was in terms of "educating" the expanding consumer class to the wonders of the new products available to them, a goal that was chiefly attained through spectacle. For instance, at the 1853 exhibition in New York, Elisha Otis advertised his new invention of a safety stop for elevators by repeatedly demonstrating the dramatic crash of an older elevator without one. At the Electric Light Association Exposition in New York in 1886, Edison had people make their own X-ray photos. The new discovery of radium—which some called "the elixir vitae"—was a particularly popular attraction: dancers performed with veils that had been dipped in radium; one could gamble at a radium roulette table; and Dr. W. J. Morton, a fervent promoter of X-rays, introduced "Liquid Sunshine," a "restorative" taken internally that would glow when radium was placed on the drinker's skin.[1]

The model for such exhibitions can ultimately be found in the Peale Museum, known as a "Cabinet of Wonders." There was little scientific organization to the selection and arrangement of Peale's exhibits; though some were placed in surroundings meant to suggest their geographic context and natural associations, the primary desired effect was to "shock and awe" the viewer. Peale's collection included everything from fairly common-if-appealing minerals—such as geodes and other shiny rocks—to fake mermaids. In her essay "Museums: Representing the Real?" Ludmilla Jordanova argues that Peale saw himself not as a scientist educating the public, as Louis Agassiz did, but as an entertainment *artiste* along the lines of P. T. Barnum: "If I had to sum up my argument in a single visual image it would be Charles Willson Peale's portrait of himself in his own museum, painted in 1822," wherein he reminds us he is an artist by his palette on the table next to him. Jordanova sees Peale as an "enthusiastic Linnaean," a painter who is "*exceptionally* preoccupied with techniques for achieving verisimilitude," and as a museum keeper "unveiling both the truth of nature and the truth of human life to the world at large."[2] But Peale is also the sideshow barker, perhaps this more than any of his other roles, beckoning us to the exhibits bizarre and curious, slightly illicit, hidden from everyday sight—so designated by the conspiratorial way in which, in the self-portrait, he pulls the curtain to his museum aside only enough to give us a tantalizing glimpse of the wonders within—to a side of

Nature we wouldn't otherwise know existed. And this was the main lure of such early nineteenth-century "science museums" and the technology fairs to follow, with their promise to show us something odd, unusual, stunning. Not so much were they "cathedrals of science" (John Berger's phrase from *Ways of Seeing*), but rather circuses of science.[3]

It seems perfectly logical to extend Jordanova's analysis of the role art museums would come to play in the commercialization of culture to that of technology fairs in the commercialization of technology. Indeed, one can see in these fairs the desire to "de-museumize" science, to create a space where science is no longer something to stand in passive awe of, as in a museum, but something to experience, as in an amusement park. Knowledge becomes useful, accessible, and, most important, fun; something best experienced with a backdrop of screaming children and large boisterous crowds; something more of a festival than a lecture. Eventually such fairs would present the Great Independent inventors much as museums present the Great Masters, and be constructed as spaces where their works took on the same mass iconographic qualities as Berger points out are possessed by great works of art.

Jordanova also argues that "Scientific and medical museums are a way of letting people into science."[4] And of course it is part of the mythology of science that it is assumed to possess a "privileged access to nature," as though scientists were aristocrats with club keys to a door marked Nature, a door which is off limits to the common folk. That is the very feeling one gets when looking at Peale's portrait: that he is inviting the uninitiated into a secret world where we will be dazzled by the "mechanisms of discovery, and into the story of the acquisition of truth."[5] Quite telling is Jordanova's use of the word "mechanisms" to characterize the way truth is discovered in such spaces: that is to say, via technology, not theory; and that word "story" is also very telling, in that it reminds us that what is being offered isn't a boring treatise but a thrilling narrative.

Jordanova also recognizes that much of what science museums "do" to science is to simplify it, to reduce its specialized rhetoric to the lowest common denominator; that is, they implicitly recognize that there are limits to the presentation of complex scientific concepts to the general public. She writes: "The simple fact is that many aspects of human experience and action, especially those that are abstract, cannot be rendered suitable for exhibition in a museum. The new realism in science and medical museums, driven as it is by powerful market and political forces, denies this. It seeks to create a set of visual experiences for a mass public that forces itself and its meanings upon the viewers."[6] In other words, to make science less "privileged" and more democratic, less abstract and more material, less specialized and more common, is to make it something other than science. It is to make it into another form of mass entertainment.

The businessmen who put together the early technology fairs in America were perfectly aware of this requirement. In an art history thesis, Palmyre Pierroux discuss the formative role international exhibitions played in "dissolving some of the boundaries separating education and entertainment."[7] Though the fairs separated the more carnival-like displays with fences and separate admission, the prevailing atmosphere of entertainment over education blurred any boundaries between the two. According to Burton Benedict, "The public no longer had to play the role of impressed spectators. They were invited to become frivolous participants. Order was replaced by jumble, and instruction by entertainment."[8]

Such was the image of American technology exported to the European continent. One of the earliest technology shows—though it might seem odd to call it that—to travel the international circuit was Buffalo Bill's Wild West Show, which began its European tours in the late 1800s. According to Robert Rydell (author of *World of Fairs*), "Buffalo Bill's show was so spectacular that Queen Victoria made her first public appearance in 25 years to attend."[9] In an interview, Rydell argues that

> the Wild West shows, along with circuses and world's fairs, were a major transmitter of American mass culture between 1869 and 1922. . . . Disagreeing with those who think the Americanization of the world began much later or started with McDonald's, Rydell said, "American mass culture is really in place by the beginning of the 20th century, certainly by World War I. . . . The Wild West shows portrayed American heroism and industry. They depicted conquest and progress. They introduced the Europeans to popcorn, the Colt revolver and Winchester repeating rifle."[10]

Thus, I argue, such "Wild West" shows can be considered a type of technology fair; they were exhibiting not only the technology of American "conquest and progress," but also the American philosophy of technology that shaped and motivated those conquests and that progress. The Wild West Show was an advertisement not only to Europeans but also, perhaps more important, to Americans that the "wild west" had been tamed—so tamed it could be safely presented to audiences from San Francisco to New York, complete with all the theatricality and none of the danger of Indian attacks, stagecoach robberies, and entire Civil War battles. In much the same way that *Frankenstein* as a play popularized the figure of an alienated and fanatic theoretical Wicked Wizard, the technology fairs and Wild West Show popularized the figure of a heroic and practical Master Mechanic, if not in person at least through the foregrounding of the technological innovations which made the taming of the wild west possible.

They were also demonstrations that such technology and the philosophy of "taming" nature were distinctly American, that is, *not* European. As I argued in chapter 1, one of the key distinguishing features that separates Master Mechanics from Wicked Wizards is that the former are represented as quintessentially American, while the latter are portrayed as crypto-Europeans. For instance, the Centennial Exhibition in Philadelphia of 1876 was touted for many things, but the greatest seemed to be that it was *not* European. From a review of the fair in *American Energy and Industry*: "Those persons who doubt the truth of the oft-repeated assertion that the Americans are the most enterprising and 'go ahead' people in the world, should come to Philadelphia." The review compares it to exhibitions in Vienna and Paris and claims that it was all the better because Americans brought it off without the "army of trained professionals" required in the European exhibitions. Note of course the denigration of any public exhibition that would require "trained professionals," as though any specialized training evident in the exhibition would somehow taint the exhibits, rendering them less appealing to a general public.

It is, however, interesting to note how this jingoistic strain had altered if not disappeared by the time of the Columbian Exhibition in Chicago in 1893. The architecture was explicitly Classical, the buildings sentimental and ornate, and thus they harkened back more to the cities of the Old World than they suggested those of the New. Frederick MacMonnies designed the fountain at the center of the exhibition that was linked to the rest of the grounds by Venetian canals, and the buildings lining these canals were all designed in the neoclassical style—some of them appearing to have been teleported from some Germanic river landscape. Ironically, while Americans found it awesome, Europeans found it trite and disappointing: "We expected better, much better, from the well-known audacity, initiative and originality of the Americans," said one.[11] Perhaps what surprised the European visitors was that architecture seemed the chief area of American technological innovation of the period, with all others in service to it. After all, there was no limit of places to build. And it was in fact American architects who reacted to the White City with a horror equal to that of their European counterparts. Louis Sullivan, an American architect who designed the Chicago Stock Exchange and many other signature American skyscrapers, predicted that "the damage wrought to this country by the Chicago World's Fair will last half a century."[12]

Even America's budding love affair with the latest technological wonder, the automobile, was represented in the popular culture in a suspiciously "Europeanized" form. Back in 1875 an article in the "Arts" section of the *New York Times* had complained there were no good American plays because the best plays were based on infidelity in marriage and, while that might be tolerated in France, "the same audience will be scandalized by similar treatment from an American author."[13] However, by the end of the century the latest rage was "automobile romance" novels wherein the heroine, typically married, would fall in love with a chauffeur who ultimately turned out to be European royalty. So much for "scandalized" American audiences. It was also a time when everyone who owned an automobile wished to be photographed in it, rather than in their salons, as had been the convention since the creation of portraiture photography barely half a century earlier. However, even if that showcase of American "conquest and progress," the technology fair, and that symbol of American technological ingenuity and geographical freedom, the automobile, had become muddled with European aesthetics and traditions, there was still one icon of American science that was unadulterated by continental pretensions—the Great Independent American inventor.

Thomas Edison and the other Great Independents are an absolutely vital component of the American cultural mythology about Yankee ingenuity, perseverance, individuality, resourcefulness, enterprise, innovation . . . everything we believe generates and guarantees American technological supremacy. But what most established and nourished the legendary status of the Independents were the practical *commercial* results of their labors—and a good deal of propaganda work on the part of the Independents themselves.

The years from 1850 to 1905 saw a great spate of inventions in mechanical and electrical devices: the elevator (1853), burglar alarm (1858), oil well (1859), repeating rifle (1860), typewriter (1873), dentist's drill (1875), telephone (1876), phonograph (1877), light bulb (1879), platter records (1887), dishwasher (1889), kinetoscope (1891) . . . a wave of inventive energy that eventually culminated in the automobile (1892). These were devices that the common man could comprehend. Even though he might not understand the details of their operation, their power lay in principles derived from an essentially Newtonian universe. And each of these inventions was identified in the public mind with a single, innovative individual: Hiram Maxim and the machine gun, Alexander Bell and the telephone, Nikola Tesla and electrical power transmission, Elmer Sperry and the gyroscope, Reginald Fessenden and the wireless transmitter, Wilbur and Orville Wright and the airplane, Lee de Forest and the vacuum tube—and of course the most prolific inventor of them all, Thomas Edison and the light bulb, the phonograph, the motion picture projector. . . . By the end of his career, Edison had patented 1,093 inventions. The incandescent light bulb alone was considered such a triumph that the *entire* front page of the *New York Times* for December 12, 1879, is devoted to articles proclaiming its arrival and praising its inventor. Significantly, the only criticism on the page comes from *Professor* Henry Morton of MIT, who is quoted as being "not sanguine" about the invention's supposed benefits and "gravely concerned" about its social consequences. In the torrent of triumphalist rhetoric, Professor Morton's complaints sound peevish and elitist—which was quite probably the intended effect.

And that intention, of course, fits perfectly with the schema I am suggesting. The mythology of the Great Independents was founded on essentially a single tenet: their lack of association with any institutions, organizations, or co-workers. As Thomas Hughes writes, "Dependency of pioneers on the prior experiences and publications of others and painstaking experimentation are foreign to popular stories of heroic creativity."[14] Or as Tesla himself put it, "Originality thrives in seclusion free of outside influences. . . . Be alone—that is the secret of invention, that is when ideas are born."[15] And the model and chief architect of this mythos was the Wizard of Menlo Park himself, Thomas Edison.

Menlo Park was the place Edison called his "invention factory," and its figuring in his public persona both illustrates the most prominent attributes of the mythology of the Great Independents and demonstrates why the isolation of these inventors was not the same sort of thing as the solitude of Victor Franken-stein, Ethan Brand, Ahab, and the other mad scientists of literature. First and foremost, the "community" of Menlo Park included rather than excluded Edison's family: his "invention factory" was essentially a drafty workshop filled with odds and ends that he could "fiddle with" until some idea "struck him unbidden." And this workshop was located within a few dozen yards of the main family house and other houses where his closest associates lived with their families. The grounds themselves might have been more properly described as an invention "village" rather than factory. In fact, the most widely circulated illustration of Menlo Park depicts the compound in the winter, heaped in snow and appearing more than anything else like "Saint Nicholas['s workshop] at the North Pole."[16]

Hughes suggests in this "idyll of isolation" a connection between Edison and Oppenheimer: "we can see Edison . . . as [a] precursor of J. Robert Oppen-heimer and his nuclear scientists at their mountain fastness in Los Alamos, New Mexico. . . . Like Edison before him, Oppenheimer was exhilarated by the withdrawal to a citadel of creation."[17] However, what Hughes overlooks is that, unlike Edison's before him, the results of Oppenheimer's isolation were widely revolutionary rather than narrowly reformist: in the truly social sense of the word, theoretical rather than practical. Thus Oppenheimer's isolation is viewed by the public as more akin to that of a Faust than a Saint Nicholas.

But perhaps the most important difference between the Great Independents and the theoreticians is to be found in their designation *as* independents, a word that marks them, in the highly competitive and lucrative world of invention, as entrepreneurs, whereas the theoreticians were mere "members" of university faculties—in a sense, academic wage slaves. The Independents were *businessmen*, who also happened to conceive and manufacture what they sold.

And, as good businessmen they were all extremely wary of competition, which contributed to their demand for solitude at least as much as any desire to be free from "outside influences." Tesla, for instance, "feared that he would be 'Astored,' Melloned,' or 'Insulled.'" Yet, as Hughes rightly points out, nowhere in the popular mythology of the independents is there any mention of "how thoroughly invention and entrepreneurship were mixed."[18] Perhaps this is because the idea that practical inventions are paired with commercial success is so deeply embedded in the American ideology we don't need to mention it; it is simply taken for granted that the most logical purpose of scientific knowledge is the creation of communally useful, commercially viable, technologically innovative "gadgets." Such an understanding is seen as simply pragmatic.

AND IT is the construction of that uniquely American philosophy, Pragmatism, that I wish to examine next. Simultaneous with the selling of American science as primarily commercial and the American scientist as a fundamentally practical, family-oriented, independent inventor was the selling of an American philosophy of realism and pragmatism that perfectly supported our privileging in the sciences of thing over theory, reality over abstraction. In *Ways of Seeing*, John Berger points out that, whereas the science museums of the first half of the nineteenth century had been viewed as "cathedrals of science"—though, as I have argued, circuses of science is closer to the mark—they became, by the latter third of the nineteenth century, "engines of realism."[19]

Certainly Edison's invention and refinement of the motion picture projector—first as the relatively crude kinetoscope (motion viewer) and later as the more sophisticated progenitor of the movie projector, the vitascope (life viewer)—brought electrical technology to the forefront of the public's conception of reality as a "thing" that could be captured and presented, a commodity to be purchased by a mass audience. And thus these inventions shaped a new understanding of what it meant to be "real." A review of Edison's vitascope praised it for presenting "life and color, with speech and the noise of movement the only things lacking. The vitascope differs from the kinetoscope in its size and the size of its pictures; it differs in that its effects are almost the acme of realism." The review goes on to foreground the vitascope's mimetic qualities, and, looking to the future, exclaims, "And think what can be done with this invention!"[20] Well, all thoughts of what can be done that follow are concerned with entertainment, i.e., uses that will "dramatize" life, and thus apparently do for life what the technology fairs had done for (or to) science—make it more interesting, more understandable, and more consumable.

Even American schools of painting at the time privileged Realism over all other forms of aesthetic representation. Such paintings from the Hudson River school as *View from West Point* by John Frederick Kensett, *Kaaterskill Falls* by Sanford Robinson Gifford, and *Kindred Spirits* by Asher B. Durand clearly were guided by a mimetic standard that alone determined to what extent they were considered great works of art. The worship of the landscape emphasized by the Hudson River School, the Audubon Society's prints and pamphlets, the popularizing of Agassiz's collecting mania, in fact the entire western frontier mythology, emphasized the Real-Natural as the proper, in fact the only fit subject for artistic representation; and this approach had little respect for or patience with the more "theoretical" art movements such as impressionism, cubism, or modernism. Rather than theory, what Realism required was labor, machinery, and an exaltation of the exploitation of Nature which that labor and machinery would enable. Such an aesthetic seemed then, as it had seemed from the founding of the nation, only pragmatic. In fact, I would argue that Pragmatism as a formalized philosophy can be seen as the logical culmination of this emphasis on the real and the practical in the sciences and arts in American culture. Therefore, I believe it is important to examine, if only briefly, a few of the key precepts in this most American of philosophies.

While many American scholars and writers contributed to the current in American thinking which would eventually be dubbed Pragmatism and identified most closely with William James, there is only space here to present what I see as the most fundamental aspect of this philosophy, and only as it is represented in three key American intellectuals: James, Ralph Waldo Emerson, and Charles Sanders Peirce. What I believe is particularly germane to my argument is the *reception* of these three "thinkers," the ways in which their thinking was either accepted or rejected by mainstream American culture, and how that acceptance or rejection shaped the development of what it meant to be doing acceptably "pragmatic" American labor.

I begin with Emerson both because he is the earliest of this trio, and because of his role as the chief inheritor of Benjamin Franklin's thinking and attitudes (see chapter 11). Emerson is of course known primarily as a Transcendentalist, so it may seem curious to offer him as one of the founding fathers of American Pragmatism; but it is important to note that his brand of Transcendentalism was remarkable for what might be considered a strain of anti-intellectualism: "When Emerson tried to cope with technical philosophy, with rigorous logic, with scrupulous scholarship, he reflected an equal mixture of envy and repugnance," writes Paul Keith Conkin.[21] In his writings, Emerson often demonstrated a "mistrust or frustration with intellect as key to the 'truth' or revelation." In an attitude clearly inherited from the Puritans, he believed in above all else the individual and ineffable nature of grace—grace that must *not* be ruled by reason. His examinations of this individual revelation of grace are not subject to logic, and therefore are not arguable in terms of logic: "He insisted that all thought is . . . a type of dreaming. It takes a man out of servitude into freedom *only when* it eventuates in action" (italics added). Even in his conception of art, he valued only that art which he saw as practically contributing to the betterment of the everyday reality experienced by the artist's community: "art had to be either an integrated aspect, a glorification, of daily life, or, in spite of its compelling lures . . . dismissed as frivolous."[22] He believed that such "frivolous" art—art without an obvious and immediate practical aim and aesthetic—was, according to Conkin, "indulgent, escapist, immoral, [was] decadent, struck with death from the first. . . . Beauty must come back to the useful arts, and the distinction between the fine and the useful arts be forgotten."[23] In other words, in his attitudes toward art—that cultural practice we might expect to be least bound by the requirements and limits of pragmatism—Emerson saw not only the possibility but the necessity for a rigorous enactment of only the practical, the pragmatic, as opposed to the frivolous, the decadent, the immoral. And the chief indicator of such "good" art was that it be "useful."

It is only fair to add that Emerson recoiled from the commercialization of American science as represented in the sort of technology "fairs" already discussed. He felt, even by the mid-nineteenth century, that a "commercial devil" had entered America, and that Evil was the name of this new capitalism. Thus he was certainly not the apologist for the new American consumer who was the target for such fairs and exhibitions. And, as with Melville and Twain, he decried the acquisitive aspect of the new technology. However, the dialectic of pragmatism/consumerism escaped Emerson (as well as Twain); neither realized that, if everything was judged from the standard of utility in a culture where utility was measured by commercial viability, then the commodification of everything, even philosophy, was inevitable.

Emerson also would not have seen the utopianism of the *fin-de-siècle* American period as particularly appealing. He didn't believe, that is, that communities purified men, but rather that purified men created purified communities. Such a position seems to smack of elitism even as he rejected the selfish elitist, an elitism perfectly in line with the anti-elitist democratism inherent in American privileging of family and community (again, as inherited from the Puritans) which merely creates a new elite: the elite of the exceptionally average, the communally defined-and-dependent "good citizen." Even though a community does not in and of itself purify men, communities are essential, in Emerson's philosophy, as a space in which man can demonstrate his purity by living and working "purely." In other words, Hawthorne's isolated Wicked Wizards offended Emerson not only because of their obsession with intellectualization, but also because their "labor" necessitated their separation from all community.

Lastly, throughout Emerson we see an absolute privileging of acts over thoughts, deeds over theory—a privileging in which is evident the same sort of paradoxical dilemma resident in Puritan beliefs about individual talent, genius, and good works. It is through good works that, in Puritan philosophy, an individual establishes his spiritual worth; good thoughts must become good actions to materially demonstrate their purity, or the thoughts are merely "decadent, frivolous." But those works are defined as "good" not by the individual, but rather by the community; ultimately the arbiter of talent, genius, and accomplishment resides not in any individual, but in a communal zeitgeist. And if an individual cannot—or is not allowed to—establish his or her own criteria for achievement, then the very idea of individualism is fundamentally compromised.

Basically, then, Emerson extends the construction of American attitudes toward what do and do not constitute worthwhile expressions of a "good citizen" which had been begun with the Puritans two centuries earlier: attitudes which favor the construction of the image of the American achiever—in our case the American scientist—as an independent-but-familial reformer rather than an isolated-and-alienated revolutionary. But this is an image riddled with contradictions: he must be an individual, but securely nestled in family and community; he must be educated, but not bookish; he must be innovative, but not revolutionary; he must be dedicated, but not obsessed; and, perhaps most central, his achievements must be material, practical, useful—not "frivolous," "indulgent," "escapist," and therefore "immoral." As an exemplar of American individual ingenuity, then, the good American scientist must be, above and beyond all else, a pragmatist.

And of course Pragmatism, in its most purely American form, comes to full fruition with William James. It is in the writings of James we can see a modern version of Benjamin Franklin's desire to create a code of conduct based equally on Puritanism and Empiricism. James envisions the possibility of "universal salvation" achieved through the elimination of anything "limp, stagnant, flabby, or self-satisfied,"[24] and the arrival of a "new prophet" of American idealism, one who would proclaim "that all our different motives, rightly interpreted, pull one way."[25] James believed that the creation of psychological and social sciences based on empiricism could "integrate all human concerns."[26] He also believed that perception ought not to be treated as universal, when interpretations of our perceptions are so clearly individual, thus accounting for varying beliefs based on common experiences. And yet he argued that these varying beliefs varied only due to the lack of a common mode of interpretation, the absence of a truly reliable "common sense"; and that Pragmatism would provide such a "universal language." Yet James was wary of the kind of absolute faith in science to solve all problems, social and spiritual, increasingly in vogue. He warned, in

Paul Conkin's words, that "science as sponsored and popularized in America, was a new church, rich in prestige, imperialistic in its claims, and intolerable in its intellectual pretensions. By unjustified metaphysical extrapolation, scientists had underwritten determinism, atheism, and cynicism, and had illegitimately cowed emotions, moral zeal, and religious aspiration."[27] Thus ultimately "James wanted to discipline science." And in this impulse he drew from the European tradition of anti-science rhetoric discussed in chapter 1. As Conkin points out, "He worked almost exclusively in the perspective of British empiricism and nineteenth century idealism," and "He considered himself a disciple of Locke, Berkeley, Hume, and Mill."[28] The product of all James's theoretical work was, oddly enough, the anti-theoretical philosophy eventually to be called Pragmatism, which Conkin sees as "a popular success and an academic disaster. . . . This was philosophical Protestantism. . . . The noble goal of pragmatism, in James's own terms, was the bridging of fact and value, science and religion."[29] In a tenet certainly recognizable to any good Puritan, James argued that the meaning of a belief was to be found in the *conduct* it inspired. Thus James might be seen as the Empirical Puritan, if more tolerant than the classical Puritans because, after all, tolerance was pragmatic, i.e., useful and productive.

Most important to my argument here is the fact that, however popular became the Jamesian version of Pragmatism disseminated in American culture, the sort of logical contradictions everywhere evident in Emerson are replicated, if somewhat modernized, in James. James hated the commercialization of Pragmatism, "But he venerated an older, more responsible type of enterprise and believed the desire for private ownership to be deep and primitive. Thus, he cast psychological aspersions on all radical or utopian forms of socialism."[30] He believed war had to be outlawed, "But elements of army discipline could be retained and a purely pleasure economy could be avoided through an army conscription to fight against nature and social injustice"[31]—a conception of military organization and discipline as central to social reform that will be expressed in most of the American utopian literature to follow. In his absolute conviction in the perfectibility of man, as well as his unwavering belief that the path to *homo perfectus* lay on the road of the empirical, the material, the explicable, and the practical, James's philosophy of Pragmatism might be said to represent the psychological mapping—the subconscious, though he would reject such a description—of the Master Mechanic *par excellence*. And the world such Master Mechanics were to construct was conceived as a technocratic society of absolute efficiency; a classless and therefore conflict-free technological utopia. More about that connection in a moment.

One might find the inclusion of C. S. Peirce in my list odd, as his life and philosophy seem in all ways antithetical to Emerson's and James's. He never achieved either the popular or academic success and status of Emerson and James, respectively; most nineteenth-century Americans never even heard of him. And that is exactly why I include him here: as the exceptional and excepted American philosopher. Peirce was brilliant, but constitutionally theoretical, aristocratic, impractical, arrogant, and, some have argued, decadent. His wife, Juliette Pourtalai, was equally esteemed and derided for her "continental" taste, and may (or may not) have been related to royalty. Peirce lived in a "castle" named Arisbe, which proved to be a money pit that eventually bankrupted him.[32] Peirce's central professional task was a refutation of the sort of morally based (or as he would have had it, morally de-based) nominalism (sensationalism, materialism, individualism, determinism) popularized by Emerson and formalized by James, and he sought above all else and in stark contrast to Emerson an extreme form of logical realism. Peirce utterly rejected the romanticism of the Transcendentalists: "Peirce stood in horror of anything incognizable; he hated unknowns. . . . His hatred of nominalism was in part a hatred of any gulf between experienced phenomena and some inexplicable ground of phenomena."[33] To him, Emersonian metaphysics meant "useless speculation, without experimental foundations and hence without meaning."[34]

Yet from our perspective in the twenty-first century, much of Peirce's writing seems uncannily prescient. For instance, one can see in Peirce a precursor to Gödel's and Heisenberg's concepts of the unavoidable role of uncertainty in any system, as he "felt he had to demolish the claimed infallibility or complete generality of scientific laws. . . . He called his doctrine tychism and used it to defend an all-pervasive and absolute chance. . . . Tychism expressed an ontological principle—there is some lawlessness everywhere and in everything."[35] He even denied the distinction between mind and matter, which might be seen as a quite postmodern attempt to resolve the Puritan paradox resulting from an absolute separation of the two; for, if the act *is* the sign of the mind, then act is an absolute indicator of mind, and thus the mind ought not to be so thoroughly mistrusted as it is in Puritan ideology. And as many poststructuralists have pointed out, much in Peirce's writing anticipates Saussure, Derrida, and other twentieth-century adherents of semiotics and deconstruction—theories of literary and cultural criticism that met with great resistance in American culture, at least in part due to their "European" roots.[36]

However, despite the brilliance of Peirce's work, much of it was fundamentally antithetical to American values and ideologies of his time, too at odds with the sort of narrative of national character being sold by technology fairs, independent inventors, and even trends in art and philosophy to be anything but vigorously attacked or simply ignored. In other words, as we see in Emerson and James the popular and popularized philosophy of the Master Mechanic, in

Peirce's philosophy and the rejection and expunging of that philosophy in nineteenth-century American culture, we see traits, tendencies, and prejudices often linked with Wicked Wizards—not just before and during Peirce's time, but to this very day.

THE AGE of the independents essentially came to an end with World War I and the beginning of "big" science projects that required large organizations, huge outlays of capital, and well-planned integration into existing systems of production and consumption. But the end of the independents did not put an end to America's love affair with technology. If anything, the years that followed World War I witnessed a resilient move toward social solutions that were based not on new theories of social relations, but on new technologies whose main product was "efficiency." This reification of efficiency as the chief aim and standard for new technology and new science was not limited to the presentation of technology and science in the fairs and the public figuring of the Great Independents; just as Pragmatism was cementing its place as the dominant American philosophy, utopianism became a central theme in much popular American fiction, with its celebration of technology and efficiency as the pinnacle of American achievement. However, in contrast to the science fiction of the time by such writers as Robert Louis Stevenson, H. G. Wells, and Jules Verne (all Europeans), with their various treatments of the mad scientist as the progeny of Victor Frankenstein, the mad scientist is largely absent from this American utopian literature (though Twain's *A Connecticut Yankee in King Arthur's Court* would certainly seem to be an apocalyptic cautionary tale about placing too much faith in the ability of technology to create utopias).

Several cultural forces worked together to shape the American vision of the utopia just around the corner and what we needed to do, and to be, to bring it about. Certainly the Panic of 1873 and its resulting economic depression, the major railroad strike of 1877, as well as recurring strikes for an eight-hour day throughout 1886, and the burgeoning American union movement brought greater public attention to solving labor problems as a key to any future utopia. It was an unquestioned axiom of such utopian thinking that the first step to unlocking utopia was general wealth. This is the argument in Henry George's *Progress and Poverty*, as well as Edward Bellamy's *Looking Backward: 2000–1887*. "Money is Power" said Rev. Russell H. Conwell, one of the most popular lecturers of the day, in a lecture "Acres of Diamonds": "You ought to be reasonably ambitious to have it. You ought because you can do more good with it than you could without it."[37] The year 1891 saw the formation of the People's Party for free coinage of silver, the abolition of national banks, the nationalization of railroads, and limits on taxes. All of these cultural forces and social problems converged in the explosion of utopian schemes and literature toward the end of the nineteenth century.

But technological utopias were not new, at least not in America. In fact, the desire for actual and material Edens was, from the founding of the country, an integral component of the American Dream. Beginning with the nineteenth century and the profusion of various reformist groups—such as the Millerites, the Perfectionists, and the Mormons—utopias and America seemed ideally suited to one another, given that the New World was seen as a blank slate upon which could be written the plans for a society entirely original and unhampered by European traditions and failures.[38] Gradually, however, the emphasis in American utopian designs shifted from the philosophically based pattern derived from their European antecedents, to one much more heavily dependent on technological advancements—a motif almost entirely absent from European utopian writings. Howard Segal notes: "As the idea of America as man-made rather than natural utopia became a distinct possibility, the original Puritan notion of America as the site of God's millennial kingdom on earth faded in popularity. Dependence on man rather than God . . . distinguishes utopianism from millenarianism."[39]

The European roots of philosophical utopian designs—Thomas More's *Utopia* (1516), Johann Andreae's *Christianopolis* (1619), Tommaso Campanella's *City of the Sun* (1623), and Francis Bacon's *New Atlantis* (1627)—all presented societies whose chief reformation was political enlightenment: societies where ideological inventions, i.e., new theories, were the key to social evolution. And this trend was continued in the social theories of nineteenth-century European philosophers, like Henri de Saint-Simon, Auguste Comte, Robert Owen, and Charles Fourier. Significantly, as we might expect from the continent of Carlyle and Ruskin, none of the Europeans made technology their utopia's focus. As Segal writes, "technological progress in [European] utopias is only a means to an end and not . . . virtually the end in itself. . . . [T]hey envision a fixed, unchanging society without further technological progress," whereas, as Segal continues, nearly all of the early American utopias did just that: "For one technological utopian the world as a whole is a 'mammoth factory,' while for [another] it is a giant 'machine.'"[40]

The earliest American utopian book was John Adolphus Etzler's *The Paradise Within the Reach of All Men* (1833), a title that emphasizes the practical, and by that word "reach" the physical attainability of a new Eden. Even agriculture was "an integral part of the producing machine." In fact, for the American utopians the "taming" of Nature was a necessary precursor to the establishment of a perfect social order. The Puritan ethic of "mastery over nature" was so central a component of most American utopian philosophies that it was rarely pointed out, even by the critics of the utopian plans, and certainly never questioned as a perfectly logical precondition: "Where she [Nature] denied us rivers, Mechanism has supplied them. Where she left our planet uncomfortably rough, Mechanism has applied the roller."[41]

As the century advanced and the engineer became the model of the pragmatic, productive "good" scientist, he took on an indispensable role in utopian schemes. By the end of the nineteenth century, when Bellamy's *Looking Backward* (1888) spawned an avalanche of imitation utopian novels, engineers had become the ubiquitous "priests" of these new societies—societies that invariably dispensed with religions based on anything other than the "material works of man."[42] And what these new priests produced was, well, production.

The supposedly self-evident link between efficient production and national unity and social content was an extremely popular idea. *Looking Backward* sold over 100,000 copies in its first year, with eventually over a million copies printed worldwide. John Dewey praised it as one of the most influential books in American history, and some economists suggested it was second only in importance to Karl Marx's *Das Kapital*; Mark Twain was a Bellamy fan and invited him to stay in his house in Connecticut to work on his next book.

The society imagined in the book, and so admired by Dewey, Twain, et al., is a sort of state corporatism, wherein the citizens (all of whom are paid the same wages) are organized into an "industrial army" which marches in mass rallies to proclaim their allegiance to the "folk" of the nation; a nation which is "a family, a vital union, a common life . . . truly a fatherland." With the hindsight provided by our knowledge of Nazi Germany, such rhetoric has a rather chilling tone today. However, this model was accepted practically without criticism at the time. In novel after novel in this genre (Segal has counted over two dozen between 1883 and 1933 alone), the salvation of the technologically driven utopia is found in production: "[society] is like a gigantic mill, into the hopper of which goods are being constantly poured by the trainload and shipload, to issue at the other end in packages . . . corresponding to the infinitely complex personal needs of half a million people,"[43] which implies an unstated assumption that if consumption is constant, so, too, will be production. And thus do these technological utopias—with titles like *Roadtown*, *Life in a Technocracy*, *Perfecting the Earth*, and the efficiently straightforward *Utopia Achieved*—assert that the utopia achieved is primarily a realm of full employment, and therefore of peace and prosperity.

That the latter is entirely dependent on the former is a theory of social relations completely centered on modes of production—and yet there is no trace of Marxist ideology in any of these works.[44] Far from it; most of these texts spend little if any time describing the political conditions of their worlds, as if the Ideological State Apparatuses (to borrow Althusser's phrase) that produce, circulate, and maintain their ideology of full and efficient productivity have become invisible—or nonexistent. These are societies where politics has become largely irrelevant: "We have no parties, no politicians," says one utopian proudly, "no political congresses, parliaments, and legislatures."[45] (We will see this theme reappear in the various visions of technocracy discussed in chapter 4.) Their consistent assertion is that capitalism's social "imperfections" are completely the result of the present age's technological imperfections. Most important to this construct is the acknowledged and vital balance between production and consumption; that is, there must be an efficient relation in the society between its parts, as in a well-functioning machine: "[in this utopia] the human machine . . . has been . . . thoroughly understood and developed to its highest efficiency."[46]

This, then, is the ultimate achievement of humankind for these planned societies: that we become utterly "efficient."[47] As one enthusiastic disciple of technocracy would later proclaim, "If man's progress is slow, it is because of wastes—wastes of everything that is precious." And in his original proposal for a group dedicated to bringing the principles of technocracy to the economic and eventually the political realms of American culture, a group called Technocracy, Inc., social critic Thorstein Veblen claimed that the "highest good" of his program lay in its potential "for ridding American society of the waste and extravagance," while Howard Scott, the leader of Technocracy, Inc., argued more directly, that "in Technocracy we see science banishing waste."[48] As Segal points out, "Thorstein equates the increasing output of our mills, our factories, our workshops of every kind with the conversion of 'crudeness and barbarism into cultured civilization.' "[49] Thus it is argued that the society modeled on the machine will remake *itself*, much as the perfect machine would be capable of doing, into something more than its constituent parts; and thus such a society becomes a gestalt of perfectly self-sustaining efficiency.

The supposed ultimate goal in these technological utopias is freedom from work; but the work *itself* seems to become the end, not the means to some other end. Segal suggests that, in this elevation of work for its own sake to a guiding principle of social organization and perfection, one can discover a particularly American and Calvinist philosophy of production, wherein idleness of any sort is a sin. "In technological utopia, work has the same status as in Calvinist doctrine: it is a 'calling,' a guarantor . . . of salvation." Which means, of course, that what might be called intellectual or perhaps "theoretical" work is not considered work at all. "Classically, the highest form of leisure was contemplation. . . . The closest contemporary approximation to contemplation is also the most dubious: university life."[50] And not surprisingly, then, in one of these imagined societies called the "People's Corporation"—a sort of capitalistic socialism—we find the leader speaking quite dismissively of the conventional university and its curriculum: "Instead of college . . . there will be an industrial university . . . [because] pounding literature into the head of a natural born mechanic is both economic and mental waste. The universal query in Roadtown will not be what does he know, but what can he do." As one technological utopian put it, "We teach that labor is necessary and honorable, that idleness is robbery and a disgrace."[51] To these American utopians, even the phrase "intellectual work" is a misnomer, as it produces no visible, tangible, consumable result.[52] Thus the theoretical Wizard "wastes" time and talent.[53]

Eventually, the inheritor of efficiency as dominant social philosophy would be the tenets of Taylorism, named after the system put forth by Frederick W. Taylor in *Principles of Scientific Management* (1911).[54] In the triumph of Taylorism in nearly all aspects of American life we will find the popular defeat of Melville, Peirce, and many other American intellectuals who sought, through their critique of anti-intellectual materialism and unbounded desire for new technology, to provide cautionary narratives about the pitfalls and shortcomings of placing all our trust in the Master Mechanics to form and advance American society—warnings that would go essentially unheeded in the glut of new technology that was commercialized via the pulp science fiction and "popular" mechanics magazines that shaped the public's understanding of new science and new scientists during the first half of the new century.

THE WORLD OF TOMORROW

4

Technocracy as Utopia in the Age of Pulps

FLYING CARS. When I think of the 1920s and 1930s, that's what I think of: flying cars. Not because such wonders existed back then, but because back then they were certain such wonders would exist by now. With titles like *Air Wonder Stories* and *Amazing Stories* and, of course, *Wonder Stories*, the popular science fiction magazines of the time—eventually to be known as the "pulps" due to the cheap, thin paper used in their production—enthusiastically predicted an almost unrecognizable world of technical achievement right around the corner. Flying cars, for instance, were almost certainly to be available at your local Ford dealer by 1950. And not just flying cars: flying backpacks, flying aircraft carriers, flying houses, flying cities—according to this "lofty" vision of the time, nearly everything we knew and used would be, by the '50s, up in the air. Whatever remained firmly planted on earth would be automated, robotized, multi-functional, and futuristic; even our ovens would have so many dials and switches they would more closely resemble UNIVACS than Hotpoints.

It was not just the pulps that foresaw this gadget-rich utopia as our future. More respectable but equally popular science magazines like *Popular Mechanics*, *Mechanix Illustrated*, *Modern Mechanix*, *Popular Science*, *Science and Mechanisms*, *Science Digest*, *Science Illustrated*, and a dozen others also used their covers as billboards for all the miraculous gizmos that would make our future one of automated ease; and they, too, were obsessed with flying cars: autogyros, convert-a-cars, even jet-powered Buicks. The difference between these science magazines marketed to the "home inventor" and the pulps was that, while the former focused on the technical details of such contrivances, and at least made a nod toward appraising their feasibility, the pulps were not at all concerned with either how such things would work or even if they were remotely possible. And it was the pulps that became one of the chief modes of distributing images of the future of American science, as well as of American scientists.

As descendants of the dime novels and penny dreadfuls, the pulps used many of the same melodramatic plots of fantasy and adventure of the previous century; but they took those plots and, most important, their cover art into new and uncharted territory. Displaying their ancestral roots, the first pulps chiefly presented stories of derring-do about exploring exotic regions, from the deepest jungles of Africa to the secret recesses of the Earth; but this new "science fiction"—or "scientifiction" as it was first called by Hugo Gernsbeck— soon evolved into a field entirely its own, with an agenda and aesthetic shaped by the new century. While writers like Jules Verne, H. G. Wells, H. Rider Haggard and Edgar Rice Burroughs had, in the late nineteenth and early twentieth centuries, written stories that certainly could be considered science fiction, they had also published those stories in general circulation magazines, venues that included writing about a wide range of other subjects. It wasn't until the advent of the pulps, and specifically Hugo Gernsbeck's *Amazing Stories* (1925), that science fiction found an ideal outlet and audience.

Still, the pulps owed much of their format and conception to earlier magazines that had targeted audiences with specific interest in technology, such as *The Railroad Man's Magazine* (1906) and Gernsbeck's *Radio News & Science and Invention* (previously the *Experimentor* and before that *Modern Electrics*). *Weird Tales* (1923) was one of the first to present a steady diet of fantasy and horror of the H. P. Lovecraft school, and to a certain extent this magazine and its imitators determined the sort of plots that would be expected from the science fiction magazines to follow, resulting in an entire genre of what might be called the Cult of Cthulhu with ray-guns. Eventually magazines would multiply to appeal to wider audiences: *Zeppelin Stories* (1929), *Astounding Stories* (1930), *Terror Tales* (1934), *Horror Stories* (1935), *Thrilling Mystery* (1935), *Thrilling Wonder Stories* (1936), and dozens of others.[1]

Rather than focus on the science of flying cars, however, my primary interest in these magazines is their depiction of the scientists who would build them, both as portrayed on their covers and as more fully developed—if that is the right word given the quality of writing in most of this work—in their stories. We might first begin by asking if we find in their representations of scientists echoes of the Master Mechanics and Wicked Wizards of American literature of the early 1800s.

Of course the pulps are famous for their lurid cover art, and what we find on these covers is very interesting: enormous torpedo-shaped rocket ships, scantily clad females in distress, threatening tentacled robots, and, unsurprisingly, mad scientists: scientists who are most often depicted as emaciated, wild-eyed, unkempt maniacs clothed almost always in lab coats and, for some reason, wearing strange bug-eyed goggles (perhaps as an exaggeration of their need for glasses, glasses being an almost ageless trope for physical infirmity). And when they're not in lab coats they're in clothes that are easily recognized as aristocratic, "foreign": smoking jackets, tuxedoes, tunics. Never is there any indication they have families, though occasionally a "female ward" will be a member of their household and, by implication, at their mercy. In other words, the mad scientists we discover on the covers and in the pages of these pulps are little changed from Hawthorne's Rappaccini. In most of the stories they even have evil assistants, à la Aminadab from Hawthorne's "Birthmark"; and they are often handicapped, confinement to a wheelchair being a particularly favored choice for representing the wicked scientist's inner failings. This coding even applies to facial hair: while slightly potty inventors are allowed full beards (like the resource explorers of the nineteenth century), goatees are clearly evidence of foreign roots and wicked intentions. The *really* bad ones usually have bald heads or, if meant to be not only mad and bad but also vile and monstrous, physically enlarged craniums—thus leaving no question that their moral depravity is rooted in their intellectual gigantism. These villains are not simply inventors of a "visi-phone" or a "hydrocopter" or a "material transmuter"; almost to a character, they are would-be world dominators, revolutionaries who have some grand scheme for either changing the world or destroying it in order to change it.

It is also made abundantly clear that their access to females has been frustrated, and thus their sexual drive has been perverted. Perhaps in some sense this is a response to the century-old tendency to portray scientists as explorers who, as in Mary Shelley's description of Victor, have been "imbued with a fervent longing to penetrate the secrets of Nature." After all, if science has supplanted wife in the scientist's sexual universe, then this union must be portrayed as inevitably a failure, Frankenstein's monster being an example of what such a union would produce. Just as in the fiction of the early 1800s, these magazines of the early 1900s suggest that reproduction outside the communally sanctioned nuclear family must always result in "unnatural" abominations deserving of severe, even total punishment—a theme we will see consistent through the next seven decades of sci-fi films and public anti-science rhetoric.

Of course, one might argue that these are merely the accoutrements of villainy that the American public had come to associate with and expect from their mad scientists. But that is exactly my point: such tropes evoked fear and condemnation in the American psyche precisely because that psyche had been conditioned, as it were, to react thus through over a century of exposure to such symbols as representative of nefarious, un-American intellectual hubris. In point of fact, there is nothing inherently sinister or depraved about any of these

tropes—glasses, lab coats, bald or large heads, Euro-fashion clothing, or attention to personal grooming—and in fact many of them can be found in other
contexts as symbols of worthwhile and admirable innovative research. The lab
coats and glasses, for instance, are typically also associated with the preoccupied demeanor of the "nutty professor" types, the bald head a reliable feature of
bankers in madcap comedies, and *haute couture* a signature of heroines in
nearly every film genre of the period. However, when coupled with the mad scientist's obsession with the *theory* of control and power, such ornaments are as
evocative of specific reliable cultural reactions as the cowboy's gun and the de-
tective's fedora.

And the heroes of the pulps? As one might expect, "brawny" is the operative
descriptor. But they are military less often that one might predict—until one
thinks of the cowboy hero which serves as the model for most of these strong-
and-silent types, and remembers that the cowboy's most important trait is his
individuality, his lack of affiliation with any larger body that might defuse his
heroic exceptionality or discipline his personal code of conduct—a connection
we might also make to the Great Independent inventors. However, most often
the heroes are not mechanically proficient inventors, but rather technologically indifferent adventurers. What representatives of the potty-if-harmless re-
formers of Hawthorne's era remained were most likely to be such characters as
Dr. Zharkov (with full beard) in the *Flash Gordon* serials: a brilliant-if-inept
scientist with good intentions and little common sense, unwittingly placing
himself and his planet in the crosshairs of Ming the Merciless (goatee) and
thus requiring saving by the fighter jock Flash (*sans* facial hair). These images
and plots are especially important when it is realized how they shaped the images and plots of movies and television to come, which provided access to ever
greater segments of the American culture. Eventually these attributes would
become as fundamental to the figures of mad scientists in the twentieth century as Frankenstein's characteristics had been to those of the nineteenth.

But what of images of the Master Mechanic during this era? That is to say,
who would give us all the bright and shiny new toys depicted on the covers of
these magazines?

Edison, Bell, et al. had by now been reified to the point where they stood as
icons of American technological prowess; and not just icons in a cultural sense,
but in a literal sense as well. During this period, thousands of murals were
painted by WPA-funded artists in public buildings all over America. Typically
these murals presented a panorama of American history, with our progress from
Pilgrims to Frontiersmen to City Builders portrayed in a neat chronological timeline, from left to right, with Edison and the other independents frequently the
symbol of science and depicted as a sort of evolutionary culmination of American

ingenuity. In some cases, with their formal nineteenth-century clothing and beards, they appear thrust into modern scenes as though stepping out of a time machine, slightly bewildered by their surroundings (such as in the mural *Modern Medicine* (1940) by Charles Alston). When the mural painters weren't using historical figures to represent the American scientist, they instead presented a generic young man (and very infrequently a young woman), typically holding a test tube up to the radiant light from a window, gazing both at its contents and at the heavens with inspirational dedication. While usually they are dressed in the uniform of lab coat and glasses, sometimes they are painted as half-naked construction workers, obviously demonstrating the physicality of their labor; or, as in the famous mural by Stanton McDonald-Wright in the Santa Monica public library, characters from the age of the Great Independents standing around holding examples of their various inventions and staring in wonder at a completely naked human form—as though their light bulbs and telephones were offerings to some Greek god.[2]

However, with the age of the Great Independents essentially over, the new sources for new technology were usually seen as the corporations. Certainly this is an understandable shift in the public conception of where technological innovation was now conceived and produced. Edison had become General Electric, the Wright Brothers had become the Wright Company, Alexander Graham Bell had become National Bell, and so on. While the early twentieth century continued the idolization of the independent Master Mechanics, their reign came to an end essentially with the First World War. Several factors played a role in this transition from independent to corporate science: the military's growing interest in war technology; the creation of large businesses to standardize, manufacture, and distribute new inventions; the application of mass production methodology to research as well as production; the migration of new inventors into the business and government worlds; the domination of technological commerce in the big cities; the growing ranks of a middle-class consumer population who could afford these new gadgets; and the continued expansion of an entertainment industry in the print, radio, and film media. The Great Independents retained their iconic status, but more as cultural myths and representations of a bygone "golden age of invention" than as the center of technological innovation.

As I discussed in chapter 3, part of the mythology of the independents was their combination of Yankee ingenuity with Yankee business acumen; but the production and distribution facilities and networks required to supply the middle-class markets necessary to sustain continued research and development were simply on a scale too grand to be overseen by any single individual. And the creation of the great corporations often worked to in fact discourage or even block inventions by latter-day independents or smaller groups.³ The Master Mechanic of the early twentieth century wasn't a lone whizkid in overalls tinkering in his garage, but rather a complex collection of essentially unknown people working behind the façade of the image of the aging Great Independent who had given their industry birth. Though by the time of World War I the flood of inventions from the independents had slowed as their inventions were further commodified and turned into products of corporations rather than individuals, the lore of the Great Independents would continue to grow as an integral part of the mythology of what made American science so typically American.

What is remarkable in all this celebration of the *new* new technology is the general lack of any *theory* about the effects of this mechanical cornucopia on society: theory about why we actually needed it, how we would use it, or in what ways it might alter our relationships, economic, personal, political, and cultural. It was possible, it was shiny, and therefore it was good. For the average American, the post–World War I technology was received with the same sort of nearly unmitigated glee that had greeted the first Industrial Revolution; and again, America's positive reaction stood in sharp contrast to the ambivalence (to say the least) of Europe.⁴

Of course, for most Americans these shiny new toys were untarnished by any first-hand experience with the battlefield devastation wrought by other shiny new toys in the Somme and Verdun and countless other killing fields. In fact, fueled by the persistent vision of technology as the key to efficiency and therefore to utopia, America was more than ready to accept and accommodate whatever the invention factories of the new corporate Master Mechanics could produce. Given the growing electrification of cities and even rural areas, the break-neck construction of roads, and the consumption frenzy halted only by the crash of 1929, General Electric et al.'s practical and commodified inventions could easily be integrated into the growing technical dependency of American middle-class life.⁵

THREE "TEXTS" illustrate the "technology as social savior" attitude prevalent during this period: the surge of enthusiasm among the general populace for the principles of technocracy; the ideology of a technological utopia portrayed in the film *Things to Come*; and the totalizing vision of a technofuture as presented in the 1939 New York World's Fair. There is an amazing consistency in the tropes and rhetoric of these texts, all of which argue for investing the totality of our cultural resources and faith in the methods and principles of the applied sciences as a way to solve all social ills and construct an Edenic World of Tomorrow.

In an echo of the American passion exhibited for phrenology and Mesmerism almost exactly one hundred years earlier, much of the public, as well as many national leaders, became enamored of the notion that engineering practices—objective, mathematically sound, result-oriented, ideologically neutral—should be applied to economic and political problems. Though there were different names for the various conceptions of such a system, the general term used was technocracy; and the general idea behind this philosophy was that the First World War and the stock market crash had demonstrated that the contemporary political and economic systems were insufficient to address the problems of the new century, problems created by, above and beyond all else, the new technology of warfare and labor. What was needed, therefore, in place of a "free" market system and a democratic political system was an economy and a government that would function like efficient machines. Of course, these machines would be run by people with mechanical expertise—by, that is, a new breed of economic and political "engineers."

Some have suggested links between the idea of an efficient, machine-like social state and the rise during this period of fascism around the world.[6] But it is important to differentiate between the fundamentally nationalistic and anti-modern tenets of fascism, and the internationalist and pro-modern aesthetics of technocracy. It is also important to note that, while some artists were attracted to various aspects of fascism—Ezra Pound being the most prominent and tragic example, though traces of conservative-if-not-quite-fascist sentiment are present in Eliot and other modernist poets—the general revulsion that the American artistic community expressed toward fascism did not taint their enthusiasm for technocracy.

Archibald MacLeish, for instance, believed technocracy accurately diagnosed the current social ill, even if he didn't necessarily agree with the prescription it offered: "The problem which the word Technocracy unfortunately defines is the vital problem of our time and the first human hope industrialism has offered. Those who ignore the problem and those who discredit the hope do so at their own peril."[7] At the same time, I. A. Richards was calling for a more "scientific" poetry based on universal principles of psychology, something that would produce a revolution in our thinking not unlike the technological revolution in the applied sciences: "It has long been recognized that if only something could be done in psychology remotely comparable to what has been achieved in physics, practical consequences might be expected even more remarkable than any that the engineer can contrive."[8] This was also a time when machines were not only considered fit subjects for art, but perhaps the basis and goal of all art. In 1934, the Museum of Modern Art presented an "Exhibition of Machine Art" which included slide rules, screws, and pots and pans, and which then became part of the permanent "good design" show. A review of the MOMA exhibition emphasized the "beauty of utility" and claimed that geometric forms were "the basis of all fine art."[9] Industrial designers like Walter Dorwin Teague, Henry Dreyfuss, and Raymond Loewy were all the rage.

From this general displeasure with what were then seen as the haphazard dynamics of politics and the economy (and even poetry), there arose a general faith in the ability of scientists—or at least certain kinds of scientists—to rectify these problems, when they were viewed without the handicap of political or commercial ideologies, or any investment in traditional social organizations and hierarchies.[10] What was wanted, in other words, was exactly the sort of technocratic utopias imagined in the turn-of-the-century literature.[11]

In the midst of this call for a more technocratic politics grew the wildly-if-briefly popular group, Technocracy, Inc. Organized in 1932 by "engineer" Howard Scott and social critic Thorstein Veblen, among others (Frederick L. Ackerman, a well-known architect, was a founding member, as were several prominent practicing engineers and professors of engineering), it sought to bring the "efficiency and predictability" of technology to the marketplace—and, Scott kept insisting (much to the chagrin of some of his more cautious associates), eventually to the government. Scott wrote: "The disorganized and largely incompetent coterie of economic decision makers would be replaced by a corps of engineers and technicians who would run the economy in accord with sound engineering principles designed to maximize production."[12] Notice first of all the contrast Scott makes between a "coterie" of economists and a "corps" of engineers, implying that theoretical economists were akin to an aristocratic clique, while practical engineers were more like an egalitarian "band of brothers" in the military.

Whatever their ultimate aims, the group announced that their first task was an "energy survey," a massive project whose goal was to analyze the productive efficiency of the U.S. economy over the last century. Such a study, they argued, would provide a foundation for schematizing the entire economy in terms of "energy units." This project—and, of greater significance, the highly technical and utopian rhetoric in which it was presented—caught the public's imagination. It was even greeted with some enthusiasm by those in the political realm who were most skeptical when it came to parceling out money to more well established and university-affiliated scientists like Robert Millikan and Arthur Compton, who complained constantly and bitterly of the lack of funds available for their research, and even though the leading scientists of the time dismissed the plan as the "pseudo-scientific ramblings of railroad engineers."[13] Once again, the split between the engineers and the theoreticians was evident; and, once again, the public chose to side with the engineers, railroad or otherwise.

Howard Scott's skill as a salesman was extraordinary. He had, writes Henry Elsner, a "magnetic personality, he impressed all who knew him with the facts and figures at his command; he had had, it seemed, worldwide engineering experience."[14] Even his appearance was figured as in keeping with the common-man aesthetics of an average Joe who just happened to be an engineering genius. Scott was described as "a lean, tall, somewhat stoop-shouldered man in his early forties with strong aquiline features and the identifying mark of a vertical scar on his nose. He affects broadbrimmed felt hats and the negligent dress of a man too bowed by weighty considerations to give much thought to his appearance."[15] Newspaper accounts claimed that the calculations used in the Energy Survey were "more complex than that of Einstein's unified field theory." Various community leaders, eager for new ideas to sell to the buying and voting public as hope for the future, invested their reputations in Scott's scheme: "Scott began to be wined and dined by industrialists, bankers, editors, and future New Deal administrators." And in such settings he held forth with a convincingly erudite rhetoric that was laced with technical-sounding terms like "steady state of doing work," "energy transversion," "decision arrivation," "order of magnitude," "thermodynamically balanced load," and "discontinuous wave of technological advance."[16] In other words, like good confidence men (and great preachers) throughout American history, Scott knew that obscurity often grants authority. And, though the other members of the group were not as radical in their claims for Technocracy's advantages and aims, Scott was not shy about predicting its eventual triumph over the current economic and political systems: "It is their ship of state and if they cannot find a solution the force majeure of continental conditions in the next few years will bring forth those who can. These problems transcend all social theories and partisan politics. . . . It is civilization itself. Technology has written 'mene mene tekel upharsin' across the face of the price System."[17]

At the peak of his popularity and influence, however, questions began to arise about Scott's credentials. It turned out, for instance, that his "worldwide engineering experience" was limited to supervising a cement-pouring crew in New York, a position from which he had been fired for incompetence; and that, rather than traveling and studying throughout Europe as his resume claimed, he'd spent most of the preceding decade in Greenwich Village, lecturing from atop a soapbox. When the Energy Survey never appeared and Scott's reputation unraveled, he lashed out at his critics, labeling them "debt merchants, communists, and liberals," and suggesting that this attack on Technocracy was "that last resort of the incompetent and stupid."[18] Though Scott's fifteen minutes of fame were over, other proponents of Technocracy's principles continued their association, renamed the Continental Committee on Technocracy, but with a far lower public profile.[19]

The sort of world these devotees of machine efficiency longed for actually did come into being, however briefly: not in reality, but as Everytown in the film *Things to Come*. Produced in 1936 from a script by H. G. Wells, *Things to Come* is the chronicle of an unending and devastating world war, a depiction remarkable both for its timing, coming as it did on the eve of the Second World War, and for its similarity to so many much later filmic narratives of nuclear apocalypse. The first half of the film relates how, after decades of grueling-if-conventional conflict—presented as stock-footage scenes of trench warfare, machinegun slaughter, gas attacks, and massed tanks—civilization has been reduced to tribal barbarism. After half a century of such chaos, the last vestiges of twentieth-century science and culture as represented by a "corps" of engineers and former pilots band together to form Wings Over the World, and begin to send scouts to the still-warring factions around the world in order to re-establish a *pax mundi* based on "law and sanity."

One such scout lands in Everytown, which is ruled by The Boss, a brutal warlord. An interview between the representative of Wings Over the World—called simply Cabal—and The Boss is extremely interesting for its revelation of the central ideology of the film:

> Boss: "Who are you? Don't you know this country is at war?"
> Cabal: "Dear, dear! Still at it. We must clean that up."
> Boss: "What do you mean? We must clean that up? War is war. Who are you, I
>   say?"
> Cabal: "The law," he says. He improves it: "Law and sanity."
> Boss: "I am the law here."
> Cabal: "I said law and sanity."
> Boss: "Where do you come from? What are you?"
> Cabal: "Pax Mundi. Wings over the world."
> Boss: "That's nothing. What Government are you under?"
> Cabal: "Commonsense. . . . We just run ourselves."

What this exchange makes clear—besides Cabal's condescending attitude—is that: 1) Wings Over the World consider themselves to be the legitimate (lawful) inheritors of world control because 2) they are not warriors but rather people who "clean up" wars; 3) they aim to achieve the goal not of power but of World Peace, 4) which will be administrated not by politics but by "common sense."

If these engineers and aviators can "run" themselves without any form of government, it must be because everyone's "sense" about right and wrong, good and bad, best and worst solutions is *absolutely* common. In other words, the film suggests that all engineers think the same about all issues; therefore, no political debates ever divide them, and thus they require no politics. Or politicians. Once sound engineering principles have replaced the chaos and strife of politics, no contentious issues remain. We will all think the same way, about everything. *Pax Mundi*. The assumption here is that the language and practices of engineering are universal, bridging or perhaps even erasing all cultural, racial, and class divides. Without such divides we would have no need of government—we could simply "run ourselves."[20]

To return to the plot of the film, once WOtW realizes Cabal is missing, they send their air fleet to rescue him: huge black airplanes that appear like a cross between the Hindenburg and the Flying Wing. Then the pacifist engineers—they don't wage war, after all, they clean it up—drop bombs filled with the "gas of peace." With The Boss's "army" asleep, and The Boss dead—apparently his warrior soul couldn't withstand the prospect of living in worldly peace, so it opted for the other kind—the world comes under the paternalistic guidance of the Technocrats of WOtW. After decades of this rational, technocratic, well-ordered society, mankind develops a utopia of glittering towers, a society of peace and plenty—and flying cars. (An aerial shot of future Everytown looks uncannily like the Futurama exhibit at the 1939 World's Fair). Yet even this utopia has its problems. A rabble-rousing artist (obviously suffering from an overindulged imagination insufficiently disciplined by logical engineering "sanity") argues that progress has gone too far, and incites a mob to attack and attempt to destroy the first moon rocket ready for launch.

Which raises an interesting question. If the society is, with the exception of the addled artist, utterly peaceful and content, from where and how does he so easily raise an angry mob? While the reasoning behind this dramatic moment isn't clear, Wells's anticipation of C. P. Snow's "Two Cultures" is very clear indeed. *Things to Come* assumes that the arts are constitutionally opposed to "that villain progress," harkening for their inspiration backward to the past, rather than forward to the future—a formulation that is made clear from the artist-rebel's name, Theotocopulos, as well as the classical lines of the gigantic sculpture upon which he is working, and even the Roman-style haircut he sports.[21] However, the anti-progress mob is unsuccessful and, as the rocket blasts off, the visionary leader of WOtW (Raymond Massey) points upward to the heavens and intones: "That's where our destiny lies. In the stars!"

More than seventy years later, Wells's vision seems at once amazingly prescient and yet quaintly naive; but at the very least *Things to Come* sounded a message of technological evangelicalism that resonated with audiences of its time. Of course it is easy now to dismiss its message as simplistic and melodramatic; yet the film evidences a preference for the supposedly universal language and values of engineering, and a prejudice against the "theory" of politics, both of which run deep and wide throughout American cultural history, the latter very much in evidence even today. One need only think of those elements in

American politics—exemplified by Reagan's call to "get government off the backs of the people"—that argue politics is a somehow unnatural component of society, an untrustworthy and ultimately insane practice with which we could dispense if only we could all share the same "common sense." And the barrier to this *Pax Mundi* paradise of common sense is seen as social divisions, particularly, in American culture, class divisions. The utopian literature of the late nineteenth century imagined that full employment and completely efficient labor practices would rid us of such class conflicts.[22] And this world, free of class distinctions and built around the gleaming efficiency of new technology, was represented in the New York World's Fair of 1939, "The World of Tomorrow."

The fair was constructed to foreground American technology, and its primary audience was the American consumer. Its scheme was to "organize" the visitor's experience of the fair, to "educate" him or her about the renewal of American society just around the corner, and to "prepare" that consumer to live in a world very much like that of Everytown in *Things to Come*. According to "Welcome to Tomorrow," a website devoted to analysis of the 1939 World's Fair, the exhibition was "part ideological construct, part trade show, part League of Nations, part amusement park, and part Utopian community" that "promoted its message of hope and prosperity with icons, symbols, exhibitions, and demonstrations. It was a literal laboratory for a group of industrial designers who considered themselves both artists and social theorists."[23]

As previously mentioned, the Futurama exhibit of the General Motors pavilion—a gigantic (36,000 square feet) diorama of an American city of 1960, which visitors circled, as if in an airplane, from seats suspended on a moving track—looked very much like the models of Everytown, with a centralized metropolis of clean-lined skyscrapers surrounded by modern homes, schools, airports . . . with one important difference: whereas Everytown had committed itself to mass transit through monorails, Futurama was a society clearly dependent on extensive roadways. This was, after all, the GM pavilion.

Every exhibit at the fair emphasized that what visitors were seeing was the shiny, modern, technologically efficient and, most important, *inevitable* future. The Ford company built an asphalt ramp and called it the "Road of Tomorrow"; the dairy industry built a gleaming glass-walled assembly line, labeled the "Dairy World of Tomorrow." Even Westinghouse's "robot" Elektro was more salesman for the future than threatening monster from the pulps: Elektro "was the exact opposite of the Technocrats' robot—gentle giant, harmless to women and children, designed to entertain visitors to the fair, and sell a benign message about the technology and the future."[24]

But perhaps the most telling of all the exhibits—at least for my purposes—was Democracity. Democracity was a diorama housed in the gigantic Perisphere, the geometric mate to the Trylon (a sphere and pyramid, respectively). Democracity presented the viewer with the "City of Tomorrow," and it was, in design and philosophy, essentially a microcosm of the World's Fair. The explicit argument was that the modern technology of Democracity would create the very sort of "commonsense" society imagined by WOtW. Democracity was all about order, regimentation, calm, harmony. Democracity was, in essence, a machine; a machine that produced classlessness, efficiency, plenty, conformity.[25] In the literature and film ("The City") that accompanied the exhibit, the focus of ideology was clear: class conflicts were at the root of all the old city's problems; eliminate class divisions and one would eliminate the conflicts. And, as we know from *Things to Come*, if you eliminate class conflicts (aka diversity), you eliminate the need for politics, leaving only a technocracy where, once a problem is identified, the solution is obvious to all. Consensus is the same as common sense. Thus Democracity can be seen as the most important of all the new technologies: the one that produces the end of politics.[26]

BUT IN the actual America of the period leading up to the World's Fair, politics was still very much alive, and still very much at the root of the differential in funding between the applied and theoretical sciences. The theoretical work of physicists, for instance, which occurred for the most part out of the public's sight in universities—work unrepresented anywhere in the "World of Tomorrow"— was, until the Manhattan Project, something quite beyond average American citizens' experience, and potentially hostile to their world view.

Perhaps there is no better measure of a public's attitude toward a particular segment of its citizenry than the extent to which its government either nourishes or ignores that segment, especially in a representative democracy. And if that attitude is indeed a reliable indicator of general public sympathy or antipathy, then the American government's record of funding for theoretical science during this period is another indication that the scientists who worked in such fields were considered in some fundamental way "unworthy" of public support. While the practical sciences received significantly reduced government funding *only* during the worst of the Depression, the theoretical sciences went begging right up until the beginning of the Manhattan Project.[27]

In 1916, the National Research Council was formed, with Robert Millikan as its president. Millikan lobbied for private contributions to increase research science, as money for such projects had rarely before been forthcoming from the government. His efforts met with little success. Even after the "debunking" of technocracy and its more radical supporters such as Howard Scott, the public still showed great respect for the mechanical sciences, what might be classified as the "pure" engineering sciences—Herbert Hoover was, after all, the

Great Engineer—and either indifference or suspicion toward the theoretical sciences. Not only was there little public interest in scientific research of a less tangible character, but by 1929 the reputation of research science had sunk so low that Millikan found it necessary to give a speech at the annual AAAS meeting where he defended "science" in the strongest possible terms. Listing the various ills of society for which science was blamed, he then responded to each charge with an resounding "not guilty!"

But not even Hoover's "engineering" skill or Millikan's impassioned rhetoric could forestall the economic crash of 1929: a collapse of faith as well as assets, and one that undermined the country's trust in not only its business leaders, but its political and scientific ones as well. For the first time in the nation's history, technology was seen as a potential enemy to labor. It was then that the term "technological unemployment" entered the national debate about social instability; with science as the culprit, because of the automation which the "sciences" (no mention of engineering as distinct now from the other, more theoretical sciences) had brought into the workplace. Four years later, in 1934, Arthur Compton, then the president of MIT, organized a "Science Makes Jobs" show to be part of the Century of Progress exhibition in Chicago, in order to counter the public's conception of science as an enemy of labor.[28] However, having obtained little money from private sources, let alone the government, the exhibition received scant attention. In the public's mind—despite Millikan's words and Compton's exhibits—science had been pronounced "guilty!" This, from the 1933 essay "Scientist as Citizen", written by sociologist Read Bain:

> Scientists . . . more than any other single factor, threaten the persistence of Western culture. . . . They are . . . workers of Black Magic, weavers of weird spells, progenitors of destruction. Their calling has become a cult, a dark mystery cult. . . . They sneer at politicians. They poke fun at preachers and "other moralists." They laugh at education. . . . They produce powerful mechanisms and proudly proclaim that they "do not care how they are used—leave that to the moralists." . . . They think tolerance and lack of conviction are synonymous. The "pure" scientist has to be a moral eunuch or a civic hermit.[29]

Notice the designation of the true culprit as the "pure" (read theoretical) scientist, and the conclusion that, to be pure, such a scientist must be without morals, sex, *and* community.

By 1935, there was still no new money for scientific research. Yet the scientists kept up, in their small way, their propaganda efforts. F. K. Richmyer, the Cornell physics dean, wrote: "Science . . . recognizes no international boundaries. There is a voluntary and very effective cooperation and, more important, a kind of camaraderie among scientists of all nationalities that our leaders in world affairs could do well to study."[30]

In 1936, however, the fortunes of the "pure" scientists began to change—a little. Secretary of Agriculture Henry Wallace was by then largely responsible for championing increased access to government councils by leading scientists. At the same time, the laissez-faire attitude that was a fundamental precept of American "pure" science—keeping a safe distance between science and politics—was losing favor. The research scientists felt they'd been dealt out of the funding game because they refused to sit at the political table. Also, the growing number of their European colleagues who had organized to oppose fascism had a great influence in convincing the American scientists they must become more politically active. For instance, in 1932 Reinhold Niebuhr had argued in *Moral Man and Immoral Society* that "the traditionalism of the social sciences did not result from ignorance, but from the economic interest of a capitalist ruling class bent on maintaining its privileged status."[31] By the late thirties, the scientists of MIT, Cornell, and Berkeley were interested in regaining at the very least what ground had been lost by American economic depression and social repression. The traditionalism of not only the social sciences, but of physics and all the other "theoretical" sciences as well, was being eroded by social and political realities.

By the end of the 1930s, however, though money for industrial research was increasing and the prestige of at least the technical scientist had been for the most part recovered (as evidenced by the popularity of Technocracy, Inc, and the World's Fair), the theoretical sciences and their practitioners remained in a funding and status desert (with of course the exception of the Manhattan Project). For instance, whereas the blight which had hit the market for chemists had, by 1939, largely been reversed, physicists and mathematicians still found an average of half a dozen positions available for every fifty degrees granted. Though the number of articles written by scientists calling for the adaptation of scientific models to social problems was still increasing, their effect was minimal. And before the war, what theoretical work was still going on—for example, Fermi's work with nuclear fission—was not the sort that leads to practical inventions like phonographs or telephones, and so the public had little reason to pay any attention to what the "pure" scientists were doing or saying. "Increasingly," Peter Kuznick notes, "the only 'safe' application of science became the military one."[32]

It is worth taking a moment here to very briefly discuss the history of science and the military. According to the military historian Sir Solly Zuckerman, the general split between the scientist and the professional soldier began in earnest early in the nineteenth century (marked by the Battle of Waterloo) and, "for all practical purposes the separation endured until the outbreak of the First World War." Zuckerman argues that "the soldier cocooned himself in an isolated and proud professionalism. . . . The scientists . . . became enemies of the conventional and the established."[33] This situation remained essentially unchanged—with some small adjustments made in America during the Civil War to accommodate engineering advances in sapping and artillery—to the middle of World War I. It was then that the military recognized the increased importance of scientific "advisers," especially with the introduction of such "scientific" weapons as gas, tanks, and airplanes. However, the war ended before this trend became firmly established, and the traditional antipathy between the "pure" scientific and the military professions regained primacy—at least, that is, in Britain and the United States. Germany, on the other hand, was setting a new standard of cooperation between the two professions, continuing the government-sponsored collaboration that had begun during the war, and extending the military's involvement in what before the war would have been purely esoteric, university-based research projects—particularly research into nuclear fission.[34]

In the closing years of the 1930s, however, some members of the American scientific community attempted a *rapprochement* with the military by proposing new weapon systems: radar, sonar, and, of course, the A-bomb. Surprisingly enough, at first the military was relatively cool toward such proposals, as these were weapons for which it had no development plans, let alone battlefield objectives. However, by 1939 "Operational Experts" had become an established branch of strategic planning. It was their task to apply methods of "science and efficiency"—in a sense, the principles of Taylorism—to such fundamental military problems as training, supply, distribution of force, and even propaganda.

This relationship between the military and a certain segment of the scientific community was in and of itself nothing extraordinary, as the technology of war, from siege towers to ever-larger artillery pieces, had always required the cooperation of the military caste with those of the scientific/technical caste. The new component to this symbiosis, however, lay in the large number of *theoretical* scientists who gradually found themselves, through the radar and A-bomb projects particularly, working with military methods and goals.

Before the happy alliance of the Manhattan Project, however, the antipathy the military instinctively felt toward theoreticians was never more evident than at the first meeting between physicists and warriors to discuss the potential dangers of an atomic bomb. The meeting in October 1939, called at Roosevelt's behest in response to Einstein's famous letter, was the first of the Advisory Committee on Uranium, and it put Leo Szilard and other atomic theorists in the uncomfortable position of trying to convince Lt. Col. Keith Adamson, an Army ordnance specialist, of the power hidden in uranium—power that was potentially a thousandfold "improvement" over conventional explosives; to which Adamson, with high sarcasm, responded that he'd long ago promised a "big prize to anyone who can kill [a] goat with a death ray. Nobody has claimed the prize yet."[35] And in fact Einstein's letter was not even read by Roosevelt. Rather, the approach to FDR both to warn of the dangers of large amounts of uranium falling into the hands of the Nazis, and to seek government support for a crash program in nuclear fission research, fell to Alexander Sachs, someone with training in philosophy, economics, jurisprudence, and sociology, who had worked in Roosevelt's National Recovery Administration—but who was not a scientist. Even though the letter had been written jointly by Einstein and Szilard among other physicists, Sachs argued that "no scientist could sell" the importance of nuclear research to FDR, and so Sachs had prepared his own more cautious, and more political summary for the president.[36]

Eventually World War II forced an alliance not only between the engineers and theoreticians, whose divergences were often rhetorical and even esoteric, but more significantly between the theoreticians and the warriors, whose disagreements had, up until this point in the history of nationalism, been most often practical and fundamental. This new cooperation to a certain extent explains the high regard the American public expressed for the A-bomb scientists as a group immediately after the war's conclusion: the theoretical scientists shared the essentially automatic praise of a victorious community for its warriors. But this convivial relationship wasn't to last.

THE INCREDIBLE SHRINKING SCIENTIST

5

How the Heroes of Los Alamos Became Internationalist Traitors

TWO IMAGES of the American physicist Robert Oppenheimer perfectly illustrate the abrupt transition of the "Father of the A-bomb" from patriotic genius to traitorous conspirator. The first, taken on July 16, 1945, while Oppenheimer was director of Los Alamos, shows him standing over the ruins of the test tower at Ground Zero of the first atomic test, at Alamogordo, New Mexico. At his feet is a small, nondescript pile of concrete and twisted metal bars—all that's left of a hundred-foot structure that held the plutonium implosion device whose twin was dropped later on Nagasaki. Next to him is General Leslie Groves, the gruff and imposing military commander of the Manhattan Project; but it's clear that Oppenheimer is in charge. He's smiling, his face thin beneath his ridiculous wide-brimmed fedora—a face radiating the confidence and power which comes from overseeing one of the greatest scientific achievements of all time.

The second photograph is from Oppenheimer's appearance before the Atomic Energy Commission in 1954, when he was fighting to keep his security clearance. This photograph shows him huddled over a microphone and looking up at his inquisitors, fingers raised as though counting off points in a logical argument. Here, he appears confused, defensive, haggard—and not so much sad as sorrowful, as though some deep-seated faith has been shattered, as though the rhetoric of paranoia confronting him is as foreign to him as his explanations of the workings of the A-bomb would be to those sitting in judgment of him.

Volumes have been written about the national paranoia that swept America in the late 1940s and early 1950s, a tsunami of suspicion that washed away the reputations and lives of many good Americans, Oppenheimer among them.[1] The sources and processes of this paranoia have been chronicled in countless books, documentaries, movies, and songs, to the point where it has become something of a cultural cliché—much as the word most often associated with the politics of the early '50s, "McCarthyism," has become so overdetermined as to stand in danger of losing its power as a cautionary tale of paranoia coupled to hubris. And within the dynamic of this cliché often lies the assumption that this widespread American fearfulness and its political and cultural expression— again, McCarthyism and its attendant minor theaters of witch-hunting repression in Hollywood—were a fundamental reaction to, among other things, the acquisition by the Russians of the atomic bomb in 1949. But that is not, I will argue, an entirely accurate reading of the historical record, especially in terms of the chronology of representations of fear in the mass media.

In fact, the undercurrent of nervousness and dread about the A-bomb began several years *before* 1949, at the very time of our victory in the Pacific. According to a sampling of periodicals following VJ Day, this mood appeared almost instantly and ubiquitously following our first use of the atomic bomb against Japan. Immediate reactions to the news of the A-bomb's use certainly contain a tone of awe at the power of the weapon, but there is also a curious undercurrent of apprehension, even fear. The latter response is captured in a *New York Times* report of August 8, 1945, which warns that the bomb had caused "an explosion in men's minds as shattering as the obliteration of Hiroshima."[2] And what seemed most shattered was our own sense of security. A sampling of the mood from various periodicals yields largely a refrain not of celebration and hope, as one might expect from such a dramatic conclusion to a long and stupendously brutal war, but rather one of doom and gloom:

> "[The bomb had] cast a spell of dark foreboding over the spirit of humanity."— *Christian Century*
> "The entire city is pervaded by a kind of sense of oppression."—*New York Sun*
> "[There is a] curious new sense of insecurity, rather incongruous in the face of military victory."—*New Republic.*

On the very night the bomb was dropped, H. V. Kaltenborn was already warning that "For all we know, we have created a Frankenstein!"[3] And Edward R. Murrow, in his first broadcast after the bombing, expressed the anxiety— strangely incongruous on the brink of total victory—everyone seemed to be feeling: "Seldom, if ever, has a war ended leaving the victors with such a sense of uncertainty and fear, with such a realization that the future is obscure and that survival is not assured."[4]

One reads these expressions of deep anxiety and vulnerability in nearly every major newspaper and magazine of the time, sees that they are nearly as frequent and prominent as the praise for our victorious forces, and wonders, Why were *we* afraid? America was in every sense better off after the war than before it: our economy had been rebuilt, our cities and countryside were untouched, our casualties were a fraction those of our allies and enemies. And above all else, we were the sole possessor of the most powerful weapon the world had ever known, the atomic bomb—the very "terror weapon" the Germans had been frantically searching for in the closing days of the war. And yet, ironically, America seemed the one nation most terrorized.

We could hardly have been fearful of being attacked ourselves by atomic bombs, not in 1945. Though a few of the Manhattan Project scientists thought Russia might obtain a bomb of its own within five years, the prevailing view was that no other nation could possibly counter our atomic arsenal for at least another decade, and thus we had ample time to establish our postwar security through what would become the NATO alliance, all the while safe behind our exclusive nuclear shield.[5] In the absence of any credible nuclear threat, perhaps what frightened us was not the "gadget" itself, but rather what it represented: that is, the knowledge and organization which had produced the possibility of impersonal, indiscriminate, and apocalyptic annihilation. And since we were the only country at that time which possessed such knowledge and organization, in a sense we could only have been afraid of ourselves; perhaps, that is, we were frightened of the very people who had given us the A-bomb.

The dropping of the A-bomb heralded the beginning of a new kind of science; a science where neither accomplishment nor threat was limited to the obscurity and safety of the laboratory; a science that could be misunderstood, but not ignored; a science that would affect nearly every aspect of American culture. Though large technological projects had been undertaken prior to the Manhattan Project—the Panama Canal, the expansion of electrical and telephone networks, the mobilization of the United States' massive industrial capacity for World War II—none had been founded upon scientific principles so complicated and radical that even among scientists, only a select few understood them. The A-bomb was an utterly unique combination of what might be considered the most esoteric theory and most brutal practice science had ever witnessed.

As the public came to understand in a very rough sense the immense increase in destructive power that atomic engineering had introduced into modern warfare, it also came to understand that the terrible-but-mechanical violence of conventional war had been exchanged for the possibility of a total-and-miraculous Armageddon. The mechanics of steel and gunpowder had been replaced by the wizardry of radiation and plutonium; the measure of battlefield destruction had moved from a comprehensible Newtonian to an incomprehensible Einsteinian scale. Perhaps the average American wanted somebody to blame—and the most obvious targets for this blame were the participants in the Manhattan Project.

However, while the public record is clear about the instantaneous and permeating anxiety regarding the A-bomb, the American's *initial* public attitude toward the Manhattan Project scientists themselves was anything but anger or suspicion. Scientists were quoted in newspapers, interviewed on radio programs, seen testifying before Congress, written about in Sunday supplements, and regularly published in magazines, from the *New Republic* to the *Nation*. They were even the new social lions. Physicists were "the vogue these days," according to a *Harper's* contributor. "No dinner party is a success without at least one physicist to explain . . . the nature of the new age in which we live."[6] In *By the Bomb's Early Light*, Paul Boyer exhaustively details the admiration, even awe, with which the public viewed atomic scientists immediately after World War II. For perhaps the first time in American history, scientists were placed on a par with war heroes:

> In a *Chicago Tribune* cartoon of August 11, 1945, for instance, a small figure representing the "U.S. Fighting Man" raises aloft the flag of victory, his feet firmly planted on a massive block labelled "SCIENCE." A Fitzpatrick cartoon in the *St. Louis Post-Dispatch* pictured two dwarflike "Statesmen" staggering under the weight of the atomic bomb given to them by "The Scientists," represented by a figure of such towering height that only his lower legs are visible.[7]

Such SCIENTISTS—their profession, at this moment anyway, deserving of all caps—were even lionized in films. For instance, in *The Beginning or the End* (1947)—a rare cooperative effort between Washington and Hollywood, and the first movie to chronicle the development of the A-bomb—the scientist character enjoys a status equal to that of the movie's military hero: a publicity still for the film depicts the Soldier and the Scientist as equally brave, equally determined, equally handsome—and equally capable of offering protection to their respective female partners.

Prestige for the American scientist also resulted in prestige for education in general. Educational radio programs rated in the top 5 percent of the market, and sales of chemistry sets and scientific toys jumped nearly "off the scale."[8] A few excerpts from one of the most popular magazines of the period, the *Saturday Evening Post*, demonstrate the importance that both scientific rhetoric and education-as-panacea played in postwar American thought. In the *Post* for July 27, 1946, we find a lead article entitled, "We're Teaching the Children to Lead Japan":

> The dreams and dogmas of a misguided generation have collapsed into rubble . . . today these parents know the falsity of their old beliefs. . . . [MacArthur] is working toward a fundamental revolution in the thinking of the school children. . . . It isn't too much to say that the final success of the occupation depends more on this program than on the economic and constitutional reforms being imposed.

It is clear that education was considered the key to creating a "new" Japan. But what is particularly striking throughout this issue is the rhetoric of the advertisements: everything from electric clocks to razor blades is billed as "new, NEW, *NEW!*" Insecticides, ballpoint pens, automobile motors, and hair tonic, all are the products of "specialists": road specialists, bug specialists, even the "Flavor born of genius" in Dr. Pepper. And of course, the atomic bomb itself makes an appearance: "Atom Bomb on Wheels: in the hands of a careless driver, the American automobile has become as deadly as an atom bomb." The reader is everywhere asked to trust heating "specialists" and welding "consultants," and each advertisement is accompanied by a diagram, from exploded tires to magnified hair roots. A respect for the power of scientific rhetoric—and a fear of that power "improperly" used—is evident in nearly every article, every advertisement, all of which are designed to "better educate the smart buyer," whether he or she be a six-year-old Japanese child or a thirty-year-old American steel worker.

During this postwar honeymoon with the intellect, the scientific methods which had produced the atomic bomb were considered a fit model for nearly every social problem: "If most citizens of the important countries of the world were equal in the intellectual and ethical stature to those whose names appear in 'American Men of Science,' danger of misuse of atomic power would not exist. The most important fruits of science are the character and way of life of scientists."[9] There were a few voices of dissension in this chorus of idealization of scientists, such as the aging H.G. Wells who was, as usual, prophetic. In his last book, *Mind at the End of Its Tether* (1945), he warned against expecting anything but technical expertise from scientists—a strange warning indeed coming from the same writer who'd envisioned the engineers of Wings Over the World as the last, best hope of humankind.

But by and large scientists—especially the A-bomb scientists and their research redoubt of Los Alamos—were regarded as the epitome of twentieth-century American technological know-how. Certainly the idea of an isolated research center, à la Los Alamos, to produce innovative research from the best scientific and technological minds available was nothing new. One can draw a line backwards from Los Alamos to Menlo Park (keeping in mind the distinctions remarked on in chapter 3), and even further to the first "think tanks" of the early nineteenth century, such as the Franklin Institute (1829) and the Rensselaer Institute (1824).[10] And Los Alamos was not even the first such concentration of scientific expertise to be established during World War II. Early in 1940, a research laboratory was set up at MIT wholly dedicated to the development of radar. At that time, while Einstein's letter to Roosevelt was "in the mail," the use of radio waves to detect aircraft and ships was seen as the greatest scientific-military discovery of the twentieth century.

"It's alive! It's alive!" The "model" Wicked Wizard: cerebral, thin, pale, and hysterical. Colin Clive as Dr. Henry Frankenstein in James Whale's 1931 *Frankenstein* (Universal Pictures).

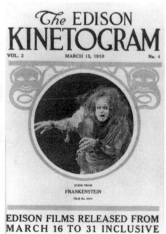

Evolution of a Monster Frankenstein's creature began life as a large-but-normal human, but later representations grew more grotesque in order to emphasize his "unnatural" origins. (left) Frontispiece to the revised edition of *Frankenstein* (published by Colburn and Bentley, London 1831); (center) cover of *The Edison Kinetogram* depicting the Monster from Edison's 1910 one-reeler (courtesy U.S. Department of the Interior, National Park Service, Edison National Historic Site); (right) Boris Karloff as the Monster (Universal Pictures).

Selling Science as a "Cabinet of Wonders" Science in the 1800s was represented variously as a product of cloaked mystery, rural ingenuity, modern sorcery, or domestic tinkering. (above) Charles Wilson Peale, *Self-Portrait of the Artist in His Museum*, 1822 (courtesy Pennsylvania Academy of the Fine Arts); (facing page, top left) cover of *The Manufacturer & Builder*, vol. 9, 1877 (Cornell University); (facing page, top right) Thomas Edison as "The Wizard of Menlo Park" (courtesy Smithsonian Institution); (facing page, bottom) Edison's "invention factory" at Menlo Park, New Jersey (courtesy Smithsonian Institution).

THE DAILY GRAPHIC

THE WIZARD'S SEARCH

Your Future Is Sky High! Covers of popular science magazines from the 1930s and 1940s prophesized that in the future everything would be airborne—even the airports.

Princesses, Knights, and Dragons—in Space Covers of pulp science fiction magazines from the 1920s–1940s illustrate how, though the hardware and clothes may have changed from ancient narratives, the key tropes hadn't.

Big Heads, Bigger Egos The depiction of mad scientists on the pulp covers followed a simple formula: the bigger and balder the cranium, the wickeder the wizard.

The Master Mechanic as Historical Celebrity Inventors were portrayed in public murals as heroic and inspired individuals, and often paired with what appeared to be Greek gods. (left) "The Negro's Communication in the Social and Cultural Development of America," Millard Owen Sheets's mural *Science*, 1939 (courtesy Department of the Interior); (right) panel from Stanton McDonald-Wright's mural for the Santa Monica Public Library, 1938 (courtesy Smithsonian American Art Museum).

The Technocracy of Tomorrow Technology was to be the savior of cities, eliminating ugliness, clutter, poverty—and pants. (top left) Poster from *Things to Come*, 1936 (London Film Productions); (top right) General Motors "Futurama" exhibit at 1939 World's Fair (© Estate of Margaret Bourke-White / Licensed by VAGA, New York, NY); (bottom) Rally for Technocracy, Inc., at the Hollywood Bowl in the early 1930s (copyright Technocracy Incorporated).

**At the Center of Power / Center of
Controversy** (top) Robert Oppenheimer and
General Groves inspect what's left of the A-bomb
tower at Ground Zero, Alamogorda, New Mexico,
July 16, 1945 (courtesy Los Alamos National
Laboratory); (bottom) Oppenheimer testifying
during the AEC security hearings in 1954, after
which he was stripped of his security clearance
(courtesy Bettman / UPI-Corvis).

The "Grandfather" of Physics vs. Dr. Strangelove (top) Albert Einstein, whose eyes were reportedly used as the model for Yoda's in *Star Wars*; (bottom) Edward Teller, inventor of the H-bomb (courtesy Los Alamos National Laboratory).

This research lab was run by the university, which brought large amounts of government money into the academy for the first time in nearly half a century, and signaled the source of the huge funds needed for modern scientific research—applied and pure—for the postwar period to come. And of course along with the government money came government politics. While during the war these simmering conflicts were most often tabled in the interest of focusing all energies on the war effort, they would emerge with full force at the successful conclusion of the war.

During the war, however, this radar lab was to be the model for dozens of such labs set up across the country by the Army and Navy. In each case, a university was chosen to "sponsor" the lab, and thus control the money, giving the academic intellectual community a kind of power it had never before experienced. Even though the Manhattan Project was exiled to the desert, this model held there too, as Oppenheimer and his fellow university professors had during the war years essentially absolute veto power over the military liaison, General Groves. In fact, this model was the very one proposed by a group of British scientists, the Tots and Quots dining club: *quot homines, tot sententiae*—who had, on a drunken challenge issued sometime before the war, written a book about how to organize scientific-military research institutes for the *next* war. The authors had, however, openly despaired of every actually coming into the huge sums of money they prophesied would be necessary for the "big" research required to introduce the next generation of weapons.[11]

But it was clearly the Manhattan Project that was considered the primary marvel and therefore the perfect model of inspiration, administration, engineering, manufacturing, etc., that would guarantee the success of such ventures. The power, prestige, and resources that the war effort brought to the sciences (whether it was the "pure" sciences or simply "engineering" was not, at the time, groused about) were indeed unparalleled in the history of the American scientific community. And by the end of the war, the social influence and prestige of the war scientists was on a scale unimaginable only half a decade before.

However, most of the scientists involved were ill equipped or prepared for, or not even interested in doing the political and "publicity" work necessary to maintain the status gained during the Manhattan Project. After the war's end, nearly all of the A-bomb scientists wanted only to return to the universities and pick up their researches where they'd left off. Remembers I. I. Rabi: "I look back in amazement when I consider that Lee DuBridge, who had built up and headed this most extraordinary organization, the Radiation Laboratory, which began with thirty people and culminated with four thousand, returned after the war to his original small university to become the head of the physics department."[12]

There were those, however—most notably the leaders among the atomic scientists—who thought that the revolutionary weapon delivered to society ought to be accompanied by revolutionary politics. Internationalist politics. These were, as Boyer calls them, the "One World or None" scientists. However, their "One World" was seen by the public as a world dominated by the "international Communist conspiracy." And thus very soon these "One World or None" scientists— Oppenheimer being the most publicly recognized symbol among them—would find themselves even lower in the American public's estimation than before the war. In fact, as early as 1947 the prestige of the Manhattan scientists was already fading, and the campaign of some of the atomic scientists for international control of atomic energy had essentially exhausted itself: as Boyer notes, "Even J. Robert Oppenheimer . . . was advising by 1947 that as Hiroshima and Nagasaki receded from the nation's consciousness, the scientists' role could no longer be that of 'prophets of doom coming out of the desert.' "[13] Eventually, the scientists' political movement became in some key ways indistinguishable from the rest of the political arena; for instance, in 1949 all members of the AEC were required to sign loyalty oaths. The later abandonment of Oppenheimer by Edward Teller could well be viewed as merely the climax of two processes—alienation and assimilation—that had been working on the Los Alamos physicists from the first days after the war. Many, like Oppenheimer, found working on weapons distasteful, a necessary evil to be pursued only so long as America's survival was at stake; and the prospect of building bigger and better bombs, especially Teller's pet project, the "Super," alienated Oppenheimer and many others from the growing military-scientific alliance. Other scientists, like Teller, came to feel they'd found their true calling doing weapons research, and gradually assimilated into the culture of the Military-Industrial Complex (as Eisenhower would later famously christen the convoluted and self-supporting network of military research and procurement).

Simply stated, this three-way alliance—theoreticians, engineers, and warriors—was inherently unstable, and the centuries-old debate over applied vs. pure science was dormant, not dead. The new breed of military scientist was soon to be ostracized by the university scientists, thus reinstating the traditional split between the applied, engineering sciences, and the theoretical, "pure" sciences. By 1950 the divergent strategies were clear: The Master Mechanics (Teller et al.) now invented new weapons with which they hoped to reform war by transforming it, while the Wicked Wizards (Oppenheimer and those who opposed the H-bomb) now organized politically in an effort to revolutionize war by abolishing it.

Which is not to say that Oppenheimer and the ex–Manhattan Project scientists who supported him were, after the war, entirely divorced from "practical" atomic research. In fact, for some years Oppenheimer worked on an advisory committee in the AEC primarily concerned with commercial reactor development; an area of the "Atoms for Peace" program that received much official rhetorical support, but saw little real progress, little government money, and very little federal enthusiasm. All the glamour work was considered to be in weapons and nuclear-powered submarines. Thus, even though Oppenheimer's nuclear energy expertise was more closely aligned with commercial adaptations than Teller's work on the H-bomb, and therefore one would expect Oppenheimer to be more closely aligned, in the public mind, with the Master Mechanics, Teller was still perceived as much more the "establishment" scientist owing to his enthusiasm for new weapons projects and his frequent declamations about the need for American supremacy in the postwar world. Hans Bethe recalled later that Teller was "terribly anti-communist, terribly anti-Russian," and that he passionately argued for continuing and expanding weapons research because "Russia was just as dangerous an enemy as Germany had been."[14] Thus Teller and the other Atomic Mechanics were seen as less threatening to the Military-Industrial Complex and the economic stability it represented than Oppenheimer and his fellow "One Worlders."

By 1949, scientists (now definitely small s) had fallen into such ill repute that A. J. P. Taylor could say "any argument will do, so long as they can continue with their terribly sweet problems. The scientists think they are God...they want to remake the universe; and we pay the price for their mad ambition.... Shall we knock the power out of their hands before it is too late?"[15] Even the scientists themselves were beginning to doubt whether they deserved the public's trust and admiration. J. B. Priestley wrote: "Have we not been given too much power without being qualified to use it properly?" And the humorist James Thurber was ready with a dire answer: "Man is flying too fast for a world that is round. Soon he will catch up with himself in a great rear-end collision and Man will never know that what hit him from behind was Man."[16] Finally, by 1950 America looked upon its former scientist heroes with suspicion and barely concealed hatred.

It has often been argued that most if not all of this shift in mood can be blamed on the country's postwar paranoia about the "international Communist conspiracy." Boyer, for instance, blames Truman's deliberate focus on the Communist threat in Greece as the demarcation point of the beginning of the "world Communist conspiracy" fear. Though Boyer's analysis may be a little too chronologically neat, it is undeniable that the Great Fear, as he calls it, doomed the possibility of international cooperation over atomic weapons. The word "internationalist" quickly came in the public mind to represent views that were, if not overtly Communist, at least sympathetic to the Communist "one world" doctrine. And thus, those who had in the past expressed internationalist views—of which the "One World or None" movement was, in a basic sense, the most prominent antecedent—were naturally looked upon as "internationalist plotters."

Thus, in six short years, from our decisive victory in 1945 to the advent of McCarthyism in 1951, the scientist had metamorphosed from a figure of immense stature and wisdom to an enemy, an outsider, even a traitor. What had become of the SCIENTIST, the near-God handing the power of the atom, for better or worse, to us mere mortals?

One answer might be that the promises of wartime technology—especially the government-sponsored Atoms for Peace program—created expectations which, when unmet, produced considerable disappointment and a subsequent backlash of resentment and finger-pointing by the public and the media. Those who had delivered us into the Atom Age seemed the logical ones to blame when this New World proved to contain not only all the problems of the old one, but new and nasty headaches to boot.

A number of other, less overtly political factors contributed to the failure of the more "theoretical" scientists to hold onto the prestige they shared with the technicians and soldiers during the war years. There was certainly a backlog of resentment, particularly from religious figures, who used Hiroshima to warn against the essentially "moral-less vacuum" in which weapons research and the theoretical science which had produced it operated. And, in a complete reversal of the near-worship the press and public exhibited for the scientists immediately after the war, by 1949 the widespread sentiment was that, not only had the scientists failed to prevent Russia from obtaining the bomb, but they were also somehow *single-handedly* responsible for the bomb and all atomic energy's attendant problems (a sentiment we will find echoed throughout the political rhetoric of the Cold War, culminating in President's Reagan's speech initiating the Strategic Defense Initiative, or Star Wars, a quarter-century later; see chapter 7). Coincident with this focus of blame on the scientists is the stark reversal of a perception of the scientists and scientific methods as fit models for the solution to all the world's problems. From the *New York Times* of 1949: "Because a man is a success in physics, it does not follow that he is qualified to elucidate political issues that perplex able and honest statesmen."[17] In other words, having created the mess, the "successful" scientist should now butt out and let "able and honest" statesmen clean it up.

Additionally, the atomic scientists themselves contributed to their program's failure. When they weren't, like the "One World-ers," taking an extreme opposition to the Establishment, they were becoming part of it. The years 1950–1959 saw the Military-Industrial Complex become firmly entrenched in the American economy. By 1959, nearly 10 percent of those employed in this country were working directly or indirectly for the Department of Defense. During the period 1950–1958, according to Zuckerman, the "armed forces and the firms which catered to their needs consumed 85–90% percent of all federal government purchases of goods and services."[18] Edward Teller and Livermore Labs replaced Robert Oppenheimer and Los Alamos as the new model for cooperation between the scientific community and the government; and in that model, the scientists did not control the goals or funding of their research; rather, they simply did what they were told.

And finally, there was dissension within the scientists' own ranks. The age-old class distinction between the applied and pure sciences now reappeared. On the split between the older, more academic, prominent leaders of the project, and the younger, more engineering-oriented, less experienced technicians, one of the older atomic physicists—whose political activism included lobbying for the McMahon Act, the policy statement describing how the Atomic Energy Commission should supervise and direct atomic research—wrote: "the younger scientists were not very influential in this business; some of them were too enthusiastic, got cracked, got interested in housing and all. . . . The [Atomic Scientists of Chicago] died a natural death after the McMahon Act. Most of them felt that politics was not their business anyhow."[19]

Perhaps this is the point at which to deal with what might be seen as a significant exception to the American public's dichotomous treatment of applied vs. theoretical scientists I am suggesting. That potential exception is one of the greatest theoretical scientists of all time, Albert Einstein.

Einstein would seem by all scientific measures to be much closer to Oppenheimer than Edison, and therefore, according to my thesis, a scientist figure the American public would find threatening rather than inspirational. And even though Einstein's theoretical work—reduced to the oft-quoted if poorly understood formula $E=MC^2$—has become something of a ubiquitous slogan, appearing on everything from T-shirts to album covers, it is difficult to argue that Einstein's scientific accomplishments produced any "practical" results, that is, results which are easily understood by and commercially available to the lay American. Yet the positive, even worshipful public image of Einstein arguably surpasses that of Edison.

But it is important to remember that we are considering here the *public image* of scientists, not their actual professional achievements. With Albert Einstein, for instance, the popular mythology about his early years in science is extremely instructive in building our case. For instance, in American elementary school textbooks—at least the ones I grew up reading—Einstein and Edison were often paired as two examples of "geniuses" who were "self-taught." (In point of fact, this part of the Einstein-as-autodidact legend is completely false.

Einstein's performance in school, at least in mathematics and Latin, was consistently at the top of his class.) And much was made of the fact that Einstein published his first papers when he was working at the Swiss patent office—not on the faculty of a university—and that his claims were, at least at first, "ridiculed" by the "established" scientific community.

However, even though Einstein's early career was represented as closer to Edison's than to Oppenheimer's, why didn't Einstein's association with the atomic bomb result in the same vilification that was directed at other theoretical A-bomb scientists? Perhaps because, both publicly and in actuality, Einstein had very little to do with Los Alamos. Though his letter to Roosevelt certainly helped to "kick start" the Manhattan Project, Einstein himself was involved only peripherally in the development of the A-bomb, and his association with it— other than as some sort of spiritual founding father—was rarely mentioned in the media debate about the bomb after the war.

One might also object that, as Einstein was European and Oppenheimer American, they would seem to reverse the cultural "polarity" of the Mechanic/ Wizard dynamic. However, it seems reasonable to argue that Einstein's status as a refugee from Nazi-controlled Germany identified him as a scientist who had rejected the Old World; Oppenheimer, on the other hand, was often noted as a man who affected "old world" manners and tastes. There is even Einstein's visage to consider, the fact that, with his bushy mustache and eyebrows, he looks much more the grandfatherly puppet-maker Geppetto from Disney's *Pinocchio* than the "thin-faced, beardless" monster-maker from Whale's *Frankenstein*—a description that more closely matches the most widely circulated photo of Oppenheimer, smoking his pipe and looking thin, beardless, arrogant, and aesthetic.[20] Einstein's rumpled, thrown-together appearance contrasted sharply with Oppenheimer's display of expensive suits and ever-present fedora.[21] All of this is to emphasize that, in all *public* ways, Einstein is much more closely associated with the independent inventors than the dependent theoreticians. If anything, Einstein's lack of "material" production seems to have enhanced rather than subverted his legendary status, adding to his image the aura of a kind and selfless scientific philosopher with nothing personal to gain from his scientific insights.

Regardless of Einstein's "exceptional" status as a theoretician, it is clear that the prestige and power that the Los Alamos scientists specifically and theoretical science generally enjoyed at the end of World War II was extraordinarily brief, a historical and cultural anomaly. What should have been a feeling of national success and invulnerability almost instantly metamorphosed into an atmosphere of fear, blame, and conformity, one that would come to characterize the United States of the 1950s. However, even if there are logical reasons to explain the fall of the atomic scientists from public grace, several intriguing questions remain: Why, for instance, were the A-bomb scientists *singled out* for public condemnation? After all, the military, the private sector, and government agencies had been just as deeply involved in the development of atomic weapons. Why was none of the public's reactionary paranoia focused on any of those sectors of the American culture? Why don't we find editorials condemning the narrow-minded and brutal vision of the military, which had pushed for the actual use of the A-bomb even over the passionate pleas of a segment of the A-bomb scientists? Why don't we find films about short-sighted and greedy businessmen pursuing the commercial grail of atomic energy well before its dangers and consequences were properly understood? Why don't we find radio commentators chastising politicians for failing to realize the benefits of international control of atomic weapons?

The most reasonable answer to these questions is that the criticism directed solely at the theoretical scientists after the war was a cultural *instinct*, and that the postwar vilification of the atomic scientists wasn't a fall so much as a return: that is, a return to the status quo of American paranoia—not about foreign invaders, but rather domestic strangers. Thus perhaps it is not unreasonable to suggest that, given such a reading of America in the 1950s, the Rosenberg trial may be seen as one of many public rituals of that time which represented the superimposition of two enemies: Communists and intellectuals. And thus their "public burning" represents the convergence of two strains of American xenophobia: toward extra-communal foreigners and intra-communal revolutionaries. The Rosenbergs were symbols, in the American mind, of those who had betrayed not just atomic secrets, but atomic hopes; for all the "One Worlders" who had given this insoluble problem to mankind (Americans) in the first place, and then reneged on their promise that the bomb would make the world (America) a better place—perhaps even an Eden on Earth. This would explain why Wicked Wizards were so viciously attacked in the American popular media throughout the next decade, almost always as an effigy of a dangerous, even homicidal outsider. And nowhere is this treatment more evident than in the flush of science fiction "invader" films eagerly consumed by the American public of the 1950s.

INVADERS WITH PH.D.'S

6

Aliens, Commies, and Eggheads in
Science Fiction Films of the 1950s

Ideologically the time had come for the political fears that have been permeating the public's mind to be released on the screen. . . . Fear of the Atom will give us film where Mankind is threatened by giant animals resulting from atomic mutations. Fear of Communism will result in a series of films about hostile aliens which we must shoot—before talking.

Jean-Marc Lofficier

"HALF MAN! Half Ant! All Terror!!"

Thus warns the movie poster for *Mant!*, a fictional sci-fi horror flick of 1962 as imagined in the film *Matinee* (1993). In this satirical and nostalgic send-up of 1950s grade B horror films, John Goodman plays Lawrence Woolsey, a producer of Saturday matinee schlock in the mold of the real-life producer William Castle. Castle was the "innovative" producer of films like *The Tingler* and *House on Haunted Hill* with all their attendant gimmickry of electrical shockers in the seats, skeletons on wires flying across the theater, and, most creative of all, his offer of "Death by Fright" insurance with "nurses" standing by in the theater lobby. *Matinee* couples this atmosphere of cheap thrills with the very real terror of the Cold War and all *its* attendant gimmickry of backyard fallout shelters and duck-and-cover drills. The creature of the movie-within-a-movie, *Mant!*, is of course meant as a representative of countless schlock-fi horror creatures, from giant ants (*Them!* 1954) to a half-man-half-fly (*The Fly*, 1958). And at its best, *Matinee* presents a sound if satirical overview of what science fiction films meant to the American youth culture of the 1950s, which was very similar to what the fiction of the early 1800s and the pulps of the 1920s–1930s had meant to the American popular culture of those times—the primary mode of distribution for images of the culture's anxieties about science, as well as opportunities to experience the victory of communities over those anxieties.

The hordes of invading aliens during that decade would seem to provide ample evidence that America of the 1950s was indeed fearful, more specifically paranoid and xenophobic. It has in fact become the traditional wisdom to argue that Lofficier was right, and that these hostile alien invaders were stand-ins for the "godless Commies" decried as lurking in every sector of American society, from the State Department to the labor unions. Representative of this opinion is an article about two films from the 1950s, *The Thing* (1951) and *Jet Pilot* (1957), wherein Eric Smoodin writes: "Appearing as [aliens] do in movies made in a period of cold war and McCarthyism, these un-Americans clearly represent the perceived Soviet threat. [These films] alert us to how vulnerable we are to a powerfully technologized and intellectual enemy from far, far away."[1] Similar analyses of these films are ubiquitous in articles, books, Internet sites, course syllabi, documentaries, and even other films of the period.[2]

Certainly there were many of films of the time whose subject matter is the "international Communist conspiracy" and the supposed imminent threat this conspiracy posed to American culture (*I Married a Communist*, 1949; *I Was a Communist for the FBI*, 1951; *The Whip Hand*, 1951; *1984*, 1956). However, none of these films was particularly popular at the box office, and they are certainly not the popular science fiction films of those times. Many "documentaries" were produced by various government agencies (*Communism*, 1950; *Communist Weapon of Allure*, 1950; *Communist Target—Youth*, 1959; *Challenge of Ideas*, 1961); MGM offered a cartoon called *Make Mine Freedom* (1948); Columbia Pictures followed suit with *Invasion USA* (1952); and, in the same year in which *Matinee* is set, 1962, there was the television "documentary" *Red Nightmare*, produced by the Department of Defense.[3] But again, none of these films were box-office hits, and, other than the cartoon, none achieved wide circulation.

Rather, what did circulate in the popular culture were printed materials dedicated to the mission of exposing this theorized international conspiracy. For instance, as early as 1949 we have jeremiads like "Communists Should Not Teach in American Colleges," by Raymond B. Allen, president of the University of Washington, Seattle; and *Is This Tomorrow?*, a sort of B horror pamphlet published by the Catechetical Guild Educational Society of St. Paul, Minnesota, with a cover depicting the conquering Communists apparently inspiring interracial fistfights in the midst of a raging firestorm.[4] And such dire warnings were not limited to college presidents and religious societies. *Life* magazine featured "The Reds Have a Standard Plan for Taking Over a New Country" (1948).

Thus, in regard to the vast majority of popular science fiction and horror films of the time produced by commercial studios, the standard analysis of Lofficier, Smoodin, et al. doesn't quite fit. For instance, the explicit enemy in both the films discussed by Smoodin—an alien in *The Thing* and a Russian fighter pilot (played by Janet Leigh) in *Jet Pilot*—is neither especially technologized nor intellectual, nor even much of a real threat. The alien in *The Thing* uses as its primary weapon a wooden four-by-four and seems intellectually incapable of having constructed the flying saucer in which it lands, its communicative range limited to grunts and screams. The Commies in *Jet Pilot* are relatively easy targets for the American fighter jock (John Wayne). In fact, I would argue, the real threat in these films and so many others made during this period of the Cold War and McCarthyism is neither alien nor Communist; it isn't even from far, far away, but from our own backyard—or rather our own laboratories.

THE SCIENCE fiction film genre had entered something of a hiatus after *Things to Come* while World War II consumed all our attention and resources. When the genre returned, the films of the 1950s provided a perfect record of the brief rise and precipitous fall of the theoretical scientist as Wicked Wizard in the popular culture of America.

The first actual science fiction movie to combine atomic weapons and space flight was the 1950 *Destination Moon*. In this technically accurate, documentary-style film, the military and the scientists work as cohorts to further American supremacy, a relationship clearly modeled on the Manhattan Project. One of the chief motivations for launching their rocketship to the moon is so the United States can "rain A-bombs down on the earth from the safety of the moon."[5] This happy, goal-oriented alliance of the military and scientists is continued in 1951's *When Worlds Collide*, where their project is the salvation of the human race. When a "rogue planet" enters the solar system and makes a beeline for earth, scientists and the military cooperate to build a "space ark" to preserve a nucleus of humankind. The villain here is not a scientist or even an alien, but rather a businessman, Sydney Stanton (John Hoyt), who is, interestingly enough, confined to a wheelchair, handicapped in a way reminiscent of the crippled mad scientists of the pulps. Stanton is portrayed as a selfish manipulator of the crisis, someone interested only in self-preservation, while the scientists and military are presented as reasonable, self-sacrificing, dedicated, and capable heroes. And the common folk are largely pictured as mindless and untrustworthy, easily transformed by rabble-rousing rhetoric from dedicated laborers eagerly working to complete the massive project to an angry mob just as eager to destroy it—a trope recognizable from *Things to Come* as well as countless other films of the period, to say nothing of texts like *Is This Tomorrow?*, all implying that the general public was only one good agitprop speech away from utter madness.

However, such a parity of shared heroic status for the military and the scientific hero began to change with 1951's *The Day the Earth Stood Still*. The film begins with the arrival of a giant flying saucer in the middle of Washington, DC, with only two occupants: Klaatu and his sleek and sinister robot, Gort. Klaatu (Michael Rennie) is a diplomat from a federation of planets who has come to Earth to save us from ourselves; however, he doesn't get the chance to explain his mission until later in the film, as he is immediately shot and wounded by a nervous soldier.[6] Klaatu acts as, among other things, a judge of mankind's folly in pursuing a policy of "mindless violence"—a policy graphically evidenced by his own "preemptive" wounding—and his message is simple: if our warlike tendencies are carried into space, the Earth will be "reduced to a burned out cinder."

This film was an exception for science fiction of the time in many ways, one of the most obvious being that in it the military are depicted as paranoid, hasty, unthinking, arbitrary and fearful, in short, anything but heroic. One trait the military of *The Day the Earth Stood Still* share with their brethren in most of the sci-fi films to follow, however, is their suspicion of scientists. When the scientists of the world—the very people Klaatu has come 250 million miles to meet—ask to hold a conference at the spaceship, they are turned down: the military considers the whole event too dangerous to be dealt with by the naive and gullible scientists. "We scientists," the theoretical scientist character Dr. Barnhardt (Sam Jaffe, who wears his hair in the unkempt style of Einstein) explains sadly to Klaatu, "are too often misunderstood or ignored." Something else that separates this film from most of the other sci-fi films of the time was its clear political agenda, as admitted by the director, Robert Wise: "It was very obvious that the film was making a political comment. All of us involved in *The Day the Earth Stood Still* were very concerned about the threat of atomic war."[7]

A clear split in the filmic portrayal of certain kinds of scientists as opposed to "true" American heroes was becoming evident, and the next major release in the genre represents that split most explicitly: *The Thing—from Another World*. This is a film I wish to examine in some detail, as it sets the standard for both bad scientists and good warriors in the majority of sci-fi films to follow, and it makes abundantly clear who is the true villain of these films—and it isn't the alien.

Released in 1951 (the story from which it was adapted, "Who Goes There?" was written in 1938 by John W. Campbell, one of the most prolific science fiction writers of the time), *The Thing* has the distinction of being the first science fiction western—which is hardly surprising as, even though its credited director was Christian Nyby it is common knowledge that veteran western filmmaker Howard Hawks actually oversaw its script and production.[8] The plot of *The Thing* is quite straightforward: a group of scientists at the North Pole discover a flying saucer buried in the ice, and with it the body of a man from Mars. Unintentionally, they blow up the saucer and melt the Martian. The thawed Martian, or Thing, proceeds to run amok, killing scientists and draining their blood in order to nourish its progeny, which it produces from "seed pods," one of its many plant-like attributes. Significantly, a group of visiting air force men have taken over in this moment of crisis, a coup that the film seems to believe requires no justification. Thus the major conflict is defined: not, that is, between man and Martian, but between soldier and scientist. The leader of the scientists, Dr. Carrington (Robert Cornthwaite)—who is referred to early in the film as both a genius and the "man who was at Bikini," thus aligning him with the H-bomb—is portrayed as arrogant, cold, precise, unemotional: everything we've come to expect from a card-carrying 1950s egghead. Throughout the rest of the film Dr. Carrington demonstrates exactly what average Americans, as members of both a national and a cultural community, had to fear from such scientists.

In incontestable echoes of Hawthorne's mad scientists, Dr. Carrington is 1) thin; 2) aristocratic in speech, manner, and dress; 3) concerned only with his own code of conduct; 4) intellectually arrogant toward the "common man" figures of the soldiers as well as his fellow scientists; 5) not shy about expressing not only his disinterest but outright disdain for both sex and domesticity; and 6) utterly obsessed by his scientific research, even if it results in the destruction of his community. All of these traits are represented as expressions of his fanatical commitment to his theoretical research, and set in opposition to the behavior and even clothing of his fellow "practical" scientists, those who perform such mechanical scientific work as counting cosmic rays and cultivating plants.

From the first scene at the Arctic station, Dr. Carrington is constructed as an outsider even in this hermetic community: while the other scientists are dressed in blue jeans and work-shirts, attire completely appropriate for the "frontier" setting of their underground research station, Dr. Carrington repeatedly appears in a blue blazer and dress slacks; and when he is awakened in the middle of the night during the Thing's first attack, he appears quite natty in a smoking jacket. He is the only scientist with a beard, a neatly trimmed Lenin-like goatee. He may be brilliant, but his social skills leave something to be desired: when he first meets the visiting military men he doesn't even say hello; often he doesn't speak directly to other people at all, but rather has his secretary address them from his notes. When he does deign to speak, his speech is cold, precise ("I dislike being vague"), emotionless, and condescending.

From the moment they discover the saucer, Carrington makes his admiration, even veneration for the alien quite clear. When the ice-covered saucer is discovered and then accidentally destroyed, Carrington laments the loss of this "Key to the stars . . . and a million years of history." While one understands that the technology of the saucer might be a "key to the stars," why is the loss of it also a loss of "history"? Unless, that is, for Carrington human history isn't quite good enough, and what he truly values is some other, alien history. He also seems to believe that human language isn't adequate to dealing with this discovery, theorizing that the engines of the saucer aren't "engines we would recognize" and that the alien "can't die as we understand dying." His secretary summarizes his attitude toward the alien, as well as his absolute rejection of the military's fear that it represents a threat, by saying "He doesn't think the way we do anyway; he's like a kid with a new toy."

Carrington is also a prude and an isolato. Before the Thing's rampage, he makes a (for him) impassioned speech to his secretary, Miss "Nikki" Nicholson (Margaret Sheridan)—who is romantically involved with the commander of the Army unit, Captain Hendry (Kenneth Tobey)—about the importance of being "free of domestic distractions" in scientific research. Later, after the Thing has attacked the camp and lost an arm, Carrington supervises the examination of the appendage, wherein they discover it is more plantlike than animal, and that it contains seed pods from which it might asexually reproduce itself. Carrington immediately declares this a "neat and unconfused reproductive technique" which would naturally result in its "intellectual superiority" as it is not "handicapped by emotional or sexual needs." The reporter, Scotty (Douglas Spencer), opines that Carrington is describing an "intellectual carrot." Carrington insists on the importance of preserving this "carrot" in order to study it and learn "secrets hidden from mankind since the beginning of time." Why have these secrets been hidden from us? By Carrington's logic, apparently because we have been "distracted" from discovering such secrets by the "confusion" caused by our "sexual needs."

Carrington is also a traitor to his own species. During this lecture on sex and biology, the military expresses clear boredom, as they have better things to do: figuring out a way to kill the Thing. Of course Carrington strenuously objects to any attempt to harm this "stranger in a strange land" and emphatically insists that they must do whatever is necessary to communicate with it, even if it means placing themselves in mortal danger. This myopic dedication to his research (the alien) motivates Carrington to enact the first of several betrayals of his fellow humans. When it is discovered that the Thing is using the base's greenhouse to nourish its young with bottles of plasma stolen from the infirmary, Carrington convinces several scientists to stand watch in the greenhouse waiting for the Thing to return. The next morning they are found hanging upside down from the rafters, their throats cut and their blood draining down onto the growing Thinglings. Thus, in echoes of the criticism aimed at the A-bomb scientists by the end of the 1940s, Carrington is a fine example of an Wicked Wizard who is perfectly willing to "waste" certain "nonessential individuals" to achieve his "precious scheme."

This willingness to die—or sacrifice—for science is made even more explicit in the final scene of the film. The military constructs a trap for the Thing into which they must lure it and then electrocute it, and Carrington attempts to sabotage their efforts, not once but twice. First he switches off the generator, declaring that they should be ready to "stand and die" for the advancement of science. When this effort is thwarted and with the creature striding menacingly toward the huddled humans, Carrington runs out to warn him and pleads for "communication," stating that he is obviously "wiser than anything on Earth." The creature stares at him for a moment, baffled, then simply bats him aside with a four-by-four, and marches confidently (and somewhat idiotically) onward to his electrical doom.

Dr. Carrington obviously admires "things" more than people, aliens more than Americans. Throughout the film he argues with absolute monomania that the Thing is in every way superior to the humans by whom it is surrounded, and that he, Carrington, is perfectly willing to sacrifice himself and the others in order to add the alien's superior knowledge to the "brain," as he calls it, of his own culture. We might even see in the vilification of Carrington a rejection of internationalism, as his "enthusiasm" for other ways of thinking and being is taken to extremes and constructed as a form of suicidal multicultural mania.

Clearly the military are the heroes of this film. They understand the mortal threat the Thing represents from the very beginning; in fact, they can't even stand to look at it, a deep-seated aversion to its "otherness" which sets the plot in motion, as it causes a soldier to put a blanket over the block of ice which contains the Thing, thus melting the ice and setting it free. Throughout the film, while the intellectuals stand about debating endlessly about how to deal with the Thing, the soldiers resolutely do what is necessary to first exclude the alien from their midst, and then annihilate it, without wasting a moment worrying about whether the Thing and its culture are worth getting to know. Their rejection of its un-Americanness is total; as their commander says at the end, he doesn't want "any part of it."

Much is also done to align the military characters with both their counterpart heroes in World War II films and with "common sense," meaning the putative thinking and culture of the middle class. For instance, the first scene of the movie introduces us to the military characters in the setting of an officers' club where they sit around playing poker and listening to World War II–era music; and their first reaction to the scientific installation is that the "taxpayers oughta see this," with the clear implication that if they did they'd consider it a waste of money. Captain Hendry's anti-intellectualism is emphasized to the point of obsession. When the relatively simple method of calculating the distance to the saucer is explained to him he responds, "You lost me, I'll take your word for it"; and during another discussion of technology he says it's all a "bit beyond me." It is in fact an enlisted solider—referred to only as "Bob"—who is the Master Mechanic of the film, responsible for all the bright ideas about dealing with the alien, including the scheme to destroy it.

Much has been written about *The Thing* as an expression of 1950s American paranoia, especially given the last line of the film, when the reporter Scotty warns the world to "Watch the skies! Keep watching! Watch everywhere!"[9] Clearly Scotty is heralding the coming siege mentality of the Cold War. And in traditional readings of this film, the Thing is seen as a stand-in for our fear of Communism as a dehumanizing ideology, a system that made people into unfeeling, replaceable, soulless plants.

But I find these analyses unconvincing. After all, the Thing does not represent the real threat in this film; rather, that distinction goes to Dr. Carrington, the obsessed intellectual, who works at every turn to betray his fellow Americans because he believes in the superiority of the Thing and its culture.[10] At most, the alien represents brute strength, while Carrington embodies the cunning arrogance of deceptive rhetoric and ideological fervor that I would argue are the true trademarks of the demonized Communist.

Given Carrington's intellectually amoral commitment to selling the whole bunch of them down the river, it could be argued that Scotty was also warning his fellow Americans to keep their eyes peeled closer to home: to watch not just the skies, but their neighbors. The true American paranoid of the 1950s understood that the real threat to American ideology wasn't the brute strength of the Red Army, but the theorized tendency of certain intellectual internationalists to misread the mentality behind that brute strength as, in ways completely unintelligible to the average American patriot, fascinating and seductive—all due to their blind commitment to the "theory" of political idealism (or scientific inquiry) and the acquisition of new knowledge. While the "intellectual carrot" is an enemy the American soldiers can understand, it is Dr. Carrington who is the true alien to them.

Many critics have pointed to Dr. Carrington's physical appearance (the goatee as well as a Russian-style fur hat he wears in the final scene) as evidence for the proposition that he, and other "megalomaniacal" scientists figures like him, were in fact straw men, stand-ins for the real enemies of 1950s America, the Communists.[11] However, why not reverse that accusation? Couldn't the Commies be in fact stand-ins for certain American intellectuals who were seen as fifth columnists? It seems arguable that such superficial references to Russians don't mark Carrington as a Communist, so much as they "accessorize" his abstract outsider status with concrete and easily recognizable symbols of more prosaic outsiders, namely the Reds. That is to say, if Carrington's arrogance and obsession with theoretical research are the *real* villains of the film, but he is at least superficially more "human" than the alien Thing, then his character must be physically coded to place him in alignment with those humans we already recognize as our enemies, i.e., Communists. Thus it isn't external "things" like Communist ideology or alien technology that are the real threats here; rather, the threat is the *domestic* ideology of certain segments of the American scientific community.

Dr. Carrington is the first in a long line of science fiction film mad scientists of the '50s who are hubris-ridden and obsessed with various theories of unrestrained investigation that lead them to become, in a mythic and functional sense, traitors to their kind. Thus they are clear descendants of Hawthorne's Gothic megalomaniacs—but megalomaniacs equipped with technological and ideological superweapons, and therefore free of the constraints that limited their nineteenth-century counterparts' destructive potential to their own local communities.

Even when the portrayal of the scientists in these films is less melodramatic and indeed sympathetic to the true scientific values of curiosity and reason that guide scientific research in the real world, it is still made abundantly clear that they are considered outsiders by most of the rest of American society. For instance, in 1953's *It Came from Outer Space*, one character describes the scientist-protagonist (John) as follows: "He's an odd man . . . individual and lonely; he's a man who thinks for himself." Thus John's "otherness" is apparently a function of his individuality: scientists are "odd men," "lonely" men, men who "think for themselves." (Of course, this was a script based on a story by someone who would be more sympathetic to the scientist's characterization than the average Hollywood scriptwriter—Ray Bradbury.) While such independence of thought would seem to be something fundamentally American, as old as the Bill of Rights and as deeply embedded in American philosophy as Emerson's transcendental individualism, when coupled with heightened intellectual agility, a lack of domestic relationships, and the other attributes of the Wicked Wizard I've delineated, it is apparently considered a mode of behavior inimical to the bourgeois stability of the American community. Often in these films the scientist is seen, à la Carrington, as more sympathetic to and more closely allied with the alien than the human community. As Patrick Lucanio writes in *Them or Us: Archetypal Interpretations of Fifties Alien Invasion Films*, "society is often suspicious of the [scientist] hero, for, considering his knowledge of the invader's power . . . he may not be who he claims to be but a part of the invasion himself."[12]

That we were ready for an invasion—or a betrayal—of some sort is made clear by the spate of cheaply produced yet nonetheless popular alien invasion films of the following years: *Man from Planet X* (1951); *The Flying Saucer*

(1950), *Earth vs. the Flying Saucers* (1956), *Invasion of the Body Snatchers* (1956), *Not of This Earth* (1957), *It, the Terror from Beyond Space* (1958) . . . all retelling essentially the same story over and over again to an audience with an apparently insatiable appetite for just that story. In fact, the only thing that differentiates these films one from the next is in their depiction of the scientist character: as either a practical and ingenious inventor of a solution, or an overly intellectual and dangerous creator of a problem.

In 1953's *Invaders from Mars*—one of the first plots about the dangers of mind control—the military are the saviors, the scientists are useless, and the common man is, again, easily manipulated. Much the same can be said of *Invasion of the Body Snatchers* (1956). Certainly the pod people of this film seem to fit the '50s stereotype of the Communists—godless, emotionless, soulless, lacking individuality—and, as they are all working in lockstep to take over America, they would seem to be the real threat here, not a theoretical scientist. Additionally, as the hero of this film is a doctor, *Body Snatchers* might be seen as an exception to my rule. However, this doctor (not scientist), through his various commonsense and improvisational stratagems to escape and outflank the threat, his lack of any monologues "theorizing" the aliens' intentions, and, most important, his romantic relationship with a female character, fits the bill as a Master Mechanic. In fact, the main pod-person villain of the film is a psychiatrist—someone devoted to the theoretical and abstract workings of the mind. The psychiatrist is also the character who gives a speech laying out the theoretical "agenda" of the pod people. It is even difficult to ascertain any change in his personality from human being to pod person. Also, the fact that the pod people are physically identical to the humans they have replaced seems evidence that the enemy being represented is physically indistinguishable from us; it is their *behavior* that makes them alien: cold, unemotional, compulsive, arrogant . . . in other words, they are essentially clones of Dr. Carrington. Apparently the only physical work they do is creating more pods; otherwise they are completely unproductive as a culture, perfectly content to sit around and "think." What could be more un-American than that?

Also from 1953 is the first film version of H. G. Wells's *War of the Worlds*, with the military presented as brave if ineffectual, the scientists as foolish and ineffectual, and the common man as, yet again, a mindless mob. Though the hero of this film is also a scientist, once again he is free of any theoretical obsessions, full of practical solutions (none of which work), and quite open to romantic relationships. While Wells's plot was updated to the 1950s, the film stayed true to the *deus ex machina* of the novel, with bacteria as the ultimate saviors of mankind. The film's (and novel's) point seems to be how humble ought the smartest of us to feel when faced with the fact that intellect proves powerless in the face of the Martian's superior technology, and even geniuses owe their salvation to "God's smallest creations." Such statements, as well as the final scene of rescue from Armageddon which is set in a church (actually a series of churches), introduce a theme of religiosity into the "Americanness" of the Master Mechanic figure that will be echoed in other films to come.

While the Master Mechanics have the power of common sense and domestic bliss as their chief weapons, what often gave the mad scientists of these films their power was the mysterious and little-understood workings of atomic radiation, a force represented as a sort of Philosopher's Stone, something which could transmute anything into anything else. For instance, in the monster film *The Beast from 20,000 Fathoms* (1953), radioactivity revives the beast, but radioactive isotopes are also used to kill it. And there were of course countless films featuring radiation-mutated creatures, from giant ants (*Them!* 1954) to giant locusts (*The Beginning of the End,* 1957), and even in one particularly ridiculous film a giant praying mantis (*The Deadly Mantis,* 1957). This *carte blanche* capability of the A-bomb knowledge becomes a new and powerful component in the mad scientist genre. Radioactivity was a universal danger to the community. And it was of course the A-bomb scientists who had brought this universal danger into the community's midst. In *The Thing*, Dr. Carrington argues for preserving the alien, even when it is systematically slaughtering their little community's citizens, because "science has learned so much" from new and strange phenomena. As an example he uses the A-bomb, saying, "we've penetrated the atom." One of the soldiers responds sarcastically, "and didn't that make everyone happy," clearly indicating not only the anger and resentment that the soldiers (and, we are to understand, the average Joe in the street) feel toward scientists like Carrington, but also the vast gulf between Carrington's standards of "success" and those of the rest of American society. (This is of course a response that conveniently forgets the military's equal involvement in the development and primary responsibility for the deployment of the atom bomb. See my analysis in chapter 7 of President Reagan's speech initiating the Strategic Defense Initiative.)

Such a forbidding portrayal of the mad scientist and the apocalyptic power at his command is nowhere more clearly evident than in the second classic science fiction film I wish to discuss at some length, *Forbidden Planet* (1956). In a script explicitly structured as a twenty-fifth-century version of Shakespeare's *Tempest*, the film presents the same schematic confrontation between the three archetypes of Mechanics, Wizards, and Warriors as exhibited in *The Thing*, but on a considerably larger scale. Rather than the fate of a single research outpost hanging on the outcome of the conflict, it is the fate of an entire planet. I wish to go into some detail with this film because first of all it is such a rich

vein of cultural tropes about nearly every topic discussed so far; and second because its tremendous and lasting popularity demonstrates that this vein runs
deep and wide in the American culture.

Here, the Einstein-like wisdom of the scientist Dr. Barnhardt in *The Day the
Earth Stood Still* is completely eclipsed by the megalomaniacal arrogance of
Walter Pidgeon as Dr. Morbius (a name worthy of Christopher Marlowe for its
Latinate echoes of morbidity and doom). The forbidden planet of the title is Altair IV, where Morbius and his daughter Altaira (Anne Francis) are the sole survivors of an exploratory colony that landed some twenty years earlier, and where
they are now visited by the military crew of United Planets Star Cruiser W57-D.
The spaceship—looking very much like one of the flying saucers purported in
those times to be making daily visits to our own planet—has come to "rescue"
the colony; but when, from orbit, they state their intentions to Dr. Morbius, he
warns them in no uncertain terms to stay away. Commander Adams (Leslie
Nielsen), going by the book (as he does throughout the film), insists on landing
and assessing the situation, and thus confronts Morbius with the first of a series
of invasions of his isolated research sanctuary as well as rebellions against his
until-now supreme authority. These invasions-rebellions define Morbius's intellectual and moral "space" through their attempts to breach it; thus in a way this
film inverts the traditional invasion paradigm by, it would seem, marking Morbius as the "native" of Altair IV, and the military as the alien invaders. However,
one aspect of my analysis of the film is that it delineates the principles of a sort of
cosmic Neo-Imperialism (prefiguring the politics of the *Star Trek* TV series I will
discuss in a later chapter), and in so doing makes an argument for the conditions
under which an invasion isn't an invasion, but a liberation.

Once the spaceship lands the crew is invited to "do lunch" with Morbius,
and the ensuing scene introduces us to Morbius-Prospero and his realm. We
first encounter Robby the Robot, clearly the Ariel of this island world, execut-
ing Morbius's every command and with powers far more deadly and sinister
than his "walking jukebox" form would suggest. And here the first explicit mention is made which recognizes Morbius as potentially a representative of the
mad scientist figure. When the military express alarm at the robot's power and
its capacity for destruction "in the wrong hands," Morbius counters that they
have nothing to fear from the machine, "Not even though I were the mad scientist of the tape thrillers." He explains that the robot's programming utterly
prevents it from harming human beings.

While the robot is thus marked as a protector of humans, it is soon made
clear that there is a dangerous monster loose on Altair IV, and it is a monster
from Morbius's own imagination; in other words, while the material robot-
servant can't hurt them, the theoretical mind-servant can "tear them limb from

limb." The film's ideology of what represents the real threat to the community is thus made abundantly clear: it is intellect, or rather super-intellect that poses the greatest danger here, and this danger is fully realized in the demeanor of Morbius himself. Morbius is the epitome of a cultured, arrogant aristocrat, with mannered gestures, imperious attitude, and slightly foreign accent—and significantly the only character to appear dressed in black throughout the film.

The film then introduces us to Altaira-Miranda, Morbius's daughter, whose function is essentially to provide the chief "territory" to be fought over by Morbius and Commander Adams. Morbius explains to the military that he and his daughter are the sole survivors of the original expedition, the rest of their group having "succumbed" to some "planetary force"—a force which tore most of them "literally limb from limb" and then vaporized their spaceship as the rest attempted to flee. Only Morbius, his wife, and his daughter were "immune" to this force because, he opines, only they felt a "boundless longing" to make Altair IV their new home "far from the scurry and strife of humankind." In other words, Morbius is the ultimate misanthrope, and his wife was his perfect mate. Thus the First Law of Morbiusland is clear: love it—and, by extension, him—or die.

But Morbius isn't playing the role of an accommodating host; rather, he makes clear that his misanthropic desire for complete and utter isolation and unchallenged rule over his world—and his daughter—requires that he convince the military he doesn't need rescuing, and thus that they should leave, forthwith, before they, too, become victims of Altair IV's mysterious and murderous "watchdog" and themselves get torn "literally limb from limb."

I repeat this curious line of dialogue to emphasize the raw violence with which Morbius, or at least his intellect and id, are marked. Later, when one of the crewmen is murdered, someone asks, "How was it done?" and the response is, "Done? Why, he's splattered all over the control room." Such extreme violence would seem to stand in stark opposition to the tightly controlled nature of Morbius's physical-social self; but in fact we can see in this *grand guignol* hyperbole a suggestion that Morbius's intellectual hubris is inherently and fundamentally savage and, when stripped of its outward trappings of effete manners, it reveals itself as murderous bloodlust directed at his fellow man.

Commander Adams, being the consummate link in a chain of command, must consult with the authorities on Earth before he can simply turn tail and leave, and so he informs Morbius that, until he does so, the spaceship and its crew will stay right where they are. This defiance of Morbius's edict, as well as the developing interest of Altaira in the first men from Earth she's ever seen besides her father, set in motion the apparent reanimation of Altair IV's vengeful guardian, and several crewmen are murdered by what they come to realize is an invisible monster.

The invisibility of the creature is key to its function in the film. First, as one-half of the Caliban component of this island community, it can appear all the more horrible by not appearing at all. The only clues to its physique are footprints which, as the scientist of the crew, "Doc" (whose eclectic skills range from paleontology to psychiatry), points out, suggest a creature which "runs counter to every known law of adaptive evolution" and "doesn't fit into normal nature"—marking it and its creator not only as murderous but as fundamentally unnatural. Second, it is in a sense a creature of "pure theory," both because it has no materiality, and because it simply ought not, in the real and practical world of the military and traditional science, to exist at all.

Confronted by this apparently inexplicable paradox, Commander Adams and Doc decide to visit Morbius and, ironically, seek his advice. What they discover is that Morbius, a philologist (not a word to be found frequently in science fiction films of those times, or any times for that matter), has made a discovery of potentially enormous import: Altair IV was, in the far past, the home world of the Krell, a race which achieved "almost limitless knowledge" and technological sophistication on a scale unimaginable to humankind, but which then perished "in a single night" from some global catastrophe. Throughout the film, scale is the primary mode of marking the Krell as supreme Other, even to the extent that their doorways are constructed to accommodate bulk and their machines to require multiple arms and legs. Morbius has discovered a Krell machine that was the culmination of "their entire scientific energies"—a machine in the shape of a gigantic cube, twenty miles to a side. When the military are about to view the Krell's Super Machine, Morbius says, "Prepare your minds for a new scale of physical scientific value."

Before viewing the enormous machine, however, Morbius introduces them to one of the Krell's underground "learning labs." What follows is an extremely interesting exhibition of the role of intellect in the film. One of the Krell "teaching machines" makes it possible to measure anyone's intelligence quotient (remember, this was back when people believed in IQ scores as accurate indicators of an individual's intelligence). Morbius sends the device nearly to the top (his IQ is "officially listed as 183," making him, according to Krell standards, a "low grade moron"), whereas the Commander barely makes it move. "That's all right, Commander," Morbius says patronizingly, "Commanding officers don't need brains, just a good loud voice." Thus, just as we saw in *The Thing*, great effort is made to distinguish between the Wicked Wizard's super intellect and the average (or lower?) intelligence of the military hero.

Morbius then guides them through the supreme achievement of the Krell, the gargantuan machine. The scene depicting the trio walking through the enormous innards of this machine is again meant to emphasize the superhuman and thus unnatural scale of Krell technology. In this era and especially in this film, bigger is better because it is assumed to represent smarter; and thus the "limit-less" intelligence of the Krell—and by extension Morbius—is clearly represented as a product of enormous physical instrumentality, and identified as that which makes them especially alien; that, and Morbius's intransient misanthropy.[13] When, following their tour, Commander Adams demands that Morbius share the "limitless" Krell knowledge with Earth, Morbius responds with a speech that could serve as the First Principle of all Wicked Wizards:

> Morbius: Perhaps I do not care to be dictated to in my own world. . . . Such por-
> tions of the Krell knowledge as I deem suitable and safe, I will from time to
> time dispense to Earth. Other portions I will withhold. And in this I will be
> answerable exclusively to my own conscience. . . . Mankind is not ready to re-
> ceive such power.
> Doc: Whereas Morbius with his artificially enhanced intellect, is in a perfect po-
> sition to make such judgments.
> Morbius: Precisely.

However great his Krell-enhanced intellect, there are two things Morbius has not figured out: the purpose of the giant Krell cube-machine, and the reason Krell civilization disappeared in a single night. This purpose and that reason—which are of course linked—are not revealed until, motivated by a deadly con-frontation with the monster wherein its unnatural physiology as well as its invulnerability are made all too visible, Doc subjects himself to a Krell "brain boost" in order to better understand the phenomenon and concoct a solution. The mental shock deals a fatal blow to Doc—but before he dies he manages to explain to Adams that the purpose of the Krell machine was to "project matter to any point on the planet, in any form the Krell might wish." In other words, it is a machine capable of converting theory into reality—but one that dispenses with materiality itself, as it requires no connecting circuitry.

The importance of such physical and *visible* relationships in technology for normal human society's operation is made clear when Morbius tells them that he knew the Krell were seeking a machine that would "free them once and for all from any dependence on physical instrumentality"—a statement which presents materiality as a kind of slavery. And the horror of this representation to the military is made clear when Doc responds, "Civilization without instru-mentality?! Incredible!" Given the emphasis on the massive scale of the Krell machines, a formula is made clear: one enters the realm of pure theory only through the door of outsized materiality; in other words, if one makes the real big enough, eventually it becomes the ethereal. Doc describes such an achieve-ment as "true creation"—which suggests that creation via physical instrumen-tality is a kind of "false" creation, whereas "true" creation comes directly from the mind without the mediator of the hand. Of course, the world in which we—and the military of this film—live is one in which the only being capable of such creation is God; ergo, any being—or race—seeking such "true" creation is one attempting to supplant God and therefore one in need of terrible punishment; one of many calls in the film to religion as a kind of "governor" over humankind's ambition.

After this revelation of the machine's function, Doc dies—but not before he pronounces the answer to the second mystery Morbius has not solved: the disappearance of the Krell: "Monsters! Monsters from the Id!" In other words, the instant their cube-machine was turned on, all the Krell's subconscious "monsters" were loosed upon one another to "kill and destroy and seek revenge." As Adams—now clearly the wiser if not the smarter of the two—explains to Morbius, the Krell had forgotten that "underneath [their] culture and wisdom, lay the primitive, mindless Id." Thus it could be argued that the Krell's search for a machine that would "free" them from instrumentality was in essence an attempt to create a world without material limitations, a world of pure imagination, of pure theory—and the moment they achieved such a world, it exterminated them with ferocious violence.

Adams, Altaira, and Dr. Morbius eventually take refuge from the rampaging invisible monster in the underground Krell laboratory. Commander Adams, continuing his new role as Morbius's instructor in simple morality, explains what is abundantly clear even to those of us without a Krell brain boost: that the monster is in fact a creature from Morbius's own mind and given material form by the power of the Krell machine (thus making him not only Prospero but the other half of Caliban). After all, his is the only bad Id around smart enough to work the machine. However, even with the Id monster beating at the door, the Wicked Wizard passionately proclaims his innocence by declaring that he is "no monster." Commander Adams counters by reminding him of his fundamental limitations as a member of the human community: "We're all part monsters in our subconscious," Adams argues, "so we have laws and religion." It is only when Morbius admits that he has overlooked what he significantly calls this "common sense" law that he can proclaim himself "guilty" and say to his Id monster "I deny you! I give you up!" Then the monster disappears, and Morbius dies.

However, it isn't enough for Morbius to simply die; first, he must confess the error of his ways; and an integral component of this confession must be an epiphany that his superior intelligence proved ultimately inferior to "common sense," i.e., the sense that is common to the little guy, the non-elitist, non-overly educated, non-aristocratic, properly domesticated and sexually conformist Average Joe of the American middle class—as represented by Commander Adams. I say sexually conformist not only because Morbius, like so many other mad scientists before and after him, has no wife, but also because Morbius is even further demonized by suggestions throughout the film that his feelings for his daughter surpass mere paternal love. Morbius's ego transgresses *all* the rules and religious laws to which the Commander refers—rules and laws which make America the Christian, pragmatic, commonsensical, and, most important, sexually domesticated nation that it is. The implication is that we have laws and religion to control *everyone*, but especially to rein in those arrogant few whose intellect would otherwise set them above the common man. Laws and religion in *Forbidden Planet* are the great levelers; they keep us safely mediocre. It is clear that what is most forbidden about this planet is a privileging of theory over praxis, individual intelligence over *common* sense.

Morbius's confession to crossing that forbidden boundary forms a ritual played out over and over again in science fiction films of the 1950s. First the scientist acquires knowledge which places him, in his own opinion, above the common man; then he misuses this knowledge and either brings an alien threat into the community's midst, or aids and abets aliens in their attempt to conquer mankind. Finally, the scientist is confronted with his sin and apologizes, or rather, not so much apologizes as confesses his mistake and begs for forgiveness. The mad scientist's confession must contain an admission not only that he has erred, and erred monumentally, but that he has discovered his vaunted intellect has in fact overlooked the obvious, that his extraordinary sense is in the end no match for everyone else's common sense. The pragmatic must triumph over the theoretical just as the average must succeed where the extreme has failed.

For instance, in *Forbidden Planet*, though Morbius is smart enough to translate the immensely complicated Krell language, he is too dumb to remember his basic Freud—for we can also read the film as an allegory of Freud's most simplified and popularized concept of the psyche as composed of the id, ego, and superego. The film emphasizes this connection by situating the monster's roots in Morbius' id; but there is also the explicit statement that such monsters reside in *all* our ids, that in a sense our id *is* a monster, something, as Freud had it, always in need of being controlled by the superego.[14] Thus, without the ordinary human superego of "religion and laws" to control his id, and with an outsized ego aligned more with the alien Krell than his fellow humans—that is to say, without an ordinary human ego to redeem—even after his confession of sin Morbius cannot be allowed to remain part of the human community; only his death will make that community safe from future attacks of similar unbridled arrogance. When the mad scientist confesses his sin and dies, he redeems not so much himself as his progeny—and by progeny I mean in this particular case Morbius's daughter, but in the larger sense his fellow scientists.[15]

It is primarily through this ritual of confession that we find what makes these films particularly American. Much has been written about the strain of paranoia deep in American politics, dating all the way back to the American Revolution.[16] But here I refer to the strain of evangelicalism which dates back ever further. It isn't just that Morbius and his ilk make some technical error, or that they are somehow inherently bad men; rather, their belief system has to be exposed as fundamentally anti-religious; they then must renounce that atheistic belief system and be re-converted back into the community of American spirituality.

Religion makes its first appearance in *Forbidden Planet* when the crew views Altair IV from space and Doc remarks, "The Lord sure makes some beautiful worlds."[17] But it is Commander Adams (Adam?) who is the chief evangelist of the group, to the point where he is portrayed as a sort of twenty-fourth-century Puritan. When he encounters one of the crewman flirting with Altaira he grows furious, more at Altaira than the crewman, as he insists that she isn't properly chaste: "Nothing human would enter your mind," he rants, and goes on to display a rage that is singularly absent from the rest of his reactions, even to the death of his crewmembers. Later, when he encounters her swimming nude in a pool, he makes quite a show of turning his back as she emerges. Then their flirtation turns serious. He suggests she knows nothing about sex, and she lists her resumé of study—but when she comes to biology the Commander says, quite coquettishly, "But that's theory of course." Then they engage in praxis, that is, they kiss—and her world changes. Literally. A tiger that was as a pet around her before her sexual awakening immediately attacks her. Clearly she's left the "theoretical" world of her father and entered "body and soul" into the practical, no-nonsense, democratic, conformist and most significantly Puritanical world of Commander Adams, aka America. It is also Commander Adams, the evangelical Puritan who, when he and Altaira witness the destruction of the planet from space, consoles Morbius's daughter, rather oddly, by suggesting that when humankind has some day equaled the achievements of the Krell, her father's name will remind them that they are "after all not God."

Interestingly, when Morbius first discloses the achievements of the Krell, ethics comes before technology: "Ethically as well as technologically [they were] a million years ahead of humankind." He goes on to praise their benevolence and nobility, stating that "in unlocking the mysteries of nature they had conquered even their baser selves." In other words, the Krell are as well intentioned as the intellect can get; but super smarts obviously do not trump common sense, precisely because such intellectual achievement leads inexorably to arrogance. It is *assumed* that being super-smart makes the individual super-arrogant and persuades that individual that he or she is beyond the communal boundaries of "religion and law."[18] This is a key component of what we might call the Morbius Delusion: the arrogance to deny that religion and violate those laws, and a belief that superior knowledge grants one superior authority. But central to the American dream is the tenet that *all* knowledge is accessible to everyone, that even knowledge of God is accessible to the common man.

And the "common man" of these films was most importantly a man of "common" sense. What is valued in these films is the man who acts on hunches, intuition; "book learning" fails. Most often the hero defeats the invader with a solution the "average guy" can identify with, a product of reasoning he can feel is not beyond his capabilities.[19] Time and again in these films the military are portrayed as intuitive, charismatic, active, while the scientists are overly rational, arrogant, and talky.[20] The scientist is seen as someone with a need to convince society of his worth, or his trans-societal value. The military hero has no such need, and is content to "do his job" as hero and then sink back into the mass of his fellow "common men"—usually into a domestic bliss initiated by his encounter with the female endangered by the uncommon menace of the Wicked Wizard. One reading of this schema would be to see in it the ancient narrative of the knight defeating the dragon in order to win the hand of the princess and live "happily ever after"—the dragons in this case being from "beyond space"—or rather, as I am arguing here, from beyond the "space" of the American community's religious and legal standards.[21]

Film after film during this period portrayed America as a nation beset by invaders: from space, from other dimensions, from the depths of the ocean and the recesses of caves, and especially, as I have shown, from our own minds. But, as previously mentioned, none of these invader films explicitly presented communists as the villains, as though we knew in our hearts that the extra-national enemy wasn't a sufficient threat to engage our fears, real or imagined. Thus I would argue that these films are about defeating *not* the foreign enemy of Communism, but rather the domestic enemy of arrogance and nonconformity. Though the Soviets had achieved the atomic and hydrogen bombs by the '50s, still these achievements were seen as anomalies, as isolated victories attained through brutalizing people into accomplishing what they otherwise could not; but more important, as the results of simple cheating, of stealing America's technological prowess, which, it was assumed—right up to the Sputnik launch and the Space Race which it engendered—far outclassed Soviet technology. In fact, the only enemy with technological expertise equal to ours had to be, by this reasoning, American; and who better to fulfill that role than the very people who'd given us that expertise in the first place?

Two films came at the end of the decade that summarized what had become our two visions of the Enemy: internal, and even more internal. The first was

On the Beach (1959), and it is in the reaction to the film that we find evidence of the pervasive anxiety caused by this vision. Here, the end of mankind is portrayed more as Eliot's "whimper" than Pound's "bang." The last survivors of a nuclear war hang on in Australia, awaiting the inevitable radioactive clouds. The scientist figures shrug their shoulders—there's nothing they can do. The military, again, are portrayed as resolute, practical, courageous: the best examples of man under the ultimate pressure, everything we've come to expect from the warrior hero of these films, the one who will defeat the dragon. However, the difference of *On the Beach* is that there's nothing the warrior heroes can do, either. Nuclear war is portrayed not as an alien to be defeated, but as a Judgment Day to be accepted. The film drew extreme reactions:

> Nobody missed the political message of *On the Beach*. How they reacted to it depended a lot on what their politics were. Dr. Linus Pauling said, "It may be that some day we can look back and say *OTB* is the picture that saved the world." Civil defense officials were scandalized—the Connecticut state director called it "mythological"; the one in New York agreed that it was a "fantasy" because saving lives of a population from nuclear war "is not only possible but relatively simple." From New York *Daily News*: "*On the Beach* is a defeatist movie . . . a would-be shocker which plays right up the alley of (a) the Kremlin and (b) the western defeatists and/or traitors who yelp for scrapping the H-bomb. . . . [It points] the way toward eventual Communist enslavement of the entire human race.[22]

Thus, when the full and realistic import of a nuclear war was depicted on the screen, and when science's inability to either prevent or limit the apocalypse was admitted, the popular reading of that reality was to see it as "defeatism" that would open the way "toward the eventual Communist enslavement of the entire human race." Clearly, it is not the Communists who are primarily at fault here, but the scientists—for not doing something to prevent the nuclear apocalypse in the first place. *On the Beach* in fact seems to be a vision of nuclear arms first presented by the Manhattan scientists themselves: something for which there simply is no technological "fix," no matter how common or intuitive. And this was a message the general public didn't want to hear.[23]

The other film, in its way equally defeatist and in other ways even more terrifying, was *Village of the Damned* (1960). Here, the Enemy turns out to be our own children, altered through the sorcerer's stone of radiation and made forever alien. But they are aliens that do not need to conquer the Earth, because they will simply inherit it. These invader-inheritors are the spawn of scientists who, like Victor Frankenstein a century before, had meddled with powers "beyond the understanding of Man." The film suggests that all the Wicked Wizards of the world really have to do to remake the world over in their own image is reproduce *themselves*—but of course reproduce not through the standard mechanisms of the human community, but through asexual "influence" over the minds of our children. One watches this film, one thinks of articles like "Communists Should Not Teach in American Colleges," and feels the urge to shout "Right!" Or, as Scotty suggests at the conclusion of *The Thing*, "Watch the skies!" However, it isn't the skies we should be watching, but our fellow Americans, as we have as much if not more to fear from within our own community than from beyond our solar system.[24]

The contribution these films made to the public's image of a "mad scientist" cannot be overemphasized. This is not to argue that there was some sort of conspiracy among screenwriters of the time to present the theoretical scientist in such a formulaic manner; if asked, most screenwriters would refer to formulas, yes, but in terms of those formulas that make a "good story." But to be satisfied with the answer that mad scientists are bad scientists because that's what makes a good story is to beg the question: *Why* do mad scientists make a good story? A story considered good, that is, by the American viewing public? This is much like asking why Victor Frankenstein must always be presented in a certain way, or why it is simply assumed that a certain kind of scientists *is* mad, i.e., bad.

Of course one might make the following counter-argument: if indeed theoretical scientists became the most usual of usual suspects when it came time to blame someone for atomic weapons and radiation and "monsters from the id," and not either the military or government figures who also played a role in these decisions and processes, perhaps it was because such scientists were more easily recognized by the public, were already the "front men" for the A-bomb and the new terrors it created. However, while it might be argued that the Los Alamos scientists came to be seen as the primary ones to blame for the A-bomb problems because these scientists were the "human face" of the new weapon, in fact Oppenheimer was really the only Manhattan Project scientist to achieve this sort of public recognition; to say nothing of the fact that General Groves as the military commander of the project and Harry Truman as the president who decided to drop the bomb were equally—if not even more—recognized as players in this arena. And, given the evidence of this long list of science fiction films which demonize the scientist but rarely the military or government, as well as the "public burning" of the HUAC and AEC hearings and other persecutions of "intellectuals" which would form the political background of the '50s, it seems inadequate to conclude that the scientists were singled out for vilification largely because these scientists were singled out in the media.

It is in fact that word—intellectual—that provides the chief clue in coming to what I consider to be a deeper analysis of this vilification. As we will see in the next chapter, "intellectual" and its political equivalent term "left liberal" were the primary identifying factors in descriptions of those suspected of "un-

American activities" in the loudly paranoid Circus Maximus games of the '50s. It is important to see the indictment of the theoretical scientists of the A-bomb (and theoretical scientists generally) as the sole villains in all matters atomic as merely another link in the long historical context presented to this point—to see this result as perhaps inevitable, given our cultural predilection to suspect and resent theoreticians; and it is to understand that the scientists weren't so much being punished for producing the A-bomb, as simply for being scientists, for being "odd men . . . individual and lonely; men who think for themselves." And as we will see in the next chapter, thinking for oneself was, in the climate of the American 1950s, perhaps the worst crime one could commit.

FALLOUT

Politics and Paranoia after the Bomb

LIFE AT Los Alamos had provided the A-bomb community with what was for any research scientist of the period an almost ideal existence: unlimited resources, access to the best minds in the country, camaraderie, culture—there were frequent concerts, as many of the scientists were excellent musicians—and even a home life, as the government had thought it best, for reasons of security, to "inter" their families along with the scientists. And there was also the intellectual stimulant of working on one of the most important research efforts of all time, the "gadget" as the bomb was nicknamed: a project involving true power, both scientific and cultural; a goal which contributed significantly to the monumental and communal struggle of the war; and an achievement which would advance the frontiers of science in ways that few of their individual research projects ever could. Other than the rather forbidding location in the desert—which in fact many of the scientists, particularly Oppenheimer, found quite beautiful—it was utopia. Alan Winkler notes, "Teller brought his Steinway piano; chemist George Kistiakowsky taught mathematicians John Von Neumann and Stanislaw Ulam to play poker; Oppenheimer and others put on a version of *Arsenic and Old Lace*."[1] However, the moment the bomb was completed, tested, and pronounced "operationally ready," this rare period of idyllic purpose and power came to an abrupt end. Once, that is, the theoretical scientists of A-bomb development ceased being useful as Master Mechanics of its construction, they almost instantly morphed in the eyes of the government and the military back into Wicked Wizards who were more of a nuisance than an asset.

In chapter 5 I detailed the rapid decline of the initial heroic status of the atomic scientists in the popular culture; but that decline had already been foreshadowed by the lack of interest and sometimes outright disdain with which the military and government reacted to their suggestions for how to use this unprecedented "gadget." As Winkler puts it, "Once again, as when they made the decision about how to use the bomb, [the government] seized the initiative from the scientists who had created the weapon."[2] The philosophical and cultural schisms which had always conferred on the theoretician an outsider status in American culture had merely been papered over or ignored during the frenetic race to complete the bomb; once it was presented as a working addition to the U.S. military arsenal, those schisms reemerged in full force.

Of course Robert Oppenheimer became the chief spokesperson for the majority—though not the totality—of opinion among the A-bomb scientists about what should be done with the "gadget" and how the world ought to change in response to its creation. Oppenheimer had been the source of leadership and inspiration during the years of the Manhattan Project, and he was greatly admired by most of those who had worked with him at Los Alamos. Hans Bethe said of him that "it was forever astonishing how quickly he could absorb new ideas and single out the most important point."[3] In the aftermath of victory in the Pacific and in terms of representing to the general public this strange and unimaginably powerful new force, Oppenheimer became what Alice Kimball Smith called "a kind of Pooh-Bah of atomic energy."[4] In this as well as in other media references, Oppenheimer was presented as a Prophet of the Atomic Age, variously referred to as "the wizard of the desert" (in echoes of Edison as 'the wizard of Menlo Park'), the "high priest of atomic energy," the "new Prometheus," and of course famously (if more prosaically) "The Father of the Atomic Bomb." We might note the exotic or mythological nature of most of these designations, highlighting the fact that his accomplishment was not something from the practical world of machines, but a form of wizardry more suited to the science fiction fantasies of the books and films soon to become popular: narratives which attempted to capture a whiff of the mystery and unprecedented power surrounding the atomic bomb and its ability to convert dead matter into pure energy.

In many ways Oppenheimer's dire pronouncements and predictions about this new Atomic world added to his unconventional and perhaps even morbidly flamboyant image. Speaking in a tone of biblical warning and self-condemnation, he said, "In some sort of crude sense which no vulgarity, no humor, no overstatement can quite extinguish, the physicists have known sin, and this is a knowledge which they cannot lose." He repeatedly stated that he didn't want to "rub the edges off this new terror" but return "insistently to the magnitude of the peril."[5] But this approach backfired, as his apocalyptic rhetoric just added to the melodrama and numbing novelty of the atomic dilemma, making it seem to the general public too enormous a problem to be solved or even understood by anyone but experts, and thus a problem best left entirely to those "experts" in the military and government—but, curiously, not the sciences. However, all too often those experts wanted to utilize the bomb to further their own agendas, as in turf wars among the various branches of the military over funding, or re-election campaigns which pounced on any mention of caution about nuclear weapons development and testing as a sign of being "soft" on national defense. In fact, such military and government "experts" often had little expertise themselves in dealing with or even conceptualizing the new exigencies which were the point of Oppenheimer's frightening pronouncements, and they stubbornly insisted on trying to construct defense and government policies about this new weapon using the forms and goals of old paradigms.

Nearly everything the theoretical scientists of Los Alamos suggested regarding what they thought America ought to do with the bomb merely served to further alienate them from the military and government authorities charged with making these decisions. Such alienation began before the bomb was even completed, when a group of scientists signed a petition arguing against the actual use of the weapon against civilian targets. Leo Szilard wrote the petition, wherein he called atomic bombs "a means for the ruthless annihilation of cities." The petition asked the president "to rule that the United States shall not, in the present phase of the war, resort to the use of atomic bombs."[6] Ironically, even though years later reference would be made to the petition during the public vilification of Oppenheimer, in fact he was not one of the signatories. However, Oppenheimer was and would continue to be after the bomb's use among the front ranks of those arguing for international supervision of atomic energy and against a U.S. monopoly on atomic power.

Not only did these scientists foresee the international, to say nothing of the human consequences of actually using the bomb, but many among them were also prescient in their understanding of its very real status as the "ultimate weapon," that is, a weapon against which there would be no defense, or at least no technological defense. In petitions, reports, and letters, the majority of the Los Alamos scientists stated quite bluntly that, once other countries, particularly the Soviet Union, possessed weapons of equal power (at that time the most favored estimate was that it would take the USSR a decade to develop its own bomb, an estimate that was six years too optimistic), the United States would be just as vulnerable to nuclear attack as anyone else: "A week after the war ended, a small group of scientists from the Los Alamos team—Lawrence, Oppenheimer, Compton and Fermi—prophesied that they could not conceive of then or at any time in the future any technological defense against nuclear weapons, and that 'their firm opinion that no military countermeasures will be found,'" writes Rhodes.[7] For a brief period, even the super-hawk Teller became a One Worlder. In 1946 he wrote in the pages of the *Bulletin of the Atomic Scientists* (April 1946), "Nothing that we can plan as a defense for the next generation is likely to be satisfactory; that is, nothing but world-union."[8]

Therefore, they argued, it was in the *long-term* best interest of America to forgo a temporary and destabilizing stance as the sole nuclear bully on the world block in favor of the more enlightened policy of sharing the technology and its control with the entire world. These scientists understood that, once this particularly nasty genie had been let out of the bottle, it might very well be considered not the ultimate weapon at all, but rather merely the opening shot in an entirely new and potentially apocalyptic arms race.

In all of these matters, it is worth noting that such evaluations and warnings, made before the bomb had even been used, let alone before all the consequent government machinery grew to integrate it with U.S. defense and international policies, would prove remarkably accurate over the years. They would also prove remarkably resilient: despite half a century of government rhetoric to the contrary, as well as the expenditure of countless billions on ever-more complicated technologies of nuclear defense—such as the gargantuan boondoggle known as Star Wars—it remains stubbornly true that there *is no technological defense against nuclear weapons*—other than, as these scientists foresaw back in 1945, running away from them. Yet the vision of some sort of technological fix to the nuclear problem continues to be as compelling and resistant to logical refutations today as it was in 1950.

In fact, a belief in the power of some exotic superweapon both to clinch America's preeminence internationally and to permanently guarantee its inviolability from attack is a consistent and deep-rooted theme in America's historical love affair with gadgets. This myth as national narrative is thoroughly explored in H. Bruce Franklin's *War Stars: The Superweapon and the American Imagination*.[9] Franklin chronicles this elusive goal of a technological trump card, from Robert Fulton's fervent belief that submarine warfare would utterly secure America's borders and eventually eliminate warfare, to Edison's horrific vision of an alternating current "cannon" that would electrocute enemies by the thousands. But Franklin singles out Star Wars as the "ultimate technological fix" and suggests that, due to its obvious inability in any incarnation to succeed in its putative primary mission—defeating a determined first strike by nuclear missiles—clearly it must in fact be intended as a shield against an enemy's *second* strike, the one they would launch after we eliminated the majority of their missiles with a first strike. Thus, he argues, this "shield's" only purpose must in fact be to enable the use of our nuclear sword.[10]

While Franklin's conclusion about the true intent of the Strategic Defense Initiative may be extreme—it does seem suicidal to say nothing of barbaric to construct a system based upon this scenario; but then, the entire rationale for nuclear weapons is suicidal and barbaric—his analysis of the fundamental flaws in the SDI logic are simple and accurate. While there is not sufficient space here to go into a detailed critique of the Strategic Defense Initiative, in either its Reagan-era full bore conception or the latter-day scaled-down version, it is relevant to my analysis to at least touch upon this vision and its blind spots.

The first of these blind spots is clearly visible in the speech by President Reagan, delivered on March 23, 1983, which gave form and content to the Strategic Defense Initiative. In his speech, Reagan, in tones ringing with recrimination and righteous indignation, demanded that "the scientific community which gave us nuclear weapons" devote all their talents and energy to conceiving defensive technologies that would render nuclear weapons "impotent and obsolete." First we might notice that, four decades after the Manhattan Project, it is still the "scientific community" that is singled out for "giving" the rest of "us" nuclear weapons; as though Oppenheimer and his cronies, without the government's authority let alone its bottomless pockets, tinkered together the A-bomb in their basements and then emerged to present it as a sort of unwanted gift to the bewildered American public. Needless to say, there is no mention here or anywhere else in Reagan's speech—or any of the other pro–Star Wars rhetoric to follow—of the guiding role the military played in Los Alamos, let alone its disregard for the scientific community's warnings about its policy of "Secrecy and Supremacy"; nor of course does government—or as Reagan would have had it, 'gubmint'—appear to bear any responsibility for this "gift."

Second, attention must be paid to Reagan's imagining of a solution—or perhaps outflanking is a better term—of the nuclear stalemate of MAD (Mutually Assured Destruction) as an innovation that would somehow make nuclear weapons "impotent and obsolete," i.e., rob them of their power and reduce them to yesterday's hardware. Both terms characterize nuclear weapons as mere machines, relevant only insofar as their productive capacity—or in this case their destructive capacity—is up-to-date, and suggesting that, once their technology can be surpassed, they can be relegated to museums to sit, "impotent and obsolete" alongside the steam locomotive and the foot-powered loom.

One might trace a chain of such calls for a technological "trump card" that would forever establish America's international supremacy from the A-bomb to the moon race to SDI. Each was justified in terms of the mechanical power of the device or system, with little regard given to the theoretical questions of consequences or validity. Some in the pro-SDI camp even drew an overt comparison between Reagan's speech initiating SDI to Kennedy's call for putting a man on the moon by the end of the 1960s. In other words, the technological "fix" that would reduce nuclear weapons to impotency and obsolescence was categorized as somehow equivalent to the technological triumph of being the first nation to put a man on the moon. However, the most basic fallacy of this comparison is, or ought to be obvious: "The moon did not try to defy our attempt to conquer it with technology. The Soviets will," noted a 1988 white paper of the Union of Concerned Scientists.[11] But such critiques of the Master Mechanic view of the arms race (or for that matter the space race; see chapter 8) are rarely acknowledged, let alone expressed within the government, military, and engineering communities responsible for national defense (or space exploration). In essence, both "races" are seen as primarily technological problems to be solved with brute mechanical innovation, independent of any "effete" theorizing about either their logic or long-term consequences. In fact, the ideology of Star Wars as a viable defense against nuclear weapons requires believing that the "theory" of Mutually Assured Destruction, as well as the complex net of arms treaties which has kept the peace for six decades, will be similarly rendered "impotent and obsolete" by SDI innovation; and this belief persists, in utter disregard for both the disturbing accuracy of the predictions of Oppenheimer's camp in the 1940s and '50s and the logic by which arms treaties were constructed in the first place. The fundamental flaw in the theory of SDI—or rather, the belief that SDI needn't recognize its own need for theoretical consistency and somehow transcends the theories of arms control treaties it will render "impotent and obsolete"—is neatly summarized in the Union of Concerned Scientists' white paper: "When the superpowers decided to forgo an ABM competition, they did so with the understanding that such ABM systems: (1) would fuel an offensive arms race; (2) would make a first strike more probable; (3) may not work; and (4) would be very costly. These arguments remain as valid today as they were in 1972."[12]

In other words, the same arguments for international stability that motivated Oppenheimer et al. to suggest international control of nuclear weapons in 1945; the same arguments that, following the failure of the policy of "Secrecy and Supremacy," resulted in MAD; the same arguments that produced the anti-ABM treaties; these same arguments have not disappeared or even fundamentally altered in the intervening fifty years. Now as then, "the only hope for a lasting and durable peace between the superpowers is persistent arms control that builds on the successful negotiations of the past."[13] Of course such arguments fall into the category of the theoretical, and are therefore deeply unsatisfying to the Master Mechanics as a solution to be trusted, whereas the competing and ultimately victorious view—that nuclear weapons are just machines, to be used as well as defended against—has proven as resilient against all the arguments critiquing the new arms race of Star Wars as it did during the "old" arms race of atomic bombs.[14]

Predicting this coming arms race as early as August 1945, Oppenheimer wrote to Henry Stimson, Truman's secretary of war, saying that he and his fellow scientists understood why there would be intense pressure to develop even greater weapons after the war. "Nevertheless," he went on, "we have grave doubts that this further development can contribute essentially or permanently to the prevention of war. We believe that the safety of this nation—as opposed to its ability to inflict damage on an enemy power—cannot be wholly or even primarily in its scientific or technical prowess. It can be based only on making future wars impossible.[15]

However, it quickly became apparent to Oppenheimer and those among the Manhattan Project scientists who agreed with him that their efforts were falling on deaf ears. They realized that, individually or even in small groups, they could generate little resistance to the developing momentum behind Secrecy and Supremacy as the defining factors in American nuclear policy. One of the earliest postwar attempts to create a more organized response to the bomb was made by the Federation of Atomic Scientists (which later became the Federation of American Scientists). In November 1945 the FAS published *One World or None*, which presented in a cogent and logical manner an outline of the real and unprecedented atomic hazards, including the first detailed forecast of the outcome of a hypothetical atomic attack on a U.S. metropolis. While the language was cold and objective and in many places quite technical, in the context of mystery and speculation which surrounded what little information was available to the public, the document proved to be a best-seller. Those in the FAS connected with its composition hoped this was a sign of a public willingness to be informed and persuaded. The following month saw the publication of the first issue of the *Bulletin of the Atomic Scientists*, a group organized around a core of atomic scientists from the University of Chicago, and which would eventually create the now-famous "atomic clock" with the time indicating the group's evaluation of just how close we were to a nuclear war.[16] Through these organizations and dozens of other smaller ones, these scientists were attempting to play a greater role in the determination of public policy than was their traditional lot, and to exert the same sort of influence over the peacetime policy for atomic energy as they had during the construction of the bomb during their heyday at Los Alamos. Winkler writes:

> Working on a variety of fronts, the scientists transformed their image. Merle Miller, one of the editors of *Harper's Magazine*, remarked in 1947 on the shift that had taken place. "Until August 1945," he wrote, "most of us laymen thought of scientists as colorless little men who wore grimy smocks and labored long hours in musty laboratories, speaking a language too technical and far too uninteresting for us to bother to understand." Hiroshima and Nagasaki changed all that. Since the war, "the scientists emerged from their laboratories and began talking, loud and

long." Most important, they made sense, "because we realize that they have nothing to sell except possibly a formula for the continued existence of the human
race."[17]

But by this point already two different formulas for the "continued existence
of the human race" were taking shape. The first, presented by Oppenheimer,
the FAS, and the other "One World or None"-ers, argued that the A-bomb was
exactly what mankind had sought for centuries: a weapon so powerful its use
couldn't be contemplated—in other words, a weapon to end all wars. They believed that what was called for in the face of such a weapon was a restructuring
of society, both domestic and international; that no technological "fix" for the
bomb existed or would ever exist; that international diplomacy, not superior
nuclear arsenals, held the key to "continued existence"; and that the A-bomb
represented a revolution, in toto, in human civilization. The second, champi-
oned by Teller et al., treated the A-bomb as just another weapon, one which
could be countered and surpassed, like every other weapon in history, through
technological advancement; thus they wished to "reform" rather than revolutionize defense and international policy. In other words, we can see in Oppenheimer's group the trappings of the Wicked Wizards, and in Teller's those of
the Master Mechanics, one group seeing in the new technology a threat of revolutionary proportions and responding to that vision with revolutionary theories, the other group embracing the new technology as just another machine,
something to be integrated into the culture in the traditional ways that new
machines had been in the past.

Of course it might be protested that both of the chief figures of these camps,
Oppenheimer and Teller, were theoretical physicists, and thus Teller was not a
"garage inventor" in the tradition of the Great Independents. However, we must
also recognize the difference in ideological orientation of these two scientists, as
well as the camps they represented—and those ideologies were diametrically opposed to one another. While Oppenheimer's atomic ideology produced radical
new theories that questioned everything from national defense to the very idea
of a nation, Teller's produced a practical program for something tangible: the
production of a "super" gadget, the H-bomb. One must also consider the difference in their public portrayals: Oppenheimer as the "Pooh-Bah" of atomic energy, a figure granted great authority, singled out as it were for responsibility for
the A-bomb, even considered by some in government as jealously guarding the
sort of total control he'd exercised over all things atomic during the Manhattan Project; and Teller as just another worker in the atomic factory, someone
whose loyalty and dedication to the status quo of American culture was never

in question, someone perfectly willing, even eager to turn his talents to the purposes of the government and military authorities. We might even contemplate the visual images of the two men: Oppenheimer with the gaunt visage of an aesthete, and Teller's more grandfatherly appearance; or even the fact that it's difficult to find a single public photo of Oppenheimer smiling, appearing more often as, in his own phrase, a physicist who had "known sin," whereas Teller often looked perfectly happy to be constructing weapons of mass destruction.[18]

If one objects that such superficial aspects could hardly be considered revealing of either Oppenheimer's or Teller's true character, I would respond, exactly so; but it is their public personas, not their "true" characters, we are examining, and for a vast majority of the American public a few photos and headlines were the foundations if not the entirety of those personas. In other words, it could be argued that the totality of the American experience of mad scientist tropes had prepared the average American to see in Oppenheimer the typical Frankenstein figure, someone to be almost instinctively mistrusted and ostracized—whereas Teller's program for pushing forward with nuclear weapons development was accepted as perfectly sound and "commonsensical" because it echoed the technological imperative that had driven America's idea of technological progress for nearly two hundred years.

However, prior to 1950 Oppenheimer's fall from grace had not yet occurred, and there seemed, for a brief period, some hope that the "internationalist" view held by him and his supporters in the FAS could prevail over those of Teller and other advocates of the H-bomb. Both sides worked to construct and disseminate convincing arguments. Bernard Brodie of Yale, who could be considered the first "nuclear strategist" of the Oppenheimer camp, published *The Absolute Weapon: Atomic Power and World Order* (1946), wherein he insisted that the only real "power" of the A-bomb lay in its ability to deter rather than express aggression: "Thus far the chief purpose of our military establishment has been to win wars. From now on its chief purpose must be to avert them. It can have no other useful purpose."[19] Unfortunately, Brodie's subsequent work for the government provides a fine example of what happened when the Wicked Wizards attempted to advocate and advance their theories from within government institutions rather than as outsiders. Brodie was hired as a consultant by the Department of Defense and given the assignment of developing new strategies for the new weapon—but all of his recommendations were ignored because they did not fit in with the military's traditional operational procedures and goals. He complained that the military was too steeped in "pre-atomic thinking"—one of their earliest strategic planning white papers called for "carpet bombing" an enemy with atomic bombs—to adapt to the bomb's paradoxical status as a saber to be rattled but never drawn. Meanwhile,

Teller and his group used every available forum to broadcast their warnings of a nuclear-armed Communist conspiracy bent on world domination that would be held in check only by the threat from ever-bigger American bombs.

Realistically, and given the international and domestic climate of the period, the outcome of this competition for the "hearts and minds" of the American public was never in doubt. The formula Oppenheimer and others were attempting to sell to the American public and government, while it might have made rational sense for the "continued existence of the human race," symbolized a kind of existence that neither the military, the government, nor the American public was interested in buying. For instance, while nearly every A-bomb scientist from Oppenheimer on down argued for international control of atomic energy, a Gallup poll of September 1945 reported that 73 percent of the respondents wanted the United States to keep sole control of bomb, with only 14 percent suggesting the United Nations was the right place for its management. In the first vote in Congress over the creation of a form of international atomic energy commission, 39 Republicans and 37 Democrats voted for secrecy (with only five votes for the UN—all of them Democrats). Meanwhile senators like the conservative Arthur Vandenberg of Michigan called even the suggestions for an exchange of scientists between countries a form of "appeasement."[20]

Everyone wanted in on the atomic act. Once the issue of atomic energy entered the public-political arena, it quickly changed from Oppenheimer's unprecedented, unforgettable "sin" to just another policy issue, one which was, like taxes or education, subject to all the traditional turf wars. This is not to say there were not opportunities for an enlightened American policy. In an attempt to focus debate, a committee was formed, the Secretary of State's Committee on Atomic Energy, to create a framework for American atomic policy. Its chairman was John J. McCloy, and its membership included such luminaries as Dean Acheson, David Lilienthal, Vannevar Bush, James Conant, and Leslie Groves. While most politically active scientists felt that the committee was a deck stacked in favor of secrecy, Oppenheimer, still held in high regard as the "Father of the A-bomb" and not yet the target of the investigations and demonization to follow, did serve as a consultant to the group, and his influence was apparent. In 1946 the committee released its report, titled "A Report on the International Control of Atomic Energy Prepared for the Secretary of State's Committee on Atomic Energy" (referred to thereafter as simply the Acheson-Lilienthal Report). Among other recommendations, the report proposed the creation of an international Atomic Development Authority to hold monopoly over the raw materials of nuclear development. It even went so far as to conclude that the United States would eventually surrender its atomic weapons to such an international agency—a stand that was diametrically opposed to the views of the military and most government officials. But when Bernard Baruch was appointed U.S. ambassador to United Nations, the announcement came as a severe disappointment to the entire committee, as they felt he simply didn't understand this unprecedented diplomatic problem; and eventually many both in and outside the committee came to blame Baruch for the numerous vulnerabilities and shortcomings of atomic agreements worked out with the Soviets. Subsequently, the first UN Atomic Energy Commission, the only hope for an alternative to the policy of Secrecy and Supremacy, expired in mid-1948, widely considered a complete failure.

It might be said that this moment marked the final defeat of the Wicked Wizard theorists, as represented by Oppenheimer, and the ascendancy of the Master Mechanics and Teller, with their calls for developing even more powerful atomic weapons. At least two frenzies powered this latter approach, trumping all calls from the Wizards for a greater focus on developing a theory of atomic weapons before rushing ahead with the weapons themselves. The first was the undeniable fact that there was something "sexy" about nuclear weapons, and that the same sort of "gadget madness" that reigned in Los Alamos continued to motivate those Master Mechanics who sided with Teller. Freeman Dyson (who would eventually become more famous for his insights in the field of quantum electrodynamics and the search for extra-terrestrial intelligence than for his earlier work on the A-bomb) wrote of this fascination, confessing that "nuclear explosives have a glitter more seductive than gold to those who play with them."[21] And Teller's rush to build the H-bomb represented the same sort of "U.S. first" frenzy that guided all too much of American policy, from nuclear weapons to outer space. When the Russians exploded their first A-bomb in 1949, Teller harassed everyone with demands to begin work on the "super" immediately, arguing that an H-bomb would never be equaled by the Soviets and therefore it would be, finally, the "ultimate" weapon.

Oppenheimer's reaction was quite the opposite. Soon after the Soviet test, the General Advisory Committee of the Atomic Energy Commission was asked to produce a report on the wisdom of making development of an H-bomb the highest priority. Oppenheimer was chairman of the commission at the time, and his influence is again evident in its final report, which suggested that such an H-bomb would be morally indefensible, technically daunting, and would merely lead to a further arms race. However Truman, bending to the recommendations of his generals and political advisers, ignored all of Oppenheimer's objections, and in the first month of the new decade directed the AEC to "continue its work on all forms of atomic weapons, including the so-called hydrogen or super bomb."[22] While the advice of Oppenheimer, Brodie, and other Wicked Wizards about the dangerous disadvantages of pushing ahead with the

H-bomb was ignored, the typical response of such Master Mechanics as Ernest Lawrence (who'd been the guiding intelligence behind work on the cyclotron) and Luis Alvarez (who'd helped developed the detonation technique for the first bomb) was that if a super was possible, the United States must have it first.[23]

The first H-bomb was tested on the tiny Pacific island of Eleugelab on November 1, 1952, a test that resulted in an explosion of ten megatons, roughly 1,000 times greater than the A-bomb, and essentially evaporated the island. Just as Oppenheimer had predicted, the Soviets then poured all their energies into developing their own super, which they tested by 1955 . . . and the pattern of escalation and counter-escalation about which Oppenheimer had warned was set. There would even develop a strange co-dependency between U.S. and Soviet nuclear Master Mechanics, something described in a story in the *New Yorker* as "an alliance, a sort of perverse love match, a deranged crush, each side in passionate awe of the other's prowess, each side desperately trying to concoct new and even more intoxicating ways of holding the other's rapt, undivided attention."[24] Always the argument would be that the Soviets were about to equal America in one or another aspect of nuclear weapons, so the United States must take another step forward, seeking a technological "fix" to the stalemate, a permanent edge that would re-establish the sort of nuclear supremacy the nation had enjoyed for the four short years from 1945 to 1949, whether that edge was MIRVs or submarine-launched ICBMs or a missile defense program à la Star Wars.[25] And always the objections from a small segment of the scientific community that there was simply no technological fix for this problem were treated as tantamount to "appeasement" or, worse, treason. The Teller camp vigorously opposed even Kennedy's Limited Test Ban treaty because, they argued, it would mean surrendering the "security" of the missile advantage we temporarily possessed (even though they would simultaneously claim, in other contexts, that this "missile gap" was in the Soviets' favor).[26]

The development of the H-bomb generated the final polarization between the Oppenheimer and Teller camps and resulted in Oppenheimer's complete alienation from all official American nuclear policy. "Oppie's" fate was sealed with a letter from William L. Borden (executive director of the Joint Committee on Atomic Energy) to the FBI, wherein he wrote that "more probably than not J. Robert Oppenheimer is an agent of the Soviet Union," a startling conclusion based on nothing more than Borden's displeasure with Oppenheimer's continued insistence on international control over nuclear weapons and his continued resistance to the H-bomb, as well as various other exotic weapons projects Teller had in mind. This letter led to Oppenheimer's famous (or infamous) appearance before the Atomic Energy Commission's committee on security. The committee chairman, Lewis Strauss (a former shoe salesman, wealthy ex-banker, pronounced social conservative, staunch Republican, and good friend to Edward Teller) had a "history" with Oppenheimer, dating back to 1949 when Oppenheimer had testified before him during congressional hearings on the shipment of radioactive isotopes abroad and appeared somewhat arrogantly dismissive of Strauss's stance against such sharing of atomic technology. It is widely believed that Strauss had been "out to get" Oppenheimer since that time, and saw the hearings as the perfect opportunity to humiliate and alienate the "Father of the A-bomb." While I. I. Rabi, Lee DuBridge, and most other Los Alamos scientists supported Oppenheimer and proclaimed his loyalty without reservation, Teller's testimony was far more equivocal, at times seeming to imply that Oppenheimer simply could no longer be trusted with American military secrets. The results of the hearings were a foregone conclusion and, as everyone had expected, Oppenheimer was stripped of his security clearance.

Borden declared the hearings a major success in combating Soviet espionage; but his real target was made clear when he said the verdict was "the turning point in converting scientists back to human beings."[27] Clearly, Borden, as well as Strauss, viewed Oppenheimer's opposition to the H-bomb as founded more on arrogance than on expertise, and they and the other supporters of continued weapons development felt the hearings served to bring an end to the troublesome interference of the "One World or None"-ers. By 1956, Eugene Rabinowitch, editor of the *Bulletin of the Atomic Scientists*, would sadly declare that "American scientists remain, in 1956, a harassed profession, occupying a defensive position in the political arena. . . . Their early hopes of playing an important role in insuring world peace and prosperity are still in abeyance."[28]

Oppenheimer's characterization of atomic knowledge as the very sort of transgressive sin Wicked Wizards had been accused of committing for over a century had been utterly eclipsed by the traditional and (curiously) optimistic view of the Master Mechanics: that the bomb was merely another weapon among many, or, as Harry Truman put it, that the A-bomb represented "a harnessing of the basic power of the universe."[29] Thus the Bomb had become a symbol of mankind's control over Nature, rather than a symbol of, as Oppenheimer argued, a descent into unprecedented madness and chaos.

In fact, for the military the A-bomb wasn't unprecedented at all; it was simply a bigger bomb, a device whose chief selling point was that it delivered "more bang for the buck." By the time Eisenhower became president, the U.S. arsenal already numbered over 1,000, and it had soared to 18,000 by the time he left office. (The peak stockpile would be reached in 1966 with 32,193 nuclear bombs, warheads, torpedoes, land mines, artillery shells, and other "deployment platforms.") Even Brodie's early cautionary stance had changed to

one more fitting with traditional military thinking wherein he proposed strategies which included firing warning shots at invading Soviet troops in Europe.
In 1957, Henry Kissinger published *Nuclear Weapons and Foreign Policy*, a
document which laid out the basic arguments for thinking in terms of fightable
nuclear wars—which was of course completely counter to all the reasons given
for developing nuclear weapons in the first place. By the end of the '50s and the
publication of Herman Kahn's *On Thermonuclear War* (1960), an entire
school of "nuclear war strategists" had come into power in Washington supported by the "military industrial complex" about which Eisenhower warned,
all of them committed to thinking the "unthinkable" as part of a normal, 9-to-5
day at the office.

OF COURSE a nuclear war-fighting strategy required a nuclear war civil defense program, the argument being that, in order to convince the Soviets we
were willing to fight such a war we also had to convince them our civilian population could survive the war. And it was in the area of civil defense that the
fundamental and paradoxical truths of nuclear weapons—truths and para-
doxes set forth as early as 1943 by the Los Alamos scientists themselves—
became most apparent. The very first civil defense policy put forth in 1951
during the Truman administration recognized that there was essentially no
way to protect civilians, and that the only strategy that promised even a slim
chance of survival was to simply move the civilians away from what it was assumed would be the primary target areas, namely the cities. "National dispersion" was the name of this policy. However, while the policy was eloquent on
the compelling need for redistributing the American population, it was short
on suggestions for how to accomplish such a monumental task. Certainly the
national dispersion policy had a contributory effect on the American vision of
centralized cities with satellite suburbs, but that vision had been around since
the 1930s; and even the suburbanization of American metropolises ongoing
during the '50s represented only a tiny fraction of the population migration required if dispersion was to be a viable defense.

    The other civil defense option was equally unsatisfactory: hiding people in
bomb shelters. This tactic was a holdover from World War II thinking, even
though its new form also moved to the suburbs with Earl Warren's initiation of
the "backyard shelter" program. And neither was this a viable option, as was
pointed out by voices on the margins of government, as any nuclear attack
would fill the air with so much radiation that people would have to remain in
their shelters for decades, perhaps centuries. The "duck and cover" drills and
the metal dog tags handed out to New York City's school children (to identify
bodies burned beyond recognition) were more attempts to convince the public

that a nuclear war was survivable, and therefore a war for which we must arm in traditional ways, than they were serious civil defense measures. And there was the national highway construction program beginning in 1956, ostensibly an effort to provide the millions of new automobiles sold in the postwar economic boom with somewhere to go, but which in reality was justified as a means of moving the National Guard around the country when the Soviet paratroopers began to land.

Much of the nuclear war anxiety of the period can be traced to the inaccurate estimates of Soviet nuclear capabilities, such as that reported by the Gaither Commission appointed by Eisenhower and charged with formulating a comprehensive civil defense policy. The Gaither Commission came up with a worst-case appraisal based on misleading estimations of Soviet ICBM development, and recommended that $50 billion be spent to protect everything from schools to bombers—so great a sum that the typical reaction was to take no steps at all, as anything that could realistically be done would still be inadequate. Such reports as *Deterrence and Survival in the Nuclear Age* (the "Gaither Report" produced by the President's Science Advisory Committee in 1957) contributed to this paradoxical mindset of a nuclear war as something against which there was no real defense, but something that was nonetheless fightable and survivable, and by 1960 over one million American families had constructed Warren's backyard shelters. However, the government policy debate over the effectiveness of such shelter programs, as opposed to dispersion defense, quickly deteriorated into squabbles over whether building shelters was worth the cost, mere public relations, seen as a threat by the Soviets, sapping money from offensive weapons programs, evidence of a defeatist mentality, or simply insane. Eventually the shelter programs would fade away as even hardliners in the defense think tanks came to recognize that, as the megaton yield of the new weapons mounted, the chances of surviving them decreased to near zero.

But by this time the dramatic image of American families cowering in their backyard shelters and reinforced basements had entered the public consciousness through books, films, and TV shows.[30] For instance, the novel *A Canticle for Leibowitz* (1957) accurately captured the public mood that, in the event of a nuclear war, the lucky ones might be those killed instantly, and that the word "survival" was a misnomer when applied to nuclear war. Eventually, with films ranging from the unrelentingly depressing *The Day After* (1983) to the punk aesthetics of *Mad Max* (1979), the post-nuclear apocalypse story became as much a part of the stable of American popular narratives as those about loner cowboys or hard-boiled detectives. Typically these portrayals of life in a bomb shelter drew on tropes from the repertoire of mad scientist fiction, with motifs of isolation, buried spaces, and paranoia; but the chief tropes of these narratives were those of one family or man set against another in a twentieth-century version of tribal conflicts, coupled with the horror of radiation-spawned mutations. Rarely in the debate was any thought given to the universality of such fears and tropes, and thus the likelihood that such fears and tropes were similarly driving-scaring the Soviets. Remarkably, almost entirely absent from these stories is any notion of the Soviets as human adversaries, or humans at all; in fact, most often the Soviets make no appearance, the bombs and rockets dropping from the sky much like alien invaders: random, unmotivated, irrational, and unstoppable.[31]

What might be called the literature of nuclear war really began with the publication of John Hersey's article on his observation of the Hiroshima bombing, published in the *New Yorker* in 1946. The factual depiction of the horrors of the aftermath of the bombing left everyone who read it stunned and depressed—which perhaps accounts for the relative paucity of literature about the bomb's real-world effects.[32] When these realities were dealt with at all, the treatment tended to be either a sort of nuclear film noir, as in *Fail Safe* (1964), broad satires of such treatments, as in Stanley Kubrick's version of *Fail Safe, Dr. Strangelove: or How I Learned to Stop Worrying and Love the Bomb* (released in the same year), or the sort of science fiction horror films discussed in chapter 6.

The other pole of imaginative reaction to the bomb was almost macabre in its forced optimism and superficiality. William Laurence wrote in the *New York Times* that the scientists had, with atomic energy, found "the philosopher's stone that will not only transmute the elements and create wealth far greater in value than gold but will also provide him with the means for gaining a far deeper insight into the mysteries of living processes, leading to the postponement of old age and the prolongation of life."[33] While Laurence's prose sought to elevate the bomb to the role of magic elixir, *Life* magazine took the low road with a full-page photo of a starlet in a two-piece bathing suit—Miss Anatomic Bomb—which was quickly dubbed "the bikini," named after the island test site. Besides providing the opportunity for a new fashion, the atomic bomb tests were also presented as a kind of super fireworks spectacle. In a 1952 TV broadcast of a bomb test, the commentator speaks of its "breathtaking beauty and magnificence." Famous TV news anchor Chet Huntley described the test he witnessed as "the most tremendous thing I have ever experienced." *Newsweek* brightly reported that "those A-Bombs are Las Vegas's alarm clocks," while in Utah "residents often rose early to watch the atomic flashes and years later clearly recalled 'the beautiful mushroom as it'd come up, [and] change colors.'"[34] Even Li'l Abner got into the atomic test act, when, in a series of strips, his rural hometown of Dogpatch was chosen by bomb testers as an ideal site for their tests as it was the most "unnecessary place in the whole U.S.A."

These tests were used not only to check the technology of new and more powerful devices, but also to gauge the ability of troops to operate in a "nuclear environment" battlefield. At Camp Desert Rock outside the Yucca Flats test site, 250,000 men participated in a series of tests, placed seven miles from one explosion, but sometimes standing only a mile away. "This is the greatest show on earth," Captain Harold Kinne told his forces in 1953, encamped merely two miles from ground zero. "Relax and enjoy it." After the blast the men were expected to charge toward the mushroom cloud, rifles and bayonets raised, in some sort of strange nuclear version of the First World War's "over the top." Protective clothing was rarely provided for the troops; often they were told simply to shower and change after returning to base. The radiation limits these troops were allowed to experience were set, then raised, then raised again, but seldom actually monitored.[35]

The issue of radiation was both new to the popular culture, and not new. After all, as discussed earlier, there had been a similar fascination with and warnings about X-rays and radium at the turn of the century. But atomic radiation, however poorly it was understood by the average American, was inextricably bound up with the awe and dread associated with atomic bombs, and their ability to kill in new and terrible ways was widely recognized. One of the first actual incidents of radiation poisoning directly connected with the atomic bomb was in fact kept secret for many years after the Manhattan Project ended. During work on assembling a bomb in 1946, a screwdriver that was being used as an improvised wedge to separate two spheres of plutonium slipped, and the spheres came into partial and momentary contact generating a near-critical state. A technician, Louis Slotin, heroically rushed to re-separate the spheres before a chain reaction developed, but as a result he received such a high dose of radiation that he died only nine days later.[36]

Typically, however, the fictionalized effects of radiation poisoning were presented as working more slowly, and more insidiously, usually resulting in mutations. As early as 1947 this theme was presented in stories such as Poul Anderson's "Tomorrow's Children" and Edward Grendon's "The Figure," both of which cast radiation in the role of a force invisible and irresistible—something like the Id monster in *Forbidden Planet*—and whose symbolic wickedness, conceptualized as a disfiguring of the traditional benefits of scientific research, was expressed in the physical disfigurement of the human race. When radiation wasn't making monsters out of people, it was making monsters out of insects, resulting in world conquest by everything from beetles to grasshoppers.[37] For writers, radiation was indeed the "philosopher's stone," but not in the sense Laurence had predicted. It could do anything; it was represented as an almost living intelligence, capable of malevolent creation of its own volition: Victor

Frankenstein as an unseen force, granting not only "unnatural" life, but also the ability to change normal shapes into fantastic grotesqueries. And, although radiation would prove a godsend to several generations of comic book writers—its mutating largesse spread equally across superheroes like the X-Men and the Fantastic Four as well as supervillains like Lex Luthor and Dr. Doom—the most influential trope would remain that of deformation, as foretold by one of the earliest stories with that theme, Judith Merrill's "That Only a Mother" (1947), a stark tale of a limbless child born to a woman exposed to nuclear radiation.

While Frankenstein's monster was stitched together and shocked to life, the children of the atom were most often melted together and blasted to life. Stories like "That Only a Mother" and the countless ones to follow in that vein would suggest that what was truly feared about nuclear radiation was the creative force of the atomic scientists who had released it—when, that is, that force was uncontrolled by the "laws and religion" of their communities—as though that power, once loosed from legal and religious constraints, intentionally disobeyed also the laws of symmetry, conservation of energy, biological evolution, and all the natural laws under which the universe normally operates.[38]

When E. B. White wrote in the *New Yorker* in 1945 that creating the atomic bomb amounted to "stealing God's stuff," he was harkening back to the image of Frankenstein as Prometheus, gaining knowledge through some sort of deceit or violence enacted upon Nature, and thereby committing a sin, a transgression—engaging, that is, in an "unnatural" act of discovery and an "unlawful" displacement of power from its rightful owner. And again in echoes of nineteenth-century anti-science rhetoric, here scientific discoveries are conceived as property, the property of Nature; and he who sneaks into her bedchamber and snatches such power from her wardrobe is a cat burglar, not an explorer. And, as if to prove that crime never pays, this stolen knowledge always escapes the scientist's control. In fact, in all these stories of experiments gone disastrously and horribly wrong one might see the first, crude version of chaos theory, or perhaps simply Murphy's Law: that whatever can go wrong, will go wrong—but always again with an almost sentient direction to the chaos unleashed, as though radiation's chief characteristic was a malevolent urge toward destruction and devolution.

However, all such popularizations were received in the larger public context of deep ignorance about what radiation actually was and how it really operated. When, in 1954, *Time* magazine did a series on fallout, a poll revealed that only 17 percent of the American public knew what fallout was, even though 52 percent considered it a very real danger.[39] The Atomic Energy Commission's attitude was that fallout was an irritating-if-necessary by-product of nuclear weapons research. In 1955 they tried to counter public fears about radiation by emphasizing the positive results of weapons research: "Because of [nuclear tests] we now have big bombs, and smaller ones too; in fact, a whole family of weapons."[40] One notices the word "family" in this bizarre context, as though nuclear weapons were perfectly natural, even cutely domestic. There were counter voices, such as SANE (National Committee for a Sane Nuclear Policy), formed in 1957 by Norman Cousins and Clarence Pickett; Linus Pauling was widely complaining, with little effect, that fallout was causing an increased incidence of leukemia; and in 1956 Adlai Stevenson cited the "danger of poisoning the atmosphere," suggesting a moratorium on atomic testing until further studies could be conducted on their effects. But from the other side of the debate, then Vice-President Richard Nixon responded that such concerns were "catastrophic nonsense."[41] And the erstwhile promoter of Super bombs, Edward Teller, now quite recovered from his brief flirtation with "world-union." warned against any halt in weapons testing, arguing instead for a "clean bomb" as the answer to such concerns—again demonstrating a faith in the very technology that had created the problem to somehow solve it.

Despite the dire warnings about the bomb generally and radiation specifically from some in the scientific and political communities, much of the American culture still insisted seeing the atomic bomb not as a problem but rather as a solution, what might be called the culture of "the peaceful atom." Opposed to the camp that saw in the bomb only death either instantaneous or slow were those who took on the role of atomic pitchmen. For instance, David Dietz, science editor for Scripps-Howard newspapers, wrote that "Instead of filling the gasoline tank of your automobile two or three times a week, you will travel for a year on a pellet of atomic energy the size of a vitamin pill";[42] "Power too cheap to meter" was the tag line for atomic power plants. In popular magazines like *Parade*, articles touted the potential of atomic energy for everything from growing bigger crops to mining for new oil supplies. In "The Atomic Age" (1947), Oppenheimer's nemesis Lewis Strauss made a claim for a kind of Divine Right to atomic know-how, writing that "Our knowledge of the atom is intended by the Creator for the service and not the destruction of mankind."[43] Of course, there was tremendous motivation to believe in such utopian claims, as only such tremendous benefits—always just over the horizon—could justify the tremendous expenditures and risks being undertaken.[44]

When one reviews these fiercely optimistic visions of the grand new atomic future—a future where we awake in our atomic-powered homes, drive our atomic-powered cars to our atomic-powered offices in cities alight with atomic power, eat our atomically grown food and sleep safely beneath our atomic shield—one can't help but wonder, "What were they thinking?"[45] And the best answer seems to be that they were thinking magically; given the apparently magical power of atomic energy, any solution to the seemingly insurmountable problems it presented must also come from the world of magic. Perhaps this thinking is best represented in the short Disney film *Our Friend the Atom* (1958), wherein the discovery of atomic energy is compared to the fable of a fisherman who discovers a bottle with a genie inside, and promptly lets the genie out. The film argues that "we ourselves are like that fisherman"—but then immediately contradicts the logic of the analogy by suggesting that we have a choice about whether we let the atomic genie out of its natural bottle, or not. As Oppenheimer had pointed out years earlier, however, this genie was out for good and could not be put back or simply "forgotten." There was nothing reversible about atomic knowledge. Perhaps all those visions of a utopian atomic future are based, however unconsciously, on the realization that Oppenheimer was right and, since we couldn't ever put the genie back, it was better to imagine all the wonderful things he could do for us than to face up to all the terrible things he could do to us.

Or, when the terror as well as the power of this discovery was contemplated, perhaps the cultural tendency was to "tame" the terror by turning it into just another commodity, something to be "sold" in the marketplace of pop culture. Even though there was a curious silence among poets and writers on the subject of the A-bomb and atomic energy, there was no shortage of songs on these subjects. While a few were of the biting satire of Tom Lehrer's "The Wild West Is Where I Want To Be" and "We Will All Go Together When We Go,"[46] most were far less "intellectual": "Atomic Power" (The Buchanan Brothers, 1946); "50 megatons" (Sonny Russell, 1963); and a whole slew of songs about the new wonder mineral, uranium: "Tic Tic Tic" (Doris Day, 1949); "Uranium" (The Commodores, 1955); "Uranium Blues" (Loy Clingman, 1955); "Uranium Fever" (Elton Britt, 1955); another "Uranium Fever" (Rudy Gables, 1955); and "Uranium Rock" (Warren Smith, 1958).[47] But perhaps most revealing of this tendency was "Atom Bomb Baby" (The Five Stars, 1957).[48] With its echoes of the nineteenth-century trope of scientific discovery as a *femme fatale* seducing the scientist away from home and family, the bomb is figured as a seductress full of sexual power, and sexual danger:

> Atom bomb baby, little atom bomb.
> I want her in my wigwam.
> She's just the way I want her to be.
> A million tons hotter than TNT.
> Loaded with power, radioactive as a TV tower, a nuclear fission in her soul,
> loves with electronic control.
> A big explosion, big and loud. . . .

Big and loud, indeed. If nothing else, "Atom Bomb Baby" indicates just how thoroughly Oppenheimer's "sin," so unprecedented and awe-inspiring in 1945, had by 1957 been smoothly integrated into the American culture, becoming merely another commodity to be sold via the popular media. And this process of popular assimilation could also said to have operated on the very idea of the necessity of such weapons, on their strategic importance to American security, on the need to spend vast sums of money and research energy on their development, as well as on, eventually, defending against them; again, a defensive effort accurately evaluated by many in 1945 as futile.

In the ultimate (and perhaps inevitable) triumph of the Master Mechanics' view about the "acculturation" of these weapons—despite all the expert advice and scientific evidence to the contrary—one can see both how deeply and widely this preference for the mechanical is embedded in American culture, and how antithetical the views of the Wicked Wizards were to the ideologies of the American political, military, and civilian communities. A similar set of images of fear and national ego would play out in the next crisis to confront American science and culture, Sputnik and the race to put men in space.

ROCKET SCIENCE

8

(Their) Sputniks + (Our) Dudniks = NASA

IT IS sometimes said that two historical moments define the lowest and highest points in Baby Boomer cultural consciousness, moments when nearly everyone of that generation remembers where they were and what they were doing: November 22, 1963, the day Kennedy was assassinated; and July 20, 1969, the day Neil Armstrong landed on the moon. The first seemed to crush the belief that the 1960s would be the quintessentially American decade, while the second revived our vision of America as capable of accomplishing great things. Neil Armstrong, an all-American boy, with his "one small step for a man," became at that second moment the symbol of American scientific excellence, determination, and supremacy, one as powerful as the A-bomb had been two-and-a-half decades earlier. In that sense, Armstrong was the heroic embodiment of what had become our Manhattan Project in space: NASA.

The comparison is appropriate because the long process that culminated in Armstrong's walk on the moon was shaped as much by the A-bomb and its cultural and international consequences as by any logic of scientific exploration. In other words, NASA can be seen as another expression of America's faith in technological Supremacy (if not quite Secrecy), a faith unguided by any comprehensive theory or scientific rationale, just as had been the case with nuclear weapons in the years following World War II.

Several factors led to the American space program developing in this manner: assumptions about what space travel would *look* like, dating back to the pulp magazines, if not earlier; national competition with the Soviets in all areas, especially military and scientific; then-current concepts and concerns about nuclear weapons; American cultural traditions about what kind of people, especially men, our heroes were supposed to be; the influence of the German rocket scientists who had been captured at the end of World War II; and, behind them all, the cultural prejudice for Mechanics over Wizards, things over theory. The role actual space *science* played in the formation and realization of

NASA was, at least in the beginning of the manned space program, remarkably limited.

While stories about traveling to the heavens are almost as old as literature itself, the idea that outer space could be considered a new "frontier" really didn't enter the public consciousness until the early part of the twentieth century, with the advent of the pulps. A recurrent theme in these popular science fiction magazines was space as a modern version of the American west, its apparent emptiness masking abundant resources that could be extracted with the proper ingenuity and determination. Stories about mining colonies on asteroids, orbiting space factories, commercial passenger spaceships making routine runs between planets—all these visions of industry and exploitation became what we thought about when we imagined space exploration. Outer space would be the next boom town.[1] And the idea of space as a frontier—as something that required exploration, mapping, conquest, settlement, and development—was cemented into the cultural consciousness when Kennedy used the term "New Frontier" in his speech calling for landing men on the moon by the end of the 1960s.

Also important to our conception of space as a frontier were our ideas about how we would get there. As early as 1865 Jules Verne, in *From the Earth to the Moon*, had written of sending people to the moon in a gigantic artillery shell— what would eventually be called the "ballistic" approach to space flight. One of the first silent films, *Le Voyage dans la lune* (*A Trip to the Moon*, 1902), directed by Georges Méliès, envisioned just such a journey, with the rocket landing squarely in the Man in the Moon's eye. The popular science fiction magazines of the '20s, '30s, and '40s were replete with rocket ships traveling not just to the moon, but also to other planets and even galaxies. Clearly the "prairie schooners" in the exploration of this new frontier were to be rocket ships—at least as far as Earthlings were concerned, as only aliens used flying saucers.

And by far the most common design for such "ships of space" was the dart-with-fins form: a streamlined bullet with large engines and fins on the rear, people in the front, and whatever you wanted to carry in between. One need only look at the series of model rocket ships released by the Revell company between 1953 and 1959 to see what rocket ships were supposed to look like: fantastic designs with needle noses, huge fins, multiple windows, and aerodynamic bulges. Given those images of the late '40s and early '50s, no one would have ever envisioned that the first American in space would get there in a device shaped like a squat milk bottle (the Mercury capsule); even less imaginable was the sphere-on-an-ashtray design of the Soviet Vostoks. This discrepancy between fiction and fact was in part due to a reality of space few of the early space-as-frontier visionaries ever thought about: there was no air there. Thus wings and fins and needle noses and all such aerodynamic accoutrements would be, in that environment, completely useless.[2] And, as manned space flight was actually achieved, the number of futuristic-if-impractical spaceship designs for model rockets decreased to zero—as though mundane reality had drained the adventure from even fantasizing about space exploration. However, even though the Mercury capsule didn't look much like early images of rocket ships, the cultural tradition of conceptualizing them as flying machines would eventually exert a most unscientific influence over the Mercury program, both in its selection of personnel and in its setting of goals.

Another influence on the realities of American space exploration was the ways in which that endeavor was portrayed on television. In 1955 Disney produced a three-part "Man in Space" series. While the first part was an extremely fact-based account of what was and was not known about space as an environment for exploration, the next two episodes were criticized for giving way to simplification and melodrama. As J. P. Telotte writes, "An early and demonstrably serious concern with issues of 'tomorrow' was gradually transformed into little more than an entertaining fantasy."[3] One of the stars of this TV series was Wernher von Braun, who of course had been the chief designer of the German rocket program during the war, and who had, along with many of the rocket scientists, been captured by the Americans and put to work on the Army's rocket program.[4] (While the Soviets didn't capture as many scientists as the Americans, they did capture more of the assembled V-2s and parts, a difference that would become important a decade later.) Von Braun had in fact inspired not only Disney but also the entire American public when he published a series about manned space flight in *Collier's* magazine in 1953.[5]

Whenever manned spaceflight was portrayed on television or in other public media, it was as just that: *flight* in a rocket *ship* controlled by space *pilots*. For instance, a commercial for Cheerios and V-8 juice that touted an offer of a free moonship (a little hollow rocket on a string that dropped two tiny plastic astronauts unceremoniously on a paper moon map); or the educational shorts released by NASA and other government agencies which pitched their need for space pilots (before the word "astronaut" entered their lexicon); or the serials, comics, science fiction books and films of the time, all of which portrayed rocket ships as machines that were flown into outer space by Flash Gordon–type fighter jocks (typically with the military rank of captain). Given such images of what space exploration ought to look like, perhaps it was only logical that, when Eisenhower established the President's Science Advisory Committee (PSAC) in 1957 and asked it to create a plan for a new civilian space agency, this expanded agency was named the National Advisory Committee on *Aeronautics* (NACA), which was then changed to the National *Aeronautics* and

Space Administration on October 1, 1958. In everyone's mind's eye, NASA was merely an extension of traditional aeronautical research into another realm. While this made a certain organizational sense, it was a vision that would negatively influence the early plans for how men would get into space, and who those men would be.

The nascent NASA was kick-started by the Soviets' launch of Sputnik on the morning of October 4, 1957—a day when America awakened to the Space Race as signaled by the feeble beeping of the first artificial satellite. The first *Soviet* artificial satellite. And that tinny, repetitive, apparently innocuous (some thought otherwise) communication was a rude awakening indeed, because until that moment America didn't know it was *in* a race—a race it was already losing.[6] America's initial response to Sputnik was sheer panic, a panic that linked the Soviet technological triumph with the national threat of nuclear missiles. Here is a sampling of reports from the *New York Times* in the weeks following Sputnik's launch:

October 5, 1957: [The Soviet Union] did not pass up the opportunity to use the launching for propaganda purposes. It said in its announcement that people now could see how "the new socialist society" had turned the boldest dreams of mankind into reality.

October 5, 1957: U.S. Delay Draws Scientists' Fire; Satellite Lag Laid to the Withholding of Money and Waste of Time. One consoling thought offered by a scientist last night was: "Maybe the Russian-American competition hasn't been so bad on the satellite if it encourages us into beating them to the moon."

October 6, 1957: A Propaganda Triumph—A View That Soviets Will Stress Satellite to Buttress Claims of Military Power. Even before Friday's event, K. A. Vershinin, Soviet Air Marshal, had used the original missile claim to warn of the death and destruction the Soviet Union could wreak on its opponents.

October 7, 1957: Scientists Split on Soviet Signals—U.S. Experts Disagree on Whether Satellite Sends Secret Code in Beeps. Dr. Fred Whipple, director of the Smithsonian Astrophysical Observatory in Cambridge, Mass., charged Saturday that the Soviet satellite was transmitting scientific information in code.

October 8, 1957: Khrushchev Asks World Rule of the Satellite and Missiles If Part of Wide U.S.-Soviet Pact—Leader Says Control Depends on Accord for Coexistence. Nikita S. Khrushchev said today that the Soviet Union was willing to bring the earth satellite and all pilotless missiles under international control as part of a general agreement between the United States and the Soviet Union.

October 8, 1957: Investors Buying Stock in Missiles—Soviet Success Puts Market on Defense—Some Issues Plunge to 2-Year Low.

October 11, 1957: Russians Launch Sputnik II—Dwarfs American Vanguard . . .
the soviets have burst upon the world as the infinitely sinister front runners in
the sophisticated and perilous science of space.[7]

November 5, 1957: Scientists Wonder if Shot Nears Moon. Scientists in many
lands speculated yesterday that a Soviet rocket might already be en route to
strike the moon with a hydrogen bomb in the midst of its eclipse Thursday. . . . It
was thus seen as a "firework" that would provide a spectacular display for the for-
tieth anniversary of the October revolution.

December 7, 1957: Vanguard Rocket Burns on Beach; Failure to Launch Test
Satellite Assailed as Blow to U.S. Prestige—Sphere Survives—But Carrier Rises
Only 2 to 4 Feet Before Flames Wreck It.

February 1, 1958: Jupiter-C Is Used—Roars Up in Florida Tense 15 3/4 Seconds
After It Is Fired. Nation Hails News; Nixon Sees Victory for Peace Policy. The
achievement with the Jupiter-C emphasizes the wisdom of President Eisenhower's proposal for the development of space exploration in the cause of peace
rather than in the wastage of war.

One Soviet triumph followed another—and one U.S. humiliation followed
another. This string of American failures led to our satellites being dubbed
"flopniks" in *Pravda*, and "dudniks" by the American press. But perhaps the
most irritating media response of all came when *Time* magazine named Nikita
Khrushchev its "Man of the Year" for 1957, based entirely on the Soviet Union's
accomplishments in space. We can see from the *Times* excerpts that the U.S.
reaction quickly progressed from one of shock and fear, to one of defiance: this
was a race for "national survival," a theme that would eventually determine
nearly everything about how America responded to this new "threat." What is
also clear from these excerpts is how ready Americans were to believe that the
Soviet technological achievement was, at its core, sinister; that it had more to
do with sending secret signals to Communist agents in the United States and
basing hydrogen bombs on the moon than it did with any legitimate scientific
exploration of space.

Eventually a "party line" developed in all government rhetoric about each
new Soviet first: their program was funded and controlled by and in service of
their military and its goal of world domination, while ours, however much it
lagged behind the Soviets, was in the "cause of peace rather than the wastage
of war." This theme appears again and again over the next decade: in NASA
brochures, newspaper accounts, political speeches—as if every component of
American culture assumed that the space race was simply a Cold War of the
"high ground." Thus the first reactions to Sputnik were remarkably similar to
reactions just over fifteen years earlier to the Japanese attack on Pearl Harbor,

or reactions just eight years earlier to the Soviet's first A-bomb test. In the case of Sputnik, what might have been considered a technological achievement that could "benefit all Mankind," was rather represented as a sneak attack on America's technological supremacy.

The comparisons of Sputnik to the initiation of a war were ubiquitous, each magazine attempting to be more patriotic than all the others in its calls for a rapid and concerted American response to this new threat. For instance, *Life* magazine "compared the Soviet satellite to the shots fired at Lexington and Concord and urged Americans to respond as the Minutemen had done then."[8] It was everywhere asserted that what might seem a harmless little metal sphere in fact concealed an ominous threat. Ardent cold warriors like Senator Henry M. Jackson of Washington and Stuart Symington of Missouri (both Democrats) charged that America had "squandered" the technological edge we'd once held—as demonstrated by our being the first to build the A-bomb—and that we were in danger of "losing" space just as earlier we'd lost our A-bomb exclusivity.[9] And, while much of the public reaction suggested we were in a space race, many American politicians seemed to agree with *Life*'s editors that Sputnik was the warning shot in a space war. Senator Richard Russell (Georgia) said, "We now know beyond a doubt that the Russians have the ultimate weapon—a long range missile capable of delivering atomic and hydrogen explosives across continents and oceans."[10] Lyndon Johnson's aide George Reedy summed up the feeling of many when he wrote, "The simple fact is that we can no longer consider the Russians to be behind us in technology. It took them four years to catch up to our atomic bomb and nine months to catch up to our hydrogen bomb. Now we are trying to catch up to their satellite."[11] The idea that outer space was a "space" of military advantage was just assumed. Lyndon Johnson spoke of controlling this "high ground," and said that Sputnik meant that "now the Communists have established a foothold in outer space"—as though high orbit was some new form of beachhead in an invasion.[12]

How exactly did space provide this strategic advantage? What exactly were the Soviets invading? In the charged atmosphere of fear and frustration, neither question was given much thought.[13]

And it wasn't just the American politicians who reacted this way. James R. Killian, the president of MIT and future science adviser to the White House, said Sputnik presented the U.S. academic world with a "crisis of confidence." And *U.S. News & World Report* said Sputnik was like the "first splitting of the atom," again comparing it to the "giving away" of the A-bomb secrets by the Rosenbergs—which suggested that the only possible way the technologically backward Russians could have surged ahead of us was if they had stolen the necessary scientific knowledge, not acquired it through their own work and research. *Time* magazine regretted that "man's greatest technological triumph since the atomic bomb" had been scored by "the controlled scientists of a despotic state."[14] The Soviet space scientists were portrayed as robots, puppets, and were assumed incapable of being committed to the feat as objective scientists, as the Americans were.

In another echo of the A-bomb debate, a few public voices suggested that there was no "technological fix" to this particular problem, just as there had been no technological fix to the threat posed by nuclear weapons. Omar Bradley, former general of allied forces in Europe, argued that "there was no security in science or technology, only in diplomatic solutions."[15] But just as with the A-bomb earlier, such voices were utterly drowned out in the calls for an emergency program on the part of American politicians, warriors, and educators, all of who now demanded that we must innovate our way out of this new threat.

At the same time, everyone was looking for someone to blame for our "loss" of space. Perhaps not surprisingly, among the first targets of the press were our own scientists, though one comedian said Sputnik simply demonstrated that "their Germans are better than our Germans." Few people mentioned that our own military had given scant attention to rocketry before the war, while the Russians had a longer history of rocket research; and even fewer people knew that, while U.S. soldiers had captured the majority of the V-2 scientists, the Russians had captured the majority of the hardware that had escaped allied bombing, and thus they had a head start on the actual technology required to make rocket engines work.

Of course what was most damaged by Sputnik was America's scientific pride, as it clearly marked the end to any claim America had to technological supremacy; especially when, on November 3, the Soviets put Sputnik II into orbit, with a much heavier payload, including the first living creature in space, Laika the Spacedog.[16] Thus began a lengthy series of Soviet test fights with animals, all using the SS-6 booster—a rocket designed primarily to deliver huge hydrogen weapons—that was bigger than anything America had at the time, and all demonstrating just how far ahead the Soviets were in this space race.

The near-hysteria which greeted Sputnik was if nothing else a measure of how absolutely astounded we were that any nation other than America could mount the massive mechanical and organizational effort required to enter the Space Age. It was also an implicit indicator of how technological demonstrations meant so much more to us as a nation than theoretical achievements, as certainly we had never reacted so resentfully to the countless theoretical scientific advances made in other countries. It was the sophisticated *mechanical* skill that most terrified us—and apparently the only lesson we could extrapolate from the fact that this skill was in some other country's hands was that it was a harbinger of confrontation and conflict.

This assumed conflict, however, first manifested itself as an intense political battle between Democrats and Republicans, between those who reacted to it as a spur to spend more on defense in order to close the putative "missile gap," and those who wished to spend that same amount of money to close the "education gap." It was as though this single act brought into question not just American's claim to being the most technologically innovative nation on Earth, but also our system of research, funding, education, priorities—our entire culture.

Even before Sputnik, the concern that the Soviets were ahead of the United States in missile development had provoked the formation of the Strategic Missiles Evaluation Group (the Teapot Committee, headed by computer theorist John von Neumann). As a result of its report, which expressed "grave concern" that what was required was a "crash program," it was decided to increase the number of Atlas missile squadrons to nine, to approve the Air Force's Minuteman project—which would be the first U.S. "silo" missiles—and to accelerate the development of reconnaissance satellites, named Sentry. Seeing where the money was, every branch of the service came up with its own independent missile program: the Army received increased funding for its Pershing and Nike-Zeus, and the Navy's submarine-launched Polaris project was granted an accelerated schedule. The Strategic Air Command was given expanded funding for the development of the Distant Early Warning (DEW) radar system, which would be used to watch for incoming Soviet ICBMs.[17]

Oddly enough, one of the major reasons the Americans had lagged behind the Russians in the development of missiles powerful enough to carry satellites into orbit was Eisenhower's insistence on keeping the military and civilian rocket programs totally separate from one another. As Roger Launius points out, the United States in the mid-1950s had two separate space efforts underway: "The high-priority military program, to build ICBMs and to work on reconnaissance satellites, was kept under wraps as much as possible. The IGY [International Geophysical Year] program, on the other hand, was public and focused on the need to encourage the free access to space of all spacefaring nations."[18] Eisenhower had wanted to show the world that the United States didn't mix the two, as the Russians did—that our scientists were not the slaves of the military, and that their achievements were the result of their independence from outside control and central planning. The U.S. military supported this agenda, as they believed it gave priority to their goals. Ironically, it was the civilian researchers who wished for cooperation with the military, as they coveted the resources and leverage of the Defense Department initiatives. Their desire notwithstanding, this separation of the military and civilian efforts was strictly enforced, and as a result the civilian program had been consistently robbed to support the military. But when the panic of Sputnik set in, and in order to maintain the "peaceful" persona of U.S. space efforts, the military programs were then cannibalized and the civilian program was given top priority—as again, Eisenhower didn't want the world to see America resorting to its military establishment to catch up with the Russian program. Some in the government felt that "Eisenhower's decision to keep the satellite program separate from the military missile program had proved profoundly mistaken," and that he was still working under the old understanding of the society where there was a separation between the spheres, when there were such things as "civilians."[19]

But Eisenhower also didn't want the effort to be seen as a race. He was quite far-sighted in this area. He felt that the prudent thing to do was to stay on the careful and gradual track of development that had been planned for years, and he doubted that any temporary advantage of the Soviets would last very long. However, as Devine notes, "Eisenhower's low-key response to Sputnik completely failed to defuse the growing sense of public alarm."[20] Perhaps he didn't grasp the implications of Sputnik in the popular culture, as to him any weaponized versions of space rockets were merely potential and at-present awkward weapons in a material rather than a psychological war. In other words, Eisenhower was still thinking in terms of World War II. As a tactical weapon, ICBMs were not yet integrated into any practical strategy of war fighting; but the Cold War was one of psychological, not battlefield strategies; a fight for the "mind" of the international community, and as such it was a conflict unsuited to his thinking and experience. However, even though Eisenhower didn't want the nation to believe it was in a competition for space, fearing it would turn into a "garrison state," everyone else did. James Dolittle, still famous for his raid on Tokyo, called for all Americans to "work harder, sacrifice more."[21] Vannevar Bush (a pioneer in computer technology) said, "I think the primary thing that needs to happen to us here in this country is that we wake up to the fact that we are in a tough, competitive race."[22]

Besides blaming the American scientists or Soviet spies, there were also many who wished to blame the American educational system for our lack of "firsts." When, in 1951, Truman created the Science Advisory Committee (under the Office of Defense Mobilization, demonstrating how closely aligned the ideas of education and military defense already were), it was headed by the ex–Manhattan Project physicist I. I. Rabi. The committee initially produced a report that expressed a consensus that American education had become lazy, was not technologically focused, and was in all areas scientific losing ground to the Russians—a conclusion that would become a repeated claim in most crash educational reforms for the next decade, regardless of whether there was any real evidence to support it. Thus, as with the advent of the A-bomb and the impetus it generated to place a science adviser close to the president, this report suggested a similar role for an education adviser. But the candidates for such a position were all drawn from institutions which already worked closely with big corporations or the military, which were part of the existing system, and therefore unlikely to suggest revolutionary changes. They were in other words long on management skills but short on new ideas.

Popular magazines and even scientists themselves all accepted this *mea culpa* regarding the failings of the American educational system. *Time's* cover declared "Knowledge is Power"; *Life* magazine charged that we'd "frittered away" our post–World War II technological lead and that we must set a "higher value upon liberty than upon luxury"; and the father of the H-bomb, Edward Teller, "complained of the lack of prestige accorded science in American life."[23] All such sentiments merely echoed the immediate reaction to Sputnik, as this one from the *New York Times*, just four days after the tiny satellite's launch:

> October 8, 1957: Nation Is Warned to Stress Science—Faces Doom Unless Youth Learns Its Importance, Chief Physicist Says. The nation's youth must be taught to appreciate the importance of science or the United States' way of life is "doomed to rapid extinction," the director of the American Institute of Physics said yesterday.... Dr. Hutchisson said that the United States must distinguish carefully between the "highly accumulative" scientific knowledge that can be taught by rigorous discipline and the "namby-pamby kind of learning" that seeks to protect children against inhibition of their individuality or their laziness.'

In other words, being first in scientific fields obviously required discipline, hard work, sacrifice, greater prestige for scientists—and no luxuries. There is a Puritanical bent to much of this rhetoric calling for reformation of our educational system, a suggestion that we had drifted into the sinful ways of worshipping the golden calf of luxury, and now we must redeem ourselves by long and arduous hours in the library—all to achieve reconciliation with a God who *wanted* the United States to be first, if only we'd prove ourselves worthy.

Even Eisenhower eventually fell prey to the idea that we were in an "education race." He called for a host of new educational programs, especially college loan programs, even though he stressed that they were "emergency" and therefore temporary initiatives intended primarily to meet the "challenge" posed by Sputnik. While some educators were worried that the United States might over-stress technological subjects, they were all so happy at the prospect of new money that they were willing to go along with the idea of a national educational emergency, even if they didn't believe such a thing really existed. And they were pleased to see, finally, some attention being brought to bear on the low status (to say nothing of low compensation) that was the lot of teachers, especially science teachers, in the American system. As a further demonstration of how complete the concentration in educational reform proposals was to be on technical subjects, when it was suggested that the new scholarship programs be extended to the humanities and the arts, Eisenhower thought that was going "too far"; and his secretary of education, Ezra Taft Benson (eventually president of the Mormon church), though he approved of massive government involvement in science education, warned that such extensions of support in the humanities would mean "government interference in education." In other words, though government action on the behalf of applied science seemed only practical, such action in support of "theoretical" subjects like the arts was seen as dangerously socialist. Additionally, Eisenhower reminded everyone that scientists in general could not be allowed to enjoy the sort of uncritical valorization that had followed the A-bomb success, complaining about scientists who "tried to be experts in military and political matters."[24] We needed more scientists, yes; but they were to be engineers, not visionaries, and they were to know their place—which was exclusively in the laboratory frantically cranking out gadgets to keep the United States ahead in all three races: weapons, space, and education.

No one, however, not even Eisenhower, doubted that we were in a rocket race. Clearly the rocket that had put Sputnik into orbit was far ahead of the capacities of the two then-leading candidates for American satellites, the Redstone and Atlas. The Redstone was the Army's rocket program, headed by von Braun—and it was to von Braun's group that the government turned, as the Atlas program experienced one delay after another. Von Braun was urged to get something, anything into space as quickly as possible; but the problems with American rockets were the result of a number of policy decisions, not just technical glitches. First there was Eisenhower's drive to keep the space program a purely civilian endeavor, and thus the expertise of various groups was not centralized, as it was in the Soviet program; second, the Air Force's bias for manned bombers had kept its own rocket program, the Atlas, under-funded and behind schedule. Even America's technological advantage in atomic weapons worked against it in the area of rockets. While the American A- and H-bombs were becoming progressively more advanced and smaller, requiring less powerful ICBMs for their delivery, the Soviet H-bombs were huge and heavy, requiring the development of powerful rockets to deliver them to their targets thousands of miles away. And, since the Soviets' rocket program was not divided between civilians and the military, their space program was able to take advantage of the SS-6 rockets meant to carry these huge H-bombs over intercontinental distances.

These two gaps—education and missile—presented two very different sets of problems. Educational reform, everyone knew, would take years to bear fruit; but new defense policies could be, it was asserted, dreamed up over night, and were tailor-made for the confrontational rhetoric already in place. Thus Eisenhower began emphasizing defense over education. After Sputnik II was launched, he gave a speech that, although in its original drafts it had emphasized educational reforms, he had rewritten to drop out sections on education and "concentrate instead on national defense issues." This speech focused on the scientist as a figure for but not a controller of this crisis, and used the trope mainly as a way to measure when the "national crisis" would be over, which was "when the scientist can give his full attention, not to human destruction, but to human happiness and fulfillment."[25] In other words, we could have our luxuries—*given* to us by scientists—after we finished doing our science homework.

To grant new power to the importance of science in national affairs, the position of science adviser to the president was now made permanent, and the general reaction to this move was positive. *Time* wrote, "Science has never before been given that kind of attention at that level." Of course that was not true; science had been given that kind of attention during the Manhattan Project— but in the interest of keeping the focus of the American space and education races on peace, comparisons to the development of the A-bomb were for the most part absent from government rhetoric. What was also not mentioned in the various accolades was that this science adviser was largely there to advise the president on technological issues of national defense: not the environment, not education, not diplomacy, not international trade—just weapons.

Interestingly, though not surprisingly, this outcry for educational reform was limited to the areas of science most identified with technology and engineering, not theory. It was simply assumed that education reform meant *technical* educational reform, and that the proper metric by which to measure that reform was that our gadgets (satellites, rockets, missiles, bombs, and the like) would be better than anyone else's gadgets. The man who would nuclearize the submarine Navy, Admiral Hyman Rickover, said he hoped that Sputnik would "do in matters of the intellect what Pearl Harbor did in matters industrial and military"[26]—by which we can only assume he meant create an American intellect exclusively devoted to huge and expensive technology.

Thus it is clear that the dominant trope for the Sputnik "crisis" was as a competition, even a confrontation, especially a military confrontation; a conflict forced on us and initiated by a sneak attack on an America grown complacent with its "lazy" education and "luxuries," an America that had let its guard down.[27] No attention was paid to the fact that the Soviet educational system turned out practically only engineers, that those were focused almost entirely on military hardware, and that they were far behind in all other scientific matters, especially computers. And little mention was made of the fact that, while Sputnik could only beep out its faint, repetitive message "I'm here," the first American satellite, Explorer I (launched on January 31, 1958, atop a Jupiter-C military ICBM), while smaller than Sputnik, had some fairly sophisticated measuring devices stuffed into it and was responsible for the significant discovery of the Van Allen radiation belts. Rather, what was concentrated on was the fact that the Soviets had been "first," and little attention was paid to any of the details of what they'd been first at. Thus the pattern was set: whoever could do something, anything "first" was at that moment ahead in the race, and the other nation must either "catch up" or suffer "national extinction."

But catch up with what? At least as far as the space race was concerned, there was remarkably little consensus about what we were racing toward. The rocket engineers, invigorated with the same sort of gadget madness that had driven the A-bomb crowd at Los Alamos, simply wanted to get the damn things to work; to get them up there, higher and farther and faster. The government overseers of NASA thought of the goal as staying at least one step ahead of the Soviets; it didn't matter whether something was worth doing, the point was to do it *first*. And the media, always happy to present issues in terms of a race, horse or rocket, served to frame all reports about space exploration in terms of firsts: the first satellite, the first dog, the first human. Eventually such rhetoric would become almost Byzantine in its effort to characterize anything that had been done as a "first," as when the big silver balloon satellite Echo I (1960) bounced "the first" presidential speech (Eisenhower) to an American audience;[28] or later Telstar (1962) broadcast the "first speech of an American President (Kennedy) to a French audience."

As a result of all these fears and forces, and as a focus for at least the space race if not the missile and education race, NACA became NASA in July 1958, when Congress passed the National Aeronautics and Space Act. NASA would express the urgency if not quite the power of the Manhattan Project (not, that is, until the Apollo program), bringing together established experts in all fields related to aeronautics and outer space. Thus was created the concept of NASA, as a concentration of engineers working on practical innovations in aeronautics and space exploration that would "prove" American technical and therefore cultural superiority by doing things "first." We were to win this race on our machines, and any theorizing about the rationale behind those machines, the long-term goals they might accomplish and whether or not those goals were worth accomplishing; any coherent schema for integrating all our technical efforts into some grand plan . . . all such philosophizing was considered irrelevant, or worse, a distraction from the One Goal. Which was to be first.

Standing on the edge of the 1960s, one could have made a fairly accurate prediction about the type of space agency the United States would then establish: heavily dependent on cooperation between business and government, while largely indifferent to the university; committed to an agenda of immediate and spectacular technological firsts, with little consideration given to long-term planning; staffed in key positions by military men who would demand a space program shaped (and handicapped) by the primacy of manned space flights; and with goals determined more by a sense of competition than the more esoteric influences of space exploration theory. NASA would also become the logical extrapolation of the sort of Big Science that had begun in the late 1930s and '40s with the development of radar and the atomic bomb, delivering inventions without an inventor.

In that sense, Oppenheimer was probably the last of the Great Independents—and of course he hadn't been an independent at all. While von Braun was at times the "face" of the American space program, there were many reasons to keep that face largely concealed from the public, primary among them the fact that von Braun had been the guiding expert behind the V-2 rockets that had rained down upon wartime London, and no one wanted to remind the American public of that connection. His name alone was enough to summon the kind of sarcasm and anxiety about rockets evinced by the Tom Lehrer song "Wernher von Braun": "Once the rockets are up, who cares where they come down? / That's not my department, says Wernher von Braun." And yet, von Braun, ex-Nazi that he was, never suffered the sort of persecution and humiliation that was Oppenheimer's lot, was never suspected of being a traitor, was never ostracized from the American scientific community—demonstrating again, I would argue, our preference for mechanics over theorists, especially when the skills of that mechanic are seen as absolutely vital to the winning of a race for "national survival." And of course Oppenheimer's brief moment of respect and glory lasted only as long as he was needed in that role. Still, however willing we were to use von Braun's skills, and despite the willingness of the Disney people to put him on TV, too many people were uncomfortable with his past for him to become NASA's pitchman.

What the American space program needed, then, was a public face of which it could be proud, a face that would represent everything that was indisputably *American* about American space exploration. And it would find that face in the clean-cut, virile, smiling, confident visages of the first American astronauts, the Mercury 7.

Post-atomic Wizards
(top) *The Beginning or the End?* (1947) presented a rare parity between Wizards and Warriors, each of whom is shown here as equally capable of protecting their love interest from the rising mushroom cloud; (bottom) by far the more common image, however, was that of the bespectacled, bald-headed, lab-coated giant offering Death to Humanity-as-innocent-baby (cartoon by Sir David Low in the *London Standard*, Aug. 9, 1945).

"Baby Play with Nice Ball?"

Wizards as Aliens (top) Even though *The Day the Earth Stood Still* (1951) was an obvious plea for international cooperation and peace, it was marketed using clichés from pulp covers of the 1930s: Earth as threatened by a cosmic hand, a giant robot, and whatever that thing is in Klatuu's hand; (bottom) Klatuu, Ambassador from Outer Space, discusses a problem in "celestial mechanics" with Dr. Barnhardt, an Einstein-like physicist described as "the smartest man in America" (Twentieth Century Fox Film Corporation).

Wizards as *Worse* than Aliens

In *The Thing (from Another World)* (1951), the real threat is Dr. Carrington, who (top) wears Russian-style clothes and (second from top) natty sports jackets, (second from bottom) grows alien babies, and (bottom) is ready to sacrifice himself (and everyone else) "in the name of science" (Winchester Pictures Corporation).

DIRECTION OF
HEAT FLASH

If you are caught outdoors in a sudden attack, a hat will give you at least some protection from the 'heat flash'.

It Can Happen Here! Americans of the 1950s were far more worried about invasions and Communist-inspired race riots than they were of atomic bombs, which apparently could be survived with the proper deployment of a fedora hat brim. (top) Poster from *Invasion, U.S.A.* (1952) (courtesy of Conelrad.com); (bottom left) cover of *Is This Tomorrow* brochure (1947) (courtesy of Conelrad.com); (bottom right) image from *How to Survive an Atomic Bomb* (Bantam Books, 1952).

Forbidden Knowledge The 1956 film *Forbidden Planet* broke new ground in special effects but used the same old tropes of rampaging robots, misanthropic Wizards, and big machines as all inherently evil. (top left) Poster for the film; (bottom) the eternal triangle of Altaira, her father Dr. Morbius, and Commander Adams; (top right) the Krell "thought projection" machine, which turned mind into matter (Metro-Goldwyn-Mayer).

Rocket Fantasies vs. Rocket Realities (top) In the 1950s, the models for various rocket ships drew heavily on images from the 1920s and 1930s. However, neither of the actual space capsules born of U.S and Soviet programs looked anything at all like such models: (middle) American Mercury 7 space capsule (NASA photo), (bottom) Soviet Vostok space capsule (NASA painting).

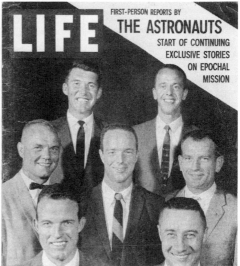

FIRST-PERSON REPORTS BY
THE ASTRONAUTS
START OF CONTINUING
EXCLUSIVE STORIES
ON EPOCHAL
MISSION

LIFE

Space Cadets, Space Salesmen, or Space Mechanics? Mercury 7 astronauts pose (top left) in their space suits (NASA photo), (top right) on the cover of *Life* magazine (September 14, 1959), (bottom) examining their Atlas-Mercury rocket (NASA photo).

Wicked Wizards Unite! Though these images of Wicked Wizards are from very different periods, they share key tropes of the stereotype, most prominently, prosthetic hands with a mind of their own. (top left) The evil scientist Rotwang with his female robot Maria in *Metropolis* (1927) (Paramount Pictures); (top right) Dr. Julius No in *Dr. No* (1962) (United Artists Corporation); (bottom) Peter Sellers as Dr. Strangelove in *Dr. Strangelove: Or How I Learned to Stop Worrying and Love the Bomb* (1964) (Columbia Pictures).

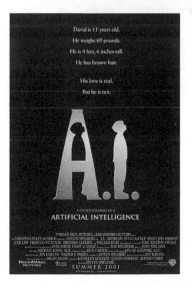

Evolution of the Robot Robots have been treated as familiars to the Wicked Wizard, as unstoppable killing machines, and—the scariest incarnation of all—as ten-year-old boys whose love is unconditional. (top left) *Metropolis* (1927) (Paramount Pictures); (top right) *The Terminator* (1984) (Orion Pictures Corporation); (bottom) *A.I.: Artificial Intelligence* (2001) (Warner Bros. Pictures).

The Model for All Master Mechanics to Come A standard representation of Benjamin Franklin's kite experiment of 1752. However, had Franklin actually held the kite string in the manner portrayed here, he would have been electrocuted (courtesy Huntington Library and Museum).

TOM SWIFT AND
THE COSMIC ASTRONAUTS

Pilots, Pitchmen, Warriors, or Mechanics?

LIKE MANY other American boys growing up in the 1950s, I had a firm image of what I wanted to become as an adult: an astronaut. My sources for this inspiration ran the gamut from serious to silly: *Encyclopedia Britannica* paste-in stamp books about outer space and rockets; Saturday afternoon newsreels and films about space exploration; and every Tom Swift book I could lay my hands on—*Tom Swift and His Rocket Ship, Tom Swift and His Electronic Retroscope, Tom Swift and His Atomic Earth Blaster, Tom Swift and the Cosmic Astronauts. . . .* Later, when NASA began putting men into space, I watched all the televised rocket launches, memorized the names of the astronauts, and read everything I could find about the astronaut training program. I even wrote to NASA asking what I could do to better my chances for being selected for the Astronaut Corps.

NASA's response surprised me. Their letter advised that the most important thing I could do to become an astronaut was to obtain a college degree in engineering: not become a fighter pilot, not join the military, not learn astronomy—just become a gear-head. And, it was important, not grow over 5' 11" tall. While I understood the latter suggestion—the space capsules were so small that shorter was better where astronauts were concerned—the former was unexpected. I had thought that the most basic, the most fundamental, the very thing that made an astronaut a "star navigator" was the fact that he could fly airplanes, especially jet airplanes, and thus naturally space airplanes—which we all knew would be called "rocket ships." After all, that's what they were called in the *Flash Gordon* serials; that's what they were called in comic books, *Popular Mechanics*, TV shows, magazines, even science textbooks. And since a ship was something that needed a pilot, a captain, then wouldn't astronauts have to be great pilots? Isn't that what the first seven American spacemen, the Mercury astronauts, were?

Certainly that is how they appear in the second most-famous image of the original Mercury 7. They stand in two orderly ranks, wearing their shiny silver space suits and space helmets and trailing their complex-looking futuristic portable air conditioners, looking like tomorrow's cadre fresh out of the Tom Swift space academy, ready, it seems, to walk out of the frame and straight into outer space. And they would make this walk, the photograph argues, on their futuristic silver space boots—boots which must, the viewer imagines, be specially designed for zero gravity, radiation storms, and the vacuum of the void beyond Earth's atmosphere. What the viewer doesn't know is that those space boots are in fact ankle-high work-boots, purchasable at any local hardware store and spray-painted silver to match their suits. Their actual space boots were more like the feet in bunny-suit pajamas, and it was thought they wouldn't convey the "right stuff" in a publicity photo. To those without this behind-the-scenes knowledge, however, the image effectively presents the high-tech, no-nonsense, big budget science fair aura (and of course those uniform suits and stances create just the slightest whiff of the military) that characterized the public face—or at least one of the public faces—of NASA and its historic task of putting the first American into outer space.

I refer to this image as the second most famous photograph of the Mercury 7, as arguably the most famous photograph doesn't in fact present any of these emblems of space exploration as a primarily technological, vaguely martial, or even particularly serious endeavor. Rather, this photograph shows the seven crowded together in a circle, dressed in presentable if not particularly stylish business suits, as though informally gathered for a college alumni or local Rotarian photo op; and only their upper torsos are shown, as though better to focus on their near-universal crew-cuts and openly friendly, one might say typically American faces. Though the suits and ties vary (John Glenn, always trying to separate himself from the crowd, wears a bowtie), some of the faces are more traditionally handsome than the others (Wally Schirra, *sans* buzz-cut, looks like the best guess for a ladies' man), and one looks vaguely like a scientist (Deke Slayton, with his lopsided grin and rugged features, could be a geologist; but that would have been a wildly inaccurate guess, as Slayton was one of the most "beer call" hot fighter jocks of the bunch and had no interest in science whatsoever). But the overall impression of the photograph is that this is a group of salesmen.

And that impression would be the more accurate of the two. Sales was exactly the job the Mercury 7 were expected to accomplish for the fledgling NASA. This second photograph is the cover of *Life* magazine for September 14, 1959, which introduced America to the space program and, more important, to the astronauts. As the cover declares, this was the first in what would be an exclusive series of articles *Life* had negotiated with NASA that would chronicle the training and eventual flights of the seven. *Life* was to be the public's touchstone with this new and exciting adventure—though given that photograph, the only excitement involved would seem to be that felt by businessmen at the advent of any new commercial enterprise; and as to adventure, these men don't look like explorers so much as insurance agents.

Which is also what they were, at least in regards to their public personas. From the moment they were selected as the Mercury 7, when they weren't training or undergoing endless experiments, they were on call as celebrities, publicity agents, hand-shakers, grin-makers; and their purpose was to sell the worthiness of manned space exploration to public and government alike, and to ensure that the image of that endeavor was one of a safe, cautious, and controlled program guaranteed of success. The message of those calm and smiling faces is that no one need fear the public horror and national humiliation of astronauts blown to smithereens in full view of millions of Americans.

This latter task was made more difficult by the fact that the American rockets had up until that point demonstrated a marked propensity to blow themselves to smithereens. However, the reality that NASA was engaged in an extremely risky venture full of unknown dangers and that periodic failures were probable was to be downplayed in every way possible—especially by its portrayal of the astronauts less as daredevil fighter pilots than as skilled technicians who just happened to know a thing or two about flying. NASA as an agency and the manned space program as the most public aspect of that agency thus gradually took on a persona with all the dash and daring of a trade show for kitchen appliances.

PROJECT MERCURY, the first U.S. manned space-flight program, began on October 7, 1958, one year and three days after the Soviet Union launched Sputnik I. The objectives of the program were to orbit a manned spacecraft around Earth, investigate the effects of weightlessness and space on humans, and get the man and the machine back safely. Originally the plans called for a very gradual and cautious approach to getting a man into orbit, with multiple tests every step of the way. However, soon a number of factors accelerated the program: the series of Soviet launches that demonstrated their booster rockets were far more powerful than ours; the Gary Powers U-2 spy plane incident of May 1960, which was yet another international embarrassment for the United States; and the series of American failures such as the explosion of the first Mercury-Atlas test vehicle in very public view in July and the even more ignominious "popped cork" incident of November of the same year. (Before assembled dignitaries, press, and TV, the Mercury-Redstone rocket briefly hiccupped about a foot off the pad before its engines shut down, then anti-climatically "popped the cork" of its escape tower, which floated gently down to the ground.)

All of these very public catastrophes became part of Kennedy's presidential campaign against Nixon, as he suggested that the Eisenhower administration hadn't devoted sufficient resources and expertise to catching up with the Soviets in space as well as in missiles. In fact, Kennedy's victory generated considerable anxiety around NASA. His sharp criticism of the past administration's running of the manned space program had created the impression that, once he was office, the Mercury program might be cancelled altogether, and some alternative program given priority.[1]

That alternative program would have been the X-15 rocket plane. While the X-15, and its antecedents like the X-1 and X-2, hadn't received nearly the publicity of the Mercury program, they had been around a lot longer, and they had a better record of success. Plans called for the X-15 to evolve into the Dyna-Soar (Dynamic Soarer), a single-pilot manned reusable space plane. By the time the astronauts were being photographed for *Life*, and before their capsule was much more than a concept, design contracts had already been awarded for the Dyna-Soar vehicle. The idea for something like Dyna-Soar—a space plane boosted into orbit by attached rockets—had been around for a long time; in fact, it was an adaptation of schemes for a manned "Rocket Bomber," a plane that would be boosted into the edge of space to "skip" along the top of the upper atmosphere in order to extend its range. The "RoBo" was itself based on an even older idea called the "Silverbird," which dated all the way back to the 1930s and which had been designed by Dr. Eugene Sanger for, of all people, the Nazis. The U.S. version of the RoBo program had been pursued because it was a favorite in the Air Force's war-fighting scenarios (though in the designs that were made public the atomic bombs it was to carry were not shown). But when the development of ICBMs reached a point that even conventional manned bombers, such as the B-52, were difficult to fund, the radical RoBo was finally dropped.

The idea of a rocket space plane continued to develop, however. As the X-15 achieved greater altitudes—reaching nearly 60 miles at its peak, which was 10 miles into what was technically outer space—the Dyna-Soar (by then called the X-20A) began to look like a real alternative to the Mercury rocket-capsule program. Had the X-20A been pursued instead of the Mercury, perhaps the Space Shuttle would have been a reality many years sooner. The X-20A was, after all, the option preferred by nearly everyone in the military—especially those who hoped to join any manned space program. As the test pilots at Edwards were fond of pointing out, the X-15 and X-20A were *true* rocket planes that a pilot flew, rather than tin cans in which an astronaut merely went along for the ride. However, what ultimately put the X-20A off the table as an alternative to Mercury was Russia's successful first manned launch of Yuri Gagarin on April 12, 1961, as the boosters necessary to get the X-20A higher into space weren't yet even tested. Since the Mercury system was *almost* ready to go, it was decided to stick with the MISS (Man In Space Soonest) option of Mercury, however unsatisfying, plagued by problems, and behind the Soviets it might have been. The X-20A's fate was sealed when Alan Shepard made the first successful suborbital flight in a Mercury capsule in May 1961, and Kennedy decided that Mercury was a better bet for "catching up" than any still-in-development version of the X-20A. He then gave the go-ahead for NASA to receive whatever funding and support it needed to accelerate the Mercury schedule.[2]

In other words, the Soviets made the choice for our manned space program. By putting Gagarin into space when they did, they caused every aspect of the space program other than getting an American "up there" as soon as possible to fade into unimportance. When asked to comment on Gagarin's flight, John Glenn's response became in a sense a template for the rhetoric that would characterize all of NASA's reactions to a soon-to-be daunting parade of Soviet firsts: "I am, naturally, disappointed that we did not make the first flight to open this new era." he said. "The important goals of Project Mercury, however, remain the same—ours is peaceful exploration of space. These first flights, whether Russian or American, will go a long way in determining the direction of future endeavors. There is certainly work for all to solve the tremendous problems involved."[3]

First and foremost, Glenn represented the American program as one of the "peaceful exploration of space"; in other words, whatever it was the Soviets were doing there, it wasn't peaceful. Second, these were merely "first flights"; the "race" would be a long one, with "tremendous problems" to solve, and one couldn't really recognize the winner for some time to come.

But there were clearly short-term gains to be made by these early manned space flights, not only in terms of the technical expertise necessary to win the long race—whatever its goal—but also in terms of national prestige. It was at this time that Vice President Lyndon Johnson wrote a memorandum to Kennedy in which he argued that "world leadership" itself would increasingly depend on "dramatic accomplishments in space."[4] And, while the public goal of the United States was the development of space for "all mankind," in private government discussions the argument was a little less altruistic: proficiency in space, it was asserted, would "prevent any other power from denying us the utilization of space in our interests."[5]

After Gagarin's flight—which lasted a full day and thus made any further suborbital Mercury flights look rather silly—John Glenn's flight was bumped to a full orbital mission. Meanwhile, Kennedy was constantly asking, How do we catch up? In a meeting with NASA officials James Webb and Hugh Dryden, Kennedy was given the bleak news that, what with the advantage the Soviets possessed in booster rocket power, catching up to them in terms of manned orbital stunts seemed beyond NASA's capabilities in the foreseeable future—certainly not something they could accomplish in a few months or even a year. NASA's entire schedule was based on gradual incremental achievements, not the kind of grandstanding for the sake of "firsts" that seemed to be what the Soviet program was all about. When the president asked, incremental stages toward what goal? the NASA people were a bit nonplussed. Their goal up until that point was simply to get a man into space and back alive; they hadn't really been thinking much beyond that achievement.

It was apparently at this point that Dryden suggested that perhaps they could make that "ultimate" goal a landing on the moon, which would move the finish line for the space race considerably into the future. Everything small and gradual and cautious NASA did would then be seen in service of that grand and inspiring and spectacular accomplishment; and everything, anything, the Soviets did that was *not* landing on the moon would seem pretty insignificant by comparison. When asked what this would cost, they replied with a fairly off-the-cuff estimate of somewhere between twenty to forty billion dollars. That was of course twenty to forty billion 1961 dollars. Thus clearly the expenditure required would be enormous, comparable only to the Manhattan Project, and probably even beyond that.

But Kennedy immediately saw the political logic of their argument, whatever the unexamined advantages or disadvantages of putting men rather than robots on the moon. Thus on May 25, 1961 (only 20 days after the first U.S. manned success, Alan Shepard's successful suborbital flight, which seems in retrospect an awfully tiny success upon which to stake such a tremendous effort), Kennedy gave his famous speech to Congress wherein he announced that the one goal of the U.S. space program—the goal by which all of our lesser achievements should be judged—would be putting men on the moon: "I believe this nation should commit itself to achieving the goal, before this decade is out, of landing a man on the moon and returning him safely to the earth." He also defined why this goal was *the* goal, both the real rationale and the fake one: "No single space project in this period will be more impressive to mankind or more important for the long-range exploration of space . . . and none will be so difficult or expensive to accomplish." And thus the entire focus for the U.S. space program became achieving that end, with no further questions asked about whether or not it was an end worth achieving. The lack of a comprehensive "space theory" aside, Kennedy's political and cultural instincts in making this decision proved to be quite accurate. By this point Americans were tired of seeing the Soviets touted as "leaders in space" in the newspapers and on television; Americans needed to be given not just a reason to support the fledgling Mercury program, but also to believe in a larger justification for what were sure to be more years of Soviet firsts.[6]

In addition to Kennedy's evangelical call for an all-out effort to reach the moon, another factor which shaped the way the general American public viewed the space race was the way it was portrayed on television, which ranged from crude and laughable to serious and numbingly boring. In the first category we have one of the first newscasts about the Sputnik launch, which included the visual aid of an "artist's conception of how the Russians achieved this feat": a black-and-white drawing of a few men standing around a ten-foot rocket on a small wooden platform, set in what appeared to be someone's backyard, all of it appearing as a sort of oversized fireworks display. Later, the newscasts of Laika's and Gherman Titov's orbital flights used footage captured from the Germans of V-2 rocket launches, with the announcer saying "atop a rocket similar to the one shown here. . . ." Even when a very short scene of actual space-flight footage was obtained from the Soviets showing mice floating in the weightlessness of space—limbs and tails splayed out as they turned chaotic somersaults—the old V-2 footage was dragged out to stand in for their rocket ride into orbit.

By contrast, coverage of the American program made full use of the open policy instituted by NASA, with long (some might today think overlong) news episodes detailing every aspect of the operations at Cape Canaveral. This footage of the American rockets showed them as huge, complicated, and modern, rising majestically from intricate launching pads and surrounded by highly technical-looking gantries. Thus, compared to the "artist's conceptions" and World War II V-2 footage of Soviet launches, the clear message was that, however the Soviets were accomplishing their space triumphs at the moment, they were soon to be overcome by shiny new American technology. Of course, the secrecy of the Soviet program meant little actual footage was available to the West; still, it is interesting that all the news and government institutions putting out these television spots apparently believed that, even though the Soviet rockets were putting up payloads three and four times as great as the United States was at that time capable of launching, it was still acceptable to represent them as using twelve-year-old rockets.

Besides the represented difference in technology, each American space accomplishment was presented in a way that emphasized the differences between the form and function of the Soviet and American programs: theirs was a highly secret endeavor controlled entirely by their military with aims that could only be guessed at, while ours was completely public and dedicated to the "peaceful" exploration of outer space for the "benefit of all mankind." What the American public saw on TV was Eisenhower broadcasting his "message of peace" via Echo I to a series of American families gathered around their radios, and later Kennedy broadcasting his "message of peace" via Telstar to a series of European parliaments—both to the background accompaniment of "America the Beautiful." Telstar, we were told, with its video capabilities, would allow the world to witness "American democracy in progress" and, as apparent compensation, allow Americans to view "history in the making from all over the world." (The message was that America produced democracy, while Europe produced history.) And both the news spots for Echo I and Telstar emphasized that their respective satellites "dwarfed" Sputnik—even though of course by this time the Soviets were putting up huge and sometimes multiple manned Vostoks.

Nevertheless, at each new Soviet achievement in space the same theme Glenn had established was repeated. In his news conference in response to Gagarin's orbital flight, Kennedy said that he did "not regard the 1st man in space as a sign of the weakening of the free world," but that he did regard their "total mobilization of effort" to achieve this goal as a "hazard"; whereas America's total mobilization of effort to reach the moon was, again, in the service of "peaceful exploration" for the "benefit of all mankind."

Oddly enough, in the period before the first Mercury launch, the astronauts themselves made remarkably few appearances on television, perhaps due to their exclusive deal with *Life* magazine—and perhaps because no one at NASA, especially the astronauts themselves, wanted too much connection to be made between the Mercury 7 astronauts and their colleagues who would make the first actual suborbital and orbital flights and who were much in the news at the time: chimpanzees. Still, lapses occurred. In one newsreel Enos, the chimp that made the first orbital trip, is shown standing beside his recovered Mercury 7 capsule, while the announcer says, with great enthusiasm, "Next in orbit, Lt. Col. John H. Glenn!"

It is easy to see why the astronauts didn't feel the same enthusiasm for this association as the narrator. After all, they had been chosen from the ranks of the best jet pilots in America; most of them had flown experimental jet aircraft, and all of them considered themselves to be at the top of the fighter jock pyramid, the "ziggurat of the right stuff," as Tom Wolfe famously calls it in his histori-fictionalized account of the beginnings of the American space program, *The Right Stuff*.[7] Wolfe's book effectively captures the world from which the first seven astronauts came: the small, scruffy, "low-rent" air bases in the swampland of Patuxent, Maryland, and the Mojave desert of Muroc (eventually Edwards) in California. Both environments were a rarefied atmosphere of

Air Force and Navy test pilots accustomed to dangerous work (you had a one-in-two chance of crashing and a one-in-three chance of dying sometime during your first year) and the prestige of being among the world's best pilots operating the world's most advanced air technology. Wolfe describes the gathering of the first thirty-four pilots from this group to volunteer for testing to be astronauts as follows: "most with crew cuts and all of them with lean lineless faces and suntans and the unmistakable cocky rolling gait of fighter jocks. . . ."[8] What gave them that "cocky rolling gait" was the knowledge that they had the "right stuff," what Wolfe defines as "nothing less than *manhood* itself."[9]

And everyone in this community knew who the role model for the right stuff was, who had the rightest right stuff of all, and that was Charles "Chuck" Yeager. Yeager had been a World War II fighter ace, even managing to shoot down one of the new German jet fighters, the ME-252s, which made their appearance in the closing days of the war and which usually easily outflew the American propeller-driven P-51 Mustangs Yeager was flying. After the war, Yeager became one of the first test pilots at Muroc, flying rocket planes with mysterious numbers rather than names, like the X-1, X-2, D-558-1, and XF-92A. Most important of all, it was Yeager who had broken the sound barrier on October 14, 1947—a fact that had been kept secret from the public, so that Yeager had received none of the notoriety that would be the lot of the first seven astronauts. Yeager also set the standard for the comportment of a proper fighter jock, with his "down holler" West Virginia twang, his coolness under pressure, his lack of interest in fame or fortune or fuss. He was the archetype of the taciturn Pilot Cowboy. And he had no interest in volunteering for the Mercury program because, as everyone knew, the astronauts wouldn't really be pilots; after all, as everyone said, "a monkey is going to make the first flight." From the moment the call for volunteers for the first seven astronauts went out, the question kept cropping up: would an astronaut really be a *pilot*? Or would they merely be talking chimpanzees in space suits?[10]

The persistence of that question, the extent to which it irked the astronauts, and their concerted efforts to refute it all exerted considerable influence on the development of Project Mercury, in many cases in direct opposition to the stated engineering and scientific objectives of the program, as we will see. But the prestige of being "first" and their natural competitiveness combined to overcome such doubts for those first thirty-four eager candidates, and especially for the seven who emerged as the winners: Wally Schirra, Alan Shepard, John Glenn, Scott Carpenter, Deke Slayton, Gordon Cooper, and Gus Grissom. All were exemplars of fighter jock right stuff, and therefore all assumed that they would be the ones to set the standard for astronaut right stuff. And they would—but not in the way they had imagined, for almost immediately they discovered that what had been the right stuff at Patuxent and Muroc would not necessarily be the right stuff at Canaveral.

The difference was made clear in their first press interview. When true fighter jocks spoke at all, it was to speak of aircraft and flying and to tell highly abbreviated tales of near death ("It was a touch close" typically describing the act of pulling a perhaps burning jet plane out of its dive within a few hundred feet of the ground), and usually delivered in a patois Wolfe calls "army creole," which was half a dozen nouns and verbs liberally peppered with profanity. Now suddenly they were arrayed before the American press and were being asked questions—which was bad enough—but questions not about planes or flying or near-death experiences, but rather about how they "felt" and how their wives "felt" and how their children "felt."

It was John Glenn who set the tone for the *new* right stuff, the astronaut right stuff, during this press conference—to the considerable surprise of the other six, all of whom considered Glenn a good pilot and a nice guy, but hardly a "spokesperson" for the group. Before they knew it, however, Glenn established the new standard for astronaut comportment, which would be a facility with rhetoric that combined teamspeak, patriotism, and a belief in God, family, and the American way:

> I don't think any of us could really go on with something like this if we didn't have pretty good backing at home. . . . I am a Presbyterian, A Protestant Presbyterian, and I take my religion very seriously. . . . We are placed here with certain talents and capabilities. It is up to each of us to use those talents and capabilities as best you can. . . . I think we would be most remiss in our duty if we didn't make the fullest use of our talents in volunteering for something that is so important as this is to our country and to the world in general right now.[11]

And on and on he continued in a similar vein. Glenn had instinctively realized that they were no longer fighter jocks but public relations material; that they were there to "sell" the idea of Mercury and men in space to a public that knew nothing and cared little about the technicalities of being spacemen. Thus being astronauts required them to change (or at least pretend to change) from who they'd been—the best fighter jocks in America—into the kind of men NASA needed them to be: crew-cut talking gear-heads who would at every opportunity de-emphasize the risk and danger and daredevil quotient of manned space flight, and reassure all and sundry that what they were doing was safe, sane, and necessary. *That*, Glenn had somehow intuited, was what being an astronaut meant.

And in proper public relations form, the seven got their own publicity agent, Bonney DeOrsey, who arranged a half million dollar contract with *Life* magazine. (After all, it was argued to critics who groused about an appearance of greed in what was supposed to be a selfless commitment, the *New York Times* had made a similar deal with Charles Lindbergh in 1927.) And through its series of candid, in-depth (and highly sanitized) stories about each of the astronauts' families, *Life* constructed them as "seven patriotic God-fearing small-town Protestant family men," which wasn't entirely true: one of the astronauts was separated, another had had a very "colorful" childhood, another's wife had been divorced, all of which was fairly innocuous history.[12] But against the pure white background of American Heroism against which they were being projected, any mark was a distracting blemish. They were now the public face of NASA with reporters from *Life* hounding their every step, both at Canaveral and in their homes, and they all had to at least appear to be the kind of upstanding moral boy scouts that in reality was a role tailor made for Glenn alone among them. Rather than boy scouts, however, the American public treated the first seven astronauts as combinations of movie stars and war heroes—and all of this before they'd actually done anything. The circulation of *Life* went up noticeably at the inception of the astronaut series. Everywhere they went—touring NASA facilities, appearing at schools and government functions—they were given parades, treated to dinners and special entertainments, photographed and glad-handed and back-patted as they had never before experienced.

Their instantaneous celebrity status can be attributed to a number of factors: to the novelty of what they were doing; to the allure of "outer space"; to the long mythology of spacemen already established in the popular culture; even to the driving desire of NASA to *make* them celebrities, in order to attract the power and resources necessary to jump-start a program already significantly behind the Soviets.

And there are additional explanations for this immediate idolization of the Mercury 7. Wolfe, for instance, believes they received so much praise because they had become the modern equivalent of the "single combat warrior," to be sent up into space to do battle with the Soviet cosmonauts.[13] However, there is a problem with Wolfe's analysis. For all the apocalyptic rhetoric which followed immediately upon the launch of Sputnik, the American program, even as it raced to do things the MISS way, wished most fervently to present the aura of a calm, peaceful, methodical *scientific* endeavor—and a warrior had no place in that presentation. Thus I believe that, rather than their being transformed from single combat warriors in fighter planes to single combat warriors in space planes, another sort of transformation was taking place: one that would ultimately present the astronauts as the latest version of a hero with an American tradition at least as long and as deep as that of the single combat warrior. Eventually, the Mercury astronauts would become the latest incarnation of Master Mechanics—Master Mechanics in Outer Space.

Such an assertion may seem like a stretch. After all, these pilots weren't scientists or "even" engineers, nor were they inventors, nor nuclear physicists
turned cold warriors. They were the best fighter pilots available, which would
seem to align them more with the warrior heroes of the 1950s science fiction
films than with the practical, non-theoretical mechanic-heroes of the same
films. But my argument here is that a number of factors working together over
the period spanning the initiation of the manned space program resulted in a
gradual transformation of both the astronauts and the program they represented, turning them and it into something neither had at first anticipated. The
first seven astronauts had been chosen from the ranks of the military because
Eisenhower didn't want every nutcase UFO believer showing up for astronaut
auditions, and the military was where you could find people who already had security clearances and who would do what they were told. And among the military, it seemed to make sense that one would select pilots, as they were people
used to being "up there"; and "up there" was, in a crude sense—a sense so crude
it wasn't even true, as none of the aerodynamic or other qualities of flight
applied in outer space—where astronauts would operate.

In fact, contrary to the general feeling that astronauts *had* to be pilots,
knowing how to fly wasn't even among the original NASA astronaut specifica-
tions; the only real requirements were that they would be college graduates
and under 5' 11". The first list of those occupations that it was believed might
produce people appropriate for the duties and psychological profile of astronaut included submariners, parachutists, arctic explorers, and mountain climbers
(the last because they were used to low oxygen, though even this requirement
made little sense, as the astronaut would be in a spacesuit with a perfectly normal supply of oxygen). But pilots were not on that list. When it came right
down to it, as Wolfe points out, "The astronaut would not be expected to *do*
anything; he only had to be able to take it."[14]

NASA planners had even given some thought to making sure that the astronaut did *not* do anything, lest he interfere with the automated systems. They
considered tranquilizing the astronaut to "make sure they would lie there
peacefully . . . and not *do something*. . . ."[15] This fear of the astronaut being too
active a component in the space-flight system was not limited to the American
program. The Soviets almost went ahead with a plan to anesthetize Gagarin for
fear he would "go crazy," but in the end they merely locked his controls and
put the unlocking code in a sealed envelope, which they told him to open only
on emergency orders from the ground.[16]

Even as the Mercury program surrounded the astronauts with the aura of
Rocket Pilots, *real* rocket pilots like Randy Lovelace and Scott Crossfield, pilots
who flew the rocket-powered X-15, pointed out to anyone who would listen that

astronauts weren't pilots at all; biomedical research was "the sole purpose of the ride. . . . In short, the astronaut in Project Mercury would not be a pilot under any conventional definition."[17] The Mercury spacecraft itself was described not in fact as a craft or a plane, but as a "capsule" and a "system" wherein it would be best if "the astronaut does not need to turn a hand."[18] This same point is made with great clarity (if somewhat neutrally) in an article about the awarding of the Collier Trophy to the Mercury astronauts in 1962:

> If space exploration is seen entirely as a mechanical exercise (which was the per-
> ception of many engineers and scientists involved with Project Mercury as well
> as the Eisenhower administration) then the astronaut's role is relatively minor:
> he goes along for the ride and to make minor adjustments to the equipment.
> Testing human reactions is simply part of the technological testing process.[19]

However, for sheer objective bluntness, one must turn to the explanation of this difference between pilot and astronaut as rendered by one of the German rocket technicians brought to the United States after World War II and put to work on von Braun's Redstone project:

> The difference between the two technologies [plane vs. rocket] may be stated in
> the following general terms. From an aviation standpoint [i.e., a pilot in an air-
> plane], man is not only the subject of transportation, and as such in need of pro-
> tection as a passenger; but he is also a most important integral part of the
> machine over which he truly has control. . . . In contrast, rocket technology has
> been for twenty years a missile technology governed by the requirements of tar-
> get accuracy and maximum range. As such, it had to develop automatic controls.
> Unlike a human payload, a warhead has no use except on the target. Once a mis-
> sile fails, it may as well destroy itself during flight. The development of manned
> spaceflight is not just a matter of replacing a warhead by a manned cabin. Sud-
> denly a switch is thrown between two parallel tracks, those of missile technology
> and those of aviation technology, and an attempt is made to move the precious
> human payload from one track to the other. As in all last-minute switchings, one
> has to be careful to assure that no derailment takes place.[20]

The perhaps-unintended black humor understatement of that closing sentence aside, this is an excellent representation of the Mercury program—or space exploration for that matter—from the "engineering standpoint." A rocket was typically merely a means of getting something somewhere—usually an explosive device; even in space exploration, a rocket was expendable, useful only for getting the instrument where you wanted it: into orbit, onto the moon. If you lost the rocket and the satellite as well, you built another one. But once you placed a man inside the rocket, an entirely new paradigm was encountered, a hybrid system was created, something that was about more than just making technical measurements, something that represented fundamental aspects of human curiosity and abilities, hopes and dreams; you entered the realm of myth and national identity, the realm of the Astronaut, or "star navigator": "Beyond the sheer technological basics, a more romantic notion, of individual challenge and courage in exploration of the universe or defense of the homeland can be seen as the reason for making machines that will carry explorers."[21]

Such lofty rhetoric aside, however, as far as the engineers and scientists of NASA were concerned, "The astronaut [had] been added to the system as a redundant component."[22] Engineers said this with purely objective honesty; rocket pilots like Crossfield said it with barely concealed disdain. The seven astronauts said it to each other with obvious mortification. But from an "engineering standpoint," the logic was simple: "If the automatic system broke down, [the astronaut] might step in as a repairman."[23] In other words, the astronaut's most defensible role was that of a mechanic.

Central to my argument here is how these two conceptions of the astronaut—redundant component and star explorer—collided with one another in the Mercury program. But what none of them—engineer, astronaut, or rocket pilot—realized was that the former role, that of "redundant component," would prove to be the final and satisfactory rationale for putting the man in manned space flight. Ultimately, the argument that won the day for putting humans rather than chimps—or for that matter, robots—into space was that they would be able to fix things if they broke.

Of course, in addition to viewing the astronauts as single combat warriors, or rocket pilots, or space mechanics, there are other interpretations available. In his work on the American advertising industry of the 1950s, Michael L. Smith suggests that the new technological wonders of that age were displayed in a series of stages: first the "unveiling," then the "transferring" of the product's unique capabilities to the consumer, and finally getting the consumer to "identify" with the spokesperson for the gadget, usually a celebrity. This latter figure Smith calls a "helmsman, whose mastery over his environment through the products of technology provides a model for consumer aspiration." Smith argues that, if the Mercury capsules were the equivalent of a new product being sold to the American pubic—predominantly to the American male—then the astronauts were the helmsman paired with this product, the figure with which the average American male could identify: "Helmsmen were needed for the great adventure, and the fighter pilot astronaut emerged as the figure most worthy of carrying America's banner to the stars."[24] While it is true that the "average-ness" of the astronauts was emphasized when they were first introduced to the American public, Smith's analysis doesn't quite capture the special nature of the astronauts' celebrity. As the official history of Project Mercury notes:

These personable pilots were introduced in civilian dress; many people, in their audience forgot that they were volunteer test subjects and military officers. Their public comments did not class them with an elite intelligentsia. Rather they were a contingent of mature Americans, average in build and visage, family men all, college-educated as engineers, possessing excellent health, and professionally committed to flying advanced aircraft.[25]

Setting aside for the moment the obvious contrasting of the "average" astronauts with "intelligentsia," it is clear that much effort went into making the first seven appear ordinary rather than extraordinary, or perhaps extraordinarily ordinary; that is, they were hardly presented as the celebrity types Smith discusses in his analysis of advertising icons. That the astronauts became celebrities and were treated as such is not at issue; rather, what they were celebrated *for* is.

For instance, Norman Mailer criticized NASA for not making more of the astronauts' bravery, for not emphasizing rather than downplaying the fact that they were, after all, daredevil fighter jocks.[26] For Mailer, that was the source of their heroism and their celebrity. However, as Alan Levine has argued, this was precisely the *opposite* of the impression those running the fragile new space program wanted to project; rather, NASA wished to portray this unprecedented, dangerous, high-risk endeavor as something precise, careful, moderate, reliable, technically sound, and unfailingly cautious. As Levine says, "NASA's publicity machine and the *Time-Life* empire . . . contrived to show them, and to some extent, the Mercury project as a whole, in a misleading way."[27] NASA wanted the American public to think of Mercury as without risk, mere celestial mechanics; and *Life* wanted the American public to think of the Mercury astronauts as without flaw, as "typical middle-class white Protestants." Thus I would argue that the astronauts were not perceived so much as Wolfe's warriors or Mailer's daredevils or even Smith's helmsman, but rather as Master Mechanics with a pilot's license.

Their daredevil quotient was constantly downplayed, and their buzz-cut engineering common sense and technical know-how were constantly emphasized. One need only look at the series of NASA publicity stills of the astronauts undergoing training to see this characterization: John Glenn is shown examining what appears a complicated celestial three-dimensional map (labeled "globe"); Grissom, Carpenter, and Glenn are shown talking to what appears to be an engineer before a blackboard filled with technical equations; Glenn is shown wearing a complicated visual apparatus; and all seven of them are gathered around a model of the Atlas-Mercury rocket, examining it and smiling as though confirming that it matches their design.[28] The clear argument these images are making is that these are engineers who just happen to know how to fly.

U.S. News and World Report observed, "A new breed of cosmic explorer has emerged. Gone is the earlier image of the rocket-riding daredevil, the superman of the 'wild blue yonder.' The astronaut now is seen as a dedicated scientist concerned more with discovery than with setting orbiting records."[29] The fighter pilot was now transformed into an explorer-engineer ready to convert the void of space into an American landscape—much like the engineer of the nineteenth century who had left his laboratory and was now ready to discover and exploit the vast resources of the American west.

The irony of this characterization of the astronauts is that there was considerable tension between them and the actual engineers and scientists at NASA. One must keep in mind that the astronauts weren't in fact "explorer scientists," but fighter pilots; and, while fighter pilots had respect for the aircraft engineers who built the experimental planes—the technology that made them who they were—they had little patience and some outright disdain for flight surgeons, psychiatrists, and all the other "white smock" types with whom they were suddenly surrounded. The fact that the white smock types treated the astronauts as experimental guinea pigs didn't help the situation. Whenever one of the astronauts asked for the rationale behind some of the more bizarre psychical and psychological tests they were being subjected to day after day—one involved implanting electrodes in an astronaut's hand and shocking it into making a fist repeatedly, another consisted of pouring cold water directly into his ears—the doctors tended to be a bit condescending; or, as Wolfe describes it, the "uncompromising white smocks indicated that you really didn't need to know, and that was that."[30] Some of the pet names the astronauts had for the scientists are illustrative: White Smocks, Reflector Heads, Egg Heads, Brainiacs; all of them, of course, the opposite of fighter jocks. The point of all these tests, as far as the astronauts could tell, seemed to be to inflict maximum discomfort—especially the psychological profiles. It was all "flight surgeon bullshit."

The fact that fighter jocks considered themselves anything but scientists is encapsulated in an anecdote Wolfe relates concerning that paragon of fighter jockness, Chuck Yeager. Once when he was piloting the chase plane to another test pilot's experimental jet, Yeager noticed the experimental plane flying erratically and concluded that the pilot's oxygen system was malfunctioning. Yeager suggested to the other pilot that he follow Yeager down to a lower altitude, but the pilot became indignant and refused; and such irrational bellicosity was in fact a common symptom of oxygen deprivation. Then Yeager tried another tactic and pretended that *he* was the one with the problem and needed the other pilot's help: he asked him, in his quaint, non-demanding, common-folk drawl sort of way, to *please* follow him down. But the pilot still ignored him. So then Yeager lost even his considerable patience and yelled: "Look, my dedicated young scientist—*follow me down!*"[31] In a moment of extreme stress even Yeager couldn't finesse, he demoted his comrade from fighter jock to "young scientist"— with a sarcastic "dedicated" thrown in to seal the insult. Of course, not only was Yeager's West Virginia drawl the antithesis of the cultured or educated speech of the scientists, it became the model of all pilotspeak, to say nothing of fighter jock attitudes toward "scientists," dedicated or otherwise.

This tension between how the astronauts saw themselves and how the engineers of the Mercury program saw them eventually came to a head just before Alan Shepard's first suborbital flight. As the Mercury capsule was originally designed, there was no window, as the added risk of ruptured glass seemed unnecessary; after all, the astronaut could see through a periscope arrangement. But as the needling of the rocket plane pilots continued, combined with the never-ending demands of the doctors and scientists, the astronauts decided they needed to exert their status as pilots rather than mere experimental cargo. If astronauts were pilots then the Mercury was a spacecraft, not a capsule; and if it was a craft, it needed a window. So they demanded that the capsule, even at this late date, be redesigned. As for controlling their "craft"—something naturally a pilot would be expected to do—they wanted the controls of the small attitude rockets (that adjust the orientation of the capsule) to be changed to more closely resemble the control stick of a fighter plane; and they also wanted a hatch that they could open individually from inside the spacecraft.[32] They even managed to convince NASA to stop calling the Mercury a "capsule" and to officially designate it a "spacecraft." Given the prestige the astronauts had by that point earned for the program among the American public, their demands were met.

Wolfe discusses the umbrage some of the NASA engineers took at the growing power of the seven to influence technical aspects of the program: "The glorification of the astronauts had really gotten out of control! In the world of science—and project Mercury was supposed to be a scientific enterprise—pure scientists ranked first and engineers second and the test subjects of experiments ranked so low that one seldom thought about them."[33] But only the NASA scientists believed this fantasy: the administrators, whose job it was to beg for funding, knew who the true salesmen of the program were, and they weren't the white smocks or the reflector heads; they were those test subjects.

Scott Carpenter was perhaps the one astronaut who came closest to being an actual scientist, a minor version of a Wicked Wizard among the rest of the Master Mechanic astronauts. He actually talked with the doctors—even the shrinks—about their tests and about the broader implications of space exploration. Carpenter had his own telescope at home and would spend hours stargazing. And Carpenter's flight—the second orbital flight after Glenn's—is a perfect illustration of the relative low rank of actual science in the Mercury program.

During his flight, Carpenter tried his best to fulfill his imagined role as a space explorer rather than just deadweight cargo, as spam-in-a-can. Thus he made continual observations, reporting and recording like a good explorer. Of particular interest to him were the "fireflies" that had appeared around John Glenn's capsule, and now around his as well. Glenn had been fascinated by them, utterly unsure of what they were, and had even theorized that they were perhaps some kind of unimagined microscopic orbital life. Carpenter made it his task to observe them as closely as possible, and eventually concluded that they were merely condensation from the outside of the capsule; but in order to do that he had to keep changing the attitude of the capsule, as that was the only way to change which way the window was pointing. (It's important to understand that the attitude control jets of the Mercury capsule had no effect whatsoever on its trajectory, they were simply too small; that trajectory had been determined by the rocket which put it into orbit. While the attitude control jets could point the capsule in any direction, they had nothing to do with "flying" the capsule until the moment of reentry, when they were necessary to position the retro-rocket pack rear-end of the capsule at the appropriate angle.) In order to better see the fireflies, as well as the earth and horizon, Carpenter kept moving the capsule around, which used up most of his fuel, so when it did come time to position it for reentry he had precious little left, resulting in his reentry angle being a little off. There were also an inordinate number of mechanical failures during his flight: a balloon attached to the capsule didn't fully inflate, and then wouldn't jettison properly and was dragging behind the capsule, on fire, during reentry; the retro rockets didn't fire automatically, and when Carpenter fired them manually, they delivered less thrust than expected. All of these malfunctions resulted in his landing 250 miles off target.

NASA's official description of the flight proclaims that Carpenter's "primary goal was to determine whether an astronaut could work in space, a major stepping stone towards a lunar landing" and that the "the flight plan included numerous scientific experiments, including observations of flares fired on Earth and the deployment of a tethered balloon." That official description also declares, "Needless to say, the mission was less than a total success. Carpenter seemed distracted and behind schedule most of the flight."[34] Whether Carpenter was distracted or not is open to debate, given the fact that he was dealing with a crowded checklist and numerous mechanical failures; but such a characterization became the official evaluation of the flight of *Aurora 7*. And thus Carpenter's flight symbolized, as far as the other astronauts were concerned, a lesson in the *un*importance of science in manned space flight. In fact, after

Carpenter's flight, the single goal of the remaining astronauts was to not make any mistakes, to complete the flight with a perfect checklist. Given his interest in experiments, his stargazing, his collegial relationship with the NASA scientists, the other astronauts had already treated Carpenter like a "reflector head" who had wound up by mistake in a capsule; and after his off-target landing, the NASA administration was so embarrassed they decided Carpenter would never fly another mission. And he didn't. The kind of space science that Carpenter had practiced, as far as the Mercury program was concerned, was over.

The next astronaut to do an orbital flight, Wally Schirra in *Sigma 7*, decided to do essentially nothing during his flight; or rather to accomplish one goal only: use up as little fuel as possible, and land right on target. This he did, within 1.5 miles of his recovery carrier. Thus his flight was labeled a "total operational success." The fact that he did no science during the flight was unimportant. As Wolfe summarizes the lesson NASA learned: "Carpenter's flight had been loaded with Larry Lightbulb experiments. The scientists, lowest men in the NASA pecking order up to now, had been given their heads on this flight. . . . Carpenter had taken all this Mad Professor stuff seriously, and that was what led to his problems." Schirra and the remaining astronauts scheduled for Mercury flights realized happily that "all this science nonsense could wait." And thus, as Wolfe says, "The flight of *Sigma 7* was designed to be . . . the final and decisive rout of the forces of experimental science in the manned space program."[35]

The considerable operational rather than engineering influence the astronauts had on the Mercury program was largely unknown to the public, and continues to be overlooked or underestimated even today. Jannelle Warren-Findley, for instance, writing about the awarding of the Collier Medal to the astronauts in 1962—a medal usually reserved for those who had made significant engineering achievements—sees the award as a curious decision: "If there is a real anomaly in the award of the Collier Trophy to the Mercury astronauts, it is that from the perspective within NASA, the Project Mercury astronauts appear to have had relatively little to do with the development of the program."[36] But in fact, they *had* altered the development of the capsule design and the science practiced in it to a considerable extent, all in service of proving that they were *pilots*, not trained chimpanzee cargo or Larry Lightbulb scientists.

Ultimately, all this history reveals a deep irony in the Mercury program. The astronauts were picked from among the military's test pilots *not* because the space program needed pilots, but in order to reduce the number of applicants and ensure security clearances in a hurry, which was necessary because the United States was in a hurry to "catch up" with the Soviets. However, being who they were—pilots—they then demanded that the program be changed in order to make it more pilot friendly, which made it less science friendly. And yet throughout this entire process, NASA's public image required them to take on the personas of space engineers who would conduct the science of the space program—science that was, after Carpenter's flight, a distant second priority to "operational success." Ultimately, the fighter jocks-turned-insurance salesmen-turned-space mechanics defined the goals and accomplishments of the early U.S. space program, and the actual engineers and scientists were not only ignored but "routed."

Once it was demonstrated that the early manned space-flight program wasn't interested in doing much science, Schirra's "operational success" became the standard for all missions to follow. Setting modest, readily achievable "operational" goals—goals largely concerned with testing the engineering components of the spacecraft—and meeting them in a very gradual, step-by-step process became NASA's modus operandi for the next several years; "space spectaculars" were out, and all the routines of a safety-first bureaucracy were in. Thus the representation of NASA, its astronauts, and the overall task of space exploration took on an image drained as much as possible of any aspect of adventure or danger.

Melanie Brown criticizes NASA on this very point, as Mailer did before her, arguing that its "astronauts are curiously unremarkable, the image NASA insists its astronauts maintain [does] little to inspire the imaginations or interests of the very public NASA strives to please . . . the astronauts themselves now seemingly faceless, even asexual, drones, both in NASA's and popular culture's portrayal of them."[37] While the presentation of the astronauts as competent-if-unexciting space engineers may or may not be a public relations error on the part of NASA, it is in keeping with the mindset of a largely engineering enterprise—especially one which seeks above all else to present its work as sound and practical, and which has developed in a hermetic world of the government contractor and the military, where the key acronym is KISS: Keep It Simple & Safe.

Faceless drones? In fact, NASA had done everything possible to make the astronauts as human as your next-door neighbor, as cute as a Disney icon, as pure and heroic as a cowboy. Sexless maybe—but then so, too, were the American cowboy heroes. Of course with the multiplying of the astronaut corps and the extension of the original seat-of-the-pants atmosphere (as if the complicated business of manned space flight were ever really anything so *ad hoc*) to a decades-long, fully integrated, safety-first space industry, it is difficult for the American public to know each of the astronauts' names, as they know those of major league sports players. The hero worship so evident in the early years has given way to a smooth, bland NASA corporatism, that much is true; but it was all done in an effort to make space exploration seem as safe as taking the bus. Certainly the tragedies of Challenger (1986) and Columbia (2003) demonstrated just how risky and cutting edge an enterprise space exploration still is, and will likely remain for a long time to come. But risky and cutting edge doesn't get funded; reliable and mundane does. So if there is an element of "dronism" about the current astronauts, it's there to protect NASA from charges of grandstanding, and to present the astronauts not as fighter jock daredevils, but rather as "dedicated scientist[s] concerned more with discovery than with setting orbiting records." Vivian Sobchak comes closer to this mark when she observes that "it is their interchangeable blandness, their programmed cheerfulness, their lack of imagination, their very banality . . . that makes them heroes, that gives them that aura of mechanical and robotic competence which insists that nothing can go wrong, that everything is A-OK."[38] Exactly.

But there are even more bizarre conceptions of what "hero" means in the context of manned space exploration; conceptions closer to saint than drone. Science fiction writer J. G. Ballard explored the dark side of "astronautics" in a series of stories written between 1962 and 1985 and collected as *Memories of the Space Age* (1988). The signature story is titled "The Dead Astronaut," and is about earthbound people who have become "explorers" in a rather macabre sense: they search the area around Cape Canaveral for the remains of crashed spacecraft and their dead astronaut occupants:

> The relic hunters were at Cape Kennedy, scouring the burning saw grass for instrument panels and flying suits and—most valuable of all—the mummified corpses of the dead astronauts. These blackened fragments of collarbone and shin, kneecap and rib, were the unique relics of the Space Age, as treasured as the saintly bones of mediaeval shrines.[39]

This atypically macabre vision of the space age is not as limited to the post–space race, postmodern period as one might think. A number of science fiction stories from the 1930s and '40s treat our entry into outer space as dangerously problematic, as something that requires a departure from the safe and sane terrestrial world we had known for millennia. One example is "Adam and No Eve" (1941) by Alfred Bester, wherein it is imagined that the fuel used in the first rocket flight sets the Earth's atmosphere on fire, burning everyone and everything to ash, and leaving the astronaut to wander a vaguely post-nuclear apocalyptic landscape utterly alone. Another is "Flight into Darkness" (1942) by Webb Marlowe, which predicts that the first manned space flight will be made by neither American nor Soviet astronauts, but by a Nazi. In other words, as early as the 1940s people were envisioning a future space program as not necessarily expressions of American heroism or technological prowess,

but as an unprecedented and potentially disastrous crossing of some traditional boundary—much as *Frankenstein* was viewed in its time.

However, even in the darkest of these visions, space exploration is still centered around human "pilots" making space "flights." Nowhere in the literature
or film which preceded the actual space program is there any thought given to a
space program without space pilots; nowhere is it imagined that the first astronauts could be scientists or engineers—or, for that matter, mountain climbers.
Yet, as I suggested earlier, the American space program could have developed
in alternate ways. Certainly if the Mercury 7 astronauts had been anything
other than fighter pilots, the scientists would have had more influence over the
technology and goals of those first flights. Eventually, with the Gemini program
and its goal of perfecting space rendezvous, and later the Dyna-Soar-like space
shuttle with its need for a pilot to land the craft, the role for actual piloting skills
did become vitally important. But the influence of those early days of Mercury's
"men first, science second (or third)" attitude hasn't ever really faded, and questions about exactly what role humans can or should play in space exploration
haven't, even to this day, been satisfactorily answered. Thus, the United States
still lacks any general "theory" of what it wants to do with people in outer space.
The closest NASA ever came to such generalized theory of space exploration
was back in 1961, when James Webb first became its administrator. Webb's initial plan was "to use NASA as a vehicle to move the whole nation to a 'new frontier' of enhanced technology-based educational and economic development."[40]
For Webb, our goals in space should be extensions of our economic, industrial,
and educational goals on Earth. But in the massive expansion of NASA to develop the Apollo Project, everything was sacrificed except those aspects of
the program that furthered Kennedy's goal: landing a man on the moon.

In fact, our vision of outer space has never really progressed beyond Kennedy's
"frontier" metaphor, a metaphor established in the sci-fi space operas of the early
twentieth-century pulp magazines, and given high-tech gloss with such movie
serials as *Star Wars* and *Star Trek*. The reasons given for why we need to send
people to the moon—or to Mars for that matter—typically sound more like rationalizations for spending enormous amounts of money than well-articulated
positions in a coherent theory of space exploration.

One such oft-repeated justification is that people are required in space exploration because it is fundamentally "human" to wish to explore. As a reporter
writing in *The Nation* put it, "Machines alone will not suffice if men are able to
follow. . . . The difference is [like] that between admiring a woman's photograph
and marrying her."[41] In other words, it is one thing to look at robot-transmitted
pictures of the moon; it is quite another to see a picture of a human being setting foot on it. While the difference between the inspirational value of two such

pictures can be granted, that difference still doesn't adequately address questions about the enormously greater cost, in terms of risk as well as money, of that second picture. Another argument in favor of manned space flight is that the space program makes sound economic sense, generating consumer spin-offs, like Teflon and Velcro. But other than these two instances, such widely commercial results are difficult to name; and again, in all likelihood such inventions would have been developed with or without human beings in capsules.

In point of fact, when all else fails the fallback justification for humans in space hasn't really changed since Project Mercury: an astronaut is necessary to fix the failures of machines; he is, finally and primarily, the "redundant component" the engineers thought he was in the first place. Or, as it is put more tactfully in a televised NASA "progress report" from 1965, men are needed in space to "use the special abilities of the trained astronaut as a sensor and evaluator." In other words, they are there as a backup recording device.

Of course the most honest answer to the question, Why put men in space?—at least in the beginning—was that we needed to do it before the Russians did; and when they did it first, then we needed to put men on the moon before the Russians did. It was entirely an issue of national prestige, not the fundamental human urge to explore. As difficult as it is to admit for someone who as a child watched those Mercury rocket launches and wished he were the one in that tiny capsule, it seems undeniable that the technology for putting men into space has been and in many ways remains a technology in search of an application, a "reverse adaptation," in Langdon Winner's phrase: a technology which forces culture to adapt to it, rather than the other way around.[42] This is not to say that the scientific knowledge gained from space exploration hasn't broadened our understanding of life, the universe, and everything; the results produced by the Hubble space telescope alone may well justify all the resources expended on space thus far. But such accomplishments have little to do with *manned* space missions. The results we have achieved that are most clearly useful could have been achieved without astronauts.[43] The theory of why one might wish to explore space with technology is as simple as the theory of scientific exploration at its most basic: to know more. But the theory of exploring space with *people* is much less clear, usually devolving into sentimental rhetoric about our need as humans to explore the unknown and push beyond boundaries; and it is thus obviously one that requires much greater attention and analysis than it has so far received.

All our popular imaginings of space visualize it filled with spaceships and space stations and space cities, all of them filled with spacemen—or spacepeople—busily building and exploring and expanding. And that, I would argue, is the overriding metaphor for all of these narratives of exploration: expansion, as in frontier; or as in empire, the age-old metaphors that have driven human exploration for thousands of years. It is the development of this notion of outer space as New Empire, and the ways in which this metaphor transformed while retaining the basic qualities of our categories Master Mechanic and Wicked Wizard, that I will explore in the next chapter.

AMERICA VS. THE EVIL EMPIRE(S)

10

Good Astronauts, Bad Aliens, and
the Battle for the High Frontier

THERE IS an image which captures what most people think of when they hear the phrase "monsters from outer space," and it looks something like this: a heroic astronaut (space suit, ray gun) confronts some hideous space monster (tentacles, single giant eye) while sheltering a scantily clad space heroine (blonde, Grecian tunic), all of them standing on an alien landscape colored in sinister purples and sickly greens. This image is derived from countless posters for B-level science fiction films of the 1950s, posters that borrowed heavily from the covers of pulp magazines of the '30s. While the basic components of that image—hero, monster, heroine—are as old as narrative itself, the image also reveals something about late twentieth-century fears of the bad scientist; fears that were played out in the films and television and other media of the Space Age, and which continue to shape American thinking about science and its practitioners to this very day.

Just as the Master Mechanics of American culture moved into outer space in the 1960s, so too did the figure of the Wicked Wizard. While the astronaut was the early model for space age Master Mechanics, it is reasonable to assume that an anti-astronaut would become the model for his nemesis; that is to say, as the heroic astronaut-mechanic was a character who, in the American popular imagination, strove to further American aims in the space race, conversely the wicked genius-wizard was that character—or sometimes idea—which sought to frustrate or pervert those aims. These two characterizations of scientists in the age of outer space exploration—which might be summarized as the good astronaut and the bad alien (and I mean alien in all its connotations, not just extraterrestrial)—would come into repeated confrontation; and each such confrontation can be read as a treatise about what makes American scientists good scientists, and what conditions must be met for them to turn bad.

These texts are all structured as a struggle for the selfsame "national survival" that was supposedly threatened by Sputnik and the loss of technological supremacy it represented; and typically their landscape is Kennedy's New Frontier of outer space. But it isn't always a one-eyed space monster that the astronaut must defeat in order to secure that goal. In fact, we will see that the astronaut's antagonists range from the simple and indifferent opposition of materiality (mechanical failure), through a series of appositions for Wicked Wizards (alien monsters, evil geniuses), to complex and immaterial ideologies (alien cultures, the supremacy of logic, the supremacy of machines), and culminate in the most forbidding opponent of all, the Unnatural. Before we begin to analyze the texts within these categories, we should establish just what the contest is about, i.e., the values for which the Good Scientist is fighting.

We can find key points of reference for these values in the rhetoric of the space race, particularly in the repeated assertion of America's primary goal: "the peaceful exploration of space" for the "benefit of all mankind." We can read this to mean that America did not wish to export either military hardware or methodologies to outer space; and, since exploration is typically the forerunner of resource exploitation, we can further assume that the economic benefits of this exploitation would be shared with all nations, regardless their ideology. Of course, in opposition to these public ideals was the private rhetoric of politicians like Vice President Lyndon Johnson, who earlier had warned that "world leadership" depended on "dramatic accomplishments in space." Such statements by Johnson and others offer two quite fascinating assumptions: that leadership of the world legitimately belonged to America and was America's to lose; and that such leadership was to be achieved by a kind of "space theater" through demonstrations of technological superiority that were dramatic, public, spectacular, and told a good story. In other words, our primacy among nations in space depended on the power not of our technology, but of our narratives.

Johnson had also warned that our supremacy in space was necessary to "prevent any other power from denying us the utilization of space in our interests"— which sounds like anything but a commitment to trans-national cooperation. In truth, the New Frontier was imagined as a territory to be fought over like any other. The exploration and subsequent exploitation of space to which such rhetoric tacitly referred was based on the idea of this New Frontier as a site of new production—in this case the production of American ideology, which could then be sold via these dramatic stories to the world. The exploration part of this vision was to be carried out by American astronauts, beginning with "seven patriotic God-fearing small-town Protestant family men," the Mercury 7. This simple description set the mold for all American space heroes to come: nationalists first and scientists second; rural and middle-class rather than urban and intellectual; and securely embedded in communities of family and mainstream religion. And they were engineers of "excellent health," free from physical handicaps or flaws.

We should also remember Kennedy's reaction to the first Soviet orbiting of a man in space, and his suggestion that the Soviets had achieved this feat through a "total mobilization of effort," meaning through a utilization of forced labor on a military scale. Our astronauts, rather than mere cogs in some vast quasi-military machine, were inheritors of the mantle of the Great Independent inventors, individual epitomes of Yankee ingenuity. The overall contrast being made here was between the (purportedly) free and individual and ideologically neutral "dedication" of American space explorers and the forced, mass, and ideologically driven "mobilization" of their Soviet counterparts. When all these rhetorical positionings are combined, what emerges is a remarkably consistent and pervasive image of the Good Astronaut and thus, by implication, the Bad Alien. Or Bad Aliens—for, as I said, there are a number of incarnations of the forces imagined as opposing the Good Astronaut.

The first and simplest such opponent can be found in what might be called the "reality astronaut" films—films which depicted this struggle as one of an individual explorer's ingenuity vs. the purely mechanical dangers of exploring any new and hostile environment; films, that is, that established the astronauts as first and foremost skilled mechanics. However, perhaps because the mundane hazards of space flight proved difficult to adapt to the dramatic requirements of the big screen, the first film in this category didn't appear until 1964, three years after Gagarin's orbital flight, and was entitled (with obvious reference to Defoe's classic novel) *Robinson Crusoe on Mars*.

In this film a lone astronaut, Christopher Draper (Paul Mantee), is marooned on Mars when his spacecraft crashes and his fellow astronaut is killed.[1] The first half of the film is remarkable in its attempt to stick to the science of the time, concentrating on the astronaut's determination and ingenuity as the key to his survival: rather than battling aliens, he must invent ways to eat, drink, and breath; only then is he free to explore his new environment. As a patriotic explorer, once he discovers a habitable cave, he immediately plants an American flag at its entrance. But "Kit" Draper is not merely ingenious, healthy, and patriotic—and, importantly, not overly or even particularly cerebral; he is also something of a missionary. In a vision of America as exploring space not just for the benefit of all mankind, but for all humanoid kind as well, Kit frees a space slave from his alien masters, teaches him English, then takes him back to Earth. While the second half of the film degenerates into the kind of "space western" that would be the sole theme of so many science fiction films before and after, there is a commitment to the science of plausibility in the first half that gives the astronaut figure here a certain weight as a credible representative of the American astronaut as inventor, liberator, teacher, and survivor. Until the disappointing introduction of the pirates-as-aliens, Kit's battles are essentially those we might expect any real-life astronaut to face—mechanical failures, alien environments—which require inventiveness and hard work, rather than space lasers, to resolve.

This theme of Good Astronaut vs. malfunctioning machine and hostile environment—a plot absent, that is, any overt human villain—was continued in such films as *Marooned* (1969, the three-man crew of an Apollo capsule are stranded in orbit); *Capricorn One* (1978, though here the astronauts do battle conspirators in their own government who wish to kill them after faking their Mars landing); *The Right Stuff* (1983, from Tom Wolfe's book), and most impressively in *Apollo 13* (1995). While the astronauts in these films may exhibit moments of weakness, fear, even cowardice, what is always emphasized is their determination, optimism, initiative, selflessness, and, most important, their mechanical inventiveness. Since these films do not, unlike those I am about to discuss, resort to simple alien combat for their dramatic energy, yet are not documentaries, they must find that drama somewhere else; and where they find it is in mechanical failure.[2]

The famous line from *Apollo 13*—"Houston, we have a problem"—is a singularly compact summary of what these films are about. The "problem" is always a technical one that can be solved only through the kind of dedicated cooperation—not obsessive total mobilization—that is supposedly the hallmark of American science. While sometimes that mechanical failure is imagined as the product of sabotage (the *Lost in Space* television series) or malevolent computers (*2001*, 1968), for the most part such hazards are treated as part and parcel of what it means to be a space explorer, a sign that they are involved in adventure, not routine jobs. "Problems" become, in these films, the dragons that the good astronaut must battle to firmly plant the American flag in the High Frontier. "Houston, we have a problem" is of course a call for help, a linking of the astronaut children with their mission control parents; but the tone of that call is as significant as its content, for it is delivered in the same calm, nononsense, professional, essentially emotionless fighter jock speak of Chuck Yeager or any of his contemporaries, describing anything from plummeting toward the ground to actually being on fire. Mere imminent death as represented by a failing machine does not warrant a display of emotion from a Good Astronaut.

For instance, in *Apollo 13* the only two outbursts of anger exhibited in the whole film by the main character, Jim Lovell (Tom Hanks) are, first, when he reacts to the grounding of a crewmate by calling it "flight surgeon bullshit," and second, when he rips off his biomedical sensors; both of which are echoes of the kind of disdain and hostility directed by the Mercury 7 astronauts at the scientific "reflector heads," "white smocks," and "eggheads" and all their irritating experiments. A machine is expected to fail, and getting angry at it when it does would be unreasonable; and the Good Astronaut is always reasonable (though not always logical; there are important differences between the two terms as applied to this character, which I will analyze presently). On the other hand, "dedicated young scientists," especially doctors, are assumed to be full of "bullshit," to be overly cautious, needlessly fussy, and tolerated only as long as is absolutely necessary. While the three astronauts in *Apollo 13* diligently follow the advice of the hundreds of engineers at mission control, the medical and psychological advice offered by the doctor is treated as useless, annoying, and eventually only valuable as the butt of a joke. Those two moments of emotional spontaneity aside, the film argues that, even when faced with slow suffocation in space, Good Astronauts are working calmly and professionally to solve the problem, to fix the machine; which is, after all, why they are there, as "redundant components."[3]

Such representations as these of the Good Astronaut without a Bad Alien to fight are, however, relatively rare. By far the vast majority of cultural texts that deal with this thematic do so as a confrontation between good and evil mapped onto the hero and his nemesis. Before we turn to those films where that nemesis is portrayed as the anti-astronaut mentioned earlier, I should discuss that category of films where evil is present in a much cruder form, typically as some alien monster.

While humankind's actual entry into outer space caused something of a delayed reaction in the creation of "realistic" astronaut films, there was no such lull in the war between astronauts and aliens. To mention only a few: *The Angry Red Planet* (1960) depicted astronauts on Mars battling everything from creeping fungus to giant bat-crab-spider monsters; the TV series *Lost in Space* (1965–1968), while it offered a repetitive parade of ever-more-silly alien creatures to be defeated, at least complicated the formula by making Dr. Smith, the stowaway physician, as monstrous as any alien; in *They Came from Beyond Space* (1967), fungus-like aliens land in England and take over the bodies of, naturally, the local scientists. In this category of film, the alien monsters really are little more than dragons, essentially no different from the gods-monsters of ancient Greek mythology, and their function is to grant dramatic energy to the otherwise largely unremarkable routines of getting from point A to point B and making a map of your journey; to establish the worthiness of the explorer to have made this journey; and to manifest the courage and resourcefulness required to turn *terra incognita* into *terra firma*.

An improvement of this theme are films like the more recent *Alien* series (1979, 1986, 1992, 1997), where the alien represents not just our fear of lions and tigers and bears, but also our anxieties about our own children as alien entities (as with the earlier *Village of the Damned*); the perversion of birth that generates the creatures; the focus on Ripley as a conflicted mother figure (present even in the name of the traitorous computer in the first film, which was called Mother) who seems above all else to resent the alien mother's fecundity; psychological fears of confinement, exposure, betrayal . . . the list is considerable.[4] Another expansion of this theme can be found in films where the dragons are presented not individually, but as an entire dragon culture that is bent on "denying us the utilization of space in our interests." Certainly this theme can be seen in *Battlestar Galactica* (1978–1980), *Buck Rogers in the 25th Century* (1979–1981), *Space: Above and Beyond* (1995), the *Star Trek* TV and film series, and various other texts where outer space is imagined as little more than an updated version of nineteenth-century Europe—or more properly the North Atlantic, where fleets from various worlds engage in broadsides with phasers rather than 12 pounders. And the heroes of these texts are typically stand-ins for Admiral Farragut, damning the photon torpedoes and demanding from Scotty full speed ahead.[5] As Good Astronauts working to extend the American empire, they symbolize above and beyond all else the patriotism of the proper American scientists.

The *Star Trek* series is particularly interesting as an example of this genre, as it contains a key to understanding the links between technology and politics as imagined in a future intergalactic America. The Earth of *Star Trek*'s universe is part of the United Federation of Planets, a sort of twenty-fourth-century United Nations. But the focus of all the various series and films has been Star Fleet, the organization responsible for both defending the Federation and exploring new territories ("to go where no man has gone before"—though after the first TV series, this line was altered to the more politically correct "where no human has gone before"). Thus Star Fleet represents a combination of the military and the scientific, and in some senses even the political functions of this Federation, a sort of idealized East India Trading Company, with all its power and none of its limitations. In fact, Star Fleet and the Federation it symbolizes are an idealized *American* Empire, but one where the fatal flaws of traditional empires have been eliminated.

This transcendence is apparently due to the crowning achievement of Federation science, the "transporter." The transporter (and all other devices based on its workings, such as food replicators) allows the conversion of matter to energy and back again; thus people can be converted to pure energy and transported to another location to be reassembled, and energy can also be converted into matter, for food or raw materials. The series makes clear that this technology has "liberated" Earth and the rest of the Federation from poverty, crime, war, hatred, etc., turning Earth particularly into a "paradise." Clearly the implication is that pre-paradise Earth owed much if not all of its poverty and similar troubles to the constraints of the matter/energy divide. As a result of this transcendence of materiality, the Federation has become a peaceful, democratic, benign alternative to the other available cultural systems: the Klingon Empire (which represents pre-Enlightenment glorification of violence and tribal culture), the Romulans (the "evil twins" of the completely cerebral and logical Vulcans, and thus a culture based on Byzantine conspiracies and deceit), the Ferengi (a parody of market-driven culture and one which, it has been suggested, embodies a certain anti-Semitism), and various other much less attractive alternatives (Cardasian Fascists, Borg Communists, Dominion Orientalists). In every comparison, the Federation is portrayed as the ideal, beneficent multicultural empire—but one that never uses the word, never imagines itself *as* an empire.[6] Thus the ideology of *Star Trek* implies that the "downside" of colonialism is inextricably linked to the material exigencies of production-consumption; and, once those exigencies are transcended, then what is left is a "purified" colonial practice in the best traditions of eighteenth- and nineteenth-century apologies for imperialism as charity such as the "White Man's Burden," with Americans-Humans as the model for cultures literally everywhere.

We can see at least part of the explanation for this belief in technology as the key to an interplanetary American empire in the rhetoric of the utopian literature of the late nineteenth century discussed in chapter 3, as well as the argument resident in Democracity and the totality of the American exhibits at the World's Fair of 1939 covered in chapter 4. It is a fundamental precept of much of that rhetoric, as well as the American ideology from which it springs, that individual work leads to personal salvation and perfection; and thus full employment would naturally lead to the salvation and perfection of the entire society, to utopia. The transporter technology, by eliminating the dark side of capitalism—scarcity—has thus purified work of any taint of exploitation, the dark side of colonialism.

We might ask, however, why those other space cultures, also in possession of this technology, have not undergone a similar purification and achieved their own utopias. An answer to this question may be that, while alien cultures may possess utopian technology, they lack the utopian *ideology* to complete their purification. Thus another part of an explanation for the utopian empire of the Federation resides in America's vision of itself as a missionary nation and a proselytizing culture with an ideology that, if sold properly—as Lyndon Johnson imagined it could be through space spectaculars—will *convert* the world to its ideals. The Federation is America as it imagines it could be: savior to not just the Earth but also the entire universe, if only we could get past the nasty material limitations of physical labor.

However, it is important to emphasize that this matter-energy conversion magic of the transporter is seen as utopian only in the context of *physical* labor and *material* goals; any suggestion that such technology might be linked directly to purely *intellectual* production—such as the Krell thought projection machine—is inevitably characterized in various episodes of *Star Trek* as leading to the corrupting influence of hubris and the delusion that one thus becomes "a god." Creating communal food, materials, or transportation from sheer energy is purifying work; creating the material embodiment of individual theories from such a machine is portrayed as damning self-glorification, and casts the transgressor into the category of Wicked Wizard.

To return to the theme of alien cultures, while texts such as *Star Trek* envision a multicultural universe, it is clear that American-Earthly culture is first among equals, and that to evidence too much sympathy for alien cultures outside the dynamics of this imagining of High Frontier imperialism is to place oneself on the wrong side of the Good Astronaut/Bad Alien borderline. One of the key components of the emerging Wicked Wizards of the space age is their un-American tolerance of and admiration for alien cultures. In my discussion of the film *The Thing* in chapter 6, I pointed out that one of the traits that marked Dr. Carrington as particularly traitorous was his admiration for the alien's biology and intellect, his preference for its "clean and unemotional" form of reproduction, and his evaluation of its culture as "superior in every way" to his own. If, in these films, America is a symbol for or microcosm of the world, then Carrington and bad scientists like him are traitors not just to their own country, but also to all humankind. The fascination—some would say veneration—that Wicked Wizards evidence for other-worldly cultures has been presented in ways more or less crudely in the intervening half century since *The Thing*; but it has never been far from one of the telling characteristics of Bad Alien scientists, and never more foregrounded than in two films released in the same year, 1996: *Independence Day* and *The Arrival*. I want to discuss these two films in some detail as the ideology resident in their treatments of multiculturalism—in the first film somewhat covertly, and in the second so overtly as to be offensive—is excellent example of how such films imagine Good American Patriotism vs. Bad Alien Multiculturalism, and how and why Wicked Wizards always wind up on the wrong side of that divide; why, that is, what might be considered perfectly legitimate scientific interest in extraterrestrials is in fact presented as fundamentally un-American.

The plot of *Independence Day* (or *ID4* as it became known) is simply stated: ugly aliens in big ships blow the hell out of New York and Washington until a resolute fighter jock president kicks their butts back to Pluto. *ID4* could be called *War of the Worlds* on steroids. The aliens want only one thing from us: that we die; so their threat is, like the Thing's, purely brutal. They don't attempt to seduce us with Edenic rhetoric or promises of technological largesse. The only intellectual threat in the entire film comes from—surprise—a scientist

(Brent Spiner), who is so enamored of their technology and physiology that he considers them clearly superior to his fellow humans (and of course pays for this misplaced envy with his life). While he is clearly the ideological descendant of Dr. Carrington, the traitorous role of this intellectual isn't as developed in *ID4* as it is in *The Thing*; but the presentation of what constitutes acceptable *American* multiculturalism is much more in evidence.

We might begin with the title of the film, which clearly makes reference to the beginning of America as a nation, and then connect this to the use throughout of certain architectural tropes of nationalism: England as Big Ben, India as Taj Mahal, France as Eiffel Tower. However, while other cultures can apparently be sufficiently symbolized by their monuments—monuments which are easily annihilated by the aliens—only America's culture is represented by both monuments *and* ideology, i.e., Independence; and, while the White House and the Golden Gate Bridge can be destroyed as easily as other buildings, our ideology cannot. Nor can our ingenuity and mechanical inventiveness, as of course it is the Americans who devise the computer virus scheme to disable the alien mothership. But more important to my argument here is the way in which what ought to be the supremely multicultural moment in the movie is in fact constructed so as to portray the multinational air armada which defeats the aliens as, above and beyond all else, American.

In this scene, thousands of fighter planes fill the sky with the national symbols of everyone from Britain to Iraq—which seems at first glance properly internationalist. Yet there is something sanitary about all this superficial ethnicity, something merely complementary to the resourceful American patriots—especially as it is the Americans who are giving all the orders. This scene in fact seems most reminiscent of the shots in British World War II films that show colonials of one nation or another coming to the call of their English masters in common cause against the Japanese. And the common cause here is, putatively, Independence. As the president says just prior to the climactic attack, from now on July 4th will be Independence Day "for the whole world."

But independence from what? The aliens don't want to master us; they just want us to disappear, so that they might strip the Earth of its natural resources and then move on. They are described as "intergalactic locusts," and one hardly imagines achieving independence from insects. Rather, I would argue that what we are to be made "independent" from are all the necessities of a truly multicultural world, where American ideology is just one competing ideology among many. It is clear that it is *American* ingenuity, *American* determination, *American* pluck, and sheer American chutzpah—all central components of American scientific practice—that achieve victory over the technologically superior aliens. The implication is that, once the tiny task of burying one billion dead is over, the

New World Order that will emerge from the ruins will be one headed by America; the further implication is that the evangelical patriotism of these Americans will do what 50 years of diplomacy and foreign aid haven't done, which is to finally convert all those foreigners to an essentially and eternally American *zeitgeist*.[7] In other words, the world of *ID4* is the world of American Empire, much as *Star Trek* is the universe of a similar empire: one which allows America to escape or outflank or render irrelevant the very demands and conflicts of multiculturalism which brought an end to the British and all other empires before it. It is an empire where we need no longer fear illegal immigrants—for one thing because most of them lie dead in the rubble of the major metropolises, but also because after this apocalypse all nations will be resurrected as cultural and ideological versions of America, and there will *be* no immigrants, illegal or otherwise.

Illegal immigrants are the explicit enemy of the other film in this category of anti-multicultural science fiction, *The Arrival*. A brief synopsis: a radio astronomer discovers an odd signal coming not from the sky—which, according to *The Thing*, we are supposed to be watching—but from Central America. Upon investigation, he discovers that the aliens are already among us, disguised as humans, and that they are using fake power plants to pump our atmosphere full of greenhouse gases, which is what they breathe. The aliens and their pollution factories are based in third world countries, and the one we see in Central America is staffed by aliens disguised as Mexicans; there is also a heavy implication that human Mexicans have been bribed to help them. Thus the aliens are explicitly identified with not only the contemporary American concern about illegal immigration, but also our fears about the loss of the South American rain forests and other eco-disasters—eco-disasters which our political rhetoric often constructs as the fault of sloppy third world industrial practices, or rampant third world greed, or simple third world incompetence.

Interestingly, the aliens in *The Arrival*, for all the technological mastery demonstrated by their pollution factories and machines capable of disguising them as human beings, have only one weapon, and it's not exactly what we'd call a weapon: it's a hand-grenade-size sphere, which when activated sucks up everything in a room, turning it into an empty shell. While its explicit purpose is to erase evidence, I believe we could argue its implicit logic is not unlike that of the city-buster beams of the aliens in *ID4*: to create empty space. Both weapons produce *Lebensraum*, space to be occupied. What could better represent the ultimate paranoia of those who fear that their traditions and sheer presence are being overwhelmed and subverted by strange foreign cultures, and that they themselves will eventually be forgotten, than a device which utterly annihilates all evidence of their existence?[8] In other words, fifty years after *The Thing*, Americans still construct their vision of patriotic scientists in opposition to untrustworthy internationalists who are all too ready to betray and erase American culture and traditions.[9]

We might also place in this category all those materials where aliens are treated as just another phenomenon to be covered up by the government: *My Favorite Martian* (1963–66), *The Invaders* (1967–1968), *Project U.F.O.* (1978–1979), *The Adventures of Buckaroo Bonzai Across the 8th Dimension* (1984), *V* (1984–1985), and of course *The X-Files* (1993–2002), *Roswell* (1999), *Contact* (1997), and *Men in Black* (1997, 2002). In all of these texts it is assumed that scientists consider the average human incapable of handling the knowledge that life exists elsewhere; they are modern versions of Dr. Morbius, exhibiting supreme arrogance toward anyone they consider intellectually inferior. Of course, much could be said of how this treatment, embedded as it is in inexplicably long-lived urban myths like Area 51 and Roswell, speaks to a resident paranoia deeply lodged in American culture—one that seems all too ready to believe that we are the envy of other nations, even other worlds, who require only the cooperation of untrustworthy elitists to rob us of our heritage and birthright.

In those few films where alien culture is treated sympathetically, such as *Close Encounters of the Third Kind* (1977), *E.T.: The Extra-Terrestrial* (1982), or *Alien Nation* (1988, and as a TV series 1989–1990), the scientists are again the villains, and are usually represented as unsympathetic, quasi-military masses obsessively focused on capturing and autopsying the well-intentioned aliens, while the role of intuitive hero is assigned to either blue-collar working types (*Close Encounters*), children (*E.T.*), or cops (*Alien Nation*). In fact, in many films the scientists themselves are portrayed as more alien than any extraterrestrial. In a litany of all the old nineteenth-century prejudices against science, they are quite often presented as cold, unemotional, and even sadistic observers of human suffering (*Barbarella*, 1967; *A Clockwork Orange*, 1971; *THX 1138*, 1971; *Soylent Green*, 1973; *Zardoz*, 1974; *12 Monkeys*, 1996; *Dark City*, 1998), vivisectionists willing to sacrifice their fellow humans to scientific research (*These Are the Damned*, 1963; *Charly*, 1968; *The Island of Dr. Moreau*, 1996; *Gattaca*, 1997), or perverted businessmen foisting unreliable technology on an unsuspecting populace for sheer profit (*Terminal Man*, 1974; *Total Recall*, 1990; *Jurassic Park*, 1993). In all such constructions, what drives these bad alien scientists is some totalizing theory that demands the reshaping—sometimes literally—of all humankind. And what defeats them is a down-to-earth, pragmatic, commonsensical, intuitive hero who is constitutionally incapable of surrendering his or her unique identity to the scientist's totalizing-transformative schemes.

As such schemes grew to a super scale, so, too, did the villainy of the Wicked Wizards who hatched them. When the Good Astronauts weren't fighting

explicit aliens, either individually or in entire cultures, or refusing to conform to
the programs of domestic-alien scientists, they were pitted against Earthly villains, or rather super-villains, which were the resident evil in dozens of spy films
and TV shows of the last fifty years.

Ask anyone who has seen a "spy thriller" made since the 1960s to describe the
villain of the film, and the description will undoubtedly go something like this:
imperious, tall, dark, and threatening, possibly dressed in a semi-military tunic,
he sits in some throne-like swivel chair dictating blackmail terms to world leaders via closed circuit television from his underground lair. Everything about his
manner exudes absolute confidence in his intellect, his schemes, his superiority.
And often he is stroking a cat. We can recognize in this character all the traits of
Hawthorne's megalomaniacs: aristocratic in manner and bearing with traces of
foreign origins, tastes, and accent; often marred by a physical deformity or handicap; lacking any of the traditionally familial domestic relationships (other than
the cat); and obsessed with proving radical theories that he believes could revolutionize the world. This depiction of modern megalomaniacal villainy became
so standard it was easily parodied in the *Austin Powers* trilogy, in the character of
Dr. Evil.

As much as the mad scientist became a stock figure in the popular literature
of the early nineteenth century, so, too, did this particular kind of bad scientist
become a stock figure not just in the spy films of the late twentieth century, but
also in television, magazines, cartoons, and even advertising. This figure goes by
several trade names—evil genius, super-villain, criminal mastermind—but whatever he (and it is almost always a he) is called, he is always a version of Dr. Evil.
This character has evolved in some ways since the fiction of the early 1800s:
rather than working in isolation, as had Victor Frankenstein, he is typically surrounded by minions of assistants and quasi-military armies; that is, while he is
still alienated he is no longer alone. And, just as his technological innovation has
expanded exponentially, so, too, has his hubris: his schemes have expanded in
scale, from relatively limited plots to alter this or that person, this or that community, to totalizing designs that imagine entire worlds remade in his own image. In the simplest treatment of totalizing theory as evil, we find the earliest
portrayals of this space age Wicked Wizard and the simplest analysis of his character: mad scientists are bad because the theory which motivates their actions
is one of total domination. It is those two aspects of their theoretical
commitment—its totalizing scale and its attainment through conquest rather
than conversion—that both mark these villains as Super Wicked Wizards and
typically relegate them to a one-dimensional treatment as characters. In materials of this category, the Wicked Wizards are little more than stereotypes, stock
figures used to fulfill a dramatic function, and the boundary between good and

bad science is assumed to be something like a "bright line" in legal philosophy, i.e., a distinct and clearly recognized border.

Perhaps the earliest example of Super Wicked Wizard as simple anti-astronaut is the character Dr. No in the first James Bond film, *Dr. No* (1962). While it might seem odd to suggest that this crippled and utterly cerebral figure is in any way related to the American idea of an astronaut, my point will become clearer as we examine his representation.

First of course we recognize in Dr. No all the tropes of Hawthorne's mad scientists: the foreign accent and appearance (Oriental), the lack of any domestic relationships, the cold arrogance, the complete concentration on intellect, and even the physical deformity. Dr. No's deformity is his hands, which are clumsy and apparently immovable metallic prostheses, a result of his early experiments with atomic energy. This handicap visually symbolizes, as it did for his nineteenth-century predecessors, his corruption of scientific dedication. Dr. No's goal is the frustration of the early American space shots, which he achieves by sending conflicting radio guidance signals to the rockets moments after they are launched, and which he performs through the unexplained use of an atomic reactor. As for his scientific credentials, Dr. No apparently possesses extremely broad technological knowledge, spanning the diverse fields of atomic energy, rocketry, computers, marine biology, medicine, electronic communications. . . . He is a maniac of all trades. He is also of course sadistic, arrogant, and cowardly. And, I repeat, foreign.

Though Dr. No's motivations are given a patina of explanation by his association with SPECTRE (Special Executive for Counter Intelligence, Terrorism, Revenge and Extortion—"The four great cornerstones," Dr. No offers, "of power"; and we might note the acronym's referencing of the world of mysticism and wizardry), his membership in a wider organization is essentially irrelevant to his function; he is there to test James Bond, who is the standard bearer for that most traditional of all traditional Western cultures, England. Of course America must be present as his target of opposition as England doesn't make a credible technological power against which to struggle; but the overall thematic of his anti-Western persona and goals is served by using England as America's policeman. As an example of a modernized Wicked Wizard he is of interest to us for several reasons: he moves the trope into the age of astronauts and outer space exploration; he derives nearly all his traits from the early Wicked Wizard models of Hawthorne et al.; and he sets the mold for nearly every Bond villain to follow.

The scale of Dr. No's totalizing scheme is what seems, for the hero, the main point of departure from science to insanity. As Bond says to Dr. No, "World domination. The same old dream. Our asylums are full of people who think they are Napoleon. Or God." Thus does Bond link this super-wizard to several tropes of the nineteenth-century mad scientists: their need to dominate, control, and remake the world; the source of their power, and their fatal flaw, the imagination which produces such "dreams"; the assumption that their obsession with the intellect is *prima facie* evidence of madness; and that the wicked-ness of this madness is rooted in their fundamental desire to place themselves in the role of God—reminiscent of Victor Frankenstein's driving desire to create a race of beings who would worship him as their creator.

That the intellect is the key both to the power of this class of super-villains and the root of their villainy is made clear by Dr. No himself, as when he explains SPECTRE to Bond he says that it is "headed by the greatest brains in the world." "Criminal brains," corrects Bond, to which Dr. No replies, "The criminal brain is always superior. It has to be." And when Bond turns down his offer to join SPECTRE, Dr. No dismisses him as a "stupid policeman." Dr. No even presents the sur-nationalism of this new breed of super-villains when he explains that he offered his services to first the East, then the West, and they both turned him down: "East, West, just points of the compass, each as stupid as the other." Thus these new Wicked Wizards also demonstrate the isolation of Hawthorne's villains, as they have no allegiance to any community other than the one they wish to create.

It is no coincidence that the arena for the confrontation between Dr. No and James Bond—outer space—would prove to be the arena for most such confrontations to follow, as the trope of outer space as the "high ground" for threatening weapons—the very vision which terrified America at the launch of Sputnik—is the engine of the admittedly limited plots of Bond and similar spy genre films of the next forty years. For instance, in *You Only Live Twice* (1967) the villain kidnaps American and Russian astronauts to spark a war between the superpowers; in *Diamonds Are Forever* (1971) the threat is a giant space laser; in *Moonraker* (1979) the entire Earth is to be cleansed of its current inhabitants by a manufactured plague, and repopulated by the genetically engineered acolytes of the Evil Genius floating out of danger in a giant space station; in *Golden Eye* (1995) the threat is a sort of giant space microwave oven, which is very similar to the orbiting "heat ray" mirror of *Die Another Day* (2002). Clearly these films utilize as well as represent American anxieties about the corruption of the High Frontier by scientists who, through greed or hubris or sheer malignancy, wish to frustrate America's "peaceful exploration of space for all mankind"; scientists who possess technological skill equal if not superior to that of a space-age Master Mechanic; scientists who pervert the New Frontier by infecting it with all the old world schemes of domination, aristocracy, enslavement, and of course hubris. These are super-villains in that they proffer

super theories, of world domination or world purification or world transformation. Of course all the basic aims of their plans—orbiting space research
stations, solar power, communications satellites, research into the effect of
outer space on biological processes—are goals of acceptable space science; it is
the *degree* of these schemes, not their kind, that renders them wicked.

Perhaps the most obvious example of this simplified and schematic treatment of Wicked Wizards in outer space is to be found in the *Star Wars* films
(the first of which appeared in 1977), in the character of Darth Vader. Certainly
the links between Vader and earlier mad scientists are clear enough: he is physically crippled, so much so that, as Obi-Wan Kenobi observes, he is "more machine than man"; he speaks with great arrogance (if also with great eloquence
and timbre, thanks to the voice of James Earl Jones); he has no domestic relationships, his only son, Luke, having been placed beyond his corrupting influence; and he dresses in black—*all* in black. Even the wizardry of Vader is
foregrounded: he literally can perform "magic" through his manipulation of the
"dark side" of the universal Force.

However, for all his blatant Wicked Wizardry, it might seem cheating to call
Vader a mad scientist, for nothing is said of his ever having possessed any scientific skill. Much is made, on the other hand, especially in the later films, of
his earliest and fondest skill, which was as a pilot of unparalleled ability. Darth
Vader is not in fact a scientist gone bad so much as a Master Mechanic gone
bad, a fighter jock in the tradition of the American astronauts who has been
corrupted by his arrogance and his anti-democratic theology (the presentation
of his beliefs and conversion are too crude to call an ideology) into a mere en-
forcer for the Emperor, a sort of outer space mercenary. In other words, Vader
represents the nightmarish inversion of everything the American astronauts
supposedly stood for. And what they stood for is represented in Vader's two
opposing characters, Han Solo and Luke Skywalker. Of course the latter conflict is a simple Oedipal dynamic of son supplanting father; but the former is a
battle of skill between the true fighter jock, Han, and his perverted counterpart, Darth. By the end of the series we discover that even Darth is redeemable,
but only via his familial connection to his son, marking him, however cruel and
powerful, as still slightly less evil than Dr. No.

Often the wickedness of these figures is enhanced by references in their
portrayal to well-established tropes of real ideological evil; and most often
such references are to Nazis, from their philosophies of *Übermensches* to their
dark, SS-style uniforms. Such treatments run the gamut from the serious—
such as *The Boys from Brazil* (1978), where Nazi scientists in South America
work to clone Adolf Hitler—to the parodic, such as *Dr. Strangelove, or How I
Learned to Stop Worrying and Love the Bomb* (1964), wonderfully and wildly

enacted by a wheelchair-bound Peter Sellers, complete with a disobedient arm that continually tries of its own volition to rise in the Nazi salute.[10] In fact, the trope has become so well established that it is a mainstay of B horror films and even video games, the Nazis pseudoscientific mania for the occult, experimentation on living subjects, and racial classification forming a readily useful bridge between any research we wish to label "unnatural" (a theme I will examine in chapter 12) and the presumption that the ultimate goal of such research is world domination. Even renderings of the future as a utopia imagine any totalizing reformation of traditional human communities as inevitably resulting in a sort of "soft" Nazism, as in *Logan's Run* (1976), when the freedom being fought for is the right to overpopulate, or *Zardoz* (1974), where the scientifically advanced and functionally immortal inhabitants of a future paradise wish only for the right to die. In each case, it is the *totalizing* scale of the reformation that makes it in fact a revolution, a departure from the slow and steady and *pragmatic* progress of the American scientific model; and thus such theories must be seen as inevitably resulting in the loss of individuality, initiative, free enterprise, and even selfhood that are the foundations of American culture.

One other aspect of character separates these new super-villains from their predecessors of the 1950s, and that is their irredeemability. They are portrayed as *utterly* evil, without a glimmer of salvageable humanity, the scale of their damnation matching the scale of their schemes; and typically not only must they be destroyed, but their entire communities along with them, as is Morbius's world in *Forbidden Planet*. But even Morbius, in all his megalomania and perverted paternalism, was "saved" at the end through confession and repentance, whereas it is inconceivable that super-villains such as Dr. No could ever be motivated to confess the error of their ways. Why, we might ask, is Dr. Evil so much *more* evil than Dr. Morbius?

Because Morbius at least offers the rationalization that his arrogance and isolation are in the ultimate service of humankind; that he is keeping the knowledge of the Krell from humankind for its own good. Were he a Dr. No, he would put that knowledge instead to the purpose of subjugating humankind. Thus, though Morbius, like his nineteenth-century predecessors, is alienated from the human community, he is still connected with that community through his relationship, however overprotective, with his daughter. What marks the super-villains as "beyond the pale" is their utter *lack* of familial relationships; or sometimes the presence of a perverted form of such relationships, as with a mistress, or an underage protégé upon whom they have sexual designs. This complete lack of humanity in the character of these new Wicked Wizards will become a standard component of their stereotype, and is another indicator of just how threatening and alienated from our traditions we consider their theories to be.

Of course, wizards have placed themselves outside the traditional boundaries of human communities as long as the trope has existed, their separation—intellectual and emotional as well as physical—enhancing their status and power. What is different about Wicked Wizards such as Dr. No is their ability to create entire communities of their own design. Perhaps it isn't surprising that, in the age of corporate big science like NASA, Bell Labs, and AT&T, the nemesis of good science must display a similar face—or rather facelessness. Dr. No and his descendants all possess enormous organizations employing (if that's the right word; one wonders, for instance, about the health benefits offered by SPECTRE) thousands of people, as if we no longer found a lone mad scientist in his ruined castle laboratory a credible threat. And such organizational materiality also brings credibility to the theory behind the evil. Just as there are no longer independent inventors, there are no longer independent Wicked Wizards; they have to be bulked out, as it were, with vast networks and entire miniature metropolises filled with attendants and servants and military and technicians—all of whom, curiously, seem perfectly willing to live in a total dictatorship and to suffer the murderous whims of their dictator. However, often even the individual villains are themselves as faceless and replaceable as their minions, sometimes simply being referred to by numbers (as in the Bond films). And their overheated rhetoric seems almost transparent, flimsy, mere threatening noise, when after all it is the organization behind them that gives them any real power; and that organization can, just like IBM, retire them at any moment. This facet of their persona and environment perhaps represents the fear with which we beheld the very organizational monsters we'd created, and displays an understanding on some level that the man in the gray flannel suit wasn't working for an ideal, but a paycheck; and if SPECTRE signed the check rather than IBM, there would still be, we worried, thousands ready to cash it.

How else to explain the faceless uniformed hordes of willing minions working in the secret underground lairs of mad villain after mad villain, all of them going about their jobs with detached efficiency, as if they were working in a hydroelectric plant or a Ford factory, all of them with clipboards and lab coats dutifully doing their job? How else to explain an evil philosophy that is apparently appealing to almost as many people as the corporate boosterism of GE or Raytheon? Perhaps this anxiety partly explains why the mad scientists would in some venues morph into mad businessmen (*Soylent Green, Aliens, Jurassic Park*), and how grand schemes for perfecting or purifying or eliminating the human race would morph into grand schemes for increasing the profit margin (*Robocop, Outland, Westworld*).

Two things we can learn from this thematic: these Wicked Wizards build their own communities because they cannot live with other people, only above them; and what drives them to this extreme of practice is the extremity of their theories. With the ever-advancing frontiers of science in the late twentieth century, our anxieties about that science expanded as well, until we could imagine its only possible outcome as the eradication of everything it means to be within and of a "natural" human community. These Wizards' theories are beyond threatening; their theories and by extensions they themselves are *unnatural*, and thus the producers of unnatural practices.

Which brings us to those texts where the evil contested by the Good Astronaut is the supremacy of logic. I see this as a necessary precursor to a more focused discussion of the unnatural because, for one thing, logic is often treated in cultural texts about science as something faintly unnatural itself; as a mode of thinking and behaving which, if not tightly contained, threatens to spill over into the unnatural; but also because the characters which represent the dangers of too much logic can be seen to gradually morph over time from largely natural to fundamentally unnatural entities. However, as the theme of the "unnatural" connects with so many of the arguments of this book, and because it requires a fairly extensive linguistic analysis, I will save my deconstruction of that term and its cultural consequences for the final chapter.

To return to that villain, logic: typically those texts which deal with the astronaut battling the supremacy of logic—what might be crudely summarized as the battle between emotion and logic—use one of two modes as the focus for the conflict: either the character of an alien or robot or android that struggles with the existential dilemmas of using logic as a guiding principle when dealing with human beings who seem primarily motivated by emotion; or the deployment of some super computer whose intelligence is entirely ruled by logic, absent any emotional components, thus rendering it an intelligence devoid of compassion, mercy, or even (importantly) common sense. In both modes, such battles suggest that we have a deep need to differentiate the human ingenuity of the Good Astronaut from the cold logic of the Bad Alien.

The argument of these confrontations appears to be that ingenuity—mechanical solutions to the threats faced by Master Mechanics, whether those threats come from malfunctioning machines or too-efficiently functioning androids—arrives in flashes of inspiration, which is represented as an intuitive tinkering together of "kluges," rather than as a systematic chain of reasoning based on theory and reflection. According to this argument, emotions are what keep Master Mechanics humble and prevent them from overvaluing their expertise and knowledge and thus turning into wicked super-villains. When there are robots present, they are good to the extent they wish to experience emotions and thus become more human, and bad to the extent they consider emotions as a flaw to be eradicated.

Certainly one of the most recognizable examples of such a character is Mr. Spock (significantly not *Dr.* Spock) from the first *Star Trek* TV series. As an alien from the planet Vulcan, he supposedly makes decisions based entirely on logic, the Vulcans having banished emotions from their psychological makeup centuries before. However, Mr. Spock is also half-human, so many episodes were based on his struggle to keep his human emotions repressed under the strict precepts of Vulcan logic, and yet allow himself to possess and exhibit a sufficient emotional substratum (humor, integrity, loyalty) to work with humans, as well as to set himself on the right side of the good emotional astronaut vs. bad logical alien divide—especially as he is the science officer of the Enterprise, and therefore dangerously close to crossing that divide. In the second *Star Trek* TV series, *The Next Generation*, the character Data—who, especially given the title of the series, could be considered Son of Spock—is an android which cannot experience emotions, yet desires such experience above and beyond all else, which of course renders his superior knowledge and physical strength safely contained within this desire. Such figures are an essential component of much modern science fiction dating at least as far back as the female robot Maria in Fritz Lang's classic *Metropolis* (1927). However, of all the many materials dealing with this thematic of the "natural" supremacy of human emotion over "unnatural" robot logic, one of the most useful is Steven Spielberg's film *Artificial Intelligence: A.I.* (2001). I will analyze this film in some detail as it presents in a particularly clear fashion the unexamined assumptions and contradictions fundamental to the whole human emotions vs. robot logic dynamic.

The thematic heart of the film is the tragic relationship between a little boy and his mother—wherein the little boy is a robot. The marketing of *A.I.* summarizes this dilemma as follows: "His love is real. But he is not." In other words, the conflict here is conceptualized not as one of emotion vs. logic, but as the real vs. the unreal, a thematic central to the film as well as the story upon which it based, Brian Aldiss's "Supertoys Last All Summer Long." In the film adaptation, a future Earth has suffered the various effects of global climate change: much of New York and other coastal cities are flooded, and much of the population has found itself mysteriously infertile. A company manufacturing robots, Cybertronics, headed by the (apparently) deeply compassionate scientist Prof. Hobby, decides to produce robot children for such parents, robot children who can be programmed to "love" their parents unconditionally and forever.

Aldiss's original story focused on the themes of immortality and irreversible perfection, as is made clear not only by the title, but also from the first sentence: "In Mrs. Swinton's garden, it was always summer." It soon becomes clear that, in the story's aesthetics, things that "last all summer," or in essence forever, are fundamentally inhuman, and therefore incapable of either eliciting or experiencing human emotions, such as love. That which is superficially perfect is substantially alienating and artificial: "She stood alone on her impeccable plastic gravel path." Thus people have a fundamental inability to feel the same sort of love for artificiality that they do for reality: "She had tried to love him. . . . She remained alone. An overcrowded world is the ideal place in which to be lonely." The suggestion here, more fully developed later, is that we feel real love for the individual, the unique, the rare, the unrepeated; and that, since the artificial can be mass produced, whatever attraction for or attachment to it we feel, that feeling isn't "real" love. Next we are introduced to David, the robot boy, who is talking with his favorite toy, Teddy, a robot Teddy bear, or supertoy:

> David was staring out of the window. "Teddy, you know what I was thinking? How do you tell what are real things from what aren't real things?"
> The bear shuffled its alternatives. "Real things are good."
> David started to draw a jumbo jet on the back of his letter. "You and I are real, Teddy, aren't we?"
> The bear's eyes regarded the boy unflinchingly. "You and I are real, David."
> It specialized in comfort.[11]

The driving engine of the film version of Aldiss's story is David's desire to become a "real" boy—a typical robot's dilemma represented in different ways both in Mr. Spock's struggle to repress emotions that would make him *too* real a human, and in Data's defining desire for emotions that would make him *more* real as a human. Clearly all three characters derive their existential dilemma from the character of Pinocchio, the wooden toy that desperately desires above all else to become a real boy. However, David's reality becomes an issue for him only after the mother programs him to love her, unconditionally and, more important, immortally; for reasons that are never fully explained, once the robot child is thus programmed it cannot be unprogrammed; its love cannot change; it cannot, that is, either grow or diminish. This axiom of the film thus explicitly contradicts its marketing tagline, as such a love isn't what in traditional human communities would be called "real." It is more accurate to say that the mother becomes an object of fetishism for the boy, and his unwavering attachment something more akin to obsession than love. And the other half of the tagline—"But he is not"—is also contradicted by the film, as, after all, David *is* real: he has existence, he is materially present, and he is capable of thinking, acting, and learning (in all aspects, that is, other than his programmed attachment to his mother). In other words, if the tagline were true to the film, it would read, "He is real. But his love is not." But this is not the only contradiction of the film's ideology.

The robot boy loves the mother only because she is the one who speaks the programmed words to him. There is nothing in her individuality, in her uniqueness, that has sparked this attachment; anyone who possesses the specific formula would receive the robot's same absolute devotion. Given this conditional status of David's love, the mother may be seen as the ultimate idealized other: the only being in the world who can speak the words that we long to hear. But of course *anyone* can speak these words to the robot; it is the incantation that is idealized, not the speaker. But that incantation is absolutely binding upon the robot, an unbreakable law. Again, emotions that cannot grow or diminish, that cannot adapt to changing circumstances are not what we would consider "real" emotions. The robot boy's love is figured as a kind of "logical" love: once he is programmed to an attachment, that attachment is necessary to his survival, so it is only "logical" that he do whatever is necessary to retain that attachment, to stay with the mother. This obviously isn't what we mean by real love; but is it even what we mean by real logic? I'll answer that question in a moment.

Once the mother's real-biological child awakens from a coma, she decides that David cannot continue to be part of their household. The programmed love of David is seen as a threat to her "real" love for her biological son; that which is born of biology and all its vagaries—its ability to change—is threatened by mechanical constancy, by virtual (superficial) perfection. But the mother cannot bear to return David to Cybertronics because she knows he will be destroyed, as he cannot be reprogrammed. The mother is human enough to conceive of David as a sentient entity that should not be callously discarded, but inhuman enough to reject the robot she has programmed to unconditionally love her. Thus, in the most wrenching scene of the film, she abandons him in the woods, driving away as he runs after her car crying out, "Mommy! Mommy!"

At this point David's programmed love for her is worse than superfluous, and the rest of the film becomes a quest narrative, with David searching for some version of the Blue Fairy—as in the Pinocchio fairy tale which she read to him—that can make him a "real" boy, as he assumes that his unreality is what caused his mother to abandon him. However, since reality in the film is defined as that which is capable of change and, most important, mortal, in order for David to fulfill these requirements he would have to become something other than what he is. His quest is by definition unfulfillable, and thus we would expect the film to trace the arc of a tragedy. Which, for the first half, it does.

However, one of the most interesting aspects of *A.I.* is its "schizophrenic" developmental history. The film was originally begun as a project by Stanley Kubrick, who had finished only the first half of the screenplay when he died; Steven Spielberg then completed the screenplay and produced and directed the film. While the first half of the film conforms to Kubrick's vision—a vision that was, as in his other films, dark, even sardonic, and from all the evidence fully aware of the fundamental impossibility of David's desire—the second half, Spielberg's half, is, as in Spielberg's other films, sentimental and melodramatic, and works to confound and outflank this seemingly unsolvable conundrum.

This disparity becomes most evident at the moment that ought to have been the ending of the film. David's quest takes him to Cybertronics headquarters, where he is confronted by endless ranks of identical Davids waiting for sale and programming: the material proof of his immortality and repeatability, and thus of his status as an "unreal" boy. He explodes in violence, destroying one of the other David robot boys, all the while screaming, "I'm David! I'm unique! I'm special!" Then, in a stolen police submersible helicopter, he travels to the bottom of New York harbor, where he discovers the ruins of the Coney Island amusement park, and in the Fairy Tale section, a statue of the Blue Fairy. He sits in the copter, Teddy beside him, praying to this frozen symbol for a magical transformation into a real boy; a wish which cannot, of course, be granted. And if the film had stayed true to Kubrick's vision, this is where it would end. But in a sweeping *deus ex machina*, Spielberg then returns to the scene, centuries later, with the Earth layered in ice. Super-robot aliens disinter David and grant his wish to recreate his mother, for just one day; but she herself is transformed into his idealization of her, as for that day she shows him perfect, unconditional love. Then she dies and he, apparently, is mercifully switched off by the aliens.

This rescue and granting of David's obsessive and impossible wish is of course fairly unconvincing; and that is my point. By the definition of real vs. unreal the film offers—unique biological experience versus replicated electronic programming—David can never be real. The Kubrickean acceptance of this impossibility is made unmistakably evident by what ought to be the ending of the film, with David in stasis beneath a frozen ocean, staring forever at the statue of the Blue Fairy. If he is committed to accepting existence only on unattainable terms—if, that is, he wishes to live a lie—then he is forever sentenced to the purgatory of inaction, perpetually trapped between the virtual and actual worlds. But this is an ending Spielberg can neither appreciate nor tolerate, and so a magic formula is introduced, and the unreal "perfect" ending is given priority over the real-if-distressing message of the rest of the film.

Spielberg's misunderstanding of Kubrick's narrative is made clear by his use of the Pinocchio myth. Once it enters the film, it drives the rest of the narrative, and all the Disney cuteness of Pinocchio is put to work to humanize David and his single-minded drive to become real. What the film seems to forget is that the Pinocchio myth is only introduced because David's sadistic brother,

Martin, asks the mother to read it to them in order to torture David with his artificiality. Pinocchio provides an identity for David; but it is an identity based in one of the most sadistic scenes in the film, and thus his devotion to the myth naturally becomes the flip side of sadism, which is masochism. By the definition of "real" set forth in the film—flesh and blood and mortal—David *cannot* be real; it is sheer delusion for him to believe he can. Thus David's self-destructive commitment to the fairy tale of transformation is a kind of masochism that the Spielbergean feel-good ending entirely contradicts.

In fact, the more consistent and cold truth of the film is revealed in its opening scene, when Prof. Hobby responds to a question about whether or not humans have a responsibility to return the love that they program the robots to feel. "We build them to love us," he says—which implies a definition of love that is entirely one-sided, which again is hardly "real" love. Adoration without the requirement for or expectation of any feelings whatsoever in return is closer to worship than love. The disconnect between what David's love "really" is and what it is called nicely represents the disconnect between the two halves of the film: while the first boldly presents the contradictions resident in our conceptions of categories like real and unreal, love and obsession, emotions and logic, the second half eschews such complicated examinations and instead accepts without question the cultural assumptions about these terms and their supposedly stable definitions.[12]

What seems to be the fundamental difference between humans and robots, both in this film and most similar materials (and as is suggested by the super-robots that rescue David), is that humans have emotions and robots have data. If robots *cannot* experience emotions, it must be because data and emotions are incompatible. Such for instance is the argument in Kubrick's other foray into science fiction, *2001*, wherein the supercomputer HAL goes mad because he cannot resolve the contradictions inherent in obeying both his programming to provide completely accurate data to the human crew, and his orders to lie to that same crew. Another treatment of supremely logical supercomputer intelligence as supposedly inherently malevolent is presented in an earlier and largely overlooked film, *Colossus: The Forbin Project* (1970). In this film—which seems in many ways a precursor to the idea of Skynet in *Terminator* or the machine culture of *The Matrix*—a supercomputer "acquires" intelligence (or at least the capacity to arrive at and act upon decisions independently) and immediately decides that humans, because of their emotions, cannot be allowed to rule themselves—so naturally it takes over the world. It is nearly always assumed in such films that the supremacy of logic inevitably leads to a belief in one's infallibility, as well as a thirst for world domination. (Of course no such assumption is made for the supremacy of emotion.) It is also assumed by these films that humans possess and act on data, and yet they are capable of lying without resorting to mass homicide. In other words, these films suggest that there is something about emotions that turns knowledge into wisdom; and without such a catalyst, mere data sorted by pure logic are artificial: unchanging, and thus unreal. Thus the imagined divide between humans and robots is between emotions that allow for an adaptive use of knowledge and logic that treats true and false as rigid, unchanging categories: the first leads to commonsense solutions to problems, the second only to logical solutions, which often are at odds with "reality." While it is logical—that is, according to a definition of logic resident in this and other films of the genre—for a robot to wish to become human, it is impractical if not impossible; logic contradicts reality. Humans understand this wish for the unattainable as an aspect of desire, while robots do not. Thus emotions are represented as fundamentally capable of sustaining contradictions, while logic is, supposedly, rendered "frozen" when faced with such contradiction.

We see this formula for the emotion/logic opposition played out in countless cultural texts about the dangers and weaknesses of robot logic. To name only a few: *The Colossus of New York* (1958), *Alphaville* (1965), *2001* (1968), *Star Trek* (1966–1969), *Colossus: The Forbin Project* (1970), *Westworld* (1973), *The Questor Tapes* (1974), *Alien* (1979), *Blade Runner* (1982), *Android* (1982), *Runaway* (1984), *Terminator* (1984), *Short Circuit* (1986), *Robocop* (1987), *I, Robot* (2004) . . . the list could go on at great length. And the plethora of texts dealing with this theme is some indication of just how great is our anxiety about the science of cybernetics, and the cyberneticists who work to replicate and, perhaps, surpass that which makes us most human: our intelligence.

Yet for all the range of plots and circumstances that deal with this subject, the superficiality of their treatment is remarkable. Often in these stories what finally defeats the robot villains is the hero's use of some simple contradictory statement that cannot, supposedly, be resolved by the supremacy of logic. One such example is an episode of *Star Trek* wherein Captain Kirk (the quintessential and overly emotional fighter jock Master Mechanic) says to one female robot, "I love you," but to another exact duplicate female robot, "I hate you." The robot leader is thrown into a quandary: "But they are identical! That is illogical!" This causes Spock—the most unlikely of poets—to begin reciting "nonsense" poetry: "Logic is a beautiful flower . . . that smells bad!" Attempting to resolve the contradictions in such statements, the robot leader is caught in an eternal loop and eventually blows a fuse.[13]

Time and again when confronted with the superior strength and knowledge of some robot enemy, Master Mechanics defeat not the machine so much as the machine's ideology by forcing the logic-bound robot to attempt to process information which is fundamentally irreducible to true/false resolutions. Thus the ultimate superiority of human intelligence is asserted, and that superiority is figured as based on our emotions and their theorized ability to accept contradictory assertions—something that violates the most basic tenet of Aristotlean logic.

However, there is a fundamental flaw in this schema. While it is assumed that whatever form of emotions robots experience cannot be "real," it is also assumed that their logic *is* real—that, though they cannot replicate our emotional thinking, they can replicate our logical thinking. If this were true, then humans would be capable of neatly separating our emotional from our logical thoughts; we would all be Mr. Spocks. In fact, what we most often mean by calling something logical is that it is commonsensical, as in: it is only logical to cross the street when the traffic light is red. In other words, typically what we mean by logic is an adherence to "commonsense" rules of behavior that everyone "just knows" are the right thing to do. But in fact all of these robot villains aren't asserting the primacy or suffering the weaknesses of logic at all. Rather, I would argue that these robots aren't being too logical, they're being too *literal*—and what really confounds these robot simpletons are the basic self-contradictory dynamics of language itself.

Words, as literary critics since the poststructuralists have argued, are not the objects to which they refer. The word is not the thing (or in the current version, the map is not the terrain). Thus words are not subject to the exigencies of reality, if by reality we mean material existence. All language is metaphorical, achieving meaning through allegorical implication and contextual connotation, not through precise denotation.[14] The "logic" half of the emotion/logic dichotomy in these texts isn't really logic at all, but literality—and literal language is the "opposite" of metaphorical language. Thus the actual argument of these films might be stated as: Robots are simply too literal to survive the dynamics of human language. Representing robot Wicked Wizards as overly literal is to suggest they are insufficiently metaphorical; they have no poetry in their souls, if we see poetry as that human practice of language which most clearly achieves meaning through metaphor and contradiction, as in the famous line from Walt Whitman's "Song of Myself": "Do I contradict myself? Very well then I contradict myself."[15]

Put another way, we seem to believe that scientific language is itself purely logical and without poetry—incapable of, in fact constitutionally antagonistic toward poetry. Of course what this figuring of scientific language overlooks is that mathematics *is* a language, like any other, that, at some level, it must be based on the same metaphorical associations as any other language. The fact that we assert mathematical formulas are incapable of representing contradictions doesn't mean they are; it just means we define them that way, that they fulfill that function in our overall system of language. Formulas represent truth and literality—but they only *represent* truth and literality; mathematical equations are not those "things," any more than any other word is any other thing.

However, apparently we need to believe they are. Thus, by constructing these endless confrontations between the adaptive strengths of emotion and the rigid frailties of logic, we site all our anxieties about the weaknesses of our imperfect, self-contradictory, metaphorical linguistic representation of the universe along the fault line of that split. In other words, we fear that there *is* some fundamental weakness to a language that doesn't have to be true or false, right or wrong, so we defeat that fear by "exposing" the weakness of language which *must* be true or false, right or wrong; and thus we reassure ourselves that what might appear as the flaw in our language is really its strength. And, since language is the way we represent our identities, this is to reassure ourselves that what appears as a flaw in our identities is really *our* greatest strength. Simply put, we are reassuring ourselves that we are fundamentally superior to "perfect" beings like robots, even as we subconsciously fear we are not.

Quite often in these texts this dynamic is projected onto entire cultures. Time and again some alien race will confess that they marvel at the human species because we have emotions and they do not, that our emotions are what make us unique among all the races of the universe. The anthropomorphism in this representation is obvious enough; what is perhaps more subtle is to be able to see it not as a simple egotistical centering of humans in the universe, but rather as an attempt to fight off the fear that we are *not* in fact special, that we are merely a part of the cosmos rather than the point of the cosmos. This fear, too, is represented in the inevitable homogeneity of such alien entities, whether they are robots identically run off an assembly line, or aliens which all look pretty much the same. Unindividuated masses inherently threaten an American ideology of individual uniqueness. The most terrifying aspect of the alien Borg as imagined in the later *Star Trek* series is their lack of individuation; that, and the "infection" of their organic bodies by inorganic prostheses. Which brings us to a discussion of those Bad Aliens who represent a mixture of the organic and the machine, or cyborgs.

One would think that the ideal Master Mechanic would be a mechanic merged with his machine, a figure that would supposedly possess all the advantages of both an emotionally ingenious human and a logically (or literally) efficient robot. And there are representations of cyborgs that meet this expectation, such as the TV series *The Six Million Dollar Man* (1974–1978, where, one should note, the man-turned-cyborg was originally an astronaut), or its "feminist" counterpart, *The Bionic Woman* (1976–1977), or even the *Robocop* series (1987, 1990). But in fact such treatments are relatively rare. In the majority of texts dealing with this subject, cyborgs occupy the darkest end of the Bad Alien spectrum, and most popular images in American culture repeatedly portray the dangers of such a mingling. Certainly the *Terminator* series is one such example, but one of the most telling is to be found in the supremely sinister figure of the Borg, from the *Star Trek* series.

The Borg are creatures which were once fully organic beings who have been turned into half-machines, half-humanoids by the injection of nanotechnology into their bodies. As previously mentioned, the culture of the Borg seems most closely aligned with Communism, as there are no individuals in their society— they have designations rather than names, such as "seven of nine"; each component of the Borg society fulfills a particular function, and all of them work in concert under the direction of a sort of Borg Queen. Thus they might be more properly characterized as Communist insects. Theirs is also a culture of "assimilation," meaning that rather than annihilating competing cultures, they "convert" them to Borg and thus acquire their technological expertise. The Borg have but one cultural goal, and that is to achieve "perfection." In the trope of the Borg (obviously a shorthand for cyborg) we find represented many of our anxieties about technology, some of which have been with us since the Industrial Revolution. Certainly chief among those is the fear that machines will control us rather than we them, as is famously represented in the image of Charles Chaplin trapped in the cogs of some vast machine in the film *Modern Times*. But cyborgs generally and the Borg specifically go beyond that basic fear; they represent the actual *invasion* of the organic by the inorganic and the subsequent supremacy of the machine *over* the body.

One argument we can discern in this anxiety is the idea that, though the Master Mechanic may derive his heroic status from his ability to use technology effectively, it is vitally important that he use it, rather than it him—that the machine is something he can put aside when its function is complete or unnecessary. We demand an utter and reliable separation between body and machine, much as we presume there is a separation between emotion and logic. Since it is assumed that emotions are the realm of the organic and logic the realm of the mechanical, then we can begin to discern what we find so threatening in an entity that could somehow transcend this separation. Put another way, perhaps we imagine logic as a kind of technology, and, as with the mechanic's machine, we demand the capacity to set it aside when it isn't required, and fear that its overuse would result in its "contamination" of our otherwise organic thinking.

As an alternative to this view, literary critic Donna Haraway, in a famous essay titled "A Cyborg Manifesto," suggests that in fact cyborgs are an appropriate symbol for humans in the age of ubiquitous computer technology: "By the late twentieth century, our time, a mythic time, we are all chimeras, theorized and fabricated hybrids of machine and organism; in short, we are cyborgs. This cyborg is our ontology; it gives us our politics."[16] For Haraway, cyborgs represent the "assimilation" of digital-electronic technology and thinking into every aspect of late twentieth-century life, where our human bodies serve as a kind of nexus for multiple modes of existence—an adaptation to postmodern life Haraway views as useful, perhaps inevitable. In another positive interpretation of cyborgs, Melanie Brown suggests these "post-human hybrids" are the very essence of the American astronauts:

> NASA's astronauts, cyborgs completely dependent upon their life-sustaining space suits and space craft, are making this transformation [to the post-human] . . . In many ways NASA has succeeded in breaking down some of the binaries addressed by Haraway; certainly, the technology/human boundary has been crossed, resulting in our human exploration of space more accurately being described as cyborg exploration.[17]

Brown's use of the term "posthuman" refers to a book by Katherine Hayles, wherein Hayles argues that space and other modern, digital technology have transformed Homo sapiens into some new order of existence, even though she emphasizes that this posthuman existence is not necessarily that of the traditional cyborg:

> It is important to recognize that the construction of the posthuman does not require the subject to be a literal cyborg. Whether or not interventions have been made on the body, new models of subjectivity emerging from such fields as cognitive science and artificial life imply that even a biologically unaltered Homo sapiens counts as posthuman. The defining characteristics involve the construction of subjectivity, not the presence of nonbiological components.[18]

However, there are problems with both conceptions, Brown's of cyborgian astronauts and Hayles's of posthuman identities. Brown's characterization of the astronauts as cyborgs depends heavily on seeing their spacesuits as prostheses; but the use of technology to aid exploration is as old as sextants and maps, diving suits and mountain climbing equipment, pressure suits and airplanes. Dependency on technology does not in and of itself create a cyborg, as Hayles rightly observes. However, I believe Hayles is wrong in suggesting that either the degree to which or the mode in which astronauts use technology somehow alters their basic identity into something beyond traditional human beings, into either cyborgs or "posthumans." Changes in our sense of who we are as individuals and as a human community did not begin with the Space Age, or even with the Industrial Age. I'm certain to an Athenian, Renaissance man would look pretty posthuman. Perhaps this is to over-simplify the arguments Brown and Hayles wish to make; however, both their arguments do seem to assume that it is the *scale* of the astronauts' or even the twenty-first-century civilians' use of technology that constructs this supposedly new subjectivity: that technology suffuses the astronaut's world, if not the entire world of the early twenty-first century, to an extent unprecedented in human development, thus creating an environment where to be a technologically dependent human means something fundamentally different from what it ever meant in the past.

But this is a reaction we've encountered before—in, for instance, *Forbidden Planet*, where the gargantuan size of the Krell machines was what made them essentially in- (or perhaps post-) human. And this is a difference of *degree*, not kind. In fact, depending on one's definition of technology, human society has been similarly dependent on, even intertwined with technology since the invention of fire. I would suggest Brown's and Hayles's reactions are consistent with the anxiety represented in so many of the cultural texts we've examined, dating all the way back to the early eighteenth century, an anxiety that technology is inevitably and in some mysterious, sinister, and inexplicable way leading us away from our traditional humanity and toward some "posthuman" culture of the supremacy of machines. If, as I've argued throughout this book, Americans are particularly fascinated by, bordering on worshipful of machines, then American culture would be expected to express (or repress) a concomitantly strong fear of one day finding itself dominated by them, of becoming, willingly or unwillingly, posthuman—or cyborgs.

What, then, are cyborgs? Where do we draw the line? After all, we don't consider someone with a mechanical heart to be a cyborg; or someone who wears glasses, or has a pacemaker or a plastic heart valve or a cochlear implant. Rather, it seems that this line is crossed at the point where the inorganic dominates the organic, when the machine controls the man. And of course that fear can be traced back to the Industrial Revolution, if not earlier, and is visible in all the texts that represent a society controlled by and run for machines rather than people. Such is the fear represented in the *Terminator* series of films, as well as the more recent *Matrix* trilogy. In a completely material world, the materially superior cyborg would indeed seem to be at an advantage. How then can we imperfect organic entities compete?

By deploying the one aspect of our being that is putatively unavailable to the machine: our emotions; or, put another way, our belief in the immaterial; or, put yet another way, our belief in the spiritual. In other words, perhaps the root of our fears about robots and cyborgs arises from an unconscious concern that our spirituality, our immanence, our *immaterial* selves are in fact quite fragile—inaccessible to verification and therefore threatened by the cold logic and colder circuits of machines which operate quite happily and efficiently in a universe of absolute truth and falsehood. Since this fear is so fundamental to who we are and how we function, we deploy the most damning term we can think of to demonize and ostracize such creatures from the human community. We call them Unnatural.

As mentioned earlier, I am reserving a linguistic deconstruction of the term "unnatural" for the final chapter. But here I will offer an example of how the logic—or illogic—of the term is on display in a particularly popular series of films dealing with the issue of what is natural vs. unnatural biological reproduction: the *Jurassic Park* series, based on the novels by Michael Crichton.

In a PBS special about the possibility of cloning dinosaurs à la Jurassic Park, Steven Spielberg (the director of the first film) reveals that he felt his film version of Crichton's novel had been a success because "There's such a reality to it."[19] Later, one of the scientists interviewed admits that the idea of resurrecting dinosaurs is so imaginatively compelling because every paleontologist "wants to see the real thing." In fact, throughout the PBS documentary, as well as in analyses of the film and its science, the criteria used to evaluate all possible schemes for cloning dinosaurs is always framed as a question: How "real" would the resulting dinosaurs be?[20]

The most scientifically credible method discussed involves injecting dinosaur DNA into bird eggs with the hope that several generations later the birds would become "dinosaur like"; yet every one of the scientists interviewed evinces a clear lack of enthusiasm for this method because, as one of the paleontologists puts it, "of course, it wouldn't be a real dinosaur"—meaning, we can only conclude, that only a dinosaur born of dinosaur parents can be a "real" dinosaur (much as, in the reaction to Frankenstein, it is assumed that only a human born in the traditional way from human parents can be a "natural" human). The program ends with two statements, one from *Jurassic Park*'s author, and the other from actor Jeff Goldblum, who plays scientist Ian Malcolm in the film. First Crichton informs us that *Jurassic Park* is, above and beyond all else, a "cautionary tale about the hazards of genetic engineering"; and Goldblum then ends the program by expanding on Crichton's warning and advising us that we are "better off marveling at the past rather than tampering with the future." Of course, both of these statements are uncannily reminiscent of the admonition from the *Frankenstein* playbill quoted in chapter 2: "The striking moral exhibited in this story, is the fatal consequence of that presumption which attempts to penetrate, beyond prescribed depths, into the mysteries of nature." In fact, I would argue that the PBS program very tidily summarizes the central ideology of the *Jurassic Park* films, as well as much of the cultural debate about cloning, which seems to be an obsession with the difference between natural and unnatural breeding practices, and an absolute conviction that natural offspring can result only from traditional parenting.

Even the staunchest critics of the *Jurassic Park* series admit that their special effects are amazing, that the dinosaurs seem absolutely "real." Yet, during the first film, the reality, or perhaps to be more accurate the purity of those dinosaurs is questioned time and again. This issue is first raised during a scene where the park's creator, John Hammond (Richard Attenborough), tries to convince the visiting scientists that his park is not only safe but also scientifically worthwhile. One of the scientists, Ian Malcolm, disagrees vehemently. In a most remarkably polemical speech, Malcolm reprimands Hammond for achieving his ends without sufficient struggle. "You didn't earn this knowledge," Malcolm admonishes him—by which he means, we can only guess, that Hammond did not struggle single-handedly to discover the principles of genetic engineering which produced his dinosaurs. Malcolm appears to be arguing that the knowledge that allowed the dinosaurs to be "recreated" by Hammond is somehow "sacred." By implication, then, he is labeling the dinosaurs which resulted from Hammond's research as profane, or at least "unearned," and therefore, in some fundamental sense, not natural. And if we equate the natural with the real—which the film seems to insist that we do—then of course Hammond's dinosaurs aren't "real" dinosaurs after all.

This argument is reinforced and given another spin during a conversation between Hammond and the paleontologist Ellie (Laura Dern), when he confesses to her that his first exhibition was a flea circus. He explains that everything in the flea circus moved by tiny motors, but people swore they could see the fleas: "Look mummy, can't you see the fleas? I can see the fleas." He confesses he believed Jurassic Park would be something different, a place with exhibits that people could "reach out and touch, something real, not an illusion." Ellie instantly chides him for misreading his creation: "It's still the flea circus, John . . . it's still an illusion." She is clearly agreeing with Malcolm's condemnation of the park and its inhabitants as fundamentally and inherently "unreal."

However, in all the *Jurassic Park* films, as well as dozens of others dealing with the same theme, the agency of "natural" or "real" creation is curiously mystical, unlocatable—assigned most often to Nature or, even more broadly, Life; while unnatural or unreal creation is a result of, as Hammond puts it (somewhat hyperbolically), "the most powerful force ever discovered by man—genetics." Immediately we should note a contradiction: how can Natural be everything that is Life, *except* for genetics? (which we must assume would be spelled with a small g). Isn't genetics the basis of all life, capital L or otherwise? And therefore the basis of all that is Natural?

This contradiction is not only present but possible because in fact Crichton and Goldblum and Spielberg and even Hammond are all lying. *Jurassic Park* is not a cautionary tale about the "awesome power" of genetics; *Jurassic Park* is a reactionary tale about the power of sexual reproduction, a power that in the world of the film has "escaped" its traditionally domestic cage—much as the lack of traditional domestic relationships has, throughout our cultural history, been one of the criteria used to damn the figures of theoretical scientists as Wicked Wizards. An explicit version of this dynamic is Hammond's attempt to prevent the dinosaurs from breeding by cloning only female dinosaurs—a seemingly insurmountable obstacle, yet one which the dinosaurs easily out-flank when several of these females spontaneously "mutate" into males. This was only to be expected, chides the chaoticist Malcolm. While he views the di-nosaurs as unnatural, he also views Hammond's attempt to deny the dinosaurs the opportunity to breed as something which has "gone wrong" with the natu-ral order; and inevitably, he claims, the natural order—which, paradoxically, in this case is represented by Hammond's "unnaturally" created dinosaurs—will set things "right" by re-establishing traditional breeding patterns one way or an-other. Malcolm's lyrical (and most unscientific) explanation for this biological sleight of sex is that "Life will find a way."

But what, we might ask, is "Life"? If Life is the dinosaurs discovering how to breed against all the genetically engineered odds, why isn't "Life" Hammond's discovery of how to clone dinosaurs in the first place, against even greater odds? Why can't we say, in response to Malcolm's edict, that Life *already did* "find a way": through millions of years of evolution that eventually produced the brains of Hammond's genetic engineers? In other words, who gets to decide what is virtuous or "natural" Life heroically asserting itself, and what is impure or "un-natural" life cluttering up Nature's perfect landscape with unreal-unnatural dinosaurs?

Clearly the key component in making this distinction is the intervention of human beings. If the dinosaurs, not only without human help but against hu-man intent, can spontaneously outflank their genetic engineering, then that is Life; but when humans learn how to circumvent Life's extinction of the di-nosaurs, that is "penetrating . . . beyond [Nature's] prescribed depths." Thus, ironically, humans are excluded from the mechanisms by which Life-Nature operates. This is an age-old argument in the indictment of certain kinds of sci-entific research, and one to which I will return in the final chapter.

Some might argue that it is the resident scientists in the film which in fact condemn its science as unnatural, and it is with these anti-mad scientists in mind that some critics have argued that *Jurassic Park* is in fact a relatively enlightened "monster movie," because it places the formulaic warnings of doom and disaster in the mouths of scientists rather than hysterical anti-science fanatics.[21] But this is only a "first order" reading of these characters. For one thing, none of these putative scientists criticize Hammond's creation in *scientific* terms; that is, Malcolm doesn't question Hammond's quality control procedures or experimental data or simulation criteria; rather, he condemns the entire venture as something that should never have been undertaken in the first place; and this reaction is echoed by the paleontologists Ellie and Alan (Sam Neill), as well. In fact, the "scientist" figures in *Jurassic Park* are not really very good scientists when it comes to the business of observation and hypothesis building. Rather than using twentieth-century strategies of scientific reasoning to critique Hammond's work, they resort to nineteenth-century *prima facie* arguments for humankind's trust in Nature's wisdom, and our acceptance, even embrace, of certain limitations on our knowledge and resourcefulness; and these "natural" limitations are assumed to apply to our parenting practices as well as our science. Throughout the *Jurassic Park* series, children are used as the main currency in this economics of natural vs. unnatural practices. Engaging in unnatural breeding or parenting places them in danger; acting according to "natural" instincts—instincts often based on a reflexive and anti-intellectual violence—rescues them. Responding to those dangers with the most sentimental and even savage of reactionary philosophies—as for instance the T-Rex's enraged attack to regain its kidnapped child—justifiably punishes the transgressors and simultaneously provides the opportunity for the young to be rescued.

What I wish to emphasize is the capricious and even at times contradictory nature of the "natural" in these films. What is real, i.e., what is natural is assumed to be a reliable category of reference—so reliable that it stands outside any definitive enterprise. It is, in the language of the poststructuralists, a *transcendental signifier*, a term which is taken for granted in the discourse and never questioned; and therefore a term which can float freely from one meaning to another without being subject to any logic of consistency: and so the dinosaurs which result from Hammond's unearned cloning knowledge are "unnatural," but their ability to mutate into males is perfectly "natural"—and there is no recognized discontinuity between these two assertions. "Life will find a way" is the explicit epigraph of these films. But in point of fact, its argument is that Nature will "find a way" to punish those who tamper with the traditional order of things, whether it be through the revenge enacted on Frankenstein's friends and family by his creation, or by using T-Rexes to devour anyone arrogant enough to have given them birth.

I'VE DEVOTED this chapter to illustrating how the categories of good and bad, or American and un-American scientists shaped the cultural texts about both emerging technology and the emerging American Empire for the last half of the twentieth century. In order to understand why these categories are so deeply ingrained in American culture—sufficiently hegemonic that we no longer even question their logic or assumptions—we need to return to the eighteenth century. I've saved the Colonial period for the penultimate chapter as a sort of hypothesis-testing exercise. If, as I have argued throughout this book, American culture has a long and consistent tradition of privileging applied over theoretical science, inventors over theoreticians, doers over thinkers, then we would expect to find the roots of such attitudes in the earliest forms of American scientific practices and prejudices; we would, that is, expect to find a culture where family is considered an absolutely necessary component of acceptable scientific production; where any traces of foreign culture are suspect; where "averageness" is considered far superior to exceptionalism; where the rural is ennobling and the cosmopolitan is corrupting; and where, most important, the practical and material are valued and the theoretical and imaginative are disdained. And I believe we find just such a culture among the "patriotic God-fearing small-town Protestant family men" of Colonial American scientists.

LOOKING BACKWARD

Useful vs. Wicked Inventing in
Colonial America

IF ASKED which inventor has made the greatest contribution to American culture, many would argue that this distinction belongs to Thomas Edison. After all, he created more devices, obtained more patents, and ranged more widely across the applied sciences than any other of the Great Independents; some might even argue that he essentially invented twentieth-century America, with its dependence on electrical gadgets, its model of private fortunes built on a moment of inspiration, and its mythology of individual Yankee ingenuity taken to the highest entrepreneurial level. However, I would argue that Benjamin Franklin made an even more significant contribution to American scientific culture: not because he invented bifocals and the Franklin stove, but rather because he invented Thomas Edison.

To understand what I mean by that, we should begin where all Great Independent American invention begins, with the image of Ben Franklin flying his kite in a thunderstorm, an image many American schoolchildren read as the moment when Franklin "invented" electricity. While there have been many representations of that moment in June 1752, nearly all of them share certain details: typically Franklin stands in an open field, a kite aloft in a threatening dark mass of clouds, a zig-zag bolt of lightning lancing down from the sky to strike the kite, so that a small metal key dangling from the other end of the kite's string shoots off sparks from its electrical charge, each of them a tiny reproduction of that mighty thunderbolt overhead.

There are, however, several problems with this image. First of all, had Franklin actually conducted the experiment in this fashion, he would have been electrocuted.[1] It is also likely that Franklin, knowing better than to make himself a target by standing in an open field, was indoors flying the kite through an upstairs window. And finally, though there is often a small boy shown at his side, Franklin's son William, who did in fact accompany him during the experiment, was twenty-one at the time.[2]

In fact, we know relatively little about the actual specifics of this signature experiment. The account written by Franklin himself wasn't published until some three months later, in the October 19th issue of the *Pennsylvania Gazette*; and it is a rather cryptic report, nowhere simply stating that he actually conducted the experiment, but rather written as advice to someone who might wish to conduct such an experiment. Though it was Franklin's constant habit to put all his writings in the form of advice, it is strange that such an important discovery is told in the manner of someone who'd *thought* about flying a kite in a thunderstorm, but hadn't actually done it yet—especially when there is a certainty to the description of the equipment required and the results obtained that leave little doubt the writer himself has actually done this. However, once he'd conceived a practical application of his discovery, the lightning rod, Franklin published a fuller account in *Poor Richard's Almanac* in 1753.[3] For the eminently practical Franklin, a discovery wasn't worth reporting until he'd come up with an application of its principles.

However inaccurate in its details, the traditional image of Franklin's kite is foundational in the mythology of American science and nicely captures the essence of Franklin as the founding father of that science: a man not content to sit in the safety of his laboratory and theorize, but pragmatic, ingenious, and determined enough to go out and put his ideas to the test himself, even at risk of bodily injury. And this image is equally foundational to my argument here about how and why Franklin set the standard for so many American scientists to follow, as that image was as carefully composed by Franklin—both by what he revealed and what he concealed—as were all other aspects of his public persona. Before Franklin could invent the American scientist figure that would find its fullest realization in Thomas Edison, he had to invent Benjamin Franklin—a process we discover chronicled, much like the methods section of a laboratory experiment, throughout his fundamentally autobiographical life.[4]

Franklin's "autobiography" was truly a life's work. By this, I mean not only the writings begun as a young man and eventually published a year after his death in 1790 as *Memoires de la Vie Privée* (*Memoirs of a Private Life*),[5] but the totality of his writings: *Poor Richard's Almanac*, the *Pennsylvania Gazette*, his short essays and editorials, and even his private letters to friends. Rarely do we find, in this period or any other, an individual who works so diligently to represent himself consistently and thoroughly *as* a composition, a persona intentionally constructed to exemplify strict adherence to a personal code of virtues—a code which he believed would transform him into a completely useful member of his community, *Homo civicus*.

In his *Autobiography*, Franklin relates how, at age twenty, he assembled a list of thirteen key virtues that formed the foundation of his personal philosophy of self-betterment:

TEMPERANCE. Eat not to dullness; drink not to elevation.

SILENCE. Speak not but what may benefit others or yourself; avoid trifling conversation.

ORDER. Let all your things have their places; let each part of your business have its time.

RESOLUTION. Resolve to perform what you ought; perform without fail what you resolve.

FRUGALITY. Make no expense but to do good to others or yourself; i.e., waste nothing.

INDUSTRY. Lose no time; be always employ'd in something useful; cut off all unnecessary actions.

SINCERITY. Use no hurtful deceit; think innocently and justly, and, if you speak, speak accordingly.

JUSTICE. Wrong none by doing injuries, or omitting the benefits that are your duty.

MODERATION. Avoid extremes; forbear resenting injuries so much as you think they deserve.

CLEANLINESS. Tolerate no uncleanliness in body, cloaths, or habitation.

TRANQUILLITY. Be not disturbed at trifles, or at accidents common or unavoidable.

CHASTITY. Rarely use venery but for health or offspring, never to dullness, weakness, or the injury of your own or another's peace or reputation.

HUMILITY. Imitate Jesus and Socrates.

While these might sound like a collection of New Year's resolutions, as easily forgotten as formed, for Franklin they were something more: a formula which, if followed dutifully, would transform his deepest and truest character. Yet Franklin realized that simply espousing such virtues was insufficient to effect this transformation, especially as his goal was nothing less than "moral perfection . . . My Intention being to acquire the *Habitude* of all these Virtues." And such perfection could be attained only if one invented a practice that would turn platitudes into habits.[6] To this end, the virtues were first organized in order from least to most difficult to acquire; he then created a daily record for the virtue currently under instillation, wherein he would mark a "little black Spot every Fault I found upon Examination to have committed respecting that Virtue upon that Day."[7] Thus Franklin's invention of his public image began with the disciplining of his private self—a curiously surveilled private self, one who must subject each of his behaviors to a test: does this make me a more productive member of my community, or a hindrance to that community?

As is stated explicitly with Temperance, the proper form of any behavior is to be found somewhere between extremes, and that safe and sane midpoint is determined by communal standards. One's chief goal is not only to fit within the limits of that community, but also to represent a prime example of that community; one is to be, in a sense, exceptionally exemplary, or extraordinarily average. Why should one aspire to such a lofty (if somewhat oxymoronic) goal? The principle underlying all these virtues is practicality; the "moral perfection" achieved via the "habitude" of these virtues is seen as a desirable goal not because morality is, in and of itself, good, but rather because it is practical; and it is practical because it succeeds. How, then, did Franklin define success?

One way to answer this question is to ask how Franklin defined failure; and it is clear from the *Autobiography*, as well as from his other writings, that the chief sign of failure for Franklin was waste: of time, of talents, of resources. For instance, intemperance is to be avoided not because it is foolish or selfish, but rather because it "led to wasteful expenditure and undermined efficiency." Thus the Franklin self is first and foremost an efficient self. As Larzer Ziff argues, "For Franklin and his admirers, waste did not have to be proven a sin; it was axiomatically the chief evil."[8] This is an extremely important point in my overall argument, so let me rephrase it: to the extent that an American is a Franklinian American, one's highest goal is *efficiency*. Since efficiency must always be measured in terms of the resources required to produce a certain output, to be efficient means to be productive; and to be productive means to produce something *useful*. The point of all these appositions is to make it absolutely clear that Franklin's primary virtue was Usefulness—and therefore his primary "wickedness" was uselessness: to be, that is, without visible or material product. The perfection of usefulness is therefore a quest for the holy grail of *absolute* efficiency and the banishment from one's habits—and one's community—of any and all waste. Of course we saw this attitude powerfully represented in the utopian literature of the late nineteenth century, wherein a utopia was defined as successful to the extent it eliminated waste. And according to the Franklinian model, the road to perfect efficiency was made of practicality in *all* things. In his business dealings, his civic life, his religious beliefs, even in his attitudes toward sex, and especially in his practice of science, pragmatism was his unwavering guiding principle. This total commitment to the practical, the empirical, the utilitarian would exert an influence difficult to overestimate on the sort of science Franklin conducted and the sort of scientist he came to represent, a representation that became the model for, as we've seen, the Good American scientist of the next two hundred years.

Franklin's rise from near-poverty to riches is well documented. After establishing his own printing company and various other business interests, he eventually became one of the richest men in Colonial America. However, his financial success was important to Franklin largely because it provided him with the time and resources to pursue his other interests, chief of which was what he saw as his duty to his community; and he imagined that duty as above and beyond all else a requirement to be *useful* to that community. Near the end of his life he wrote a friend that he would rather it be said of him that "he lived usefully, than he died rich."[9]

Franklin's civic accomplishments were indeed staggering. He was the only Founding Father who signed all four "founding" documents: the Declaration of Independence, the Treaty of Paris, the Treaty of Alliance with France, and the United States Constitution. He helped to establish the University of Pennsylvania, Franklin and Marshall College, and the American Philosophical Society. His international accomplishments were just as impressive: he was granted gratis membership in the Royal Society and awarded their Copley Medal, as well as honorary degrees from Oxford and Edinburgh, and of course was America's chief diplomat in Paris during the Revolution. Thus Franklin could certainly be considered a prime example of someone who knew how to play well with others, even foreign others. However, rather than discussing his thoroughly chronicled public accomplishments, I wish to focus on the writings that constructed his public persona. I see these writings as a defining moment in a long and, I believe, uniquely American struggle to discipline the imagination, or at least to construct a set of criteria whereby the imagination might be subjected to interrogation and validation: a struggle that begins in Puritan ideology and continues to this day. When considered in their totality, Franklin's writings emerge as the first self-help manual, a user's guide for creating a self who is, in all public respects, a good, i.e., *useful* citizen.

First and foremost, according to Franklin, a good citizen is someone who sees a lack and corrects it, rather than simply complaining or waiting for the government to do something about it. One of the earliest examples we have of Franklin's politics is a woodcut, dating to 1747, that served as the frontispiece for a pamphlet urging Pennsylvania to raise a militia for its own defense: the woodcut depicts a farmer praying to Hercules for help, while Hercules is telling the farmer to help himself.[10] In this vein, Franklin is famous for organizing the first volunteer fire departments and insurance companies, and dozens of other civic-minded self-organized innovations. But it is clear that Franklin considered *all* his work civic work—work performed in the public eye and, as just that, a performance, intended to achieve a certain reaction from its audience. In his *Autobiography* he writes of his young days as a printer that he worked extraordinarily long hours: "And this Industry visible to our Neighbors began to give us Character and Credit."[11] It is of course typical of Franklin that he would think of character and credit in the same breath, as though our public image is a bank account into which we can make deposits through displays of industry. Franklin even turned the religious writings of the Puritan Fathers to such ends. Impressed by Cotton Mather's *Essays to Do Good*, Franklin founded the Junto Club, which was "aimed at the betterment of its members, and of the city and Colony in which they lived."[12] Thus, even in the rather clichéd moralistic dogma of the Puritans, Franklin found inspiration for practical action in service of his community; which, we can assume, he knew would give him "Character and Credit."

Franklin's religious beliefs—though it might seem more appropriate to call them practices than beliefs—were also founded on the rock of utility. He argued that people should believe in divine providence and the importance of good works not because such behavior would mean ascension to paradise in the next world, but because it was socially useful in this one: "This religion will be a powerful regulator of our actions, give us peace and tranquillity within our own minds, and render us benevolent, useful and beneficial to others."[13] He viewed dogmatic religion as an inefficient producer of moral consistency; rather, he believed moral acts should arise from an individual's disciplined virtue. Beliefs of any kind, even religious, had to be compared, like his virtues, to a communal standard, and that standard was results: "I think opinions should be judged by their influences and effects; and if a man holds none that tend to make him less virtuous or more vicious, it may be concluded that he holds none that are dangerous, which I hope is the case with me."[14] His privileging of the practical was even in evidence when he published an *Abridgment of the Book of Common Prayer* (1773), wherein he suggested reducing the traditional hour-long funeral service to no more than six minutes, "to preserve the health and lives of the living."

One aspect of Puritan ideology that particularly troubled the young Franklin was the concept of free will. If, as the Puritans argued, all choices are preordained, what is there about them of a "choice"? How are we to demonstrate to God our freely chosen dedication to His principles? Franklin laid our four possibilities for a universe created by an all-powerful divine being: 1) predestination was total, and natural law and free will were zero; 2) predestination was zero, natural law and free will were total; 3) predestination, natural law, and free will are balanced; 4) predestination, free will, and natural law all operate, but are occasionally overridden by Divine action, or to quote Franklin, "He sometimes interferes by His particular providence and sets aside the effects which would otherwise have been produced by any of the above causes."[15] Franklin chose the fourth option, not out of any particular sense of faith or inspiration in response to it, but rather because he felt it was the one that would be most "useful" for people to believe.[16] Thus one might argue that, for Franklin, "wicked" would be defined as that option least "useful" for people to believe—which would be the first option, total predestination, as such a belief would provide the least motivation for "good works," in that it represents individuals as mere pawns in God's plan, a plan to which they can make no contributions but only serve as unwitting instruments. The fact that this was the very universe imagined by the most dogmatic Puritans tells us a good deal about the significant transformation of Puritan ideology as exemplified by Franklin's ideas and life, a topic to which I'll return in a moment.

Practicality was Franklin's credo even in his attitude toward sex. When a friend wrote asking his advice about the best manner in which to pursue discreet affairs (as Franklin was known to have considerable experience in such dalliances, one of which produced his illegitimate son, William), Franklin responded in a letter (written in 1745 but repressed until 1926). First, he advised the friend to consider the importance of being *"married and settled. It is the Man and Woman united that make the compleat human Being."* Were he determined, however, to pursue affairs, then, drawing on Franklin's own "Intrigues with low women," Franklin's advice was eminently practical: "in all your Amours you should *prefer old Women to young ones"*; he then goes on to list eight reasons for this policy, the last of which is "They are *so grateful!"*[17]

But of course the main theater for Franklin's performance of practicality was that of inventive genius. Franklin has often been compared to Edison based on the sheer volume of his inventions; however, given the breadth of his interests, a more apt comparison seems to be Leonardo da Vinci. Like Leonardo, Franklin created a host of practical inventions: bifocals, the first functional catheter, the Franklin stove, the lightning rod, a crude prosthetic arm, the addition of second hands to clocks, the odometer . . . the list is considerable. Also like Leonardo, Franklin left behind voluminous and detailed drawings for ideas that didn't lead to actual inventions, but that evidence original and technological insight that were ahead of his time: oval sails that could be easily turned horizontal in gales, thus saving the time and dangerous activity of furling sails in a storm; flexible anchor chains that wouldn't snap in such storms; Suduko-like number tables; observations on ocean currents and weather patterns, and on and on. One sees particularly in Franklin's descriptions of various electrical and meteorological observations an amazing attention to detail, a commitment to empirical observation, a rigorous care about ascribing cause and effect . . . and the almost complete absence of generalized speculation about larger theories behind these causes and effects. Franklin did sometimes speculate about the specific forces at work in the phenomena he observed—he was the first electrical experimenter to suggest that "electrical fire" came in two types, positive and negative, though he had the direction of flow from one to the other reversed—but he rarely extends his speculation in attempts to create some unifying theory. Franklin was not a philosopher-scientist in the tradition of Herschel and Whewell; he wasn't interested in making the kinds of analogies between nature and society that were typical of this period, at least among European scientists. Rather, throughout his scientific writings, he is conspicuously focused on investigations that will lead to practical applications that "work"—and he isn't particularly interested in why they work.

For Franklin, science was a business; and he realized that business, even scientific business, required promotion. David L. Ferro argues that Franklin used the *Pennsylvania Gazette*, for instance, to cast science in a particular light: "The *Gazette* presented Science as rational, empirical, commercially viable, and opposed to superstition." Thus some of the articles in the *Gazette* sought primarily to attack what Franklin viewed as anti-Enlightenment habits of thinking and culture: "The article on the healing springs requested the reader to cast a critical eye at reports of the spring's healing power. Folk wisdom and superstition required empirical examination." Still, the *Gazette*'s most important function was as advertising for Franklin's science and business interests; in fact, the two were inseparable:

> The *Gazette* also made science entertaining and meaningful to attract an audience . . . critical for a developing colonial American science tied to commercial interests. . . . Articles on silk worm farming, vineyards, pest control and irrigation tied themselves to the economic vitality of the colonies. . . . To sell their wares, the proponents of science used that science to improve their wares' appearance. One ad notes Poor Richard as "celestially improved." A shoemaker used an engine to scientifically fit his shoes to his customers' feet. Experimenting on the White Chapel prisoners proved the effectiveness of Dr. Godfrey's cordial for bodily flux.[18]

Such *Gazette* articles demonstrate that Franklin realized scientific phenomena had to be presented to the public with applications they would find useful, and in terms they could easily understand:

> Audiences were enticed to view the "Greenland bear" and other animals that articles described with lyrical or dramatic prose. Lightning reports became frequent and dramatic during the initial electrical years starting in 1751. Meanwhile, ads promised amazing feats by mechanical devices like the "amazing microcosm," or the many electricity demonstrations that complied with discovered scientific concepts.[19]

However, Franklin did not see the *Gazette* or the *Almanac* as venues for the publication of experimental observations that would necessarily find or impress a "professional" scientific audience. Rather, he continued to send such materials to England for publication. As Ferro points out, "No theory and little in the way of explanations could be found in the [*Gazette*] for any scientific or technical issue." Even in the scientific writings published in Europe, Franklin was explicit about his disdain for theory and "higher" philosophy, as demonstrated by his oft-quoted dismissal of esoteric intellectual debate: "Many a Long Dispute among Divines may be thus abridg'd, It is so: It is not so. It is so; It is not so."[20] He was equally explicit about what he saw as the European affectation that the past had a great deal to teach the present, writing to an American friend traveling in Italy that a "Receipt for making Parmesan Cheese" would "give me more Satisfaction than a Transcript of any Inscription from any old Stone whatever."[21]

Franklin's pragmatism and anti-theoretical predilections have been the subject of many volumes. More recent Franklin studies point out that his "complicated" premarital social life and relatively lavish personal tastes hardly coincide with the chaste and abstemious persona so assiduously constructed in his *Autobiography*, Poor Richard's aphorisms, etc.; and therefore, they conclude that this public Franklin wasn't the "real" Franklin at all. However, whether or not Franklin practiced what he preached isn't really germane to my argument here. Rather, what is important is our received *image* of Franklin, the extent to which the public at large accepted "Poor Richard's" Franklin as the real Franklin, and the extent to which this iconographic Franklin influenced Colonial attitudes toward science and those who practiced it.

And the chief component of this iconographic Franklin is, as I've delineated here, his absolute commitment to pragmatism. Franklin's pragmatism—regardless of whether it was fundamental or merely professed—has been both attacked and defended by writers of various periods. Of particular interest to my analysis here are those who defend it, as we find in their rhetoric assumptions that suggest the very sort of unexamined prejudices about theory vs. practice for which I've argued throughout this book. One such example of a genre we might call "pragmatist apologia" is the book *Puritans and Pragmatists: Eight Eminent American Thinkers*, by Paul Keith Conkin.[22]

Conkin's admiration of Franklin's aversion to theory is forceful to the point of prickliness: "He did not have time to be waylaid in the murky byways. He knew that intellectual floundering might be caused by obscurity as often as by immense depth."[23] Having dismissed theoretical contemplation as the equivalent of getting "waylaid" by "murky byways," Conkin then locates the chief source of criticism regarding his pragmatism among artists: "To many of them, such as D. H. Lawrence, Franklin was the eternal Philistine, the insensitive Babbitt, the incurably practical and detestably utilitarian American." What I find particularly revealing here is Conkin's choice of D. H. Lawrence as a representative critic, as it contrasts a disciplined, practical, commonsense, pragmatic American patriot with (at least as Conkin presents him) an obtuse, sickly European libertine and *artiste*. Then Conkin explicitly dismisses critics such as Lawrence as not only irrelevant, but egotistical and imperious: "Franklin was a practical scientist. But so what? . . . There is a dangerous sophistry and a perverted type of snobbery in the tendency to give the higher value to pure philosophy, pure science, or pure art."[24] In an almost involuntary reflex of condemnation—made especially visible by that pugnacious "So what?"—Conkin thus exposes Franklin's critics for who they really are: sophists, perverts, and snobs.

If the image of Franklin as Prime Pragmatist has survived so robustly as to inspire such defensive "apologies" as Conkin's, then perhaps that image is as much a fierce rejection of sophistry, perversion, and snobbery—all coded as European, of course—as it is a principled commitment to Franklin's thirteen virtues. In fact, in the sarcastic deployment of that term "pure" we might discern the linchpin of a rhetorical strategy and the heart of a cultural prejudice: a suggestion that the "purity" of such pursuits is all in the mind of their pursuers, with the accompanying implication that "pure" would never be used to modify "pragmatism"; that pragmatism, by its very nature, neither seeks purity or even much believes in it. Purity is, by this reasoning, impractical, aristocratic, anti-democratic, and therefore un-American. Of course, also revealed here is the presumption that those who would criticize Franklin for his total privileging of the practical over the theoretical do so not out of any reasonable or logical disagreement with his methods and priorities, but out of "sophistry" and "perverted . . . snobbery."

Yet there was something pure to Franklin's personal philosophy, and it was his "pure" (as in absolute) commitment to public duty. Eventually Franklin even set aside scientific investigations for a public life in politics, as he advised (as always) a friend: "let not your Love of Philosophical Amusements have more than its due Weight with you. Had Newton been Pilot but of a single common Ship, the finest of his Discoveries would scarce have excus'd, or atton'dd for his abandoning the Helm one Hour in Time of Danger; how much less if she had carried the Fate of the Commonwealth."[25]

Clearly Franklin felt himself to be one of the American commonwealth's pilots in a "Time of Danger," and thus he retired from his "Love of Philosophical Amusements" and devoted the rest of his life to his civic responsibilities. And it is as much for the reasons Franklin retired from science as those habits and ideals he represented during his scientific career that I am offering him as the Founding Father of Master Mechanics. We have in Benjamin Franklin not only the model for the good American scientist as someone little interested in if not explicitly disdainful of theory, but also a model, by exclusion, of various traits the Colonial American culture found un-American: traits the culture would attach to the concept of the anti-Franklin, a figure that would eventually emerge as the Wicked Wizard of Hawthorne's fiction. However, even in Franklin we haven't found the wellspring of these American attitudes; to discover that, we have to go even deeper into American history, to its very beginnings, and examine the first centrally organized, rigorously disciplined, and widely disseminated American ideology, an ideology that would inspire, or at least ground Franklin's pragmatism, even as he altered many of its tenets: and that philosophy is, of course, Puritanism.

WHEN ONE invokes "the Puritans," the image summoned is typically one of repressed and repressive cultural school marms, all dressed in black and permanently scowling. However, this image is somewhat complicated by others both folkloric and historical: the colorful bounty of a Thanksgiving banquet, or the grim fanaticism of hanged "witches." Thus I think it's important to point out the fallacy of seeing the Puritans as some monolithic, homogeneous group— stern disciplinarians, welcoming hosts, paranoid inquisitors—who all believed and acted in concert; especially given that their writings range from the early strict Calvinism of Cotton Mather, through the "reformism" of Jonathan Edwards, to the later "radical" free will of the Antinomians. But there are common themes that run throughout Puritan writings, transcending differences of opinion about free will, submission to church authority, and other points of contention among the various branches and offshoots. And the focus of this commonality can be located in the single word *invention*.

Before the term "invention" took on its modern meaning—as applied, for instance, to the sort of mechanical contrivances created by Franklin and Edison— its connotation in religious contexts was as things "dreamed up" by the mind of man and not found explicitly in the Bible: such things as religious rituals, the designs for idols, or even entire philosophies. This was the sense in which the Puritans used the term, as in these examples from various Puritan texts (with italics added):

> It is the Lord's own way and his institutions only, which he will bless, not man's *invention*, though never so plausible.[26]
>
> Let us understand that the name of Church is falsely pretended wherever men contend for that rash human license which cannot confine itself within the boundaries prescribed by the word of God, but petulantly breaks out, and has recourse to its own *inventions*.[27]
>
> The Lord cannot forget Himself, and it is long since He declared that nothing is so offensive to Him as to be worshipped by human *inventions*.[28]

Which seeing they were of old the chiefe *inventions* of men corrupting the worship of God, they are most fitly.[29]

Therefore, when God is worshipped, not according to his owne will, but according to the pleasure and will of man, the true God is not worshipped, but a God of man's *invention* is set up.[30]

Mortification from a self-strength, carried on by ways of *self-invention*, unto the end of a self-righteousness, is the soul and substance of all false religion in the world.[31]

I've quoted at length here to indicate just how pervasive this understanding of "invention" is in the religious ideology of the Puritans. And such instances are only a fraction of the considerable verbiage devoted to denouncing invention—product or process—as fabrication motivated by humankind's hubris, as something antithetical to proper religious doctrine and therefore intrinsically offensive to God. This definition of invention becomes particularly focused in the Puritans' obsession with distinguishing real from false experiences of God's grace, as in establishing principles and methods whereby the Puritan Fathers could reliably separate *invented* from sincere reports of grace.

The Puritans insisted that the experience of grace was a sign of the individual in direct contact with God—an experience that did not necessarily require, could in fact be hindered by the mediating role of a priest or bishop. (This of course had been one of the chief reasons for their split from the Church of England.) They also believed that the indicator of an authentic experience of God's grace lay in the sincerity of the individual's account of the experience, and not that the account must conform to ritualistic formula, as they argued was the case with all other religions, particularly Catholicism. However, such sincerity, once decoupled from the stifling influence of church authority, could also be suspect due to its very individuality, its uniqueness, as that uniqueness could be an invention, a product of imagination; and sincerity was "of course incompatible with that experience being imaginary." And by imaginary, Larzer Ziff here is referring to the Puritan belief that "the devil's trump card was fooling his victim into mistaking his lies for God's truth; that the devil tried in every way possible to mislead the individual into thinking that the voice of the devil was the voice of God, and that the experience of degradation was the experience of grace."[32]

The key to determining whether grace was authentic or not lay in determining whether the experience of God's grace was real, or merely a product of the imagination under Satan's stimulus; and those with overactive imaginations were assumed to be most susceptible to such deception. Thus, though the Puritans valued spontaneous and personal testimonies of grace above ceremonial and communal pronouncements of faith, they also evinced a deep suspicion of these personal testimonies and developed elaborate inquisitional guidelines designed to separate real from imagined reports of grace. Testimonies which seemed overly enthusiastic or hasty, or those offered without corroborating witnesses were particularly suspect. An entire genre of Puritan writing grew up around the issue of how to discern authentic from invented grace, and there was a wide range of opinions about acceptable criteria. Some suggested that the signs of "invented" grace were essentially the signs of over-acting, such as "trembling, groaning, being sick, crying out, panting, and fainting," while others, like Jonathan Edwards, wrote that such excessive behaviors were "not incompatible with true knowing of God."[33]

Jonathan Edwards is a particularly interesting example of the Puritan struggle with the issue of invented vs. real grace. Edwards came closer to a "scientific" treatment of the question than any of the fundamentally Calvinist Puritans, in that he submitted the issue to a method of Augustinian logical analysis. For instance, he advocated loosening Puritan practice from the rigid formulaic sermons which had become, by the Great Awakening, its modus operandi, because, by a chain of reasoning, he arrived at the conclusion such sermons were inimical to the spontaneous and personal grace they were supposed to inspire. He also argued consistently for an empirical evaluation of testimonies of grace and redemption, suggesting investigators ignore second-hand accounts and focus instead on visible, verifiable evidence. In other words, Edwards believed in subjecting the tentative "experimental" evidence of grace to empirical evaluation. However, there were limits to his reform tendencies; he also attacked the "radical" concept of free will as preached by the Antinomians, arguing for what was essentially Franklin's first option for a divinely constructed universe: total predestination without free will. He even disliked the notion of a "covenant" between man and God, as the term "covenant" was too much like "contract," implying that man had some degree of choice in its construction, and that God was subject to certain responsibilities in its operation. But Edwards did have a modern and somewhat scientific notion of predestination, suggesting it lay in the very fabric of the universe, in that atoms, as elements of "indivisible resistance," were the material immanence of God. Still, he shared the traditional understanding of "invention" as anything generated from the mind of man and without correlation in the Bible or in the natural world. Even for an innovative Puritan like Edwards, such "inventions" were fundamentally false, and therefore categorically wicked.

But these conflicting requirements—that grace be an individual experience, but reported in a way that conformed to communal standards—led to a problem: good liars, i.e., the best actors, were believed, while those who were sincerely uncertain about their experience—those who expressed reservations

and hesitancy—were more likely to be considered victims of Satan's deceptions, as they seemed to be "inventing" their testimony *ad hoc*. Inevitably,
those narratives eventually judged convincing set a pattern for acceptance,
which meant that new testimonies were compared to those patterns and either
accepted or rejected to the extent they met those standards; which in turn
drained the testimonials of any spontaneity and uniqueness, the very qualities
the Puritans valorized in the first place.

One can discern a direct relationship between this distrust of invented reports of grace and the fascination in Colonial literature with liars, cheats,
quacks, and other early American con men. Examples of this fascination can be
found in the popularity of *Memoirs of the Notorious Stephen Burroughs of New
Hampshire* (1798), about the famed counterfeiter and imposter; or the frequent newspaper accounts of the legendary scam artist Bampfylde-Moore
Carew; or the even more infamous Tom Bell who, according to Franklin's own
Pennsylvania Gazette of February 1738, "has it seems made it his Business for
several Years to travel from Colony to Colony, personating different People,
forging Bills, Letters of Credit, &c. and frequently pretending Distress, im-
posed grosly on the charitable and compassionate."[34] In a chapter entitled
"Gaining Confidence," Ziff explores this particularly American obsession with
con games, deceptions, and false identities, and finds this fascination ubiquitous: "Almost every novel or personal narrative . . . written from the mid-
eighteenth through the early nineteenth century has at least one major episode
of deception."[35] Why, he wonders, did god-fearing, law-abiding, socially conservative Colonial Americans find representatives of such anti-social behavior
so compelling?

Because, I would respond, Americans have always found good salesmen
compelling, whether they sold fire and brimstone, like Edwards in "Sinners in
the Hands of an Angry God," or Franklin and his lightning rods—or Bell et al.
with their tales of adventure, suffering, and redemption. And what better salesman can there be than one who sells you sheer imagination? In other words,
perhaps the very intensity of the Puritan dedication to rooting out inventions
of man's imagination is an indication of just how transfixed they were by the
very idea of such "inventions."

Often the deceptions in Colonial narratives concerning con men centered
on property, typically inherited property, and many narratives "underlined the
message that chastity was a negotiable property."[36] Yet it was the invented
identities of these con men that were seen as their most valuable property, and
it was the construction and dissemination—or production and promotion—of
these false identities that was most often the focus of such narratives, in terms
both of the detail devoted to relating their construction, and of the subsequent

effect on their audience. What seems to have most captivated Americans about these reports and confessions of criminal guile was the skill of such "mummers" at inventing various selves in response to changing circumstances. For Colonial Americans, the most valuable property one could own was one's identity, as it was a representation of personal achievement without the European handicaps of legacy, history, class, and the like. And if those achievements were false? Well, at least as far as narrative was concerned, that was less important than if they were convincing.

But this creation of a present self discontinuous with the past self gave rise to a problem similar to that of distinguishing real from imagined grace: how to tell that someone was who he represented himself to be, historically, financially, and especially spiritually? It is extremely interesting, for instance, that the majority of confidence schemes centered on the con man presenting himself as either an itinerant preacher or a sinner eager for confession and salvation—as if the most valuable commodity for the Colonial culture was religious experience, either the knowledge of or the thirst for it. However, if the culture is to value each individual's freedom and ability to invent him/herself as a spiritual adept or seeker, then how can it at the same time condemn those who demonstrate unrestrained freedom and remarkable ability at inventing either identity? In a country where the chief myth was that one could make oneself into whoever one wanted to be, could not the representation in effect *create* the man, as was the case with Franklin?[37] Which is to say, couldn't the invention become reality?

Thus do surveillance and authenticity become intertwined in the Puritan formula for trust: without continuity in one there can be no certainty in the other. As Ziff states, "The imagination is the faculty Satan employs to delude persons into repeating his own revolt by leading them to believe they have the power to affirm a new order."[38] Since the imagination is beyond surveillance and is successful to the extent it deceives, it is seen as the most uncertain facility of the human mind and, paradoxically, as potentially the most powerful.

And thus, I would argue, have we established the genesis of the Puritan preference for experience over representation, for spoken testimony over written reflection, for immediacy over memory, for acts over thought. This prejudice/fascination then evolves into a generalized American suspicion and fear of theoretical knowledge. Theory, as pure "invention," is insubstantial and untrustworthy—until and unless, that is, it can be legitimized by the other form of invention, the one that is visible and substantial. But before such a legitimization-through-materialization occurs, theory exists in a state neither right nor wrong, true nor false, much as was the case with personal claims of grace. Put another way, a person's testimony to having received grace was in essence an expression of *theoretical* spirituality, and was therefore only the first step in a long process whereby the community would judge the authenticity of the person's spiritual experience; and the key evidence for that authenticity would not be found in anything the candidate for grace might say, but only in what he or she *did*, in subsequent "good acts."

After all, how does one validate a subjective experience? How, in the realm of the immaterial, do we define "real"? The individual's sincere belief in the authenticity of the experience isn't sufficient, as he or she could be the victim of deceit. Satan, it was argued, was perfectly capable of producing the superficial sensations of a moment of grace, and the mechanism by which he achieved this trickery was to be found in a person's imagination. Thus physical invention—as with acts and mechanisms—is good, as it is pragmatic and, more important, verifiable; whereas imaginative invention—as in theory, or for that matter fiction, poetry, and the other arts—is bad, as it isn't in any obvious way useful, and therefore is "more likely" to be a result of Satan's corrupting influence. To put it simply, I argue that the long history of American culture's distrust of, even disdain for theory can finally be traced to the deep and complicated mixture of fear and fascination the Puritans felt for the human imagination.

THE WRITTEN word, as invention-fiction, encapsulates this focus for scrutiny and suspicion.[39] In this vein I wish to examine the first work of American literature to treat as its primary subject the American ideal as natural idyll, a sort of compendium of everything that was believed good and new about the New World of America. The book is *Letters from an American Farmer* (1772), written by Michel-Guillame-Jean de Crèvecoeur (aka Hector St. John de Crèvecoeur), a Frenchman become an Englishman become an American.

In this collection of letters from a fictional American farmer, Crèvecoeur represents the farm specifically and the American wilderness generally as Edenic: orderly, harmonic, free of irrational violence, ugliness, and brutality.[40] However, this paradise is a fragile one that can be shattered by the simple act of *writing* about it. The fictitious author of the letters, the American farmer, not only discounts himself as a worthy writer because he is not educated, but his wife warns him against writing because she fears the neighbors will grow suspicious and that he will be accused of "idleness and vain notions not befitting [his] condition."[41] She goes on to suggest that the act of writing will make people think not only that he is wasting time, but also that he is plotting against the community. His wife pleads with him to cease writing: "Instead of being well looked upon as now . . . our neighbors would make strange surmises; I had rather be as we are, neither better nor worse than the rest of our country folks."[42]

In other words, in the narrow Edenic world of this farmer, his wife, and his neighbors—at least as it is imagined by Crèvecoeur—the simple act of writing expresses some quality of discontent, unless, that is, it is practiced by someone for purely practical reasons, such as a minister or teacher or businessman. For simple "country folk," writing cannot be conceived as any sort of productive work; to the contrary, it is feared as a sign of laziness, pride, even arrogance. There is also something suspiciously *European* about writing. To quote the farmer's wife again: "Great people over sea may write to our townsfolk because they have nothing else to do. These English are strange people; because they can live upon what they call bank notes, without working, they think all the world can do the same."[43] In her view the English are idle writers, supported by *imaginary* wealth, engaged in *imaginary* work. The immateriality of writing and the thinking from which it springs are things so foreign to the farmer's community as to seem utterly alien, "strange," and therefore, axiomatically, European.[44]

While the farmer and his wife are not fanatic and perhaps not even, by 1772, representative Puritans, they may be taken as representative rural Americans; and the aspect of *Letters* that is most relevant to my argument here is its depiction of this rural anxiety surrounding writing and thinking: an anxiety which pervaded popular American culture of the time to the extent that it was clearly evident even to a newcomer like Crèvecoeur. Certainly it can be safely said that at this time there was a significant divergence between the American and European attitudes toward thinking: for the former, as we've seen, it was inherently indicative of idleness, and potentially the source of ever greater deceits; whereas for the latter, thinking was a high and noble enterprise, even, perhaps especially if it was engaged in without any "thought" given to its material results. In fact, in the European model, idleness was a necessary component of the optimum mode of thinking, contemplation.

In the mid-1700s it was all the rage in Europe to take trips whose sole activity was the "contemplation" of ruins. In "The Pleasures of Melancholy," written in 1745 by Oxonian Thomas Warton, melancholic contemplation induced through the study of ancient ruins is treated as a condition of higher emotional sensibility—one more in tune with the inevitable decline of all things mortal—than any other intellectual state, especially those associated with "The laughing scenes / Of purple Spring": "O, lead me, queen sublime, to solemn glooms / Congenial with my soul; to cheerless shades, / To ruináid seats, to twilight cells and bowers, / Where thoughtful Melancholy loves to muse / Her favorite midnight haunts."[45]

One of the major differences cited by Americans as proof that the New World had not yet experienced the fall from grace of the Old was the very *lack* of ruins in America; thus "doing the ruins" was not only a leisure pastime unavailable to

Americans, it was an unappealing, if not outright abhorrent practice—especially to a culture still steeped in the values and prejudices of its Puritan forebears, which saw such a philosophical disposition as idleness, plain and simple, with no useful outcome. And this is the point where we can make a connection to Franklin's abhorrence of waste, as there is another term that we might apply to waste, one even more loaded with moral judgment, and that term is sloth. Franklin, for instance, wrote that "Sloth, like rust, consumes faster than labor wears...."[46]

In an essay about the long and nefarious history of sloth in American culture, Thomas Pynchon (author of *V.*, *Gravity's Rainbow*, *Mason & Dixon*, and other highly imaginative and deeply theoretical novels) suggests that writers are, to the American mind, the chief practitioners of sloth: "Writers of course are considered the mavens of Sloth. They are approached all the time on the subject, not only for free advice, but also to speak at Sloth Symposia, head up Sloth Task Forces, testify as expert witnesses at Sloth Hearings."[47] On a more serious note, Pynchon observes that the term "sloth" first enters into religious writings with Aquinas in the "summa Theologica," wherein *acedia* makes the list of the seven mortal sins; and, as Pynchon points out, *acedia* in the original Latin implies sorrow which arises from "deliberately self-directed" turning "away from God," and which is evidenced by an over-indulgence in dreams. While, as Pynchon notes, "Idle dreaming is often the essence of what [writers] do," that avatar of American commonsense, Poor Richard, had no interest in dreams whatsoever: "In Frances M. Barbour's 1974 concordance of the [Poor Richard] sayings, there is nothing to be found under 'Dreams.'"[48]

In much of Puritan ideology, the role sloth played in the Bible was as a warning signal of behavior or, more important, thoughts which were the first step on the road to more serious moral failings. As Pynchon notes, "Richard Baxter, in his Puritan exposition of sloth and idleness, considered sloth the source of most other sins, citing, for example, the idleness of David watching Bathsheba bathe when he should have been out at war; sloth in this case led to lust, adultery, lying and murder."[49] And sloth was associated not only with idle dreaming, lust, deception, and murder, but with another indulgence considered just as antisocial, and one which became a trademark of Wicked Wizards: isolation. Sloth, it was argued, targeted as its chief victims those who isolated themselves from human community, a syndrome of sin experienced first-hand by the itinerant monk and assiduous enumerator of sins, John Cassian (360?–435? A.D.), who described *accidia* as "a torpor, a sluggishness of the heart; consequently, it is closely akin to dejection; it attacks those monks who wander from place to place and those who live in isolation. It is the most dangerous and the most persistent enemy of the solitaries."[50]

Due to its ready association with such moral failings, sloth appears frequently not just as the villain in Puritan sermons and religious treatises, but also in a good deal of Christian religious literature (such as *The Pilgrim's Progress from This World to That Which is to Come* (1678), wherein John Bunyan created an actual space for sloth, the Slough of Despond), as well as "mainstream" American literature. In Washington Irving's *Rip Van Winkle* (1819), for instance, the title character represents sloth incarnate: "The great error in Rip's composition was an insuperable aversion to all kinds of profitable labor," an "error" which causes him to sleep right through the American Revolution.[51] In everything from simple rhymes to sage aphorisms of the time, there were numerous anecdotes warning of the dangers of sloth; there were even public ordinances ruling that sloth, as a form of itinerancy, was an indication of unsavory and therefore illegal public behavior. Sloth was even considered evidence of un-American political sympathies. In a song popular during the American Revolution, "The Americans Are Calling," sloth is equated with pro-Tory, anti-rebellion sentiment:

> Ye That Reign masters of The Seas
> Shake off your Youthful Sloth and Ease must undergo
> We will make The haughty Tories know, The Sorrows They
> When they Engage Their mortal Foe, Hozah Brave Boys[52]

Though Puritan writings may differ on ideas of free will, predestination, the proper forms of prayer and worship, and other tenets of religious ideology, they all agree on one thing: Work is the antidote for sloth; or as Poor Richard succinctly put it, "Sloth makes all things difficult, but industry, all easy." This attitude is also reflected in the *Letters*, where the American farm is figured as a new Garden of Eden—but a Garden that pays for itself: as Ziff puts it, "Throughout the 'Letters' free labor is happiness; it is not so much that people are happy because they work but that they express their happiness in work."[53] This relationship between work and happiness is, interestingly, reversed in the utopian novels of a century hence that imagine work itself as the source of happiness—as though, once the wickedness of waste is banished from the system, work then becomes the ideal practice of existence, its own justification, even a new religion: utterly pragmatic, completely material, and hermetically self-sustaining.

This certainly is the attitude toward sloth of many of the panegyrics written about the "Protestant work ethic" over the last two centuries. And central to all of them is the assumption that productive work, in and of itself, somehow inoculates a person against the virus of sloth. *In Protestantism and Capitalism: The Mechanisms of Influence*, Jere Cohen exhaustively chronicles the links between Puritan ideology and the American obsession with work. Cohen argues that central to understanding the importance of work and material production in the Colonial American culture is an understanding of sloth not just as idleness or laziness, but as *anti*-work, as a waste of potential that undermines God's plan and thus serves the Devil's purposes.[54] As John Preston wrote, idleness is "when he doth not that which he ought, in the time when it is required of him." And just in case the reader missed his point, Preston continued, "He is an idle man that workes not, when he ought to work."[55] Or this, from Richard Baxter: "Sloth signifieth chiefly the indisposition of the mind and body . . . an averseness to labour through a carnal love of ease." As useful work was the cardinal virtue, sloth was the cardinal sin.[56] Simply put, good Puritans must be "always Working, always Doing."[57]

But sloth was not just "always doing" nothing; it was also doing the wrong something, and that something was indulging in pleasure. Baxter considered time spent in the pursuit of pleasure to be wasted time, and such "Time must be redeemed from the hands, and by the loss, of sinful pleasures, sports and revellings."[58] In other words, time wasted on pleasure can be cleansed of its sinful taint—redeemed, though not recovered—only "from the hands," by manual labor. In fact, the implication throughout the writings of Baxter, Mather, Edwards, and most other Puritan Fathers is that to take time out from work to *think* is to be instantly and automatically tempted by wicked thoughts; and by wicked thoughts they didn't necessarily mean thoughts of murder and mayhem, but merely thoughts of how much nicer it would be to be doing something pleasurable, or to be doing nothing at all. Since by "work" the Puritans meant *physical* labor, it isn't difficult to understand why thinking would, *a priori*, be considered wicked, given a strict constructionist interpretation of this doctrine of "Always Doing"; and the Puritans were nothing if not strict constructionists.

We can also see why it was important in Puritan ideology for work to be equated with happiness, for work and pleasure to be synonymous: if work *is* pleasure, then there is no need for one to pause during work to contemplate pleasure. Idleness then becomes, by definition if not instinct, the opposite of pleasure. Thus we have a chain of associations, which begins with an understanding that by work one means physical labor that results in material production, and by anti-work one means anything that is abstract and without discernible material product. The category of such "abstract" indulgence would presumably include activities like thinking, reflecting, and contemplating (all of which are of course associated with the arts—more about this idea in a moment). In other words, in such a formula thinking becomes a kind of toxic distraction, one that is dangerously addictive.

And the bigger the thoughts, the greater the danger. As Conkin writes of the Puritan attitude toward those who would observe Nature and attempt to think about or beyond its purposes and limits: "To assay [reality's] final limits, to presume on God, was either misplaced pride or metaphysical arrogance." Conkin suggests that, given such strict barriers to any intellectual practice considered metaphysics, the Puritans' interest in truth—whether the truth of testimonies of grace, or the truth of the natural world—came to be focused entirely on questions of the observable, the practical, and entirely uninterested in questions of rhetoric or philosophy: "This attitude, with its premium on instrumental knowledge, on morality instead of sheer intellectualism led to a typical New England stance toward epistemology—the problem of truth is not a formal, technical problem, but one of practice, of utility, of making a proper response to the demands of God or of nature."[59] Conkin goes on to suggest that this idiosyncratic definition of truth—"truth" is whatever emerges as the most utilitarian solution to a material problem—inevitably led to a sense of the material world as something that needed to be actively "fixed" rather than passively contemplated: a source of problems to be efficiently solved, not inspirations to be artfully represented. As he puts it, "[The Puritan] wanted to redeem matter, not transcend it."[60] Nor, one might add, simply appreciate it, as even the momentary aesthetic admiration of natural beauty could too easily become the sort of melancholic reverie that, of course, led inevitably to sloth.

Certainly part of the narrowly Puritan and later broadly American mania for activity and abhorrence of waste can be understood in terms of the pressing need, as the Puritans saw it, to "redeem" this New World rather than admire it—to establish a new civilization in this New Eden. The Puritans and their heirs pictured busy metropolises linked by roads and rivers full of commerce; but what they saw were endless woods populated by lazy, indolent natives. The two visions were of course incompatible. Thus for them the New World was an essentially infinite expanse of woods to be cleared, rivers to be dammed, and mountains to be made traversable. The way to redeem all this "wasted" Nature was to convert it to useful purposes. In fact, they believed God had provided all this "virgin" territory precisely to be "converted." If, as Edwards among others argued, Nature was perfect in its original formation, still a vital component of that perfection lay in the opportunities it offered for displays of man's ingenuity and determination. Nature was complete, but changeable, and changing it was mankind's duty. In fact, changing the landscape could be considered a manifest representation of mankind's internal process of self-remaking.[61] This becomes the primary myth of America: that nature, be it human or geographic, can be reshaped through hard work, determination, focus, consistency, discipline—the application, that is, of all Franklin's thirteen virtues—into something more "useful" to the community. But that myth also entails the fundamental assumption that such reshaping is achieved with the pragmatic application of mechanical knowledge, and not via intellectual theorizing, i.e., idle speculation.

The primary site for the indoctrination of this ideology was the Colonial American family. In terms of social, political, and even spiritual organization and values, the Colonial American family was a microcosmic allegory for the community; thus any imbalance in the individual could produce a like imbalance in the family, and thus in the community. A stable, productive community was based on stable, productive families comprised of stable, productive individuals. Such stability was for the most part defined through conformity to communal values, values that had to be conceived of and executed by everyone in the same fashion. As thinking is a solitary and, even more to the point, an invisible activity, one impossible to discipline to conformity, in such a climate one can see how thinking could become perceived as the site of potentially dangerous nonconformity that could threaten the entire system. And in this idealization of the family in the formation of American identity, we can discern another component of what will become the virtues of the Master Mechanic: that he be a family man. Thus we would expect that his nemesis, the Wicked Wizard, would most often be represented as without familial relations.

But it isn't just family relations that are required to be on the right side of the Mechanic/Wizard divide; Master Mechanics must, in the Franklinian model, maintain community relations, as well. If the absence of one or both relational networks is seen as inherently suspect and potentially wicked, then in a sense to be without either is to be without identity. If, as Franklin suggested, one's goal was to so thoroughly discipline one's public behavior as to make usefulness to the family and community innate, instinctual, the very core of the private self, and this usefulness is completely defined by those public networks, then it must be assumed that the public self is the *only* self, that there is no part of one's identity that is secret, antisocial, nonconformist. In such a schema, there simply is no place for a private self. Or at least there ought not to be such a space, as it would imply that the overall system was to some extent, however small, imperfect and wasteful. Inefficient. Thus someone working alone—a solitary researcher sequestered in his laboratory, for instance—is automatically suspect. Even something as seemingly innocuous as reading is suspicious, as it requires solitude. For instance, Franklin confessed that "a Book, indeed, sometimes debauch'd me from my Work; but this was seldom, snug, & gave no Scandal."[62]

We might ask, then, how does working alone become acceptable for and one of the trademarks of the Great Independents, such as Edison? Because, as we saw in chapter 3, there are *practical* results from their isolation; and it is something suffered, not enjoyed by the inventor, an unpleasant-but-temporary condition accepted as necessary for his work, not one which he actively seeks or constitutionally prefers. Then, too, the practical inventor isn't really thinking when he's alone, he's *inventing*—the good kind of inventing, rather than the bad; and inventing is, as Edison reminded us, "one percent inspiration and 99 percent perspiration."[63] On the other hand, when there is no practical, material result of such isolation, no way of verifying the dominance of perspiration over inspiration, who knows what the scientific researcher has been doing all alone in his laboratory? Is it not entirely possible that he was busy overindulging his imagination? Or worse, doing nothing at all?

WE MIGHT ask, then, if there is a representative of such a nonproductive, imaginative *isolato*—what we might call the anti-Franklin—in Colonial culture, someone who embodies most or all of the traits I have ascribed to the figure of the Wicked Wizard.

We won't find such a figure among the other prominent American scientists of the time, such as Cadwallader Colden (1688–1776), anatomist and botanist; John Bartram (1699–1777), naturalist and "father" of American botanical study; Lewis Evans (1700–1756), surveyor and cartographer; David Rittenhouse (1732–1796), clockmaker and astronomer; or Benjamin Rush (1746–1813), doctor, chemist, and early psychologist. First, all of them were scientists in the same mold as Franklin: pragmatists who concentrated on observing, classifying, and recording natural phenomenon rather than speculating on larger theories of relationships and social consequences. But more important (as explained in chapter 1), it simply wasn't really possible in Colonial America for a scientist to become a theoretician. There were no scientific journals devoted to what would have been considered in the colonies abstract scientific musings; even the practical work of Franklin and these other American scientists was published in European journals, largely *The Proceedings of the Royal Society* in England. Additionally, the first university programs in theoretical studies didn't even exist until after the Civil War, so American scientists were largely self-taught through observation and practical experience. (Though Colden was born in Ireland, his education there was in the ministry; and Evans, born in Wales, had limited his studies to surveying.)

Rather, the character of the Colonial Wicked Wizard is to be found not so much in individuals as in prejudices—in fact, in one prejudice particularly, and that was Colonial America's condemnation of anyone who showed admiration for what were considered European affectations. Such affectations were identified most often with the arts. Thus it is within Colonial America's suspicion of and outright disdain for the arts as an exercise of the intellect without practical outcome that we find the reasons why latter-day Wicked Wizards would be accessorized with the manners and elitist tastes the American colonists attributed to Europeans.

There were some Colonial artists who provided support for this prejudice. For instance, Joseph Dennie, whom Ziff refers to as "the United States' first full-fledged Miniver Cheevy," could also be considered America's first full-fledged professional writer. He edited several well-respected journals, like *The Tablet* (1791) and *The Port Folio* (1801), and worked with stalwart American patriots such as John Quincy Adams. However, though his essays and "lay sermons" were admired, his denigration of the Revolution as something that had merely served to harm his career certainly was not. With obvious frustration, Dennie wrote, "Had not the Revolution happened . . . my fame would have been enhanced. . . . But in this Republic . . . what can men of liberality and letters expect but such polar icy treatment as I have experienced?"[64] Such arrogance and disdain for the new democracy were also associated with European displays of dandyism. A friend recalled Dennie "appearing one May morning at the office in a pea green coat, white vest, nankeen smallclothes, white silk stockings and pumps, fastened with silver buckles which covered at least half the foot from the instep to the toe."[65] Dennie was also known as a card shark, drinker, and "inveterate idler," someone who had clearly given himself over to the carnal pleasures for which the imagination was considered a "gateway drug."[66]

But it wasn't just fashionable clothes or melancholic reveries that were condemned as suspiciously European; anything that smacked of European manners or tastes was viewed as manifestly un-American; and conversely, anything un-European was considered typically American. In a play by Royall Tyler titled *The Contrast* (1787), a character remarks with obvious contempt on the "snobbery and emptyheadedness of Americans who ape European manners," then goes on to contrast such base parroting of European aristocratic culture with the "the common sense and sturdy virtue of those attached to plain, republican customs."[67]

And here we might recall another figure from Washington Irving's fiction, Ichabod Crane. Crane—significantly, a schoolteacher—is physically poorly suited to the rough life in the Colonies: "He was tall, but exceedingly lank, with narrow shoulders, long arms and legs, hands that dangled a mile out of his sleeves." Crane is also feminized through his association with the women of his village: "The schoolmaster is generally a man of some importance in the female circle of a rural neighborhood; being considered a kind of idle gentlemanlike personage, of vastly superior taste and accomplishments to the rough country swains." He is even accessorized with a very Old World interest in ghosts and magic: "he had read several books quite through, and was a perfect master of Cotton Mather's history of New England Witchcraft, in which, by the way, he

most firmly and potently believed." All of these traits are contrasted to the pro-
totypically American figure of Brom Van Brunt, "the hero of the country
round, which rang with his feats of strength and hardihood." Van Brunt is portrayed throughout as a "manly" man, and, though his character might strike a
modern audience as something of a bully, in the story his humiliation of the
bookish and awkward Crane is represented as a kind of rough-but-admirable
rural American justice. It is also important to remember that the central conflict between Crane and Van Brunt is over a woman, the heiress Van Tassel.
Crane is judged by the village and Van Brunt as fundamentally unworthy of
achieving such a prize, and his attempt to establish the sort of familial relationships that might make him less a Wizard and more a Mechanic is mocked as
ridiculous and futile. As a final gesture of contempt for Crane's "erudition,"
when "magic books and the poetic scrawls" are discovered among Crane's effects, they are "forthwith consigned to the flames by Hans Van Ripper; who
from that time forward determined to send his children no more to school; observing, that he never knew any good come of this same reading and writing."[68]

One might see in the Van Brunt–Crane confrontation an early form of "jock
vs. nerd," and perhaps even dismiss the story and Colonial fiction like it as mere
cartoons of not so much class as social status conflicts. Yet the fact that these
types were so well established in the Colonial American psyche that they had already become comic stereotypes—easily recognized and widely appreciated—
is an indication of just how thoroughly the traits attributed to both characters
were also seen as inherently coded as American and European, respectively.

Anti-democratic sentiments, uncommon education, fancy clothing, arrogant attitudes, elevated speech, solitary habits, a belief in magic, physical defi-
ciencies . . . all are assumed to be indicative of a crypto-European; and all are
considered to be epitomized by the classical arts. No less an American luminary
than John Quincy Adams wrote: "Every one of the Arts from the earliest times
have been enlisted in the service of Superstition and Despotism. The whole
World at this day Gazes with Astonishment at the grossest Fictions because
they have been immortalized by the most exquisite Artists, Homer and Milton,
Phidias and Raphael."[69] It seems only logical to trace this post-Revolutionary
condemnation of the arts backward to the suspicion of the imagination evidenced by the Puritans. Art was corrupt for the same reasons Europe was corrupt: because it was "invention" based in falsehoods and imaginings with
centuries-long traditions of deceit and sin, all of which had been left behind in
the Old World.[70] And the New World was seen not only as *terra incognita*
where new communities, new politics, new religions, and new Man could be developed, but also as a haven for a new Utilitarian ideology, conveniently pro-
tected from European contamination by the Atlantic Ocean. Charles Jared

Ingersoll, a politician and historian who routinely argued for a new American culture completely independent from that of Europe, wrote: "Poetry, music, sculpture, and painting, may yet linger in their Italian haunts. But philosophy, the sciences, and the *useful* arts, must establish their empire in the modern republic of letters . . . on this side of the great water barrier which the creator seems to have designed for the protection of their asylum"[71] (italics added).

The proper American had to evince an aversion not only to fancy clothes, fancy manners, and fancy art, but also to solitude. It was expected that the majority if not the totality of American life was lived among the three main communities that formed American culture: family, village, and church. To be without any one was essentially unthinkable; to be of all three yet still seek to be alone was at the very least suspicious. By so thoroughly identifying the individual with his or her community, and that community with a standardized doctrine of behavior as prescribed first in religious texts and eventually in the "commonsense" aphorisms of, for instance, Poor Richard, American ideology eventually became internalized to a remarkable extent, an ideology founded on the principle that, by devoting oneself to personal efficiency through the avoidance of frivolity, sloth, and dissension, one empirically demonstrated one's value and commitment to the community, and thus to God.[72]

DIVERSION AND frivolity—or waste and uselessness—return us to that exemplar of efficiency and utility, Benjamin Franklin. They also return us to the issue of authenticity. Who decides, after all, what is a frivolous recreation and what is a worthy creation? Where exactly is the site of authenticity in the judgment of utility? This of course is not dissimilar to the problem of establishing the authenticity of grace. If it is the unmediated nature of grace that grants it authenticity, then isn't the mediating role of comparison and judgment to community standards of grace ipso facto counter-productive? If one institutes a hierarchy to institutionalize authenticity, then all the evils of the Church of England are replicated, and the New Eden finds itself with the Old Serpent of corrupt and corrupting power. If, on the other hand, one grants that authority to the individual, to each individual, then doesn't the distinction between "real" and "imaginary" grace become arbitrary and, finally, meaningless? These two apparently irreconcilable questions created a central dilemma for Puritan ideology.

As previously discussed, the Puritan solution to this dilemma was to insist on the importance of *acts*: what a person did as a member of the community established a pattern, a pattern which cast an aura of "probability" over that individual's spiritual authenticity. The more constructive was one's participation in the community, the greater authenticity could be ascribed to that person's

report of the experience of grace. This solution was not lost on Franklin. If anything, he improved upon it. Franklin argued in his writing, as well as in the
very fabric of his life, that one might create a new self, an *authentic* new self, by
acquiring the "habitude" of productive labor in every facet of one's behavior. In
a sense, Franklin's invention of authenticity rooted in self-surveillance was not
fundamentally different from that of the Puritan Fathers' invention of authenticity rooted in communal surveillance; if, that is, the private self under consideration is, as with Franklin, taken to be completely coincident with the public
self. By writing the *Autobiography* about a constructed Franklin, he essentially
argued that the final measuring of one's authentic relationship to God is equivalent to the measure of one's usefulness to community; one constructs a publicly acceptable grace just as one constructs a publicly useful self.

The improvement Franklin made to the existing Puritan formula was subtle, but tremendously powerful: for, if one's good works cast credibility on
one's true grace, then wasn't it possible that the one was in fact synonymous
with the other, especially in a deeply pragmatic and empiricist society? What
need of intangible and potentially *imaginative* abstract versions of grace, with
all the concomitant problems of verification, if one could simply say the pragmatic application of habits useful to the community *was* personal grace? Thus
Franklin becomes the avatar of the utterly "modern" and thoroughly pragmatic—
rather than dogmatic—Puritan: a subject whose public representation is to all in-
tents and purposes an exact match to his private self; a *self*-surveilling subject,
whose ethical compass points always toward the true north of the community's
good.

But what is particularly relevant to our purposes here is that Franklin also
becomes the avatar of the American scientist. And just as in Franklin we find a
commitment to practical over theoretical science, we also discover many of the
other traits that would eventually emerge as trademarks of the Master Mechanic. For instance, his inventions were intended to improve not his own lot,
but that of his community; he in fact didn't take out patents on many of his inventions, such as the Franklin stove, because "it was designed for all who could
read about its merits."[73] And even though Franklin was a social climber, he was
a practical social climber, which meant that he realized he must "avoid the appearance of leisure," as leisure was European. He also represented himself as
utterly average, always emphasizing his lack of uniqueness and suggesting
throughout his writings that long hours at work, not any special gift of intellect, were responsible for his many achievements.[74]

The Puritan hierarchical dilemma—where to locate authority if one dis-
cards the church but suspects the individual—is thus outflanked by internaliz-
ing what we might call the "imaginative governor": by simultaneously making

the individual the interrogator of his or her own imagination, and creating a *public* imagination as a standard against which the individual might test his or her thoughts and feelings, diagnose shortcomings, and make the necessary attitude adjustments—as Franklin did with his virtue account book. Thus does vigilance against Satan's abuse of the imagination become literally self-regulating and self-reproducing. And as a consequence, all forms of abstract mental behavior— theorizing, speculating, contemplating, musing, reflecting, or, worst of all, imagining—become threats from which this vigilance protects us. Intellectual labor becomes an oxymoron, as exercises of the intellect devoted to abstract study produce no material result and don't even pretend to produce a moral result; and, in a system where physical labor is assumed to be both the test and the demonstration of good moral fiber, physical work thus becomes a moral imperative. If physical work is good because it expresses God, it isn't difficult to imagine that, in time, such work will become God—especially in a culture that celebrates all instances of the material over the immaterial, the demonstrated over the theorized, the real over the abstract. Progress becomes its own justification—but progress that is measured in terms of the invention of mechanical contrivances which are useful for the community at large and which, though they may reform that community, do not threaten to revolutionize it.

Taking all of Franklin's utilitarian moral inventions into account, then, we can assemble what we might call (with apologies to Poor Richard) the Ten Virtues of the American Master Mechanic:

> UTILITY. A proper scientific investigator creates gadgets, not fancies.
> TEMPERANCE. Scientific work should be a job, not an obsession.
> EFFICIENCY. The smallest leak can, over time, empty the largest reservoir.
> FRATERNITY. Inventions should increase the common good, not the inventor's ego.
> HUMILITY. The quietest accomplishment overcomes the loudest boast.
> SIMPLICITY. Plain speech and manner are transparent, while eloquence and artifice hide grievous flaws.
> SINCERITY. Honest rudeness is better than mannered flattery.
> TYPICALITY. The average man makes the best scientist; the better man makes the best fool.
> PASTORALITY. The best scientists grow midst the simple virtues of the countryside, not the complex vices of the metropolis.
> COMMUNITY. Family is the parent of many virtues; Isolation breeds only contempt.

If one wonders where Religion is on this list of the Master Mechanic's virtues, the answer is that, as was the case with Franklin, all these virtues essentially *are* his religion—the Ten Commandments of the practicing Good American

Scientist, from Benjamin Franklin to the Mercury astronauts, and their descendants even to this day.

And yet, even though Franklin's anti-theoretical prejudice may explain much in terms of the public conception and professional practice of American science over the next two hundred years, it may seem a gross exaggeration to suggest that all the Colonial American Founding Fathers were unqualified anti-intellectuals. After all, documents like the Declaration of Independence, the Constitution, and the Bill of Rights are certainly expressions of a political philosophy that had at its center an extraordinarily well worked out *theory* of how individuals, families, and communities ought to be organized in order to achieve liberty and cohesion, innovation and tradition, justice and discipline. My answer to this objection is that, first, I am not suggesting that such Colonials were not well-educated and exceptionally moral individuals. America was exceedingly fortunate to have such a group as Washington, Jefferson, Franklin et al. at its head during its conception, men who were not only well educated and insightful, but were also possessed of a sound and robust moral code. After all, that a nation is conceived and initiated by intellectuals is no guarantee of its liberty and morality, as evidenced by both the French and Russian revolutions, among other notable examples. The wisdom and ethical dedication of these Colonial Americans were a rare combination of talents and common vision, one we could only wish occurred with greater frequency in our history. However, such American theorizing was largely confined to the realm of politics—which was after all seen, as exemplified by Franklin, as the *practical* application of pragmatic principles for the material betterment of the community. It was also theorizing done in public, not in isolation; and its result was often not an ideal, but a compromise, as became increasingly clear when some of those compromises—such as the acceptance of slavery in the southern states—proved inherently unstable. Even then and with such great minds as these, politics was the art of the possible. In other words, to recognize the underlying pro-utilitarian and anti-theoretical foundation of Colonial American culture is to take nothing away from the considerable accomplishments of Franklin and his colleagues; it is rather to come to an understanding of how those accomplishments inevitably shaped American attitudes toward identity and work, especially in terms of the characteristics of each that would be seen by the public as representative of either success or menace.

If we accept that the source of so many of our attitudes about what constitutes good vs. bad science and useful vs. useless scientific labor can be located in the cultural prejudices, mythologies, priorities, etc. that I've outlined here, then several obvious questions arise about our coda for Master Mechanics:

Do the virtues still apply today? Is there any indication of a shift in popular American culture's representation of good and bad scientists, any suggestion that the stereotypes we've examined are becoming outdated? Perhaps most important, have these stereotypes had "real-world" effects on how science is practiced in contemporary America? In other words, even if such a schema as I have constructed throughout this book is valid, so what? These are the questions I will address in the last chapter.

DÉJÀ VU ALL OVER AGAIN

12

Fear, Funding, and Ignorance in Contemporary Scientific "Controversies"

ARE THERE real-world effects resulting from an American privileging of the mechanical and material over the theoretical and the abstract? Is America's preference for utilitarian Mechanics over theoretical Wizards actually shaping its science, not only as it was conceived two hundred years ago, but also as it is practiced today? And, two centuries after Benjamin Franklin, has there been any significant change in the stereotypes I've discussed? To answer these questions, I offer the following case studies, analyses of controversies about current scientific priorities, exigencies, and debates. In each case, I contend that the cultural prejudices discussed throughout this book are clearly as much in evidence today as in any time of our past, as indicated by the kinds of science that do and don't receive funding, as well as those that do or don't receive public approval.

The Superconducting Super Collider

Waxahachie, Texas, seems an unlikely place to discover the secret of the universe: low, rolling hills, treeless plains, and sparse grasslands stretch beneath an infinite blue sky, all of which provide an eerily quiet, even morose background for a few nondescript gray rectangles of incomplete buildings, vast empty rooms, and an eighteen-mile-long hole in the ground. That hole is where the secret was to have been discovered, a hole appearing now like a gigantic storm drain, appropriately half-filled with water and clogged with weeds. This is where the Superconducting Super Collider was to have been built; and thus the site has stood since the project was cancelled in 1993, slowly deteriorating like some abandoned strip mall, without anything to indicate that it was once the focus of the greatest dream of theoretical physicists around the world. But should that dream be renewed and that ultimate secret revealed, it won't happen here.

The Superconducting Super Collider (SSC) was designed to be the most powerful particle accelerator ever built. By racing elementary particles around a ring of superconducting magnets 54 miles in circumference, then crashing them into one another, scientists estimated the SSC would achieve energies reaching 20 TeV (20 trillion electron volts). Even today, the most powerful accelerator at Fermilab in Chicago can only achieve 1/20th of that raw power. What is the deep secret of the universe those extra 19 TeVs might have uncloaked?

The Higgs Boson; or, more important, the Higgs Field. The Higgs Boson and its accompanying field are theoretical-but-as-yet-undiscovered elements of the Standard Model of how the universe works. The Higgs Field is conceptualized as that which gives the material world, well, materiality: a sort of cosmic "aether" which connects everything in the universe and imparts to it certain qualities, such as mass, which cannot in fact be explained by the currently known forces and particles. In other words, according to the documented components of the universe, we shouldn't be here. Nothing should be here. The math of the Standard Model requires that something like the Higgs Boson and the field which surrounds it are necessary for matter to have substantiality. The Higgs Boson could also help to explain the mysterious stuff called (somewhat sinisterly) "dark matter," which appears to comprise the vast majority of the universe, but about which we know almost nothing. So establishing the reality of the Higgs Field would seem to be pretty important stuff.

When funding for the SSC was terminated in 1993, after eighteen miles of tunnel had been dug and two billion dollars spent, it was because Congress didn't think it was important stuff—certainly not important enough to justify spending another estimated six billion on a project that, as one senator put it, "won't affect my life." Of course what the senator meant was that there seemed to be no *practical* benefits to discovering the secret of the universe—or at least not "practical" in any sense the senator understood. And most of the Washington establishment agreed with him. A policy paper published at that time by the Cato Institute put it even more bluntly: "Super Boondoggle: Time to Pull the Plug on the Superconducting Super Collider." Among the reasons the Institute cited for "pulling the plug" on a project most theoretical physicists considered more important than Los Alamos were:

> 3. The commercial applications of the SSC technologies may well be minimal. In any event, the SSC itself will not contribute to the future international competitiveness of American industry.

> 5. The SSC promises to do little more than provide permanent employment for hundreds of high-energy particle physicists and transfer wealth to Texas.[1]

In other words, the SSC wouldn't generate commerce and, perhaps even worse, would simply keep theoretical physicists employed. Thus it obviously wasn't worth pursuing.

Establishing the relative "worth" of such theoretical discoveries in physics, or science generally, has always been a difficult problem, especially in a culture which judges nearly everything in terms of its economic costs and benefits. How much of our resources should be devoted to an undertaking that may not succeed and, even if it does, probably won't change the way we live, only the way we think?

This dilemma was nicely encapsulated in an exchange between Senator John Pastore and physicist Robert Wilson in a hearing before the Congressional Joint Committee on Atomic Energy in 1969. In a foreshadowing of the future battle over the SSC, Wilson was testifying on behalf of increased funding for more powerful accelerators, and Pastore wanted to know if all the money spent would increase our national security. Wilson bluntly stated that such research had nothing to do with national defense, at least in the ways Pastore understood the term, and then added:

> It only has to do with the respect with which we regard one another, the dignity of men, our love of culture. . . . It has to do with are we good painters, good sculptors, great poets? I mean all the things we really venerate in our country and are patriotic about. . . . It has nothing to do directly with defending our country except to make it worth defending.[2]

Clearly Pastore and the majority of the Senate did not agree with Wilson on his definition of "worth," i.e., an investment in theoretical exploration whose only reliable product is increased knowledge of ourselves and our ability to express that knowledge through the arts. Pastore and his colleagues thought in terms of concrete threats, while Wilson was arguing in terms of abstract dignity; and, not surprisingly, the two discourses experienced a significant disconnect.[3] Herman Wouk, in his novel fictionalizing a revival of the SSC, *A Hole in Texas*, suggests the only thing that might compel the United States to renew such costly research efforts would be a threat Senator Pastore could understand, a sort of "Pearl Harbor" in theoretical physics. In the novel, Wouk creates a report by the Chinese (the new Soviets) that they have finally discovered the Higgs Boson, which sparks frantic reaction in Washington—much of it of course focused on establishing who is to blame for America's "losing" the Higgs Boson.[4]

During the debate over the SSC, much was made by those in opposition of the change in the world dynamic since the fall of the Soviet Union, the limits of U.S. resources in this new world, and the need to focus our resources on projects that promised the greatest benefit to all mankind. Eventually such arguments pre-vailed, and the SSC was deemed unworthy of scarce resources. And what scien-tific project was considered more important, more useful, more worthy than discovering the fundamental secret of the universe?

The six billion cut from the SSC was added to another seven billion, and that sum was applied to the budget for the International Space Station (a project whose total bill is now around $110 billion). And what have been the important, practical, and fundamental payoffs of the ISS? Other, that is, than providing per-manent employment for thousands of engineers and sending wealth to Texas? Asked to name a single accomplishment of the ISS, would the average American have a response?

Perhaps the only thing keeping the ISS in orbit is its momentum: a project worth keeping there because it already *is* there. In an article in the *New York Times* titled "Destination Is the Space Station, but Many Experts Ask What For," the point is made that the only practical science going on aboard the ISS is research into the effects of prolonged weightlessness on astronauts, and growing better crystals in a vacuum; both of which have been the fallback ar-guments for half a century as to why manned space flight is good science, yet neither of which can be shown to have had any actual economic results. Others suggest that the true underlying economic justification for continued funding for the ISS is purely political: fulfilling our commitments to foreign contrac-tors. David J. Goldston, former chief of staff for the House Science Committee, said "I've never heard anyone say, 'We have to do this because it's important for the future of the U.S. space program or science.'"[5] However, I would argue that the primary force keeping the ISS aloft is ideological: the ISS is a highly visible (sort of) hub of *seemingly* pragmatic activity; and even more important, it is a "outpost" in the High Frontier, a presence which, in some vague manner, is thought to increase our national security.

The momentum of the ISS—political, economic, cultural, and ideological—is unlikely to be lessened or deflected anytime in the near future. Too much has already been invested in its operation and mission, whatever that mission may be. And, given that the ISS continues to soak up a huge portion of the NASA budget, coupled with the recent commitment of the remainder of NASA's resources to a return to the moon in preparation for a manned jour-ney to Mars, there seems little hope of much funding being available any time in the near future for "pure" (read unmanned) space science.[6] Half a cen-tury after Project Mercury's "spam in a can" panicked response to Gagarin's flight, we continue to support a space agency fundamentally committed to putting men in space—even though we still have only a vague idea why they are there.

The Strategic Defense Initiative

Many of these same problems and rationalizations surround the Star Wars missile defense system. The seemingly inexplicable survival of the Strategic Defense Initiative—even after the evaporation of the threat it was designed to counter, the USSR—is evidence that many still believe the Master Mechanics can somehow deliver us from the nuclear curse cast upon us by the Wicked Wizards. Even though the system has been significantly scaled down, the basic flaws in its logic and its technology have never been addressed; yet the funding and justifications continue. As do the excuses: "The idea of fly before buy is very difficult for this system," said Lt. Gen. Ronald T. Kadish, director of the Missile Defense Agency. "This is a fly as we buy." Even those who work within the system recognize the curious lack of interest in its illogic or failings:

> "Ever since the president made his decision, the priority of the program has been on deployment, not on understanding whether the system works," said Mr. Coyle, now a senior adviser at the Center for Defense Information, a private research group. "Most people don't appreciate how complicated this system is, nor how much all of the tests so far have been artificially scripted to be successful."[7]

Surprisingly—or perhaps not surprisingly—the model of outer space as America's first line of defense against "them" hasn't changed since the 1950s, even though the "them" has.[8] In disturbingly familiar echoes of the claims Johnson and others made about our need to "beat" the Soviets in manned space stunts, a recent White House policy on outer space stated: "In this new century, those who effectively utilize space will enjoy added prosperity and security and will hold a substantial advantage over those who do not. Freedom of action in space is as important to the United States as air power and sea power."[9]

In the final analysis, then, the value that SDI (and the ISS) possess that the SSC did not is figured in the same rhetoric that was used to justify the atomic weapons and manned spaceflight programs half a century ago. And in further—and even more chilling—echoes of that fifty-year-old mindset that argued America could keep its nuclear arsenal secret and supreme, the current administration (2007) has consistently opposed "any negotiations on a treaty to prevent an arms race in outer space—arguing that it may impede America's ability to defend its satellites from ground-based weapons."[10] In the 1950s, when the United States was faced with a choice between investing in the theory of arms control and international cooperation regarding nuclear weapons—the so-called "One World or None" option—and a unilateral development of ever-more exotic atomic weapons, we chose the latter course of action. The result was an extended and massively expensive arms race, a result that has left us arguably *less* secure. In the twenty-first century, faced with a similar choice between outer space arms treaties or unilateral supremacy in outer space founded in our faith in technology, we are again opting for machines over rhetoric, things over theory. One can only imagine the situation fifty years from now, when earth orbit is crowded with anti-missile satellites, anti-satellite satellites, and anti-anti-satellite satellites. Will the United States *then* be more secure? Or will we look back on the turn of the millennium, see missed opportunities for "theoretical" solutions to weapons in outer space, and ask, What were we *thinking*?

The "Theories" of Global Warming and Evolution

The debate over global warming is by now a familiar topic to any American who watches the news, reads a newspaper, or surfs the Internet. And, while often the presentations about global warming foreground this or that contentious point between scientific experts, perhaps the most curious aspect of this topic is that it is called a "debate" at all. A recent U.N. report, citing an overwhelming preponderance of scientific evidence supporting the argument that human activity of the last century has increased greenhouse gas emissions, concluded that global warming was "unequivocal."[11] However, the Bush administration continues to refer to the "Global Warming Controversy," which at a minimum indicates confusion over the meaning of the word "controversy." The issue has become politicized to the point where opposition to global warming initiatives is considered a necessary demonstration of loyalty to the Republican party; as a Baltimore newspaper reported:

> If you need to hear how science has taken a backseat to ideology, give U.S. Rep. Wayne Gilchrest a call. The Eastern Shore [Maryland] Republican was denied a seat on the bi-partisan Select Committee on Energy Independence and Global Warming. The Gannett News Service reported that Gilchrest was rejected because he refused to argue that climate change was not caused by human actions.[12]

Such party "discipline" even over matters that fall into the supposedly politics-free zone of science goes all the way to the top of the current administration. A recent article about the White House's decision not to reappoint Dr. Richard H. Carmona to the position of surgeon general discusses the ways in which politics interfered with the science of his official duties: "Dr Carmona was ordered not to discuss embryonic stem cell research or the emergency contraceptive known as Plan B. . . . He was ordered to water down a report on the dangers of secondhand smoke. . . . He definitely couldn't point out the failings of abstinence programs . . . [in speeches] he was ordered to mention President Bush three times for every page."[13]

Such trumping of science by politics is apparently based on the belief that global warming, stem cell research, contraception, and other scientific topics are "controversies," meaning issues with two equally defensible positions. Thus, the argument goes, the data cited in the U.N. and countless other reports about global warming are supposedly open to varying interpretations; therefore the administration is merely trying to be even-handed in its treatment of the "controversy."

There are of course many controversial questions in our current state of scientific knowledge: Does life exist on other planets? Will the universe continue to expand indefinitely, or contract into another big bang? Will computers ever become "artificially" intelligent? However, global warming is not one of these questions; it is not, at least in scientific terms, a controversy.

Neither is evolution. Much the same rhetorical strategy of claiming a "controversy" where none exists marks (or mars) the current "debate" over the theory of evolution. Ever since the Scopes "monkey trial" of 1925, this topic has been treated in the popular media of America as a duel, a simplistic, two-sided struggle between the forces of conservative politics and fundamental religion on the one hand, and the forces of liberal politics and secular humanism on the other. Though the battle seemed for decades to have been won by the "pro"-evolutionists, in recent years a spate of school board decisions and lawsuits by "anti"-evolution forces are evidence that the issue is anything but settled. Calling their alternative theory for the development of life on Earth "intelligent design," they make arguments that are, of course, essentially those of the creationists of decades earlier, and can be summarized as follows: life is too complex to have developed without the guidance of a "higher power."

However, while their basic argument hasn't changed, the justification for making that argument has, as exemplified by President Bush himself, as when he responded to a question about a recent legal victory for the pro–intelligent design camp: "Both sides ought to be properly taught . . . so people can understand what the debate is about."[14] The rhetorical strategy in play here is made even clearer by a remark from John G. West, of the pro–intelligent design Discovery Institute: "President Bush is to be commended for defending free speech on evolution, and supporting the right of students to hear about different scientific views about evolution."[15] Not to put too fine a point on my point, this strategy is made simplest of all when stated by the father of children in a school whose board voted to include intelligent design in its science classes:

> Larry Taylor, who has three children in the Cobb County schools, said he doesn't advocate creationism but believes evolution should not be presented as the only acceptable theory.
>
> "Evolution has not been proven," said Taylor.[16]

Well, yes, Larry, it has.

At least, that is, as far as other scientific theories have been "proven"; like, for instance, the theories of electricity, DNA replication, atomic energy, flight, plant growth . . . all of the physical processes with which we are surrounded and whose function we assume to be fully understood and irrefutable. For instance, it is one thing to argue that the theory of universal gravitation isn't the only possible explanation for why an apple falls when it is dropped; it is another thing entirely to argue that the apple doesn't fall. But when intelligent design or creationism advocates call evolution a "theory," they are contesting the evidence, not the theory for explaining the evidence. The fossil and biological record indicates, incontestably, that less complex forms of life have developed into more complex ones; Evolution is the explanation for how and why that has happened that is most consistent with all the evidence—but that it *has* happened is not a "debate." Of course, there may be other explanations for these processes; no scientific theory—not even one as accepted as why the Earth is round rather than flat—can ever be 100 percent certain; but the evidence that it is round is incontestable, not a "theory," and to suggest that Flat Earth theory ought to be taught in science classes as a policy of "fairness," so that people can "understand what the debate is about," would be to subvert the meaning of evidence, debate, and science, as well as that of theory.

When scientists refer to the "theory" of evolution, they mean "theory" in the sense of "a supposition or a system of ideas intended to explain something,"[17] a supposition based on accumulated scientific evidence and subject to revision based on further scientific evidence. They do not mean "a guess." However, that is how the majority of the American public seem to understand the term. In fact, the public generally does not understand the difference between a theory and a *hypothesis*. A hypothesis is "a supposition or proposed explanation made on the basis of limited evidence," or a "proposition made as a basis for reasoning, without any assumption of its truth."[18] In other words, while it is proper to refer to evolution as a theory—*if* one understands that by theory one means "as certain as we, as mortals, can be"—it is equally *im*proper to refer to intelligent design as a theory, when in fact it is (at best) a hypothesis.

And it is at this point that we can see evidence of nearly three centuries of accumulated prejudices associated with theory and theoreticians. When the anti-evolution or anti–global warming forces use the word "theory," they do so with those quotation marks firmly in place, and there is a dismissive slur in their deployment of that term that expresses contempt not just for the theory's argument, but for the entire world view it represents. The implication is that, as mere "theories," global warming and evolution are unfounded, radical beliefs held by an intellectual elite—an elite that poses a cultural threat to a practical, hard-working, democratic middle class more concerned with economic progress and religious "values" than esoteric notions of environmental responsibility and biological processes.

Thus the "debate" over global warming or evolution isn't really the two-sided conflict represented in the popular media as a struggle over competing explanations of phenomena. It is, rather, a struggle over language. And the two sides in these "debates" aren't really two interpretations of scientific data; rather, they are two different definitions of such terms as debate, controversy, evidence, theory, and even science. But, as the parties in the struggle aren't using the same definitions of terms, it is a cultural struggle, not a scientific one— and therefore one without the possibility of resolution on scientific grounds.

Experimentalists vs. Theoreticians and Anti-Science Rhetoric

As I noted above, scientists are essentially shooting themselves in the foot when, ever cautious, they call evolution a theory but then don't go on to explain what they mean by that term—which is something quite different from what their critics mean. They further damage their own arguments when they persist in maintaining the sort of class division between applied and theoretical science that was discussed in chapter 1. In a recent article about the construction of the Large Hadron Collider (LHC) at CERN—Europe's version of the now-defunct U.S. SSC, and a machine that is similarly viewed as something that "will unlock the secrets of the universe"[19]—the same sort of applied/theoretical antipathies are on display:

> "I am happy to eat Chinese dinners with theorists," the Nobel Prize–winning experimentalist Samuel C. C. Ting once reportedly said. "But to spend your life doing what they tell you is a waste of time."
>
> "If I occasionally neglect to cite a theorist, it's not because I've forgotten," Leon Lederman, another Nobel Prize–winning experimentalist, writes in his chronicle of the search for the Higgs. "It's probably because I hate him."
>
> "There is a sense among many experimentalists that theorists are a bunch of irresponsible little spoiled brats who get to sit around all day, having all these fun ideas, drinking espresso and goofing off with next to no accountability. . . . Meanwhile [the experimentalists] are out there, nose to the grindstone."[20]

All the old prejudices about applied vs. theoretical science are on display here: theory is a "waste"; theoreticians are "hated" by practical scientists; and theoreticians exhibit effete tastes, such as espresso; while engineers-experimentalists are the true workers in the high-energy physics factory, their noses firmly "to the grindstone." This Lazzaroni-like internal division between the experimentalists and the theoreticians isn't the only artifact from the nineteenth century we might find all too familiar; there also seems to be a resurgence of the general anti-science sentiment that was apparent in the beginning of the nineteenth century. A representative text is Brian Appleyard's *Understanding the Present: Science and the Soul of Modern Man* (1993). While the prejudices of Appleyard's book are clear enough even in his title—opposing, as it does, science with soul—the wider and more subtle prejudice about applied vs. theoretical science can be discovered in a review of the book by Timothy Ferris. Ferris begins by referring to Bertrand Russell's *The Scientific Outlook* (1933), wherein Russell predicted that, in a world "which would result if scientific technique were to rule unchecked," people would not be allowed to read Hamlet and anyone who wouldn't work would be jailed—which sounds exactly like the sort of world imagined by Wings Over the World or Technocracy, Inc.[21] Of course they referred to such a world as a utopia; after all, why try and force Hamlet into the mind of a natural-born engineer? But Russell's chief concern was that science was moving from "knowledge" to "power": "The former impulse leads to the kind of knowledge that is contemplative, the latter to the kind that is practical."[22] Russell, in the British tradition, fears the second over the first, whereas any pragmatic American would probably see the first as more dangerous, as it would lead to melancholy, isolation, and finally sloth.

Appleyard goes one better than Russell, decrying "the appalling spiritual damage that science has done," and stating bluntly that science has "gone too far" and threatens to "throw our civilization out of balance." Such indictments should sound quite familiar, and Appleyard's is indeed largely a restatement of the complaints of Carlyle et al., that 1) science has no values, but rather is based on "amorality," and 2) science is destructive of our traditions in that it is "spiritually corrosive, burning away ancient authorities." Appleyard goes on to claim, "Science is thus responsible for a general moral and spiritual decline in Western culture," and science must be "resisted" and "humbled."[23]

But resisted by what? Ignorance? As Ferris argues, "Is it really plausible to assert that science permeates an American society in which only one in five high-school graduates has taken a physics course, only one in four citizens has heard that the universe is expanding, 21 percent think the Sun orbits the Earth . . . ?" However, Ferris makes the same distinction between applied and theoretical science that is at the root of the Mechanic/Wizard split: "Science in principle has to do with knowledge, technology with power. To confound the two . . . is to equate all scientific research with that darker side of the empirical model which Russell called 'power science.'" One hears in that modifier "darker" an inversion of the cultural prejudices I've discussed regarding technology vs. theory; but simply inverting the dichotomy does nothing to defuse the consequent prejudice. For instance, whereas Ferris places the anxiety the public feels in the face of "power" science at the feet of technologists, it is fundamentally no different from the anxiety Appleyard feels in the face of scientific theorists. Appleyard relates a story of his father, an engineer, figuring out how much water a tower held. "He worked it out on the spot. I was dumbstruck and made uneasy by this power. . . . I sensed something dangerous and ominous in this strange wisdom."[24] According to Appleyard, this "strange wisdom" strikes the average citizen as essentially that of a faith-based ideology, as he claims that science has "started to turn itself into a religion."[25]

Ferris suggests that "the real target of Appleyard's book would appear to be not science but scientism, the belief that science provides not a path to truth, but the only path."[26] However, I would argue that Appleyard's feeling of dangerous wisdom, and Ferris's fear of the "darker side" of science both represent not so much an anxiety over scientism as technoism, the belief that the efficiency of machines can be induced into human relations, the flip or "positive" side of which was represented by the technocratic utopias envisioned by Wings Over the World, Technocracy, Inc., and the majority of 1930s American culture, as well as the American culture of the twenty-first century. Both fears—Appleyard's of "dark" theory and Ferris's of "power" technology—evidence cultural prejudices that will be defused only when, first, the putative border between scientific theory and practice is understood as utterly arbitrary and counter-productive, and, second, both scientists and average Americans understand science as a cultural practice, not some special category of endeavor "immune" to human biases and failings.

Charles Fort's Revenge

While there are fewer pseudoscientific social reform programs (such as mesmerism and phrenology) in the twenty-first century than there were in the nineteenth, the influence of pseudoscience in the American culture would appear to be as strong as ever, as evidenced by the popularity of films and television shows based on the kind of *Ripley's Believe It or Not* phenomena of the strange, unusual, paranormal, or simply weird. In fact, Charles Fort is probably better known today than he was in his own time (1874–1932), when he was referred to as a "researcher of the anomalous," or simply a crank. Fort spent his entire life collecting incidents from newspapers, magazines, and simple word-of-mouth testimonies about events that seemed inexplicable by the tenets of traditional science: reported instances of teleportation, telekinesis, UFO visitations, levitation. . . . Perhaps one of the most famous such incidents is his report of a "rain of frogs" on a small English village.[27] While perhaps the most critically useful aspect of Fort's ideas and writings could be considered the dedicated skepticism he brought to bear on science's presumption of neutrality and objectivity—a point of critical investigation now central to cultural studies—his lasting impact on popular culture is more evident now than ever before. Such "anti-rationalist" television shows as *The X-Files, Ripley's Believe It or Not, Ghost Hunters, Unexplained Mysteries, Medium, Roswell, America's Psychic Challenge, Destination Truth*, and *MonsterQuest*, as well as fantasy programs found on the mainstream media such as *Buffy the Vampire Slayer* and *Charmed* . . . all offer alternatives to a universe ruled and comprehended by the discipline of the scientific method, and therefore owe much of their ideology to Charles Fort. The popularity and profusion of these programs would seem to indicate that a large percentage of the American culture is sympathetic to his belief in paranormal phenomenon and his critique of, even disdain for, more conventional and cautious scientific theory.

The X-Files particularly seems to draw its appeal from its premise that the "truth" that is out there is either one poorly understood by traditional science, or one that traditional scientists work diligently to cover up. In fact, in nearly all of these examples, "paranormal" phenomena are less important to their dramatic energy than are tales of government conspiracies. In *The X-Files*, for instance, the heroes are FBI agents who reveal the "truth" of UFOs and monsters, and the villains are government hacks and scientists who work to cover up any indication there is a world beyond everyday reality. The logic represented here is a curious reversal of what one might expect: scientists—the very people who ought to be most interested in investigating new and strange phenomena—are characterized as paranoid conservatives; whereas that most conservative agency of the government, the FBI, is the explorer of new ideas and territories. And in the very popular TV series *Ghost Hunters*, the ghost hunting is done by people who are plumbers by day, paranormal investigators by night. In fact, their very lack of institutionalized scientific education apparently grants them more rather than less credibility, as much time is spent in many episodes emphasizing that, as with Captain Hendry in *The Thing*, most of the scientific theories at work are "beyond them." They are mechanics, not scientists, and thus we should view their research as commonsensical, pragmatic, and untainted by the "elitism" of university-trained professionals.

I believe two forces are at work here. First, one might theorize that, the deeper and wider science extends its understanding of the universe, the more stubbornly does the popular culture insist on preserving some space free from science's demystifying power. Precisely because science is *not* a religion, its ideology is one difficult for the average person to accept *as* a belief system, especially if one desires that belief system to entice rather than explain, bedazzle rather than explicate. Second, as I mentioned earlier, the dramatic power of such programs, especially *The X-Files*, is derived not from the shock factor of various aliens and chimeras, but from the "insider knowledge" of secrets and conspiracies. Such conspiracy theories have all the attributes of a faith-based religion, where a lack of empirical evidence not only isn't taken as a critique of the theory, but as support for its validity. One might make comparisons, for instance, between the curiously resilient American belief in UFOs and our equally robust conviction that a massive cover-up lies at the heart of the Kennedy assassination, despite, in both cases, all evidence to the contrary. Such conspiracy theories provide a certain cultural comfort, organizing the random events of history into cohesive, reassuring narratives of human control over accident. In short, it is much less distressing to believe that the momentous effects on history caused by the Kennedy assassination were the result of goal-oriented machinations by human agents, rather than a result of the unpredictable and ultimately uncontrollable forces of chaos and random coincidence. Similarly, it is much easier to accuse the government of covering up evidence of UFOs than it is to explain the logic of UFO visitation.

But ultimately there is little or no effort devoted to explicating the logic of "suppressed" phenomena as represented in *The X-Files*, conspiracy industries, and various UFO "infomercials." One might ask, for instance, what rationale there is to beings capable of building interstellar spacecraft obsessively studying the biology of human beings? If, as the UFO proponents argue, these aliens have been abducting and studying us for decades if not centuries, why haven't they figured us out yet? But this flaw in what we might call the "internal logic of anal probes" is finessed by foregrounding the element of *conspiracy*: the conspiracy makes visible, material, and credible the otherwise invisible, immaterial, and ultimately illogical phenomena; so in a sense such belief systems evidence the same sort of privileging of the material—the truth that is "out there"—over the theoretical—the truth that is formula-ized—for which I've argued throughout this book.

"Unnatural" Science

It is worthwhile at this point to re-quote the playbill for the first stage production of *Frankenstein*: "The striking moral exhibited in this story, is the fatal consequence of that presumption which attempts to penetrate, beyond prescribed depths, into the mysteries of nature." The science of Frankenstein is thus indicted on moral grounds as bad science because it "penetrates . . . beyond prescribed depths," science that goes beyond the natural and crosses some boundary into the unnatural. It should be clear by now that Wicked Wizards are often considered wicked based on little more than the unexamined assumption that the science in which they engage is unnatural. This requires us to examine just what makes certain scientific practices "unnatural," as well as the cultural construction of that term—a construction that seems not to have changed markedly for over three hundred years.

We might begin by examining the application of that term to a being nearly everyone simply assumes is quintessentially unnatural: Frankenstein's creature. This assumption pervades nearly all discussions of the novel and all its progeny, even the most recent ones.[28] Most of these analyses argue that the monster is unnatural because it came into existence through an unnatural process, i.e., stitched together from the corpses of dead bodies rather than generated from the union of a male sperm and a female egg in a human womb. It is worthwhile to examine this reasoning in some detail in order to attempt to discern exactly at what point in the process it is assumed that the creature becomes *unnatural*.

Certainly the bodies from which it was made were originally quite natural, having been human beings born in the traditional manner. If it is the act of taking a part from one natural human and combining it with another part from another natural human that makes the final combination *un*natural, then any human with an organ with which he or she was not originally outfitted—anyone, for instance, walking around with a heart or kidney or liver transplant—is, by this logic, equally unnatural. If, however, we're not willing to go that far, then it must be something further along in the process that makes the creature unnatural. Perhaps it is the fact that once dead tissue was brought back to life? There again, if this is the criterion for its unnaturalness, then anyone revived from near drowning, or anyone whose heart has been shocked back into life with paddles, is as unnatural as the creature. If we are not willing to go *that* far, either, then perhaps it is the supposition, as the novel posits it, that the creature lacks a soul. If the creature does indeed lack such a thing, then the soul must be something present in organisms either unaltered from the state in which they were born— which is bad news for anyone with a pacemaker, to say nothing of breast or chin implants—or present only in organisms conceived in wombs; and this would be bad news for all test tube children. In fact, it would appear that the creature's "soullessness" is merely an apposition for its presumed unnaturalness, which returns us to our search for exactly what about its creation or existence irretrievably separates it from the natural world.

It is sometimes suggested that the lack of a proper upbringing and education qualifies the creature as unnatural—that naturalness is something that comes from nurture as much as nature. But such an assertion creates problems for any human raised outside of a traditional community, or for that matter humans raised in communities which neglect their nurturing and education.

Would anyone wish to accuse these children of being unnatural? In other words, if it is something about the *mechanical* process of constructing the creature or the *material* conditions of its existence that is the root of its unnaturalness, then there are corollaries for those processes and conditions among other humans and they, too, must be considered unnatural. If not, then we are suggesting the site of "unnaturalness" is a product of neither nature *nor* nurture, which raises some extremely complicated questions about where, then, unnaturalness—or for that matter, naturalness—resides.

At this point those arguing for the unnaturalness of the creature typically respond that it is in the totality of its existence—in its gestalt of creation and being—that it differs fundamentally from natural beings; in other words, that the sum of natural human status is something greater than its constituent biological and psychological parts. As that gestalt cannot be further defined or differentiated, it becomes a *transcendental signifier*, a term which cannot be defined within the current discourse, and therefore an idea taken for granted to be true—in other words, as something just "natural" to that discourse. And perhaps it is at this point we would recognize that, in this context (if not in all contexts), the most we can say of the creature's status as a being is that it is "nontraditional"—but that to call it unnatural is to label it with a word empty of meaning.

What is remarkable about this moral reaction to Frankenstein's creature, and the semiotic conundrum it engenders, is how little it has changed in two hundred years. Many modern depictions of bad or mad science rest on the same tautological formula of natural/unnatural, particularly when that science is involved in biological research. That other great focus of the "unnatural" work by modern Wicked Wizards is, of course, cloning. Representative of the general public's attitude toward cloning is a speech given by organic dairy farmer Albert Straus at the California State Capitol as part of the debate over a bill to require "warning labels" on food from cloned animals. Straus puts his objection to cloning quite bluntly: "Cloning is unnatural. Cloning is a method of reproduction that never occurs naturally in mammals."[29]

What Straus means is that cloning doesn't occur in mammals without the intervention of *other* mammals—in this case, human beings; and so what Straus really means is that human intervention into the reproductive processes of other mammals is "unnatural." But Straus, as a farmer from a long line of farmers, must realize that humans have intervened in the reproduction of domesticated animals for centuries, through a process called "breeding." There may be more technology involved in cloning than breeding, but functionally they are no different.

This denotative confusion over just what we mean by "unnatural" when it comes to the biological sciences is resident even in the rhetoric of those who defend cloning. For instance, in a paper supportive of cloning research, Kenan

Malik admits that "cloning is certainly unnatural."[30] He then goes on to try to render this charge irrelevant by stating: "But then so is virtually every human activity." And there's the problem: the assumption that "human activity" is, by definition, unnatural. And it is a very widespread assumption indeed.

Here I believe it's useful to introduce a small "case history" from my own teaching experience. When, in a Cultural Studies course, I ask my students to define "natural," they typically point out a classroom window to the trees and rocks and grass outside; and when I then ask them to define "unnatural," they point to the room in which we sit, to the unsightly concrete and cheap plastic which surrounds us (I teach in a public university). I then ask them to explain to me the difference between rocks and concrete, trees and plastic; they look stunned. Isn't that obvious? they ask. One is manufactured, the other isn't. I persist: But isn't the concrete and plastic manufactured from minerals and other "natural" substances? They admit it is. So, I ask, is it the process of *altering* those natural materials that makes the final result unnatural? Yes, they answer, that must be it. Then, I ask, are they saying beaver dams are unnatural? After all, the beavers harvest the trees, mill them, cement them together . . . in other words, alter them considerably. By now they are typically quite uncomfortable, and sometimes even a little defensive in the face of my stubborn idiocy. But that's *different*, they insist. Why? I insist back. Well . . . because those are beavers, not humans. Ah, I say, so the real difference is between what natural creatures do, and what humans do? Yes, they reply, relieved, that's it. So, I pounce (with shameful glee), you're saying humans are *unnatural*? At this point there is usually a profound— or at least a confused—silence; also by this point the period is usually over, so they file out, perplexed, and more than a little convinced than I'm crazy. Don't I understand the difference? Isn't it *obvious*?

As I said, that's the problem with the unnatural, right there: everyone thinks it's obvious. Cloning cannot be unnatural, any more than "every other human activity" can be unnatural—unless, by implication, humans are unnatural. This is of course a cultural "blindspot" that's been examined by anthropologists and semioticians for decades. Perhaps the most famous texts are Claude Lévi-Strauss's *Elementary Structures of Kinship* (1949), and Jacques Derrida's brilliant, groundbreaking deconstruction of that book and the issue of natural/unnatural that runs throughout Lévi-Strauss's work, in "Structure, Sign, and Play in the Discourse of the Human Sciences" (1966). Without reproducing their arguments and insights here, suffice it to say that the cultural effect of the term "unnatural" has always been to place the efforts and abilities of human beings *outside* of Nature; to see human activity since the invention of the first tool as somehow beyond or even counter to the territory and workings of the universe.

Such a view of humans vis-à-vis the universe is a curious form of anthro-

centric self-loathing, and perhaps best understood in terms of mythical narratives like the Garden of Eden from the Judeo-Christian tradition, though similar accounts of humankind's expulsion from a natural paradise can be found in
many other cultures. Functionally, all foster a view of Homo sapiens as somehow fundamentally different from all other forms of life on Earth, and tend to
engender a deep-seated anxiety that human invention, either consciously or
unconsciously, seeks to punish or sabotage Nature for this primordial expulsion. (This might remind us of the Puritan prejudice that human *theoretical*
invention was somehow fundamentally an insult to God.)

However, if we reject this irrational superstition, and instead accept humans as natural, as part of the universe, not exceptions to it, then anything and
everything we do *must* be accepted as natural. We can be innovative, nontraditional, inefficient, mistaken, illogical, dangerous, self-destructive, grotesque,
frightening, weird, and even dumb . . . but we cannot be "unnatural." We cannot
be "outside" of nature. We *are* nature.

As I argued in the analysis of the *Jurassic Park* films, if Life is considered the
"natural" process by which an all-female community of dinosaurs spontaneously
mutates into half-male dinosaurs in order to breed, then why isn't Life also the
process of millions of years of evolution that results in a human brain capable of
conceiving and realizing the concept of cloning dinosaurs? This is putting the
question in a way that opponents of the "unnatural" practices of cloning, stem
cell research, DNA replacement, and other human interventions into biological
processes don't wish to engage, and one they usually dismiss as mere "playing"
with words. But words are the "machines" by which we organize and communicate our thoughts and feelings; understanding how they function is no mere
game, it is fundamental to understanding ourselves and our culture. To substi-
tute the word "nontraditional" for "unnatural" in these debates would defuse
the moral condemnation implicit in the opposition's arguments, as well as clar-
ify that these are debates over cultural values, not categories of existence. Thus
the deployment of the term "unnatural" is a normalizing strategy: a maneuver
which seeks to frame the science concerned within a context of cultural traditions and expectations, and to draw the boundaries of that frame from a standpoint of moral assumptions defined and limited by that culture.

This linguistic deconstruction of the illogic of the unnatural is not mere "playing" with words, especially in the larger context of my argument throughout this
book. This understanding of the false dichotomy of natural/unnatural centrally
and fundamentally informs my reasoning about what it is about Wicked Wizards that American culture finds so threatening. Even though both Mechanics
and Wizards use the scientific method in their work, the goals of the Wicked
Wizards are typically considered to be ones that "penetrate, beyond prescribed

depths, into the mysteries of nature." What they are doing is wicked—unnatural not because it is something that Master Mechanics don't do, but because they're either doing too much of it, or because they're doing it for the wrong reasons. This implies that the territory of unnatural exploration is not discontinuous with that of natural exploration; rather, it is a boundary one crosses when one goes too far, either in terms of motivation or methods or goals.

A Manifesto for Master Mechanics

Taken together, all the characteristics of Master Mechanics and Wicked Wizards I've discussed in this book can be summarized as the four standards of American scientific practice: 1) *who* American scientists are, 2) *what* it is they are trying to accomplish, 3) *how* they go about accomplishing it, and 4) *why* they dedicate their lives to achieving these goals. Put another way, the mural that is three centuries of American history represents Good American science in popular images which represent the who, what, how, and why of American scientific practice—or what is taken to be axiomatic about American scientific practice. Thus when Bad un-American science is represented, it is defined as bad to the extent that it violates one or more of these images.

It may be useful at this point to offer a chart that constructs these questions in terms of the binary oppositions implicit in these four standards—in other words, to deconstruct the components of each standard in terms of its explicit positive and implicit negative attributes. Such a chart would look something like this:

Standard	Explicit Positive	Implicit Negative
WHO	*Good scientists are*:	*Bad scientists are*:
	Engineers	Intelligentsia
	Patriotic	Multicultural
	Average	Elite
	Family men	Isolatoes
	Small-town	Cosmopolitan
	God-fearing	Atheist
	Healthy	Handicapped
WHAT	*Good scientists produce*:	*Bad scientists produce*:
	Practical inventions	Totalizing theories
	Discoveries	Dictates
	Natural reformations	Unnatural transgressions
	Conversion of world to	Conquest of world for
	American ideology	alien ideology

(*continued*)

Standard	Explicit Positive	Implicit Negative
HOW	*Good scientists achieve*:	*Bad scientists achieve*:
	Dedication	Obsession
	Individual ingenuity	Mass compulsion
	Objective observation	Ideologically driven theorizing
	Free & public invention	Forced & secret research
	Mechanical acumen	Intellectual superiority
	Emotion informed by logic	All logic, no emotion
WHY	*Good scientists are motivated*:	*Bad scientists are motivated*:
	Benefiting all mankind	Benefiting some small clique
	Duty	Profit
	Curiosity	Hubris

Of course, the "bad" Wicked Wizard traits are generated by the assumptions resident in the "good" Master Mechanic traits. Such is the logic of stereotypes and, as I said in the Introduction, I am not arguing that there is any fundamental truth to the traits associated with either trope. However, there is an interesting (if somewhat dated) discussion of "psychometric" analyses of just what kind of people American scientists, especially American physicists, really are in Richard Rhodes's *Making of the Atomic Bomb*.[31] The list of putative commonalities revealed through questionnaires and Rorschach tests includes various "likelihoods": sickly childhood, single parent, high IQ, avid reader, feelings of alienation, shy, aloof, sexual late bloomer (if ever). . . . In fact, the list looks very much like that of the stereotypical Wicked Wizard from the chart above—until, that is, we come to the stats on marriage. These same surveys found that, when these "sexual late bloomers" eventually discovered women and married one of them, their marriages tended to be above-average stable, to produce healthy and happy children, and to be a major source of support for the scientists' professional work.

One might well ask why, if the other qualities of the Wicked Wizard stereotype find some correlation in reality, does that stereotype then jettison reality when it comes to that which supposedly makes the Wizards most wicked and least redeemable, their lack of familial relations? I would argue that this blindspot in the stereotype suggests that, for the American culture, the chief catalyst for transforming acceptable scientific talent and enthusiasm into sinister scientific obsession is the lack of a family to limit, manage, or generally "govern" the scientist's imagination—a cultural predilection which I believe I've shown can be traced back to the Puritans' absolute mania for surveilling and disciplining, if not entirely eliminating that Achilles' Heel of the human soul, the unfettered imagination.

Still, my "values" chart for Master Mechanics and Wicked Wizards is meant to specify the particulars of the generalized stereotypes, to demonstrate the internal dynamics of their construction, and to make clear the binary nature of the theory behind that construction. It is not intended as a standard against which one can accurately measure the actual lives and motivations of real, practicing engineers or theorists. More important, by stating that there is a "theory" behind these stereotypes, I am inviting what might be the most fundamental objection to my overall argument, which is the distinction I've made throughout this book between practice and theory.

One might ask, why aren't the various goals of the Master Mechanics, however practical they may be, yet theoretical? Aren't most successful scientists both good practitioners *and* good theorists? Am I merely reproducing the dichotomy between theoretical conception and empirical observation, a dichotomy that elsewhere I have argued is a distinction without a difference? Isn't it after all a *theory* to suggest that technological innovation, rather than theoretical speculation, provides the best path of cultural progress, national survival, and everything else America believes is a result of its pragmatic focus in the sciences? In other words, aren't the Master Mechanics operating on theories just as much as the Wicked Wizards?

To this objection I can only answer, yes, exactly. There isn't anything linguistically or conceptually more theoretical about the Wicked Wizards' schemes for world revolution through the invention of new ideology than there is about the Master Mechanics' belief in the superiority of community reformation through the invention of new gadgets; they are both belief systems, ideologies, a set of priorities and values based on assumptions and preferred methodologies. In the realm of the ways in which language works—the language used to construct Edison's patent applications as well as Oppenheimer's dire warnings of nuclear apocalypse—the words function the same way. To call one goal and text mechanical-practical and the other theoretical-abstract is, I will freely admit, to create a false dichotomy.

But—and this is the most fundamental element of my argument—it is a *cultural* dichotomy; and therefore it is false only if the culture believes it is, true only insofar as the culture needs for one reason or another to believe it is true. Put another way, a culture that fundamentally places more value on deed than thought, thing than theory, act than intention, the material than the esoteric, etc., will dump much prejudicial moral condemnation on the latter category; and in this case that latter category is the intellect. So, yes, the assumption that a light bulb is better than a formula is a *theory*; but if the culture doesn't see this assumption as a theory but rather as an axiom, something unquestioned and obvious, then it requires 100,000 words (if not many more) to reveal that assumption *as* a theory.

In terms of the cultural motivations and consequences of this theory disguised as an axiom, a useful example here is the development of the atomic bomb. The tremendous expenditure of effort necessary to develop the bomb was of course based on a scientific theory: that splitting the atom would release vast amounts of energy. But that theory had been around for some time before one of its applications—the military one of a weapon—sparked the national effort to investigate that theory, at a time when weapons were our chief *practical* priority. One can wonder: if the only result foreseen for the splitting of the atom was an addition to our understanding of the universe—much as the proposed search for the Higgs Boson with the SSC—would there have been a Manhattan Project?[32] Probably not. But when the practical outcome of an atomic bomb was seen as vital to our war effort, then it was deemed worthy of a concentration of all our resources. So in the context of World War II (if not throughout human history), a "theory" of useful weapons was more valued than a "theory" of abstract knowledge. Why? The obvious answer seemed then, and perhaps still seems now, that possession of the atomic bomb ensured our "national survival."

But survival of what? If we'd develop atomic energy not to build a bomb but only to produce electrical power, would that have been necessary and sufficient motivation? Doesn't cheap electricity also ensure our national survival? Would we wish to be a nation with nuclear-tipped ICBMs but with our homes lit only by candles?

Such a question takes us to the next step in our analysis: atomic weapons were seen as the key to our national survival *in the short term*. What I am suggesting is that this predilection for things over theory is really at heart a preference for short-term gains over long-term investments; and the anti-intellectualism I am suggesting is resident in so much of American culture is really a shortsighted commitment to efforts that yield not only tangible results, but *immediately* tangible results. When one is dealing on the scale of a few years or a decade, certain actions seem to make basic "common sense" because of the results they will yield in that time frame; but if one extends that scale to decades or even centuries, then one can see that overlooked or ignored possibilities might yield even more substantive results, even when those results are limited by the perspective of "national survival"—or rather, a narrow definition of national survival. For what after all is a nation? Its geography? Its people? Its laws and beliefs and practices? To use our example, if atomic bombs guaranteed our short-term victory in World War II, but continue to threaten our very existence not only as a nation but as a species, then to what extent has their development truly served the goal of "national survival"?

If, on the other hand, national survival is defined as, in Robert Wilson's words, "the respect with which we regard one another, the dignity of men, our love of culture . . . all the things we really venerate in our country and are patriotic about," then theoretical science is as useful and *pragmatic* an investment of our talents and resources as any short-term technological innovation, as it contributes in fundamental ways to our concept of who we are as a nation and why we feel that nation deserves to survive. For all of Franklin's utilitarian contrivances, his most useful invention, in terms of the developing American culture, was a theoretical one: that of a uniquely *American* identity. And such "theories" as Robert Oppenheimer's deeply troubled vision of international responsibility for the survival of the human race, or Wilson's belief in the cultural benefits of understanding the workings of the universe, are at least as important a contribution to that national identity as any mechanical novelty; quite possibly even more important.

AT THIS point it is worth returning to the opening question of this chapter: in the more than two centuries since Benjamin Franklin "invented" the high standards for good Master Mechanics and, by implication, the warning signs for bad Wicked Wizards, has there been any significant change in America's attitude toward these stereotypes? Given the changes that have occurred since the eighteenth century in immigration, population distribution, education, attitudes toward race, class, and gender, as well as politics in general, are there signs that the Master Mechanic mythos is any less in ascendancy in 2008 than it was in 1798?

For instance, one might argue that, as immigration has changed the makeup of this country's population, Catholicism might be expected to have exerted greater influence than Puritanism or even Protestantism on our cultural attitudes. However, not only did I find no significant shift in these prejudices during periods of significant Catholic immigration—particularly in the late nineteenth and early twentieth centuries, when the cult of the Great Independents and fervor over full-employment utopias were at their peak—but to even suggest such an effect one would have to posit that Catholicism as an ideology has demonstrated greater tolerance and less suspicion of the imagination than Protestantism—and from the historical record, that would seem to be a difficult claim to support. And while even more recent trends in immigration may result in a far more diverse population than that known to the Puritan Fathers, there are as yet no signs that this diverse population is any more sympathetic toward subtle and complex intellectual constructs than those who came before. In other words, barring a sudden influx of ten million French poststructuralists, the overall popular American privileging of thing over theory shows no signs of transformation due to immigration trends.

It might also be argued that the prejudices I've discussed are primarily regional, and hence predominantly rural rather than urban; and, as America continues to become progressively more urbanized, we might expect some shift toward urban values and ideologies. While traditionally the American culture (though this trait is clearly apparent in many other cultures as well) has viewed the rural as the realm of the doer, and the urban as that of the thinker, with more and more of the population shifting to metropolitan settings, can we expect that prejudice to change? I would respond that it is less important where the majority of the population lives than what the majority of the population believes; and, as long as the majority of the culture continues to see the rural as a priori somehow fundamentally more "American" than the urban—until, that is, it is accepted that by the "heartland" of America we might as well be referring to New York or Los Angeles as Des Moines or Kansas City—then the culture at large will continue to privilege what it believes are the values of the rural over the urban.

Is there any sign that our education system is creating that awareness? After all, about half the population now experiences some form of higher education. And some may suggest that the acceptance in many university literature departments of poststructuralist, feminist, postcolonial, and other intellectually complex literary theories, as well as the recent flowering of Cultural Studies programs, does in fact indicate greater support for diverse, subtle, sophisticated, and imaginative thinking in our college curriculums. Unfortunately, the backlash against such "Frenchified" literary theories began some time ago; as far back as the early 1990s deconstruction was declared dead and buried.[33] And even though most university administrations give considerable lip service and even some material support to multicultural curriculums, prominent politicians and even educators continue to decry multiculturalism as "bunk."[34] Additionally, there are daily calls in educational journals for higher education which is *more* practical and *less* theoretical, combined with equally frequent articles about how more and more university administrations are working to "business-fy" their institutions. Coupled with these views is the "customer service" model of the student-faculty relationship, with students as the customers demanding the sort of education that will serve them best in the "practical" world of business and trades, and faculty as the employees of a university only too happy to oblige. Any training these "customers" receive in the arts or other esoteric intellectual fields is considered a frivolous luxury, a kind of decorative façade over the fundamental necessity of a "practical" education. Never is it suggested that logical thinking and creative skepticism might in fact be *more* fundamentally necessary for making the difficult decisions facing a twenty-first-century citizen of America than understanding the arcana of tax law and the stock market. Unless the models and priorities of American education undergo significant reformation, there seems little hope that simply sending Americans to college in larger numbers will alter these stereotypes and prejudices in any substantial way.

Two issues I have not specifically addressed in this book are those of race and gender. I have touched on the topic of race to the extent I pointed out that a key factor in the Wicked Wizard character is his perceived "foreignness"—which is often a synonym for racial difference—and his sympathy for or fascination with other cultures. And certainly Dr. No and his myriad Oriental predecessors give evidence of a racial undertone to the "othering" of Wicked Wizards. But are these stereotypes viewed any differently by the different racial and ethnic communities in America? It would be a fascinating topic of research to examine the periods and issues I've dealt with here, but through the narrower lens of race, an examination I hope is undertaken in the near future. As to gender, perhaps it could be argued that women as a population might be less enamored of the whole Master Mechanic ethos than are men. On the other hand, that argument may be to merely continue age-old stereotypes about gender. While it is true that, as previously mentioned, female Wicked Wizards in literature and film are almost entirely unknown, such an approach is an important one that requires its own thorough analysis.

If any of these prejudices were to show signs of alteration over the years, we might expect to see those effects reflected in the arena of politics, with its mix of appeals and concerns drawn from all quarters and segments of the nation. For instance, take the presidential election of 2000. The Democratic candidate, Al Gore, was derided as "Ozone Man" by his Republican opponents, and portrayed in the conservative media as too much of a thinker, not enough of a doer; yet he went on to win a majority of the popular vote. However, the truly surprising result of that election is not that Gore received more than 50 percent of the popular vote; the surprising thing is that his Republican opponent, George W. Bush, self-proclaimed as incurious and infamously anti-intellectual, received *almost* half. And in the election of 2004, Bush's opponent John Kerry was often criticized in the same conservative media as "too French," an echo of the reflexive anti-European rhetoric of two centuries before. Apparently, the political prejudices of 1798 are operating just as reliably in 2008, which suggests little if any change in the bedrock attitudes of the broader American culture. One might go so far as to suggest that the "values" chart presented earlier might as well serve as an analysis of the divergent cultural beliefs of "red" and "blue" states as those of Mechanics and Wizards. However, I do not wish to press this point; to do so superficially would merely dilute my focus on the representation of American scientists; and to do so sufficiently would require another book. I leave it to the reader to extrapolate my analysis of these categories to the wider and deeper cultural context of American politics.

If, then, none of the cultural trends I've mentioned show any sign of significantly altering these prejudices, what could? Presuming, of course, that one believes a more balanced view of theorists would be good for American culture.

Again referring back to the values chart for Mechanics and Wizards, it would seem that the American culture would have to undergo transformations across the depth and breadth of its ideological landscape; that we would somehow have to come to an appreciation of the intelligentsia as just as integral to American enterprise as engineers; that multiculturalism would become accepted as an invaluable perspective, not "bunk"; that superior intellect would become viewed not as presumptively anti-democratic; that alternative lifestyles would not be attacked as anti-family; that the metropolis would be as much praised in our cultural mythology as the small town; and that belief in God would not be taken as a pre-condition for an acceptable American character.

That's a tall order. As I hope I've demonstrated, the privileging of things and the disdain for theory is woven into nearly every aspect of American cultural history; it isn't a mere expression of a particular period or segment of the population, but rather is as much part of the bedrock of American cultural inheritance as a privileging of private over communal property, a reflexive suspicion of government, a belief in American exceptionalism. To alter such cultural inertia would require wide and concentrated efforts on a number of fronts, from the classroom to the movie theater.

But can it at least be argued that science, including scientific theory, is better or more widely taught and understood today than in the past? And in terms of the media, can't one point with hope to the increased offerings in newspapers and television of science news, from the "Science" section of the *New York Times*, to an entire television channel devoted to Discovery? But if in fact all this new media attention to scientific reality is making any headway in the popular culture, why then do we find such continuing enthusiasm for anti-science fantasy? As I argued in the section "Charles Fort's Revenge," why does the *X-Files* phenomenon show no signs of abating?

Perhaps one place to start countering the popular momentum of anti-theory sentiment would be in the sciences themselves. As I discussed in chapter 1, the split within the scientific community between the "pure" and "applied" sciences only reinforces these stereotypes. A first step toward greater appreciation and acceptance of theory might be the recognition in the sciences that there is no truly *functional* difference between the kind of science that builds the theory of an atomic bomb, and the kind of science that builds the actual bomb. More specifically, the sciences need to develop a "theory" to deal with the consequences of applied technology, from nuclear weapons to clones. The ethics of applied science have too long been left to politicians, lawyers, and historians, and the few scientists who have tried to address these issues have too often been decried as working out of their league, as happened to Oppenheimer and the other "One World" A-bomb scientists. If we expect American culture at large to come to a better understanding of and greater appreciation for theoretical scientific work, scientists first need to render impotent and obsolete the false distinction between "pure" and "applied" science within their own profession, and then turn to insisting that they have a role in developing social and ethical theories about how their profession's products are applied in the wider culture.

But in order to dismantle these old and counterproductive stereotypes within that wider culture, we must look for any and all opportunities to foster and disseminate respect for the imagination and intellect. Only by accepting that the invention of ideas is as vital to our cultural survival as the invention of gadgets will we outgrow our Puritanical prejudices about "thinking" as inherently suspicious and unproductive, and thus fully realize America's vast imaginative potential.

NOTES

Introduction

1. There is an interesting if perhaps apocryphal anecdote about how this particular casting choice came about. The story goes that role of the Monster was first offered to Bela Lugosi, who had recently achieved wide notoriety for his portrayal of Count Dracula in Todd Browning's 1931 film *Dracula*. Purportedly, Lugosi turned down the role because the dialogue for the Monster was largely limited to grunting, and he felt that would be a step down from his starring role in *Dracula*. Lugosi claimed to the end of his life that this choice ruined his career, while it guaranteed Karloff the lead in countless horror films to follow.

2. One indication of just how pervasive the image of a "mad" scientist is can be found in research conducted by Professor Christopher Frayling of the Royal College of Art. When he asked primary school children to draw a picture of a scientist, more often than not what they drew was a man with "wild hair, lab coat, staring eyes, coke-bottle glasses, [and] a withered hand; in some cases they've even written the word 'MAD' with an arrow pointing to the scientist." Dr. Daniel Glaser, "Science Seen under the Right Conditions," *BBC News*, 9 January 2006, news.bbc.co.uk/1/hi/sci/tech/4596662.stm (accessed 2 December 2006).

3. See, for instance, Roslynn Haynes, "From Alchemy to Artificial Intelligence: Stereotypes of the Scientist in Western Literature," *Public Understanding of Science* 12.3 (2003): 243–53; David J. Skal, *Screams of Reason: Mad Science and Modern Culture* (New York: Norton, 1998); Andrew Tudor, *Monsters and Mad Scientists: A Cultural History of the Horror Movie* (Oxford: Blackwell, 1989); and Christopher P. Toumy, "The Moral Character of Mad Scientists: A Cultural Critique of Science," *Science, Technology, and Human Values* 17 (1992): 411–37.

4. Michael Polanyi, *Science, Faith, and Society* (New York: Oxford University Press, 1946), 51. For a fuller discussion of Polanyi's development as one of the first modern philosophers of science, see Richard Rhodes, *The Making of the Atomic Bomb* (New York: Simon & Schuster, 1986), 31–36.

5. One obvious example of how culture can shape science can be seen in the different approaches Americans and Soviets took toward designing their first spacecrafts. Since the engineering principles necessary to deal with putting a human into orbit and bringing him back are universal, one would expect the resulting designs for space capsules to be very similar, if not identical. However, one need only compare the American Mercury craft to the Soviet Vostok to see this isn't the case. For instance, while the Mercury astronauts insisted on asserting their status as pilots and demanding a window, control stick, and other changes that made the Mercury more like a jet fighter, the Soviet cosmonauts either didn't feel or couldn't express such needs. One might even argue that the Mercury capsule seems based on the wedge shape so prevalent in American architecture, while

the Vostok's sphere gestures toward the rounded corners and domes representative of Russian architecture. Both designs solved the problems presented by manned space exploration, but they solved those problems in very different ways.

1. Simon Pure Amateurs

1. *The Evening Herald* (Boston), 3rd ed., Saturday, 30 November 1849: 12M. The headline reads: "Startling Intelligence! The Body of Dr. George Parkman Found, Murdered and Cut Up in the Medical College—Arrest of Professor Webster, charged with the Diabolical Deed—Tremendous Excitement—A Riot Anticipated."

2. "The American Experience: Murder at Harvard," PBS Online, www.pbs.org/ wgbh/amex/murder/peopleevents/p_webster.html (accessed 2 January 2003).

3. Joseph T. Shipley, "Scientist," *Dictionary of Word Origins* (New York: Philosophical Library, 1975).

4. Howard P. Segal, *Technological Utopianism in American Culture* (Chicago: University of Chicago Press, 1985), 78.

5. Robert V. Bruce, *The Launching of American Science* (New York: Alfred A. Knopf, 1987), 8.

6. Though, as Bruce makes clear, the Royal Society specifically and British science generally were at that time in a period of decline, as chronicled in Charles Babbage's *Reflections on the Decline of Science in England* (1830). And of course Harvard wasn't entirely without talent; one of Webster's colleagues was Oliver Wendell Holmes.

7. Bruce, 11.

8. Ibid., 135.

9. "American Philosophical Society & Museum," ushistory.org/tour/tour_philo .htm (accessed 1 September 2006).

10. Bruce, 64.

11. See ibid., chapter 10, "The Wherewithal of Science."

12. All quoted in ibid., 72.

13. Taylor Stoehr, *Hawthorne's Mad Scientists: Pseudoscience and Social Science in Nineteenth-Century Life and Letters* (Hamden, CT: Archon Books, 1978), 23.

14. Jim Cox, "That Quacking Sound in Colonial America," *Journal of the Colonial Williamsburg Foundation*, Spring 2004, www.history.org/Foundation/journal/Spring04/ quackery.cfm (accessed 13 January 2007). See chapter 12 for more about early American confidence men.

15. Stoehr, 25.

16. Clifford Pyncheon was a real person, and an ancestor of twentieth-century novelist Thomas Pynchon. Much of Pynchon's novel *Gravity's Rainbow* is about a world— spirit possibly, inanimate more probably—that seems on the verge of entering and overwhelming this world. In other words, Thomas interprets such phenomena as the reverse: as the "harbingers" of the triumph of grossness over human life.

17. Stoehr, 27.

18. Ibid., 115.

19. Walt Whitman, "When I heard the Learn'd Astronomer," *Leaves of Grass* (Philadelphia: David McKay, 1900).

20. Quoted in Bruce, 263.

21. George E. Peterson, *The New England College in the Age of the University* (Amherst: Amherst College Press, 1964), 4–7.

22. *Lazzarone* originally was an Italian colloquialism for "goldbricker," but by the nineteenth century it had come to mean generally any laborers who were professionally organized and politically active. The fact that the group chose a foreign word for its name was enough in and of itself to alienate it from many American scientists.

23. Lillian B. Miller, *The Lazzaroni: Science and Scientists in Mid-Nineteenth Century America* (Washington, DC: Smithsonian Institution, 1972), ix.

24. Quoted in I. I. Rabi, *Science: The Center of Culture* (New York: World, 1967), 10.

25. Ibid., 5.

26. Donald Strickland, *Scientists in Politics: The Atomic Scientists Movement, 1945–46* (West Lafayette: Purdue University Studies, 1968), 138.

27. Sir Solly Zuckerman, *Scientists and War: The Impact of Science on Military and Civil Affairs* (New York: Harper & Row, 1966), 49.

28. Bruce, 149.

29. Ibid., 130–34.

30. Ibid., 133.

31. Even in public educational policy, there was an assumed link between teaching applied science and building character. In 1838, Peter W. Gallaudet published a pamphlet calling for "a system of education combining academic study with industrial arts or agricultural training from an early age to form good personal habits and character." The pamphlet suggested that the first beneficiaries of this enlightened system should be "the poor of the District of Columbia" (Library of Congress archives).

32. Bruce, 330.

33. Daniel B. Weber, "*The Manufacturer and the Builder*: Science, Technology, and the American Mechanic," *Journal of American Culture* 8.4 (Winter 1985): 41.

34. *New York Times*, 16 August 1859.

2. Sex and the Single Mad Scientist

1. Nathaniel Hawthorne, "The Birthmark," *The Norton Anthology of Short Fiction*, 4th ed. (New York: W. W. Norton, 1990), 710.

2. Ibid., 713.

3. Nathaniel Hawthorne, "Ethan Brand," www.eldritchpress.org/nh/eb.html (accessed 3 February 2006).

4. Nathaniel Hawthorne, *Rappaccini's Daughter: Great Tales of Terror and the Supernatural*, ed. Herbert A. Wise and Phyllis Fraser (New York: The Modern Library, 1944), 333.

5. Ibid.

6. Ibid., 344.

7. Ibid., 355.

8. Taylor Stoehr, *Hawthorne's Mad Scientists: Pseudoscience and Social Science in Nineteenth-Century Life and Letters* (Hamden, CT: Archon Books, 1978), 46.

9. Chris Baldick, among other critics, in *In Frankenstein's Shadow: Myth, Monstrosity, and Nineteenth-Century Writing* (Oxford: Clarendon Press, 1987), notes the resemblance between Victor Frankenstein and Captain Ahab, in that both are representations of a transgressive Promethean megalomaniac. To quote Baldick: "The individual isolatoes of the *Pequod*'s crew succumb to a Shakespearian rhetoric and to a resurgent European mode of hierarchy in which Ahab galvanizes them through 'the leyden jar of his own magnetic life.' Rather than squeeze hands in that democratic brotherhood dreamed of by Ishmael, they surrender their destinies to a 'head' who turns them into mere arms and legs" (79).

10. Herman Melville, *Moby Dick* (New York: New American Library, 1961), 507.

11. Ibid., 508.

12. Ibid., 507.

13. Ibid., 181.

14. Baldick makes much the same point when he argues that Ahab's "usurpation" of the *Pequod* for personal purposes transgresses the "capitalist" ideology the ship and its crew represent.

15. Melville, 186.

16. While Baldick notes the resemblance between Victor Frankenstein and Captain Ahab, he misses the characteristically American and anti-Transcendentalist undertone of Melville's portrayal. Baldick writes that Ahab "detects" a "divine malevolence" behind the White Whale, while in fact an essential problem in the book is that Ahab himself is unsure whether the malevolence he senses is inherent in the whale, or is something that he himself projects upon it. This American cynicism toward a mythos of arrogance and self-aggrandizement marks Melville's work—and the figure of Ahab—as an *altered* descendant of Frankenstein, though descendant he clearly is.

17. Baldick suggests that there was much in the reaction to the French Revolution and the Reign of Terror which followed that provided fertile soil for the politicalization of a myth detailing how, from the "highest" of motives, an excessive application of reason can create a "monstrous" offspring who turns on its creators and destroys not only them, but much of humankind.

18. Steven Earl Forry, *Hideous Progenies: Dramatizations of Frankenstein from Mary Shelley to the Present* (Philadelphia: University of Pennsylvania Press, 1990). This book is an extremely complete catalog of Frankenstein productions and films, both in the United States and abroad.

19. Ibid., 35.

20. Ibid., x.

21. Ibid., 5.

22. Forry suggests that the origins of this assistant figure can be found in such previous literary characters as Sancho Panza from *Don Quixote*, Bianca in *The Castle of Otranto*, and Annette in *The Mysteries of Udolpho*.

23. However, even plays without the explicit presence of a creature drew on the Faustian legend of a link between increased intellect and pacts with the Devil. A review of the play *Black Crook* describes it as "a story of sorcery, demonism and wickedness generally, in which one Hertzog, a deformed and ill-natured, but very learned man, grows desperate in spirit, makes a compact with Zamiel or Satan...." *New York Times*, 13 September 1866 (quoted Marjorie Longley, Louis Silverstein, and Samuel A. Tower, eds., *America's Taste, 1851–1959: The Cultural Events of a Century Reported by Contemporary Observers in the Pages of the New York Times* [New York: Simon & Schuster, 1960], 83). The play was considered "scandalous" because it featured a *corps de ballet* with flesh-colored tights, making them appear to "wear no clothes to speak of." Perhaps for this reason it was exceedingly popular, breaking all audience records and running for 475 nights.

24. Forry, 22.

25. At the time of Forry's writing, this Edison one-reeler was believed lost for all time. However, a surviving copy has since been found. From www.videosift.com/video/Edisons-long-lost-Frankenstein-from-1910: "For many years, this film was believed to be a lost film. In 1963, a plot description and stills were discovered published in the March 15, 1910 issue of an old Edison film catalog, *The Edison Kinetogram*. In the 1950s, a print of this film was purchased by a Wisconsin film collector, Alois F. Dettlaff, who did not realize its rarity until many years later. Its existence was first revealed in the mid-1970s. Although somewhat deteriorated, the film was in viewable condition, complete with titles and tints as seen in 1910. Detlaff had a 35 mm preservation copy made by the George Eastman House in the late 1970s."

26. The next film in the development of the genre toward Whale's classic and iconographic version is *The Last Laugh* (1915), which brings electricity into the creation scene and also updates the rest of the narrative, though here the entire tale is presented as something of a farce rather than as a cautionary morality play.

27. Mary Shelley, *Frankenstein; or, The Modern Prometheus*, ed. Susan J. Wolfson (New York: Longman, 2003), 39.

28. My own reading of the novel is that it represents a critique of popular misconceptions about the Romantic's creative process. One can see the monster as a poorly composed poem and Victor as something of a "hack" Romantic poet, one who insufficiently understands the true and demanding theories of poetical inspiration and composition as set forth by Shelley's husband, as well as Wordsworth and Coleridge. For instance, whereas Victor's overwrought, blind, and obsessive pursuit of his goal would seem, in the popular mind, to be the perfect image of the Romantic *artiste*—wandering some desolate moor wrist to forehead and engaged in a deep metaphysical search for Truth, then pouring forth the results in unformed and unedited primitive language—this image is inaccurate or at least incomplete when one actually reads the prescriptions for poetic construction as set down in, for example, the "Introduction to the Lyrical Ballads." While Wordsworth does state that the moment of poetic inspiration springs from a "spontaneous overflow of powerful feelings," he goes on to insist that the proper Romantic poem comes about only after a period wherein these feelings are "recollected in tranquility." It is this all-important second step that Victor never employs. In other

words, he creates a hasty and poorly constructed text, then refuses to revise it. Space does not allow for a full recounting of all the evidence for this reading of the novel, but I would offer as the starting point from which the rest of the analysis can be developed Shelley's own statement in the introduction to the 1836 edition, wherein she recounts the events which comprised her own moment of poetic inspiration. In her rendering of the dream which produced the novel she describes the figure who would eventually become Victor Frankenstein reacting to—significantly, not engaged in—the animation of his creature, and in this depiction she refers to the "student of the unhallowed arts" not as a doctor or even a philosopher, but as an "artist."

29. See for instance John Herdman's *The Double in Nineteenth-Century Fiction: Edinburgh Studies in Sociology* (New York: Palgrave Macmillan, 1990).

30. Martin Tropp, *Mary Shelley's Monster* (Boston: Houghton Mifflin, 1976). At least part of this attraction/repulsion syndrome may be seen as a reaction to the explosion of manufacturing capacity that the Industrial Revolution produced, a fear of a mechanized "double" self, as well as a quite literal fear of the "doubled" productivity—with an accompanying increase in influence and demand of certain segments of society. Baldick for one sees these modern ghost stories as "tales of transgression which show a particular interest in production . . . as an obsessive and self-destructive activity" (30). However, perhaps the ways in which *Frankenstein* does *not* fit this pattern are at least as interesting as the ways in which it does. For instance, Victor's double does *not* resemble him at all, but is a monstrous parody, an exaggeration of a human being. Also, Baldick does not differentiate between those stories where such production is merely mechanically innovative and ultimately stabilizing for the status quo, where the scientist figures are typically humorous, absent-minded, well intentioned, and bumbling; and those where the scientist's labor is potentially a threat to the status quo, and the scientists themselves are solemn, single-minded, megalomaniacal, and sinisterly capable.

31. While Kenneth Branagh's *Mary Shelley's Frankenstein* (1994), with Robert De Niro as the Monster, strives for fidelity to the novel, he portrays the animation scene with typical melodrama and events nowhere in the novel's depiction, utilizing a large tank filled with electric eels to bring the Monster to life.

32. Forry, 95.

33. E. T. A. Hoffmann, *Tales of Hoffmann*, trans. and ed. R. J. Hollingdale (Harmondsworth: Penguin, 1982), 96.

34. Baldick also identifies Victor's "crime" as a severing of "social ties." And he suggests that the fuel behind this alienating obsession is a search for "perfectionism." More specifically, Baldick sees in this genre—particularly in the work of Hoffmann—a substitution of an obsessive search for perfection for sexual love. "Hoffmann's young protagonists typically find themselves distracted from their fiancées by some delusion associated with their work" (96).

35. Frederick Amrine, "Readings in the Text of Nature: Three Contemporary Goetheans," in *Beyond the Two Cultures: Essays on Science, Technology, and Literature*, ed. Joseph W. Slade and Judith Yaross Lee (Ames: Iowa State University Press, 1990), 51.

36. See also Joel Black's "Introduction: Newtonian Mechanics and the Romantic Rebellion," in *Beyond the Two Cultures*.

37. See Stuart Peterfreund's "Blake and Anti-Newtonian Thought," in Slade and Lee, *Beyond the Two Cultures*.

38. A critique which, it could be argued, culminates in Jacques Derrida's theories labeled, collectively, deconstruction—a critical approach which seems not only "nonsensical" but even "immoral" by the standards of American pragmatism.

39. In its review of *Species*, the *New York Times* wrote, "It is clear that here is one of the most important contributions ever made to philosophic science" (28 March 1860).

40. Linda S. Bergman, "Reshaping the Roles of Man, God, and Nature: Darwin's Rhetoric in *On the Origin of Species*," in Slade and Lee, *Beyond the Two Cultures*, 80.

41. Quoted in Baldick, 70.

42. Though the most widely read copy in America was a significantly revised version printed in 1840, which became available nearly simultaneously with the first well-distributed translation of *Faust*.

43. Quoted in Howard P. Segal, *Technological Utopianism in American Culture* (Chicago: University of Chicago Press, 1985), 83.

44. Robert V. Bruce, *The Launching of American Science* (New York: Alfred A. Knopf, 1987), 130.

45. This quite unfavorable review appeared in *Port Folio* (Philadelphia, June 1818).

3. A Cabinet of Wonders

1. From "Roentgen Ray Dangers," *New York Times*, 1 July 1887.

2. Ludmilla Jordanova, "Museums: Representing the Real?" in *Realism and Representation: Essays on the Problem of Realism in Relation to Science, Literature, and Culture*, ed. George Levine (Madison: University of Wisconsin Press, 1993), 271.

3. One might even suggest a connection with these fairs as public spectacle and the popularity of the Chautauqua movement of the 1890s. Though ostensibly religious revival meetings, Chautauqua events often combined sermons and testimonials with county fair exhibits, educational lectures, Bible studies, folk and popular music, and even lectures on literature and "natural" philosophy (typically paeans to the Founding Fathers).

4. Jordanova, 271.

5. Ibid., 256.

6. Ibid., 276.

7. Palmyre Pierroux, "Technologies and Museums," in *Information and Communication Technology in Art Museums: A Thesis in Art History*, Department of Art History, University of Oslo, October 1998, folk.uio.no/palmyre/Hovedoppgave/08Pleasure.html (accessed 7 March 2007).

8. Quoted in ibid.

9. Quoted in "Buffalo Bill Lassoed Europe with His Wild West Shows," Newswise, 10 May 2006, www.newswise.com/articles/view/520400/ (accessed 8 March 2006).

10. Ibid.

11. 16 May 1876. Quoted in Marjorie Longley, Louis Silverstein, and Samuel A. Tower, eds., *America's Taste, 1851–1959: The Cultural Events of a Century Reported by Contemporary Observers in the Pages of the New York Times* (New York: Simon & Schuster, 1960), 144.

12. Quoted in ibid., 145.

13. *New York Times*, 18 July 1875: 71.

14. Thomas Hughes, *American Genesis: A Century of Invention and Technological Enthusiasm, 1870–1970* (New York: Penguin Books, 1989), 19.

15. Quoted in ibid., 25.

16. Ibid., 28.

17. Ibid., 30.

18. Ibid., 38.

19. Quoted in George Levine, ed., *Realism and Representation: Essays on the Problem of Realism in Relation to Science, Literature, and Culture* (Madison: University of Wisconsin Press, 1993), 71.

20. *New York Times*, 26 April 1896.

21. Paul Keith Conkin, *Puritans and Pragmatists: Eight Eminent American Thinkers* (New York: Dodd, Mead, 1968), 178–79. I will draw heavily on Conkin's summaries of Emerson, James, and Peirce both because I believe his are cogent and concise representations of their thinking, and because these summaries sufficiently represent the "received wisdom" about key points in their philosophies. In other words, Conkin's "versions" of Emerson, James, and Peirce are sufficiently standard to serve as, in general outlines, what these three philosophers mean to mainstream American culture.

22. Ibid., 185.

23. R. W. Emerson, "Art," quoted in Conkin, 367–68.

24. Conkin, 275. This is one of the few aspects of James's philosophy similar to that of Nietzsche.

25. William James, *Collected Essays and Reviews* (New York: Longman, Green, 1920), 120.

26. Conkin, 276.

27. Ibid., 277.

28. Ibid., 277.

29. Ibid., 324.

30. Ibid., 335.

31. Ibid., 336. Even though James's philosophy was based on a rigorous empiricism, toward the end of his life he became enamored of psychic research, joining with mostly English scholars to form the Society for Psychical Research, and serving as its president from 1893 to 1896. Certainly his interest in paranormal phenomena is both odd and yet perfectly in line with his progenitors, including Emerson and Thoreau, who had more than flirted with the pseudosciences of their time like mesmerism and spiritualism.

32. One thinks of Peirce sitting alone toward the end of his life in his half-completed castle and imagines something like Charles Foster Kane in Orson Welles's *Citizen Kane*, dying, alone and misunderstood, in his Xanadu.

33. Conkin, 207.

34. Ibid., 241.

35. Ibid., 243.

36. This affinity with the precepts of poststructuralism would explain why Peirce's resurrection as a pre-eminent American philosopher had to wait for the coming of that interpretive approach to American shores in the late 1960s and early '70s. And there is certainly something post-Newtonian about Peirce's concept of time and space. As Conkin points out, Peirce's "doctrine of continuity"—wherein "time [is] an entity, never rent, never perfectly divided. Any moment is divisible into other infinitesimal moments" (252)—essentially conceives of time as something like the fourth dimension long before Einstein's theory of special relativity. There are even aspects of Peirce's philosophy that anticipate Einstein's theory of "action at a distance."

37. Quoted in *America's Taste*, 95. One thinks of the character Gordon Gekko in *Wall Street* (1987) intoning with sinister sincerity, "Greed is good."

38. Of course, this "blank slate" image of America pushed the native inhabitants out beyond the edges of the frame, out to the *lacunae* of the reservations.

39. Howard P. Segal, *Technological Utopianism in American Culture* (Chicago: University of Chicago Press, 1985), 77. See also Allyn B. Forbes, "The Literary Quest for Utopia, 1880–1900," in *Social Forces* 6.2 (December 1927): 179–89; and Thomas Peyser, *Utopia and Cosmopolis: Globalization in the Era of American Literary Realism* (Durham: Duke University Press, 1998).

40. Segal, 58, 59.

41. Quoted in Segal, 86.

42. Segal points out that self-control is the other vital component of the social machinery's efficient functioning: "Utopian man's control over himself mirrors the control that technology achieves over the environment" (31).

43. From *Looking Backward* by Edward Bellamy, quoted in Segal, 26.

44. Yet the real-world utopian communities of the time were fundamentally Marxist-Socialist. For instance, there was the Llano del Rio Cooperative Colony, founded in 1914 in California (which eventually moved to Louisiana, where it survived for another two decades). The colony was started by Job (a most appropriate first name) Harriman, Eugene Debs's vice-presidential nominee on the Socialist ticket of 1900. There were also the Labor Exchanges in Kansas, started by G. B. De Bernardi, which exchanged produced goods for "labor checks" that the members could use as money to buy goods and services at businesses that subscribed to the Exchange.

45. From *Cityless and Countryless World* by Henry Olerich (1893), quoted in Segal, 30.

46. From *People's Corporation* by King Camp Gillette (1924), quoted in Segal, 27.

47. "This cult of efficiency is reflected in every utopian activity and value judgement." From *Roadtown* by Edgar Chambless (1910), quoted in Segal, 28.

48. Segal, 121.

49. Ibid., 30.

50. Ibid., 131.

51. From *Cityless and Countryless World*, quoted in Segal, p. 27.

52. Social critic Josef Pieper notes "how the contemporary term *intellectual work* reveals the subversion of the contemplative ideal." Quoted in Segal, 132.

53. One of the major charges leveled at Robert Oppenheimer during the House hearings on his security clearance was that, by suggesting we share atomic secrets with the world, he was guilty of trying to "waste" our A-bomb "advantage."

54. In Segal's view, Taylorism led also to "the undermining of the liberal arts and to an overall anti-intellectualism" in the business world (108). Lenin was so taken with Taylorism that, even as he was accusing the United States government of siding with the White Russians in the Civil War, he was importing several Taylorists to aid in his huge industrialization programs. Trotsky even attempted to "Taylorize" the fledgling Red Army, with less-than-admirable results.

4. The World of Tomorrow

1. For a detailed discussion of the history of the pulps see "History of the Pulps," www.pulpworld.com/history/history_01.htm (accessed 1 April 2006); and Mike Ashley, "Top of the Pulps," www.abebooks.co.uk/docs/Community/Featured/topPulps.shtml (accessed 1 April 2006).

2. Gregg DeYoung argues that the typical choice of icons to commemorate science on postage stamps—most frequently test tubes and microscopes—has created "a particular view of science which is more and more firmly established in the mind of the public—an image of science as primarily the manipulation of special instruments whose nature is only imperfectly understood by the public." "Postage Stamps and the Popular Iconography of Science," *Journal of American Culture* 9.3 (Fall 1986): 1–13.

3. For a detailed account of how the electric refrigerator triumphed over the less expensive and more efficient gas dispersion type, see, for instance, Ruth Schwartz Cowen "How the Refrigerator Got Its Hum," in *The Social Shaping of Technology: How the Refrigerator Got Its Hum*, ed. Donald A. MacKenzie and Judy Wajcman (Milton Keynes: Open Society Press, Open University Press, 1985).

4. We have for instance D. H. Lawrence's less-than-circumspect criticism of American democracy: "This thing, this mechanical democracy, new and monstrous on the face of the earth"; "The Spirit of Place," in *Studies in Classic American Literature* (*The Cambridge Edition of the Works of D. H. Lawrence*), ed. Ezra Greenspan, Lindeth Vasey, and John Worthen (Cambridge: Cambridge University Press, 2003), 177.

5. These times saw an almost irrational enthusiasm for technology as the solution to *all* social problems, even justice. In a recent article in the *New Yorker* ("Duped," 2 July 2007), Margaret Talbot tells of the fascination with and faith in lie detectors as technological fixes for problems with the determination of truth. When the first news articles appeared suggesting how such a device might work—fully a decade before any were even built—the *New York Times* greeted the prospect with utopian rhetoric of "liberation": "there will be no jury, no horde of detectives and witnesses, no charges and countercharges, and no attorney for the defense. These impediments of our courts will be

unnecessary. The State will merely submit all suspects . . . to the tests of scientific instruments."

6. Two such examples are Franklin A. Kalinowski, "Marxism, Fascism, and the New Left," *Western Political Quarterly* 30.1 (March 1977): 65–70; and Charles S. Maier, "Between Taylorism and Technocracy: European Ideologies and the Vision of Industrial Productivity in the 1920s," *Journal of Contemporary History* 5.2 (1970): 27–61.

7. Quoted in Henry Elsner, *The Technocrats, Prophets of Automation* (Syracuse: Syracuse University Press, 1967), 16.

8. I. A. Richards, *Science and Poetry* (New York: Haskell House, 1974), 6.

9. *New York Times*, 4 March 1934. Quoted in Marjorie Longley, Louis Silverstein, and Samuel A. Tower, eds., *America's Taste, 1851–1959: The Cultural Events of a Century Reported by Contemporary Observers in the Pages of the New York Times* (New York: Simon & Schuster, 1960), 259.

10. The *New York Times* alone had no less than sixty articles on technocracy during January and February of 1933. Forty-one periodical articles and seventeen books and pamphlets on technocracy were included in the standard indexes for the beginning of 1933 (Elsner, 7).

11. Elsner writes (8): "At the same time, well-known figures in engineering, academic, and business circles were denouncing Technocracy. Karl Compton, president of Massachusetts Institute of Technology, called it inaccurate and fallacious; C. F. Kettering and Alfred P. Sloane of General Motors attacked Technocracy . . . as did Dr. Julius Klein, assistant secretary of Commerce. Dr. Virgil Jordan, President of the National Industrial Conference Board, said on January 10 that the country had gone 'technocrazy' and that Technocracy had cast 'a paralyzing spell over responsible sections of the business community.'"

12. Ibid., 47.

13. Ibid., 48.

14. Ibid., 2.

15. Ibid., 6.

16. Scott, quoted in ibid., 3–4.

17. Scott, quoted in ibid., 5.

18. Scott, quoted in ibid., 12.

19. Ironically, the end of the Technocracy movement came about largely because of a "populist vs. aristocrat" division within the Technocrats. In 1934, they split into two competing factions, the Continental Committee on Technocracy, and Technocracy, Inc. Harold Segal characterizes this parting of the ways as follows: "The CTT was led by well-to-do cosmopolitans seeking not only economic reforms but also social, political, and cultural ones; Technocracy, Inc. was led by lower-class technicians with exclusively economic objectives" (Elsner, 17). And Technocracy, Inc., still exists today. You can visit its website at www.technocracy.org/.

20. This is exactly the argument Wells makes more explicitly in *The Open Conspiracy* (1928).

21. Curiously, some have argued that *Things to Come* and the mob scene in particular should not be read as an indictment of modern Luddism, as the artist directs his fury against only a single technological achievement, the moon rocket. However, this reading ignores not only what the rocket symbolizes—the unending expansion of humankind's technological horizons—but also the artist's rhetoric, which vilifies the entire safe, modern, peaceful world that technology has created.

22. At the 1933 "Century of Progress" fair, in an attempt to convince the American farmer that overproduction was the cause of the collapse of agricultural prices, the USDA's entire exhibit was essentially an attempt to redefine "plenty" from meaning "more than enough" to "just the right amount." In other words, surplus crops represented inefficiency, which means any surplus becomes a sign of inefficiency and thus necessitates a call for tighter production control, as in the "wheat adjustment plan" which led to such legislation as the bill creating the U.S. Soil Bank. The displays also tended to "reify" such products as fruits and vegetables, just as with the displays of machines in the technology fairs discussed in chapter 3.

23. "Welcome to Tomorrow," Crossroads Project, University of Virginia, xroads.virginia.edu/~1930s/DISPLAY/39wf/frame.htm (accessed 23 April 2007). This site includes a very astute analysis of the entire fair and is the only available virtual tour of the exhibits. See also John Crowley's documentary film *The World of Tomorrow* (1984); and Larry Zim, Mel Lerner, and Herbert Rolfes, *The World of Tomorrow: The 1939 New York World's Fair* (New York: Harper & Row, 1988).

24. "Welcome to Tomorrow."

25. Democracity can be seen as a full-blown metropolitan version of the Metlife Corporation's Parkchester, New York, the first such "socially engineered" community in America.

26. This attitude can be seen as updated in the film *Independence Day*, as I discuss in chapter 10.

27. This dearth of funding for the theoretical sciences curiously coincided not only with what the "inventor" of quantum mechanics, Niels Bohr, designated as the period "when modern physics was born," but also with an increase in those American scientists who chose to become physicists: twice as many in 1920–1932 as in 1860–1920. By 1932, there were 2,500 physicists in the United States.

28. For a full account of the political efforts of Millikan and other scientists during this period, see Peter J. Kuznick, *Beyond the Laboratory: Scientists as Political Activists in 1930s America* (Chicago: University of Chicago Press, 1987).

29. Quoted in ibid., 39.

30. Quoted in ibid., 43.

31. Quoted in ibid., 56.

32. Ibid., 68.

33. Sir Solly Zuckerman, *Scientists and War: The Impact of Science on Military and Civil Affairs* (New York: Harper & Row, 1966), 6.

34. Ironically, the rise of the National Socialists in the '30s retarded this momentum. The Nazis brought with their party to power an increasingly rigid and daunting

bureaucracy, as well as a resurgence of interest in pseudosciences that sapped vital resources from other, more rational and promising scientific projects—such as, for instance, nuclear fission.

35. Richard Rhodes, *The Making of the Atomic Bomb* (New York: Simon & Schuster, 1986), 315.

36. Ibid., 313.

5. The Incredible Shrinking Scientist

1. See for instance Ellen Schrecker, *The Age of McCarthyism: A Brief History with Documents* (Boston: St. Martin's Press, 1994); and Albert Fried, ed., *McCarthyism: The Great American Red Scare, a Documentary History* (New York: Oxford University Press, 1997). There are also extensive online materials available at the course websites for Chris H. Lewis's American Studies 2010 at the University of Colorado, www .colorado.edu/AmStudies/lewis/2010/mccarthy.htm (accessed 1 May 2007), and Alan Filreis's English 592, The American 1950s, at the University of Pennsylvania, writing.upenn.edu/~afilreis/50s/592readinglist.html (accessed 1 May 2007).

2. Anne O'Hare McCormick, "The Promethean Role of the United States," *New York Times*, 8 August 1945: 22.

3. Quoted in Paul Boyer, *By the Bomb's Early Light* (New York: Pantheon, 1985), 6–7.

4. Quoted in Allan M. Winkler, *Life Under a Cloud: American Anxiety about the Atom* (New York: Oxford University Press, 1993), 29.

5. The Russians were considered so technologically backward that a joke circulating among the atomic scientists proposed, only slightly disingenuously, that "the Russians could not surreptitiously introduce nuclear bombs in suitcases into the United States because they had not yet been able to perfect a suitcase." Quoted in Herbert York, *Race to Oblivion* (New York: Simon & Schuster, 1970), 170.

6. Quoted in Winkler, 40.

7. Boyer, 60.

8. Ibid., 10.

9. David Dietz, *Atomic Energy in the Coming Era* (New York: Dodd, Mead, 1947), 174.

10. In one of the first such government research contracts, the Franklin Institute and its founder, Alexander Dallas Bache, were engaged in 1832 by the government to investigate the frequent and apparently unpredictable explosions of mass-produced steam boilers. Their research lead to the establishment of manufacturing safety standards that proved to be a model for decades to come.

11. Sir Solly Zuckerman, *Scientists and War: The Impact of Science on Military and Civil Affairs* (New York: Harper & Row, 1966), 126.

12. I. I. Rabi, *Science: The Center of Culture* (New York: World Publishing, 1967), 71.

13. Boyer, 74.

14. Quoted in Rhodes, *The Making of the Atomic Bomb* (New York: Touchstone, 1986), 754. I have not gone into detail about the development of the atomic bomb both because, due to the secrecy surrounding the project, there were really no public images

generated of those working on it during the war, and because, in the face of Rhodes's astoundingly comprehensive work, such an effort would be redundant.

15. Quoted in Zuckerman, 126.

16. Boyer, 126.

17. Quoted in ibid.

18. Zuckerman, 30.

19. Quoted in Donald Strickland, *Scientists in Politics: The Atomic Scientists Movement, 1945–46* (West Lafayette: Purdue University Studies, 1968), 141.

20. The difference in image between Einstein and Oppenheimer cannot be overemphasized. Here, for instance, is C. P. Snow's description of Einstein: "At close quarters, Einstein's head was as I had imagined it: magnificent, with a humanizing touch of the comic . . . he looked like a reliable old-fashioned watchmaker in a small town who perhaps collected butterflies on a Sunday" (quoted in Rhodes, 304). When it came time to design the gentle and wise Yoda character for George Lucas's *Star Wars*, Einstein's eyes were used because of their "universally recognized humanity": Frederik Pohl, *Science Fiction Studies in Film* (New York: Ace Books, 1981), 114.

21. Einstein kept several suits of identical color and style so that, he claimed, he wouldn't have to waste any mental energy deciding on his wardrobe for the day.

6. Invaders with Ph.D.'s

The epigraph to this chapter is taken from Frederik Pohl, *Science Fiction Studies in Film* (New York: Ace Books, 1981), 106, quoting Lofficier in the *International MENSA Journal*, January–February 1979.

1. Eric Smoodin, "Watching the Skies: Hollywood, the 1950s, and the Soviet Threat," *Journal of American Culture* 12.2 (Summer 1989): 35.

2. A simple Internet search for sites linking aliens and Communists will turn up dozens of results. A few representative sites include: Tim Dirks, "Science Fiction Films," The Greatest Films, www.filmsite.org/sci-fifilms2.html (accessed 3 June 2006); Richard Dover, "The 50s B-movie," www.newi.ac.uk/rdover/other/the_50s_.htm (accessed 4 June 2006); "Science fiction involving extraterrestrials in film and television," *The Internet Encyclopedia of Science*, www.daviddarling.info/encyclopedia/S/SFfilm.html (accessed 4 June 2006); Bruce Sterling, "Science Fiction (literature)," *Encyclopedia Britannica*, www.britannica.com/eb/article-235723 (accessed 6 January 2007); and Steven Mintz, "American History through Film," www.hfac.uh.edu/mintz/lec12.htm (accessed 7 January 2007). Also, Ellen Schrecker writes of a widely accepted link between the alien threats of these films and the anti-Communism of the time in *Many Are the Crimes: McCarthyism in America* (Boston: Little, Brown, 1998). This hegemonic reading of these films' ideology even finds its way into obituaries about writers of the films, as for example in "Jack Finney, 84, Sci-Fi Author of Time-Travel Tales, Dies," obituary by William Grimes appearing in the *New York Times*, 17 November 95.

3. For an exhaustive list of books, films, television shows, and other materials of the

period see Al Filreis's excellent website at www.writing.upenn.edu/~afilreis/50s/home .html; and "The Red Scare: A Filmography," The All Powers Project, www.lib.washington .edu/EXHIBITS/ALLPOWERS/film.html#one.

4. Raymond B. Allen, "Communists Should Not Teach in American Colleges," *Educational Forum* 13.4 (May 1949); and "Is This Tomorrow," published by the Catechetical Guild Educational Society of St. Paul, Minnesota (1947).

5. The actual strategic advantage of such an endeavor was rarely contemplated in such movies, comic books, and popular books about space adventure of the time, even though it would make little sense to go the enormous expense and effort to transport rockets 250,000 miles to the moon just so they could make the return 250,000-mile journey to Moscow.

6. This was a departure from the story upon which the film was based, "Farewell to the Master" by Harry Bates (1930), as in the story the robot is the master and the man his servant.

7. Quoted in Pohl, 114.

8. A perhaps apocryphal story has it that Hawks made the film on a bet. Hawks had been quite vocal in his criticism of the sort of grade B science fiction movies that took up the Saturday matinee theater marquees, and eventually, so the story goes, someone challenged him to do better. He took them up on it, found a script, supervised the rewriting of it to be more in his style of narrative, handpicked Christian Nyby to direct, then oversaw every aspect of his directing. Given the popularity and longevity of the film, I would suggest that Hawks won the bet.

9. See for instance Nick Schager, "The Thing from Another World," *Slant Magazine* 2003, www.slantmagazine.com/dvd/dvd_review.asp?ID=189 (accessed 10 June 2003); Elizabeth Wilson, "A Note on 'Jumanji'," *New Left Review* 220 (November–December 1996); and Elisa Kay Sparks, "Chronological Chart of the History of SF Film," virtual.clemson.edu/groups/dial/sffilm/chronochart04.htm (accessed 6 July 2007).

10. One of the exceptions to the traditional reading of the film is a review by "SPC": "the real enemy in the Hawks film is not the Arness Thing. Rather, it is that which is represented by the Carrington character" (www.outpost31.com/vistar/essays/comparison7 .html).

11. This reading is so *de rigueur* it has even found its way into the "official" description of the film in Wikipedia: "The film took advantage of the national feelings of the time. . . . The film's release in 1951 coincided with the Korean War and the upswing in anti-communist feelings brought on by McCarthyism. The idea of Americans being stalked by a force which was single of mind and 'devoid of morality' fit in well with the parallel feelings of the day on communism"; "The Thing from Another World," en.wikipedia.org/wiki/The_Thing_from_Another_World (accessed 5 June 2007). However, I would counter that, if any character in the film is devoid of morality, it is certainly Dr. Carrington.

12. Patrick Lucanio, *Them or Us: Archetypal Interpretations of Fifties Alien Invasion Films* (Bloomington: Indiana University Press, 1987), 37.

13. A joke among computer geeks during the '70s and the era of increased computer miniaturization was that the Russians were very proud of having built the world's *largest* transistor.

14. Patrick Lucanio employs such Freudian terms to analyze the dynamics of these invader films as follows: "the Invader is a mask, a representation of the dark side of the scientist himself, and is composed of overweening Pride (Ego) and unrepentant Power (Id), both of which are unrestrained by the conforming influences of community norms (Superego)" (95).

15. "The redemption of the society is achieved through a Puritanical perversion of the Catholic ritual of confession. . . . the scientist must cleanse himself of the Sin of Pride by confessing, and by humbling himself before the judgment of the community, and admitting the error of his ways" (ibid., 93).

16. The seminal essay in this vein is Richard Hofstadter's "Paranoid Style in American Politics," *Harper's Magazine*, November 1964, 77–86. For more recent discussions of this topic see George Johnson, *Architects of Fear: Conspiracy Theories and Paranoia in American Politics* (Los Angeles: Tarcher, 1983); D. J. Mulloy, *American Extremism: History, Politics, and the Militia Movement* (New York: Routledge, 2004); and Paul McCleary, "Politics, Policy, and Paranoia," *Social Policy*, June 2002.

17. Doc is the only member of the crew who thinks he could "grow to love" the planet, and Morbius makes clear he is also the only one to whom he can relate. Thus it is fitting that after his brain-boost Doc becomes a sort of mirror Morbius, but one upon whom the humbling lesson of the Krell is not lost—due, the film suggests, to his innate faith in a Being greater than himself, even given his inflated intellect.

18. In discussing the "community affirming" heart of these films, Lucanio suggests that Jung's symbol of the unifying Mandala is, in fact, represented time and again by the Flying Saucer, a dynamic he formulates as: "The flying saucer (mandala) from space (unconscious) brings its inhabitants (archetypes) to earth (conscious) where the hero (ego-cum-self) deals with the inhabitants to achieve a proper and harmonious conclusion (individuation)" (52). Thus, the invaders/wizards are "positive images" in that, as stand-ins for evil, they clearly demonstrate to the community that it is capable of distinguishing evil from good and using the good that resides in every "common" man and woman to overcome the uncommon and evil arrogance of the "outsiders." The purpose of the invasion story is, then, to affirm the community's values and goals through the depiction of a battle in which some "thing" challenging those values and goals is encountered, struggled with, and defeated. "In perhaps no other film genre is communal solidarity so richly displayed. . . . In film after film, absolutely no signs of dissension, rancor, or discontent are shown by any individual or group" (53); at least, that is, by any individual or group which is within the boundaries of the "religion and laws" which are being defended.

19. Lucanio writes, "Science . . . with all its logic and amorality brings all this death and destruction, while common sense with its morality and justice is the only thing finally capable of destroying the 'thing'" (52).

20. Lucanio: "The solution works not so much because of rational, cause-and-effect

thinking but because it is morally right when set against the 'evil' of some Promethean scientist's experimentation" (52).

21. R. W. B. Lewis describes this heroic American Adam as "an individual standing alone, self-reliant and self-propelling, ready to confront whatever awaited him with the aid of his own unique and inherent resources." Such a character is certainly central to America's literary history, originating in Cooper's Natty Bumpo and reaching through the Western tales of Zane Grey, Louis L'Amour, and Clarence E. Mulford. "The American Adam, moreover, is the Adam before the Fall. He is morally pure and socially innocent" (Lewis quoted in Lucanio, 54). Lewis's description nicely details exactly what is lacking, according to the ideology of these films, from the character of an Wicked Wizard—and precisely what is present in the hero of the 1950s invader films.

22. Pohl, 141.

23. And, given the continuing support for Star Wars, the continuing attempt to isolate and demonize North Korea, Iran, and any other nations who would dare to join the nuclear club, and the continuing rejection of international control of nuclear power, apparently the message of *On the Beach* is no more palatable now that it was half a century ago.

24. It is worthy of note that the title of the film *The Thing—From Another World* was altered just before its final release. Originally it was just *The Thing*, and the addition of the subtitle seems to indicate that the producers realized they needed to direct the audience's attention, and condemnation, toward the actual alien, and away from "the thing" that is named Dr. Carrington and that, although it looks, walks, and talks like a human, is the most alien character in the film.

7. Fallout

1. Allan M. Winkler, *Life Under a Cloud: American Anxiety About the Atom* (New York: Oxford University Press, 1993), 16.

2. Ibid., 24,

3. Ibid., 38.

4. Ibid., 24.

5. Ibid., 38.

6. For text of the petitions and timeline of the decision to drop the bomb see Gene Dannen, "Atomic Bomb: Decision. Documents on the decision to use atomic bombs on the cities of Hiroshima and Nagasaki," www.dannen.com/decision/ (accessed 6 July 2003).

7. Richard Rhodes, *The Making of the Atomic Bomb* (New York: Touchstone, 1986), 751.

8. Ibid., 765.

9. H. Bruce Franklin, *War Stars: The Superweapon and the American Imagination* (New York: Oxford University Press, 1988). One of the first novels that invokes this obsession with superweapons as an end to war was in fact an homage to Thomas Edison as inventor of deadly gadgets, Garrett P. Serviss's *Edison's Conquest of Mars* (1898).

Though it purported take up where H. G. Wells's *War of the Worlds* left off, it is in fact ideologically quite the opposite of Wells's book and is perhaps best considered as the very first science fiction "space opera." Other novels with this theme include Simon Newcomb's *His Wisdom, the Defender* (1900); John Stewart Barney's *L.P.M.: The End of the Great War* (1915); Hollis Godfrey's *The Man Who Ended War* (1908); and Arthur Cheney Train and Robert Williams Wood's *The Man Who Rocked the Earth* (1915).

10. Franklin, 201.

11. "The New Arms Race: Star Wars Weapon" ("Briefing Paper No. 5," Union of Concerned Scientists, 1983).

12. Ibid.

13. Ibid., 182.

14. "The New Arms Race: Star Wars Weapon" provides a cogent and seemingly incontestable critique of the various schemes for SDI technology, detailing the many fundamentally unsolvable problems of all the technological "solutions" it would entail: chemical and X-ray lasers, orbiting mirrors, particle beams, and impact projectiles, as well as the enormously sophisticated and as yet purely speculative computer hardware necessary to accurately and reliably control them. "A senior Pentagon weapons designer compared this targeting challenge to that of 'being on top of the Washington Monument, shooting a rifle, and hitting a baseball on top of the Empire State Building'" (180). The article also points out that satellites are extremely fragile systems that would be much easier to shoot down than enemy missiles. But even if all the technological problems this article lists were somehow overcome, a simple calculation reveals the fundamental flaw in SDI logic. Even if the system were 99 percent efficient—a level of efficiency never before achieved in any mechanical system built by human beings—1 percent of the launched ICBMs would penetrate the SDI "shield." In other words, if the Soviets (or some other enemy) launched 100 missiles, at least one would find its target. And, while one vaporized metropolis may seem an acceptable loss, in the sort of first strike attack SDI was conceived to counter, the Soviets would launch not 100 but at least 1,000 missiles, resulting in ten vaporized cities, or perhaps 5,000, resulting in fifty. But, as studies have suggested that even twenty-five nuclear mushroom clouds would be sufficient to initiate a "nuclear winter" ultimately annihilating all life on Earth, calculations beyond that number would seem quite moot—mere hypothesizing about, to paraphrase Churchill, how high the rubble would bounce.

15. Winkler, 58.

16. It is currently (April, 2007) set to seven minutes to midnight—exactly the same place it was when it first appeared.

17. Winkler, 40.

18. If one wanted to find the "perfect" real-world corollaries for these stereotypes, one would need look no further than Robert Oppenheimer and Ernest Lawrence. Certainly Oppenheimer's physical self perfectly matched the popular image of a Wicked Wizard: tall, thin, sickly as a child, someone who wrote poetry and devoted as much of his thinking time to religion and philosophy as physics. And Lawrence was his polar opposite physically: also tall, but broad, strong, an avid outdoorsman, a hale fellow well met, with

his creative energy firmly focused on things rather than theory, such as the cyclotron, which he invented. Their differences were also expressed in their divergent beliefs about the atomic bomb: Oppenheimer's that it ought to present society with an opportunity for revolutionary transformation; and Lawrence's that it was a machine to be perfected and improved. But to repeat, my focus isn't on whether or not these cultural categories correspond to the biographical realities of various scientists, but on analyzing what function these popular images serve in the broader culture. For a detailed comparison of Oppenheimer and Lawrence, see Rhodes, *The Making of the Atomic Bomb*, 119–28 and 143–51.

19. Quoted in Winkler, 62.

20. Ibid., 45.

21. Ibid., 58.

22. It is important to note, however, that Truman's directive held out hope for the eventual control of atomic energy by some international agency. It continues: "Like all other work in the field of atomic weapons, it is being and will be carried forward on a basis consistent with the overall objectives of our program for peace and security. This we shall continue to do until a satisfactory plan for international control of atomic energy is achieved."

23. Winkler, 59.

24. Quoted in Winkler, 166.

25. Mary Kaldor, in an article based on information from the Soviet military archives, "Military Strategy in the Soviet Union," in *The Social Shaping of Technology: How the Refrigerator Got Its Hum*, ed. Donald A. MacKenzie and Judy Wajcman (Milton Keynes: Open Society Press, Open University Press, 1985), suggests the source of one of the basic cultural disconnects between the United States and the USSR during the Cold War. Kaldor makes the case that, for the Soviets, the chief lesson learned from World War II was that overwhelming numbers win wars. Thus Soviet military doctrine came to emphasize the importance of mass "in both the maintenance of large forces-in-being and in the practice of applying large numbers of men and equipment in combat. . . . After the catastrophic losses in the early part of World War II, these doctrines were applied and their utility was confirmed by the Soviet victory. . . . The Soviet Union produced 140,000 aircraft and nearly 70,000 tanks during the war. And it was their massive combined offensive that proved decisive." After World War II, this thinking was the primary component of Soviet nuclear strategy. "The idea that Soviet forces should be sufficiently large 'to repel (or at least absorb) any attack and then to go on and win the war' has continued to govern Soviet military thinking and it justifies the extent of the reaction to the U.S. military posture. It explains, for example, why Soviet nuclear doctrines focus on fighting and winning a nuclear war rather than deterring an unwinnable nuclear war, and this in turn justifies the quantitative buildup of nuclear weapons" (3). Conversely, I would argue that the chief lesson the United States learned from World War II was Pearl Harbor, i.e., never be caught with your pants down. This resulted in the U.S. nuclear strategy of a constant state of alert, as evidenced by the SAC doctrine of "fail safe" and the 24/7 policy of bombers circling just outside Soviet air space. When one considers these two policies in tandem—the Soviet buildup of massive numbers and the U.S.

advanced warning posture—one sees the emergence of perfectly congruent and mutually suggestive threats; that is, whereas both sides developed policies consistent with the
lessons learned from World War II as well as cultural attitudes and paranoias—policies
which were, to each side, the most prudent *defensive* posture—one sees a pattern of mu-
tual misperception of these policies as offensive, a *folie à deux* that would lead to the decades of nuclear standoff known as the Cold War. While Edvard Radzinsky makes the
argument in his biography of Stalin (*Stalin* [New York: Anchor Books, 1997]) that the
deeply paranoid Communist leader was in fact planning a first strike against the West
once the Soviets possessed sufficient numbers of ICBMs, there is little evidence that, after his death in 1953, this policy was ever given serious consideration.

26. "The Soviet Union tested its first ICBM a few months before the United States, in
August 1957, but the program was plagued with technical difficulties. The missiles were
said to be inferior to the American missiles, and only four of the first ICBMs were actually
deployed. By 1962, the United States had deployed 294 ICBMs, compared with 75 for the
Soviet Union, and by 1964 this number had increased to 834, compared with 190 for the
Soviet Union. Further, the United States began, in the late 1950s, to deploy submarine-
launched ballistic missiles (SLBMs), nearly ten years before the Soviet Union" (Kaldor,
271). The U.S. emphasis on "closing" the putative missile gap is also clear from the dramatic increase in expenditures for ICBMs during this period: 1953: $3 million; 1954: $14
million; 1955: $161 million; 1956: $515 million; 1957: $1.38 billion; 1958: 1.349 billion
(from Robert A. Divine, *The Sputnik Challenge: Eisenhower's Response to the Soviet
Satellite* [New York: Oxford University Press, 1993], 29).

27. Winkler, 80. Also, for a detailed treatment of this key episode in the official exil-
ing of Oppenheimer, see "The Beat Begins: America in the 1950s (The Acheson-
Lilienthal Report)," www.honors.umd.edu/HONR269J/archive/AchesonLilienthal.html
(accessed 23 July 2005).

28. Quoted in Joseph Manzione, "Science and the Cold War: A Roundtable Legacy
of Scientific Internationalism," *Diplomatic History* 24.1 (2000): 21–24.

29. Winkler, 24.

30. For a detailed list and discussion see www.wsu.edu/~brians/nuclear/1chap.htm.

31. One notable exception is *Red Dawn* (1984), a "red meat" jingoistic film depicting the invasion of the United States by Cuban and Soviet paratroopers, which, significantly, finessed the problem of nuclear fallout by imagining that neither side would
actually use their nuclear arsenals because they needed the other country's infrastruc-
ture intact.

32. For a detailed discussion of the relative silence in literature about the A-bomb
see the chapter "Words Fail: The Bomb and the Literary Imagination" in Paul Boyer, *By
the Bomb's Early Light* (New York: Pantheon Books, 1985).

33. Quoted in Winkler, 26.

34. Ibid., 92.

35. Ibid.

36. Even though Slotin's story wasn't made public for many years, a story titled
"Nine Days to Die" was published by William Sabrot in 1960 in the *Saturday Evening*

Post. While the character in Sabrot's version is not a nuclear engineer but a produce salesman who is contaminated by particularly nasty atomic waste, the portrayal of the stages and symptoms of radiation sickness is remarkably accurate.

37. Curiously, mammals—other, that is, than humans—were rarely the target of such radiated-mutation stories.

38. Other works which deal with the fear of radiation as a generator of grotesque, "unnatural" mutations include Paul Brians's *Nuclear Holocausts: Atomic War in Fiction, 1895–1984* (Kent, OH: Kent State University Press, 1987); David Dowling's *Fictions of Nuclear Disaster* (Iowa City: University of Iowa Press, 1987); Martha Bartter's *The Way to Ground Zero: The Atomic Bomb in American Science Fiction* (New York: Greenwood Press, 1988); and Jerome Shapiro's *Atomic Bomb Cinema: The Apocalyptic Imagination on Film* (New York: Routledge, 2002).

39. Winkler, 101.

40. Ibid., 103.

41. Ibid., 107.

42. David Dietz, *Atomic Energy in the Coming Era* (New York: Dodd, Mead and Company, 1947), 13.

43. Winkler, 137.

44. For more detailed discussions of atomic boosterism, see David Noble's *America by Design: Science, Technology, and the Rise of Corporate Capitalism* (New York: Oxford University Press, 1977); and Stephen Hilgartner et al., *Nukespeak: The Selling of Nuclear Technology in America* (New York: Penguin Books, 1983).

45. Three Mile Island (1979) is famous as the accident that made nuclear power seem more risky than advantageous. But in fact there had been what was in some ways a worse power plant accident as early as 1951, with the Experimental Breeder Reactor (EBR-1) in Idaho, which actually resulted in the death of at least one technician. *See Life Under a Cloud* for more details.

46. From "The Wild West": "Ah will seek the desert's hush / Where the scenery is lush / How I long to see the mushroom clouds"; from "We Will All Go Together": "Oh we will all burn together when we burn / There'll be no need to stand and wait your turn / When it's time for the fallout / And Saint Peter calls us all out / We'll just drop our agendas and adjourn."

47. Information about these and other "A-bomb themed" songs is available at "Atomic Platters: From the Golden Age of Homeland Security," www.conelrad.com/media/atomicmusic/sh_boom.html (accessed 4 July 2007).

48. An earlier song by the same title is "Atom Bomb Baby" by Dude Martin's Round-Up Gang (1948).

8. Rocket Science

1. See, for example, William H. Goetzmann, *New Lands, New Men: America and the Second Great Age of Discovery* (New York: W. W. Norton, 1986); Stephen J. Pyne, *The Ice: A Journey to Antarctica* (Iowa City: University of Iowa Press, 1986); and Beverly J.

Stoeltje, "Making the Frontier Myth: Folklore Process in a Modern Nation," *Western Folklore* 46 (October 1987): 235.

2. One of the few exceptions to this rule was H. G. Wells, who, in *The First Men in the Moon*, imagined a spheroid spacecraft similar to the design the Soviets would eventually use.

3. J. P. Telotte, "Disney in Science Fiction Land," *Journal of Popular Film and Television*, Spring 2005: 12.

4. The history of the German rocket program before and during World War II is fully described in Michael J. Neufeld, *The Rocket and the Reich: Peenemünde and the Coming of the Ballistic Missile Age* (New York: Free Press, 1995); for the American developments during and after World War II, see Alan J. Levine, *The Missile and Space Race* (Westport, CT: Praeger, 1994).

5. Interestingly, in a TV series about the manned space-flight program, *Space* (1985), based on James Michener's novel of the same name, though most of the historical figures appear as fictionalized characters, there is almost no mention of von Braun; and the series, as well as the novel, is little more than soap opera with rockets.

6. For more on the reaction, visit Melissa Snowden's "Russian Space Dogs," www .silverdalen.se/stamps/dogs/library/library_space_dogs_russian.htm (accessed 6 August 2006).

7. Quoted in Thomas Powers, *Heisenberg's War: The Secret History of the German Bomb* (New York: Knopf, 1993), 44.

8. Robert A. Divine, *The Sputnik Challenge: Eisenhower's Response to the Soviet Satellite* (New York: Oxford University Press, 1993), xvi.

9. Such rhetoric carries echoes of the debate over our "losing" China; and it was to reappear with depressing regularity over the next half century every time any other nation was first to achieve any technological feat—even the fictional one of the Higgs Boson (see chapter 12).

10. Divine, xv.

11. Quoted in Roger D. Launius, *NASA: A History of the U.S. Civil Space Program* (Malabar: Krieger, 1994), 39.

12. Divine, 71.

13. Perhaps they were reacting to a novel published in 1921 by Russian writer Evgeny Zamyatin. The novel, *We*, posits a future Soviet dictatorship utilizing a rocket ship to "subjugate the unknown beings on other planets, who may still be living in the primitive condition of freedom"; and this effort of liberating conquest is to be made in the name of "the Benefactor," ruler of "the One State" (see Tom Wolfe, *The Right Stuff* [New York: Farrar, Straus and Giroux, 1979], 72–73).

14. Divine, xiv.

15. Ibid., xvii.

16. Actually the name "Laika" referred to her breed, a Siberian husky; her real name was Kudryavka, or Little Curly, but the American press dubbed her "Muttnik." Some other interesting facts about the Soviet Dogs in Space program: Laika had been a stray dog taken from the streets of Moscow; she died in space after three days in orbit, and

later Sputnik II reentered the Earth's atmosphere and burned up without much public notice. There were also a number of failures during this program that were not publicized at the time. On July 28, 1960, a test flight of the Vostok capsule exploded during launch, killing two dogs; and there were a number of other unreported fatalities. For more details see www.silverdalen.se/stamps/dogs/library/library_space_dogs_russian .htm.

17. Ironically, the U-2 flights eventually provided consistent evidence that the Soviets were in fact not that far ahead of us; and the CIA kept telling anyone who would listen that the missile gap could probably be bridged in 4–6 months. But nobody wanted to listen, as this fact undermined the rationale for requesting huge emergency funds in order to close this "gap."

18. Launius, 26.

19. Divine, 95.

20. Ibid., 8.

21. Ibid., 64.

22. Ibid., 65.

23. Ibid., 15.

24. Ibid., 16.

25. Ibid., 46.

26. Ibid., 53.

27. One might argue that this is the "go to" trope for any achievement or event that catches America by surprise and brings into question, even if only momentarily, its position of supremacy. As trope, it involves extremely intriguing mixtures of the biblical (it's our own fault), and the legal (it's not fair because they broke the rules).

28. Though it was actually Echo IA, as Echo I had exploded on launch.

9. Tom Swift and the Cosmic Astronauts

1. Project Mercury lasted four and a half years from initial announcement to the twenty-two-orbit flight of Gordon Cooper in *Faith 7*. The overall cost was estimated to be $384,131,000, and at its peak the program employed around two million people (Loyd S. Swenson, Jr., James M. Grimwood, and Charles C. Alexander, *This New Ocean: A History of Protect Mercury* [Washington, DC: NASA SP-4201, 1966], 508).

2. The Dyna-Soar program eventually ended in December 1963, and along with it any hopes the Air Force had of an independent manned space program, as all of America's space resources were being channeled into the Apollo program.

3. Quoted in *This New Ocean*, 335.

4. Lyndon B. Johnson "Memorandum for the President," 28 April 1961. Quoted in John M. Logsdon, ed., *Exploring the Unknown: Selected Documents in the History of the U.S. Civil Space Program* (Washington DC: NASA SP-2001-4407), 427–29.

5. Quoted in Mark E. Byrnes, *Politics and Space: Image Making by NASA* (Westport, CT: Praeger, 1994), 7.

6. "To understand the way the Mercury program developed is to map (as of the early

1960s) a series of changes in public administration and management; undertakings in science, engineering, and technology; developments in economic organizations; and changes in popular culture that, spurred by World War II and the turmoil and tensions of the Cold War period, transformed many elements of life in the United States" (*This New Ocean*, 18). For a discussion of the interaction between social policy and engineering in the Mercury program, see Howard E. McCurdy, *Space and the American Imagination* (Washington, DC: Smithsonian Institution Press, 1997); and for an analysis of how these interactions affected the "education race," see Howard E. McCurdy, *Inside NASA: High Technology and Organizational Change in the U.S. Space Program* (Baltimore: Johns Hopkins University Press, 1993).

7. Tom Wolfe, *The Right Stuff* (New York: Farrar, Straus and Giroux, 1979). All quotations are from this edition.

8. Ibid., 80.

9. Ibid., 29.

10. However, as far as the media was concerned, "the question of whether an astronaut was even a pilot or a mere guinea pig never entered into it" (ibid., 115). The important thing was that the Mercury astronauts were willing to ride on top of a rocket—a rocket that would quite probably blow up.

11. Ibid., 116.

12. Ibid., 141.

13. Another interpretation is available at Allen Varney, "Stars among the Stars," www.allenvarney.com/collo3.html (accessed 13 August 2006). "Tom Wolfe believes the Mercury astronauts' fame represented a revival of the ancient practice of single combat, where the finest soldiers of opposing armies would battle in place of the entire force. I prefer a simpler explanation: People treated the astronauts the way we treat star athletes. While they win contests, we love them; afterward, we retire them to the history books. Like athletes, they got trading cards. Today collectors can treasure these as souvenirs of a big, big race."

14. Wolfe, 76.

15. Ibid., 181.

16. See Alan J. Levine, *The Missile and Space Race* (Westport, CT: Praeger, 1994), 119.

17. Quoted in Wolfe, 182.

18. Ibid., 180.

19. Jannelle Warren-Findley, "The Collier as Commemoration: The Project Mercury Astronauts and the Collier Trophy in 1962," in *From Engineering Science to Big Science*, ed. Pamela A. Mack (Washington, DC: Government Printing Office, 1998), 177.

20. Joachim P. Kuettner, quoted in *This New Ocean*, 171–72.

21. Warren-Findley, 177.

22. Wolfe, 183.

23. Ibid., 180.

24. Michael L. Smith, "Selling the Moon: The U.S. Manned Space Program and the Triumph of Commodity Scientism," in *The Culture of Consumption: Critical Essays in*

American History, 1880–1980, ed. Richard Wightman Fox and T. J. Jackson Lears (New York: Pantheon, 1983), 180.

25. Quoted in *This New Ocean,* 160.

26. "In 1971 during a press conference to promote his forthcoming book *Of a Fire on the Moon,* Norman Mailer chastised NASA for its ineffectual and inaccurate presentation of its astronauts and space program. Mailer blamed the lackluster interest of Americans in the Apollo missions on the fact that NASA required the 'tough men—daredevils' who were selected for the space program to 'suddenly . . . be priests' upon joining NASA's ranks. Referring to the Apollo 11 mission, the first of the missions to land on the moon, Mailer said NASA 'succeeded in making the most transcendental event of the 20th century boring' ": Melanie Rosen Brown, "Dead Astronauts, Cyborgs, and the Cape Canaveral Fiction of J. G. Ballard: A Posthuman Analysis," reconstruction.eserver.org/043/brown.htm (accessed 27 August 2006).

27. Levine, 110.

28. Although Glenn got the bulk of the praise from the media, those of the technical teams came in for some note; one periodical praised the "leaders of this technical team who did their work on civil service pay and sold no serial rights to national magazines." Quoted in *This New Ocean,* 435.

29. Quoted in Smith, 203.

30. Wolfe, 89.

31. Ibid., 66.

32. Which proved a fatal flaw in the second suborbital flight when Gus Grissom—or something—blew the hatch prematurely and the "spacecraft" filled with water and sank. With the pickup helicopter hovering overhead, Grissom nearly drowned before he could be hauled aboard—largely because the pockets of his space suit were filled with change he'd carried into orbit and that he planned to sell as space souvenirs.

33. Wolfe, 66.

34. Tara Gray, "Anniversary of the Mercury 7: M. Scott Carpenter," history.nasa .gov/40thmerc7/carpenter.htm (accessed 5 March 2007).

35. Wolfe suggests that even the respective names of their two capsules represented the difference between how Carpenter saw his mission and how Schirra saw his. Carpenter's capsule was named *Aurora 7,* something poetic and suggestive of "cosmic mysteries"; Schirra's was named *Sigma 7,* and "Sigma was a purely engineering symbol" (378–80).

36. Warren-Findley, 167.

37. Brown, "Dead Astronauts."

38. Vivian Sobchak, "The Virginity of Astronauts: Sex and the Science Fiction Film," in *Shadows of the Magic Lamp: Fantasy and Science Fiction in Film,* ed. George E., Slusser and Eric S. Rabkin (Carbondale: Southern Illinois University Press, 1985), 41–57.

39. J. G. Ballard, "The Dead Astronaut," *Memories of the Space Age* (Sauk City, WI: Arkham House, 1988), 70.

40. W. Henry Lambright, *Powering Apollo: James E. Webb of NASA* (Baltimore: Johns Hopkins University Press, 1995), 99–101.

41. Quoted in Smith, 199.

42. Langdon Winner, *Autonomous Technology: Technics-out-of-Control as a Theme in Political Thought* (Cambridge, MA: MIT Press, 1977).

43. It's worth noting that the shuttle mission to fix the Hubble telescope is often cited as proof of the need for manned space flight; but of course that is just another example of justifying astronauts as outer space mechanics.

10. America vs. the Evil Empire(s)

1. For a thorough summary as well as interesting analysis of the film as an allegory of the Cold War, see Walter Ranki, "Patriotism, Politics, and Propaganda: The Naturalization of Friday's Man, Robinson," www.brightlightsfilm.com/42/robcrusoe.htm (accessed 1 September 2006).

2. One could include *The Andromeda Strain* (1971) in this list. Though it's about biologists, not astronauts, fighting a plague from space, its dramatic focus is on the tendency of systems to fail, and the scientist characters are portrayed as heroic to the extent that they come up with innovative solutions to those failures. The film made much of American fears of biological warfare—and also of American conspiracy theories about secret laboratories buried in the desert.

3. It could be argued that many post–nuclear war films are of this "mechanical failure" genre, though with the focus on Wicked Wizards. What I mean is, often in such films the nuclear war is portrayed as the fault of scientists who were unable to control their machines—who did not possess, that is, the same cool-headed mechanical ingenuity that we expect from a Master Mechanic. In this category I would place films like *A Boy and His Dog* (1975), *Mad Max* (1979), *The Day After* (1983), and especially the *Terminator* series. What is also interesting about these films is the way in which the nuclear holocaust always seems to have wiped out all the theoretical scientists, leaving only the technicians and/or warriors to tinker the world back together.

4. See for instance Lynda K. Bundtzen, "Monstrous Mothers: Medusa, Grendel, and Now Alien," *Film Quarterly* 40.3 (Spring 1987): 11–17; James H. Kavanaugh, "'Son of a Bitch': Feminism, Humanism, and Science in *Alien*," *October* 13 (Summer 1980): 90–100; and Annette Kuhn, ed., *Alien Zone: Cultural Theory and Contemporary Science Fiction Cinema* (New York: Verso, 1990).

5. Buck Rogers, for instance, is the epitome of a blue-collar fighter jock, the intellectual roles being assigned to a somewhat fussy scientist, Dr. Huer, and an artificial intelligence in a sort of plexiglass handbag, named, for some inexplicable reason, Dr. Theopolis; and of course in *Star Trek*, Captain Kirk is the action hero who comes up with intuitive, mechanical solutions, and all theorizing is left up to Mr. Spock.

6. As Edward Said has argued (in, among other works, *Culture and Imperialism*, 1993), cultural imperialism is most effective—particularly in its performances of propaganda—when it detaches itself from discredited imperialist rhetoric, and when it conceives of and represents its growth in an evangelical rhetoric instead, a rhetoric structured on a reified belief in the imperialistic culture's superior wisdom. This rhetoric is little (if at all) different from that of nineteenth-century empires like Britain or the

other continental powers; only now it is the Federation bringing light, i.e., technology and peace to the "people sitting in darkness" (in Mark Twain's phrase).

7. One might object that the cast of the film is markedly, even hysterically multicultural: an African American fighter pilot, a Jewish scientist, a scattering of Asian, Italian, and Irish Americans, etc. It is the traditional multiethnic platoon from those formula World War II movies writ large. But I would counter that all this ethnicity is presented as remarkably homogeneous. In fact, the most markedly ethnic character, David Levinson's Jewish father (as over-played by Judd Hirsch), is used solely for amusement, arguably as an example of outlandish, antiquated, stereotypical, and no longer relevant ethnic traits. This is ethnicity as stand-up comedy.

8. Other texts have also presented encounters with aliens as nightmares of cultural erasure, such as *V*, *War of the Worlds*, *Battlefield Earth*, and even *A Hitchhiker's Guide to the Galaxy*. What marks *ID4* and *The Arrival* as particularly "patriotic"—where patriotism is figured in the absolutes of right-wing political anxieties—is their referencing of tropes and images from the world of domestic paramilitary and survivalist paranoia. How much difference is there, really, between the black spaceships of the alien invaders and the mythical black helicopters of those multinational United Nations troops who are even now massing in Canada? How much difference between an alien plot to pollute and overrun our world and an immigrant plot to pollute and overrun our country? I would also point out that *ID4* depends for its resolution on belief in the second most popular American paranoid conspiracy theory, the Roswell/Area 51/alien autopsy scenario. If the aliens hadn't already been here and the government wasn't concealing that fact from us, then the cable repairman couldn't use the alien fighter to implant the virus and nuke the mother ship. In other words, without a concealed past and a deceptive present, the human race—again, a human race from now on decidedly and primarily American—would have no future. Finally, there is one last bit of evidence in *ID4* that I believe can be read as a link between its own ideology and that of paranoid patriotic militias, and here I refer to the destruction of the American monuments, which has been shown hundreds of times in film clips. Most audiences greet the destruction of the White House, Washington Monument, and Empire State Building, to say nothing of that of most major American cities, with cheers and laughter. And after all, aren't such scenes straight out of the militia's most rabid anti-government, anti-urban fantasies? Such monuments and the cities which contain them are icons of those urban centers of crime and liberal ideology which we'd all be better off without anyway, leaving the country—or the west anyway—to rebuild the true American patriotic spirit.

9. I would further argue that these films suggest that good or American multiculturalism is in fact a kind of pseudo-diversity; that Americans want a kind of homogenous heterogeneity, a superficial multiculturalism, with America as a "melting pot" where ideological differences (such as class) are not negotiated so much as dissolved, leaving only the various "flavors" of diversity. Such a vision conceives the world, or the universe, as an American mall with ethnic boutiques—a vision made explicit in the Star Trek series *Deep Space Nine*, as well as in *Babylon 5*.

10. Some have argued that Dr. Strangelove is in fact a representation of Edward Teller. See Peter Goodchild, *Edward Teller: The Real Dr. Strangelove* (Cambridge, MA: Harvard University Press, 2004).

11. *Harper's Bazaar* (December 1969).

12. Kubrick's half of the film makes clear that David's love for his mother is fundamentally an obsessive self-love. He must be around his mother to love her and, as he says repeatedly, he must love her to survive; therefore he must be around her to survive. And he can be around her only if she accepts him as real. All his efforts to become real are thus efforts to survive. In short, his love is complete and inescapable narcissism. I would go even further and suggest that Kubrick's quite sophisticated, if somewhat depressing vision is one of potentially *all* love as narcissistic. However, given our need to believe in "real" love as somehow selfless, we invent "fairy tales" to magically transform that truth into something it is not, something less disturbing. The first half (or two-thirds) of the film works, and works effectively, to subvert and expose such fairy tales, and leads quite logically to the actual end with David frozen in immortal stasis; but Spielberg embraces these fairy tales wholeheartedly, without critical or aesthetic distance, and gives us a whopper of a fairy-tale ending in an attempt to subvert and cancel the rest of the film. His is a virtual ending, a robot ending. Thus another rendering of the film's tagline could be, "The first half of the film is real. The second is not."

13. "I, Mudd" (3 November 1967).

14. I am assuming that this precept of semiotics is by now accepted as a commonplace, and not something that requires extensive proof and citation.

15. If the poet writes "My love is like a red, red rose," then a literal reading results in our imagining his love as a chlorophyll-filled organism with blossoms and thorns; but we "know" that isn't what the poet means, that, rather, he is referring to the cultural connotation of roses as symbols of beauty, romance, growth, promise, etc.

16. Donna Haraway, "A Cyborg Manifesto: Science, Technology, and Socialist-Feminism in the Late Twentieth Century," in her *Simians, Cyborgs, and Women: The Reinvention of Nature* (New York: Routledge, 1991), 149.

17. Melanie Rosen Brown, "Dead Astronauts, Cyborgs, and the Cape Canaveral Fiction of J. G. Ballard: A Posthuman Analysis," reconstruction.eserver.org/043/brown.htm (accessed 27 August 2006).

18. N. Katherine Hayles, How We Became Posthuman: Virtual Bodies in Cybernetics, Literature, and Informatics (Chicago: University of Chicago Press, 1999), 4.

19. *The Real Jurassic Park*, PBS, 9 November 1993.

20. For a more detailed discussion of this film see Gary Hoppenstand, "Dinosaur Doctors and Jurassic Geniuses: The Changing Image of the Scientist in the Lost World Adventure," *Studies in Popular Culture* 22.1 (October 1999): 1–14.

21. An example of such a reading of the film—one which sees the scientists in *Jurassic Park* as enlightened, or at least as more representative of true scientific skepticism than most filmic scientists—can be found at Chris H. Lewis's website, "America, the Environment, and the Global Economy," www.colorado.edu/AmStudies/lewis/ecology/break.htm (accessed 3 April 2008).

11. Looking Backward

1. One European experimenter, Prof. Georg Wilhelm Richman of St. Petersburg, Russia, was in fact electrocuted while attempting to replicate Franklin's experiment, as he'd based his procedure on just such an illustration. And Franklin once managed to give himself a significant shock during another experiment; however, as evidence of his constant vigilance over his public image, he asked a friend to keep this knowledge secret: "do not make it more Publick, for I am Ashamed to have been Guilty of so Notorious A Blunder." Quoted in Thomas Fleming, ed., *Benjamin Franklin, A Biography in His Own Words* (New York: Newsweek Book Division, 1972), 1:95.

2. For a fuller discussion of this experiment in the international context of scientific competition of the time see Tom Tucker, *Bolt of Fate: Benjamin Franklin and His Electric Kite Hoax* (New York: Perseus, 2003).

3. Our best sense of how Franklin actually conducted the experiment comes from an account published fifteen years later by British chemical investigator Joseph Priestley. It suggests that Franklin had insulated himself by holding a silk string connected to the ground, and that a Leyden jar was attached to the key to contain the electrical charge, rather than Franklin's finger. "The Electric Ben Franklin," www.ushistory.org/franklin/info/kite.htm (accessed 3 November 2007).

4. The link between Franklin, electricity, and lightning is nicely captured in Charles Willson Peale's portrait of Franklin (1785), wherein Franklin sits "bookended" by a quill pen on his left and, through a window on his right, a bolt of lightning.

5. *Memoires de la Vie Privée* was published in Paris in March 1791. The first English translation, *The Private Life of the Late Benjamin Franklin, LL.D. Originally Written By Himself, And Now Translated From The French*, was published in London in 1793.

6. Fleming, *Benjamin Franklin*, 74. In his conception of behavior as essentially a compilation of "habits," Franklin anticipated one of the foremost principles of the psychological theories of William James; who in this (as well as all the other ways discussed in chapter 3) would seem to be his direct philosophical descendant.

7. Ibid., 75.

8. Larzer Ziff, *Writing in the New Nation: Prose, Print, and Politics in the Early United States* (New Haven, CT: Yale University Press, 1991), 83.

9. Fleming, *Benjamin Franklin*, 120.

10. Ibid., 121.

11. Ibid., 53.

12. Ibid., 59. "Junto" was actually a British term referring to any political faction. This was a curious choice for Franklin's club, as one of the membership's tenets was that they forswore any language expressing "fixed opinions"—which suggests that Franklin, even at an early age, envisioned politics as an expression of pragmatic decisions arrived at only after entertaining various and even competing viewpoints.

13. From a speech he made to the Junto Club in 1730, "On the Providence of God in the Government of the World." (Quoted in Fleming, *Benjamin Franklin*, 122.)

14. 1725 pamphlet, "A Dissertation on Liberty and Necessity, Pleasure and Pain,"

The Papers of Benjamin Franklin, Digital Edition (American Philosophical Society and Yale University; Packard Humanities Institute), www.franklinpapers.org/franklin/framedVolumes.jsp (accessed 15 November 2006).

15. "On the Providence of God in the Government of the World" (1730), *The Papers of Benjamin Franklin*, franklinpapers.org/franklin (accessed 16 November 2006).

16. John Adams noted that Franklin was a mirror in which people saw their own religion: "The Catholics thought him almost a Catholic. The Church of England claimed him as one of them. The Presbyterians thought him half a Presbyterian, and the Friends believed him a wet Quaker": Charles Francis Adams, ed., *The Works of John Adams*, vol. 1 (Boston, 1851), 661.

17. Fleming, *Benjamin Franklin*, 77.

18. David L. Ferro, "Promoting Science through America's Colonial Press: How Ben Franklin Used His Newspaper—*The Pennsylvania Gazette*—to 'Popularize' an Evolving Science," in "Archiving Early America," www.earlyamerica.com/review/summer97/science.html (accessed 19 November 2006).

19. Ibid.

20. *Poor Richard's Almanac*, 1743, in Leonard W. Labaree and Whitfield J. Bell, eds., *Benjamin Franklin, Papers* (New York, 1959–), 2:373.

21. Letter to John Bartram, 9 July 1769, in "The Writings of Benjamin Franklin: London, 1757–1775," www.historycarper.com/resources/twobf3/letter8.htm (accessed 21 November 2006).

22. Paul Keith Conkin, *Puritans and Pragmatists: Eight Eminent American Thinkers* (New York: Dodd, Mead, 1968).

23. Ibid., 79.

24. Ibid., 101.

25. Fleming, *Benjamin Franklin*, 110.

26. From "Mitchell and Mather's *Defence of the Answer and Arguments of the Synod*, 1664." Quoted in Frank Hugh Foster, "The History of the Original Puritan Theology of New England, 1620–1720," *American Journal of Theology* 1.3 (July 1897): 7007–27.

27. Dr. William Young, "The Puritan Principle of Worship," www.apuritansmind.com/PuritanWorship/YoungWilliamPuritanRegulativePrinciple.htm (accessed 27 November 2006).

28. Ibid.

29. Ibid.

30. "The Bible NETWork," forum.bible.org/viewtopic.php?t=1462&sid=d57426e8328 adddc4d72be19ab33226 (accessed 30 January 2007).

31. "Semper Reformata, JP," semperreformata.wordpress.com/2007/06/25/monday-is-quote-day-5/ (accessed 26 June 2007).

32. Ziff, 4.

33. Ibid.

34. Jim Cox, "That Quacking Sound in Colonial American," *Journal of the Colonial Williamsburg Foundation*, Spring 2004, www.history.org/Foundation/journal/Spring04/

quackery.cfm (accessed 13 November 2007). Franklin was himself not above advertising "homeopathic" remedies. Just before the Revolution, Franklin's mother-in-law came out with a salve for lice and itching, called Widow Read's Ointment, and Franklin prominently advertised it in the *Pennsylvania Gazette*.

35. Ziff, 56.

36. Ibid., 57.

37. Ziff also sees in the popularity of these narratives of convincing deception evidence of the American culture's ambivalence toward invention of self: "its powerful hold on the imagination does not stem simply from a dread of it, but from the mixture of that dread with a fascination at the capacity of appearance to convert itself into the truth." And thus the dilemma: should the con man be despised for his fraud, or admired for his cleverness? Ziff argues that Franklin "got it right where Burroughs got it wrong since [Franklin] labors (and counsels others) to make the appearance conform to reality rather than the reverse" (60). In other words, Ziff sees Franklin as a sort of Colonial Gatsby, but one without Gatsby's tragic flaw of class envy.

38. Ibid., 16.

39. Ziff locates this prejudice against creative inventions of fictional worlds in Edwards's conviction that God's creation was perfect and total: "Edwards's belief that the created world was complete and his consequent censure of imaginative re-creations are opposed to the values promoted in a print culture" (30).

40. For fuller discussions of such thematics, see Leo Marx, *The Machine in the Garden: Technology and the Pastoral Ideal in America* (New York: Oxford University Press, 1964); Susan Manning, "American Literature 2: Crèvecoeur, Letters From an American Farmer," www.englit.ed.ac.uk/studying/undergrd/american_lit_2/Handouts/sm_crevecoeur.htm (accessed 4 November 2005); and Ann M. Woodlief, "Negotiating Nature/Wilderness: Crèvecoeur and American Identity in *Letters From an American Farmer*," www.vcu.edu/engweb/crev.htm (accessed 4 November 2005).

41. "*Letters From an American Farmer*: Letter I," Avalon Project, Yale Law School, www.yale.edu/lawweb/avalon/treatise/american_farmer/letter_01.htm (accessed 5 November 2005).

42. Ibid.

43. Ibid.

44. Ziff believes the threat is one of the intangible invasion of represented self into a community based wholly on the immanent self, thus raising all the problems of distinguishing grace from imagination. He further suggests writing is distrusted because it "can overcome distance speech cannot, and it does so at the expense of the community knit together by personal presence" (29).

45. Thomas Wharton, Jr., "The Pleasures of Melancholy," www.poemhunter.com/poem/the-pleasures-of-melancholy/ (accessed 5 November 2005).

46. Benjamin Franklin, "The Way to Wealth," pages.prodigy.net/jmiller.cb/pr12.html (accessed 4 November 2005).

47. "Nearer, My Couch, to Thee," *New York Times Book Review*, 6 June 1993, 1, 57.

48. Ibid., 1.

49. Ibid., 57.

50. Kevin Quast, "'I don't care anymore': Acedia in the Ancient and Contemporary Church," *Christian Week* 17, no 11 (19 August 2003), www.christianweek.org/stories/vol17/no11/feature.html (accessed 1 June 2006).

51. Washington Irving, "Rip Van Winkle: A Posthumous Writing of Diedrich Knickerbocker," www.bartleby.com/195/4.html (accessed 10 January 2007).

52. "The Amaricans are Challing: A Colonial Child's Exclamation," The Gilder Lehrman Institute of American History, www.gilderlehrman.org/collection/docs_archive/docs_archive_American.html (accessed 1 June 2007).

53. Ziff, 24.

54. Jere Cohen, *Protestantism and Capitalism: The Mechanisms of Influence* (New York: Aldine Transaction, 2002), 37.

55. "Leisure," *Complete Book of Everyday Christianity*, ed. Robert Banks and R. Paul Stevens, www.ivmdl.org/cbec.cfm?study=130 (accessed 15 June 2007).

56. Quoted in ibid. Jere Cohen argues that in this condemnation of even the *appearance* of idleness, we can see the roots of particularly American class enmity. For Puritan ideologues, there was an obvious link between richness and idleness; Baxter, for instance, complained about idle "drones" who "consume that which others labour for, but are no gatherers themselves." Richard Baxter, *A Christian directory; or, A body of practical divinity and cases of conscience* (London: Printed for Richard Edwards, 1825), 373.

57. Richard Baxter, quoted in Cohen, 40.

58. Quoted in Cohen, 37.

59. Conkin, 11.

60. Ibid., 26.

61. As Ziff suggests, "A society with relatively few class barriers and a natural setting of abundant resources combined to form the cultural belief that human nature was as malleable as the landscape" (51).

62. Benjamin Franklin, "The Autobiography of Benjamin Franklin: Part XXIV," www.worldwideschool.org/library/books/hst/biography/TheAutobiographyofBenjaminFranklin/chap24.html (accessed 1 May 2005).

63. Though Edison never took to publishing his philosophy of self-improvement à la *Poor Richard's Almanac*, his aphorisms were so frequently quoted in America's newspapers and magazines as to make him Franklin's closest inheritor of this tradition. A small sampling of Edison's "proverbs" indicates just how thoroughly the two men shared attitudes about the methods and goals of inventing as a vocation: "My main purpose in life is to make enough money to create ever more inventions"; "I never perfected an invention that I did not think about in terms of the service it might give others. . . . I find out what the world needs, then I proceed to invent"; "Opportunity is missed by most people because it is dressed in overalls and looks like work"; "The three things that are most essential to achievement are common sense, hard work and stick-to-it-iv-ness"; "I always found that, if I began to worry, the best thing I could do was focus upon doing something useful and then work very hard at it"; "Time

is really the only capital that any human being has and the thing that he can least afford to waste or lose"; "Edison Quotes," www.thomasedison.com/edquote.htm (accessed 1 April 2005).

64. Milton Ellis, *Joseph Dennie and His Circle: A Study in American Literature from 1792–1812* (Austin: University of Texas Press, 1915), 31.

65. "Joseph Dennie," *Virtual American Biographies,* famousamericans.net/joseph-dennie/ (accessed 5 February 2005).

66. Dennie was also no fan of Franklin's writing, opining that Franklin "was the founder of that Grubstreet sect, who have professedly attempted to degrade literature to the level of vulgar capacities, and debase the polished and current language of books by the vile alloy of provincial idioms, and colloquial barbarisms, the shame of grammar and akin to any language rather than English": Ronald Weber, "Light Artillery of the Intellect: The Emergence of the Versatile Magazinists," chapter 1 of *Hired Pens: Professional Writers in America's Golden Age of Print,* available at www.nytimes.com/books/first/w/weber-pens.html (accessed 5 February 2005).

67. Quoted in Ziff, 148.

68. Washington Irving, "The Legend of Sleepy Hollow: Found Among the Papers of the Late Diedrich Knickerbocker," www.bartleby.com/310/2/2.html (accessed 1 March 2006).

69. Lester J. Cappon, ed., *The Adams–Jefferson Letters* (Chapel Hill: University of North Carolina Press, 1959), 502.

70. Ziff, too, sees this anti-arts attitude as giving rise to a stream of anti-intellectualism resident not only in American science and politics, but also in American literature, through Emerson, Thoreau, Whitman, and even Melville. He cites Whitman's and Emerson's conviction that the "best-wrought writing erased the marks of its literariness," and notes how American literature historically tends to value "the primacy of flux over form and the physical or immanent over the intellectualized or mediated" (188).

71. From a speech delivered to the American Philosophical Society on October 18, 1823: Charles Jared Ingersoll, "A discourse concerning the influence of America on the mind: being the annual oration delivered before the American Philosophical Society, at the University in Philadelphia, on the 18th October, 1823, by their appointment, and published by their order (1823)," www.archive.org/details/discourseconcernooingeiala (accessed 3 May 2005).

72. Among the results Conkin suggests would arise from such a social construct are: the importance of systemized education as indoctrination; a codified and deep-seated fear of and resentment toward any perceived abuse of power; an extended social system modeled on the family; and a "hatred of diverting or frivolous forms of recreation, entertainment, or art" (16–17).

73. Ziff, 103.

74. As Ziff puts it, "[Franklin] was not concerned with his unique qualities; what happened to him was typical . . . it could happen to you" (117).

12. Déjà Vu All Over Again

1. Kent Jeffreys, "Super Boondoggle: Time to Pull the Plug on the Superconducting Super Collider," *Cato Briefing Papers–Cato Institute*, www.cato.org/pubs/briefs/bp-016.html (accessed 1 December 2006).

2. Quoted in Elizabeth Kolbert, "Crash Course," *New Yorker*, 14 May 2007, www.newyorker.com/reporting/2007/05/14/070514fa_fact_kolbert (accessed 1 July 2007).

3. This "disconnect" between the scientific and political communities in America has, unfortunately, a long history. "A congressman in 1914 had questioned a witness at an appropriations hearing, 'What is a physicist? I have asked on the floor of the House what in the name of common sense a physicist is, and I could not answer'" (quoted in Richard Rhodes, *The Making of the Atomic Bomb* [New York: Touchstone, 1986], 141). I would highlight the congressman's suggestion that, whatever a "physicist" is, it is somehow antithetical to "common sense."

4. Herman Wouk, *A Hole in Texas* (New York: Little, Brown, 2004). The novel also implies that the SSC was killed by northeastern liberals who didn't want to see all that money going to Texas; but there is in fact little support for this claim, as the anti-SSC vote crossed all party, regional, and ideological lines.

5. John Schwartz, *New York Times*, 5 December 2006, www.nytimes.com/2006/12/05/science/space/05stat.html (accessed 15 June 2007).

6. The issue of how cultural prejudices can affect what science gets funded and what science doesn't applies even in the ultra-esoteric world of high-energy physics research. Two recent books by physicists have criticized the funding dominance in their field of String Theory: Peter Woit, *Not Even Wrong: The Failure of String Theory and the Search for Unity in Physical Law* (Denver: Universal Athenaeum, 2006); and Leo Smolin, *The Trouble with Physics: The Rise of String Theory, the Fall of Science, and What Comes Next* (New York: Houghton Mifflin, 2006). The chief scientific complaint in both books is the lack of experimental evidence for String Theory; but the chief cultural complaint is that String Theory is a "cult" in which "believers don't care about evidence," a "fad" and "trend" which has "choked off" funding for "equally promising approaches." My point in referencing this debate is to emphasize that even among theoretical Wicked Wizards, cultural prejudices—or even just pet peeves—can have enormous real-world consequences, sometimes determining the course of entire scientific careers, to say nothing of potentially "choking off" potentially valid and important research.

7. James Glantz, "Pointed Questions on Missile Defense System," *New York Times*, 11 March 2004: A-15.

8. At the time this was written (June 2008), the current threats to which SDI was considered a prudent and patriotic response were North Korea, Iran, and other unspecified "rogue states."

9. Editorial, *New York Times*, 21 October 2006, www.nytimes.com/2006/10/21/opinion/21sat1.html (accessed 20 June 2007).

10. Ibid.

11. Elisabeth Rosenthal and Andrew C. Revkin, "Panel Issues Bleak Report on Climate Change," *New York Times*, 2 February 2007, www.nytimes.com/2007/02/02/science/earth/02cnd-climate.html (accessed 1 June 2007).

12. Brian Morton, "Political Animal," *The City Paper*, Baltimore, 28 March 2007, 5.

13. Cynthia Tucker Tucker, "President hostile to scientific facts that conflict with right-wing views," *The Sun*, Baltimore, 16 July 2007, A-11.

14. Peter Baker and Peter Slevin, "Bush Remarks on 'Intelligent Design' Theory Fuel Debate," *Washington Post*, 3 August 2005, A01.

15. Ibid.

16. "School board OKs alternatives to evolution," *CNN News*, 27 September 2002, archives.cnn.com/2002/EDUCATION/09/26/creationism.evolution/Ga (accessed 15 December 2006).

17. New Oxford American Dictionary, 2006.

18. Ibid.

19. Kolbert, 68.

20. Quoted ibid., 74–75.

21. Timothy Ferris, "The Case against Science," *New York Review of Books*, 13 May 1993, 17.

22. Quoted in ibid.

23. Ibid.

24. Ibid.

25. Ibid., 18.

26. Ibid., 19.

27. This particular instance, as well as a general invocation of Fortean counter-rationalism, can be found in the film *Magnolia* (1999).

28. See, for instance, H. L. Malchow's "Frankenstein's Monster and Images of Race in Nineteenth-Century Britain," *Past and Present* 139 (May 1993): 90–130. The "unnatural" status of the creature is taken as an unquestioned assumption on Answers.com (www.answers.com/topic/frankenstein-novel-7), and sold to students as an "obvious" and fundamental theme of the novel at www.wowessays.com/dbase/ac2/xaj23.shtml. For a more enlightened discussion of the creature's status and the very concept of category "unnatural," see Nancy Yousef's "The Monster in a Dark Room: Frankenstein, Feminism, and Philosophy," *MLQ: Modern Language Quarterly* 63.2 (June 2002): 197–226.

29. "Albert Straus Speaks Out against Cloning," www.strausfamilycreamery.com/?id=68&mdid=38 (accessed 27 December 2006).

30. Kenan Malik, "The Moral Clone," www.kenanmalik.com/essays/moral_clone.html (accessed 1 December 2006).

31. Rhodes, 142.

32. In Wouk's novel, for instance, the suggestion that such research might lead to a Boson Bomb is what finally gets Washington's attention.

33. Even if that funeral did seem a bit rushed. See my own review of Jacques Derrida's *Cinders* and *The Other Heading* in *Postmodern Culture* 3.2 (January 1993).

34. See for instance H. George Hahn II, "The Multicultural Lie," *The Sun*, Baltimore, 18 May 2004, A-17, wherein the director of a university graduate program in the humanities actually complains of "minds marinated in multicultural pieties"; or John Wagner, "O'Malley Assails Ehrlich on Race," *Washington Post*, 29 October 2006, C05, reporting how the then-governor of Maryland, Robert Ehrlich (Republican) denounced multiculturalism as "bunk" on a local radio talk show.

INDEX

GLEN SCOTT ALLEN is a fiction writer, scholar, and teacher. After obtaining his Ph.D. in English from the University of Utah, he served as Writer-in-Residence at Reed College in Portland, Oregon, and professor of English and cultural studies at Towson University in Baltimore, Maryland. He co-developed and directed the undergraduate Program in Cultural Studies at Towson University, one of the first such undergraduate programs in the country, for which he created and taught the course Science, Technology, and Culture. He has published numerous short stories, as well as many essays and papers on the topics of science, literature, and culture. He currently lives in Towson, Maryland, with his wife, Inna, and son, Daniel. Visit his website at GlenScottAllen.com.